Books of Merit

I'VE GOT
A HOME IN
GLORY LAND

❧ Underground Railroad Routes to Canada ❧

Inset map (Area of detail)

Lake Huron

Queen's Bush · Toronto (York)
Oakville ·
Waterloo ·
Hamilton ·
Wilberforce · Brantford · St. Catharines
London ·

Lake Ontario

Niagara River
Niagara Falls · Buffalo

Dresden
Detroit · Chatham
· Buxton
· Sandwich (Windsor)
Detroit R.
· Amherstburg

Lake Erie

Main map

Lake Superior

Lake Michigan

Lake Huron

ONTARIO

MICHIGAN

Oro ·
Lake Simcoe

Toronto (York) · Lake Ontario

Area of detail

Niagara Falls

Detroit · Lake Erie

Kingston ·

Montreal

Ottawa ·
Cornwall ·

QUEBEC

Quebec

· Trois-
Rivières

Saint John ·

NEW
BRUNSWICK

MAINE

to Halifax

VERMONT NEW
HAMPSHIRE

Syracuse · Albany

Rochester · NEW
YORK

Boston ·

Chicago ·

ILLINOIS

INDIANA

Fountain City ·

Indianapolis ·

Newport ·

Louisville ·

OHIO

Oberlin ·

Cincinnati ·
Ripley ·
Maysville ·

Lexington ·

KENTUCKY

PENNSYLVANIA

New York ·

Philadelphia ·

Baltimore ·

Manassas · Washington, D.C.

WEST
VIRGINIA

Richmond ·

VIRGINIA

MARYLAND

Atlantic

Ocean

Nashville ·

TENNESSEE

NORTH
CAROLINA

SOUTH
CAROLINA

GEORGIA

© 2006 Jeffrey L. Ward

0 Miles   300

0 Kilometers   300

I'VE GOT
A HOME IN
GLORY LAND

A Lost Tale of the Underground Railroad

KAROLYN SMARDZ FROST

Thomas Allen Publishers
Toronto

Library and Archives Canada Cataloguing in Publication

Smardz Frost, Karolyn
I've got a home in glory land : a lost tale of the underground railroad / Karolyn Smardz Frost.

Includes bibliographical references and index.
ISBN-13: 978-0-88762-250-2
ISBN-10: 0-88762-250-X

1. Blackburn, Thornton, 1813 or 4-1890. 2. Blackburn, Lucie, d. 1895.
3. Fugitive slaves—Ontario—Toronto—Biography. 4. African Americans—Ontario—
Toronto—Biography. 5. Slaves—Kentucky—Biography.
6. African Americans—Kentucky—Biography. 7. Underground railroad.
8. Antislavery movements—Canada—History—19th century.
9. Toronto (Ont.)—Biography. I. Title.

FC3097.26.B53S58 2007   306.3'620922   C2006-906368-0

Jacket design: Kwasi Osei
Jacket image: Sunny South © 1883, Library of
Congress, Prints and Photographs Division

Portions of this work were originally published, in different form, in: Karolyn E.
Smardz, "'There We Were in Darkness,—Here We Are in Light': Kentucky Slaves
and the Promised Land," in Craig Thompson Friend, ed., *The Buzzel About Kentuck:
Settling the Promised Land*, Lexington: University Press of Kentucky, 1999, 243–58;
Adrienne Shadd, Afua Cooper, and Karolyn Smardz Frost, *The Underground Railroad:
Next Stop, Toronto!*, 2nd ed., Toronto: Natural Heritage Books, 2005; Karolyn E. Smardz,
"African Americans Who Became African Canadians: The Thornton and Lucie Blackburn
House Site," in *African-American Archaeology Newsletter*, no. 13 (Spring 1995).

Published in Canada by Thomas Allen Publishers,
a division of Thomas Allen & Son Limited,
145 Front Street East, Suite 209,
Toronto, Ontario M5A 1E3 Canada

www.thomas-allen.com

Published in the United States in 2007 by Farrar, Straus, Giroux

  **Canada Council
for the Arts**

The publisher gratefully acknowledges the support of the
Ontario Arts Council for its publishing program.

We acknowledge the support of the Canada Council for the Arts, which last
year invested $20.0 million in writing and publishing throughout Canada.

We acknowledge the Government of Ontario through the Ontario
Media Development Corporation's Ontario Book Initiative.

We acknowledge the financial support of the Government of Canada through the Book
Publishing Industry Development Program (BPIDP) for our publishing activities.

11 10 09 08 07 1 2 3 4 5

Printed and bound in Canada

This volume is dedicated to Lucie and Thornton Blackburn, and to the thousands of other fugitives from slavery whose tales, unlike theirs, are lost. May this volume stand as a tribute to the courage of those who broke the chains that bound them, and so earned a place in our memories forever.

Do Lord

(traditional)

I've got a home in Glory Land that outshines the sun,
I've got a home in Glory Land that outshines the sun,
I've got a home in Glory Land that outshines the sun,
Way beyond the blue (horizon).

Chorus:
Do Lord, o, do lord, O do remember me.
Do Lord, o, do lord, O do remember me.
Do Lord, o, do lord, O do remember me.
Way beyond the blue (horizon).

I took Jesus as my saviour
You take Him, too.
I took Jesus as my saviour
You take Him, too.
I took Jesus as my saviour
You take Him, too.
Way beyond the blue (horizon).

Chorus

CONTENTS

Introduction   xi

KENTUCKY

1. Wade in the Water, Children   3

2. There Is a Land Beyond the River   15

3. On Jordan's Bank   47

4. Troubling the Waters   71

5. I'm Bound to Go   94

6. Now Let Me Fly   117

DETROIT

7. Steal Away, Steal Away, I Ain't Got
   Long to Stay Here   139

8. Tell Old Pharaoh to Let My People Go!   163

9.   Oh, Freedom!   193

10. One More River to Cross   221

11. Wrestling Jacob   241

12. At Home in the Promised Land   254

13. Soldiers in the Army of the Lord   279

14. Gird Up Your Sword   310

15. Oh, Wasn't That a Wide River?   327

     Epilogue   346

Notes   355

Bibliography   403

Primary Sources   429

Acknowledgments   437

Index   441

INTRODUCTION

In 1985, ARCHAEOLOGISTS in downtown Toronto made a remarkable find. Beneath the old Sackville Street School playground were traces of a house, a shed, and a mysterious cellar. Municipal records revealed that the original landowner had been "Thornton Blackburn, cabman, colored." He and his wife were fugitive slaves from Kentucky who had settled in Toronto in 1834 and had gone on to become wealthy and successful businesspeople. The Thornton and Lucie Blackburn Site became the first archaeological dig on an Underground Railroad site in Canada.

The discovery of the Blackburns' legacy captured the popular imagination in ways no one could have foreseen. Between June and October 1985, the site received more publicity than any dig in Canadian history. Journalists from all over the world interviewed staff, produced television and radio programs, and published articles that appeared in newspapers from Kuwait to Japan. Respected scholars traveled to Toronto to discuss the findings. More than three thousand schoolchildren and members of the public participated in the summerlong dig. Thousands of fascinated visitors came to watch, intrigued by the painstakingly slow process of piecing together the story of two human lives, written there in the soil in fragments of pottery and bits of broken glass.

As the excavations progressed, historical research revealed tantalizing clues about the Blackburns' past. The trail led to a late-nineteenth-century newspaper article entitled "The First Cab in the City," written by John Ross Robertson, editor of the *Toronto Telegram*. It credited this pair of runaway American slaves with initiating Toronto's first taxi business. An abolitionist newspaper dating to 1851 showed Mr. and Mrs. Blackburn as leaders in the campaign to end slavery in the United States and to help its refugees make new homes once they reached freedom. Thornton's tall granite tombstone in the Toronto Necropolis revealed that he was born in Maysville, Kentucky, in about 1812. But the most intriguing information came from Michigan. The "Blackburn Riots of 1831" had erupted when slave catchers tried to return a man named Thornton Blackburn and his wife to their Kentucky masters. These were the first racial riots in the city of Detroit. When the couple sought refuge in Upper Canada, a sharp diplomatic altercation between Michigan's Territorial Governor and the British colonial government of Upper Canada over their extradition had a very significant result: the formulation of British North America's first, articulated legal rationale for harboring fugitive slaves. In fact, it was the Blackburn case that formally established Canada as the main terminus of the Underground Railroad.

Yet until archaeologists discovered the site of their Toronto home, the Blackburns had been forgotten. They had no children. They never learned to read or write, and to this day not a single photo of the couple has come to light. Thornton and Lucie Blackburn were all but lost to history.

I was the director of that long-ago archaeological project. Intrigued by what our diggings had uncovered, I set about to learn all I could about Thornton and his wife. *I've Got a Home in Glory Land* is the result of almost twenty years of historical detective work. Government records in Canada and Michigan provided an all-important key to researching their lives in slavery—the names of Lucie and Thornton Blackburns' owners. All trails led back to Kentucky. As their story took shape, the Blackburn family's experiences in slavery and freedom opened a door into the world they knew and in which they played so vital a part. Set against the backdrop of antebellum America's struggle with race and slavery, the Blackburns' biography illuminates the historical trends that shaped the tangled histories of people black and white, on this continent. Thornton's mother, Sibby, was born in Virginia in about 1776. His wife, Lucie, died in Canada in 1895. The collective experience of the Blackburns therefore encompassed some 120 years of history, and on both sides of the long border the United States shares with Canada. From the impassioned liberation rhetoric inspired by the American Revolution through the catastrophe of Jim Crow–era segregation, the events and the shifting meanings of the words "race" and "freedom" over these twelve decades shaped modern North American society.

Not knowing how to begin my quest, I fell back on my early training. Archaeology is unique in that it gives voice to the inarticulate and the illiterate of any age, including, in this case, the relatively modern. Each archaeological site is a window to the past; it exposes information about people who lived and worked and died in a specific place, at a fixed time. They left behind, in the very earth, a kind of picture puzzle of their lives. There are always many pieces missing. People's emotions, hopes, fears, the dreams they dreamed, and the high-held ideals that guided their actions are not to be found in layers of dirt, however carefully sifted. But by placing the material culture of their everyday lives in historical context, one can discover an enormous amount about how the key events and larger social, economic, political, and cultural trends acted upon the people who lived through them. And sometimes, as was the case with the Blackburns, one can discover what role they took for themselves as actors in that great play.

The Blackburn saga is framed within the history of Africans in America and their ongoing resistance to the inferior and exploited status colonialism thrust upon them. This rejection of their enslavement by the turn of the nineteenth century had culminated in the establishment of well-worn paths leading out of the slave states. These clandestine routes and the courageous individuals who assisted those who traveled came to be known as the Underground Railroad.

The Underground Railroad occupies a very special place in the North American saga. Tales of hidden tunnels and false-bottomed wagons, perilous escapes by night and brazen daylight rescues all paint an enthralling picture. Yet the stories we learn are filtered through much embroidered late-nineteenth-century accounts by white authors. In the place of the daring freedom-seekers who made the perilous journey north, the heroes have become whites who helped them on their way. Yet surviving slave narratives show that most people escaped alone and unaided. Years after Kentucky-born author, poet, and playwright William Wells Brown fled slavery in 1834, he wrote, "When I escaped there was no Underground Railroad. The North Star was, in many instances, the only friend that the weary and footsore fugitive found on his pilgrimage to his new home among strangers." Mattie J. Jackson told the same story: "My parents had never learned the rescuing scheme of the underground railroad which had borne so many thousands to the standard of freedom and victories. They knew no other resource than to depend upon their own chance in running away and secreting themselves." Lost in the mythology, too, are the free blacks of the Northern states who risked far more than their white counterparts when they hid a desperate fugitive in a barn, or passed a meal over the fence to a starving family. This book is, in part, an attempt to set the Underground Railroad's record straight. The Blackburns traveled the routes of the Underground Railroad as it was, rather than as myth and legend would have it be.

No one will ever know how many African Americans fled slavery in the tumultuous years before the Civil War. Black people in the United States had been escaping those who claimed their service almost since the first Dutch slave ship landed her human cargo at Jamestown in 1619. Some runaways formed maroon communities beyond the outposts of white settlement. Others went to Spanish Florida, Mexico, and the Caribbean, and a tiny proportion reached Britain, Europe, and Africa. Estimates of those who came to Canada range between 20,000 and 100,000. Reliable contemporary observers place the number at somewhere between 30,000 and 35,000 over the entire antebellum period.

African Americans waged a daily, unrelenting battle against their enslaved condition. Well aware that their value to their owners lay in their unpaid labor, they engaged in acts of resistance calculated to undermine the slaveholder's profit margin: breaking tools, injuring livestock, or "malingering," simply pretending to be ill. Charismatic leaders arose to foment revolts always limited in scale and quickly contained, but these struck terror into the hearts of whites across the South. Such collective resistance was relatively rare, for the entire system of the slaveocracy militated against bondspeople being able to organize or arm themselves. Instead, when the beatings, hunger, and the destruction of family occasioned by sale and sexual interference became too much to bear, African Americans made the single most overtly antislavery statement possible, short of suicide or murder: they ran away. In so doing, they deprived their owners not only of their productivity and of their own market value but also that of their children and all ensuing generations. Even more potently, the thousands of slaves who "stole themselves" exploded the comforting racist myth that buttressed American slavery: that blacks were unfit for freedom, too lazy and unintelligent to care for themselves without white supervision, and that they preferred the kindly oversight of benevolent masters—that they were, indeed, "happy in their chains."

In a Christian nation founded upon republican principles, the commodification of black labor required moral justification. White America found ways of separating itself from blacks as fellow human beings. No lesser an authority than Thomas Jefferson wrote, "I advance it therefore, as a suspicion only, that the blacks, whether originally a distinct race or made distinct by time and circumstance, are inferior to the whites in the endowments of both body and mind." A beneficiary himself of the plantation system, he deemed slavery a "necessary evil." In the years immediately following the American Revolution, biblical and scientific justifications were sought to "prove" blacks irredeemably less capable than whites, uneducable, inherently indolent, and immoral, the eternal "other." Even in Northern states where slavery gave way to wage labor soon after the Revolution, black skin came to be considered emblematic of bondage. People of color were required to carry with them papers attesting to their free status, lest they be taken up as fugitive slaves under harsh federal laws that enabled slaveholders to seek out their absconding property anywhere in the United States. Slavery in America was inextricably intertwined with the concept of race.

By the time a young enslaved Kentuckian named Thornton Blackburn came of age in 1830, self-serving pro-slavery ideology had transformed Jefferson's "necessary evil" into a system slaveholders professedly believed to be a "positive good." Apologists maintained that white "wage slaves" in Britain and the northern United States were worse off than blacks living in Southern slavery. John C. Calhoun of South Carolina, who with New England's Daniel Webster and Kentucky's own Henry Clay formed the "Great Triumvirate" of antebellum American politics, summed this up in a speech he made before the U.S. Senate on February 6, 1837: "Never before has the black race of Central Africa, from the dawn of history to the present day, attained a condition so civilized and so improved, not only physically, but morally and intellectually." Yet nowhere was such nonsense better contradicted than in the lengths enslaved African Americans were willing to go to free themselves. The exodus of black men, women, and children from the slave states was a vast, collective rejection of their circumstances and of the racially biased rationalizations that supported slavery.

Whippings, mutilation, rape, and varied forms of physical and mental torture were ways in which the slaveholding class maintained its hegemony over its unwilling workers. But slave narratives show that a majority of runaways fled for a more specific reason: they were about to be parted from those they loved. Colonial-era planters had maintained the fiction that they cared for their "black families" as they did their white. When selling off slaves, they paid lip service to keeping couples or at least mothers and children together. The death knell to such paternalism sounded when the invention of Eli Whitney's cotton gin in 1793 gave birth to the cotton-growing boom of the early nineteenth century. As cotton-growing expanded in the Deep South, the older farming districts of the more northerly slave states found it very profitable to ship their "surplus" slaves south for sale. These so-called Border States became a slave-producing resource for the larger, more prosperous plantation economy of the Lower South. Wives and mothers, fathers, and even tiny babies were taken from their loved ones and sold far away.

At the same time, the rift between North and South was widening into an irreparable chasm. Increasing Northern and foreign criticism of the American slave system and resistance to the expansion of slavery into the newly added frontier districts resulted in a hardening of pro-slavery positions. A series of slave revolts terrified slaveholding whites and intensified efforts to control supposedly contented local black populations. In addition to the escalating threat of being sold away from their families, enslaved African Americans in the first decades of the nineteenth century suffered from enhanced surveillance, ever more limited mobility, and a host of other indignities and restrictions. Slave flight to the Northern states and to destinations outside the borders of the United States turned from a trickle to a flood as conditions deteriorated in the South. Proslavery advocates blamed the progressively more vocal abolitionist movement for slave discontent and minimized the numbers of runaways officially reported, but the fact that mounting numbers of black Americans were taking terrible personal risks to flee bondage was difficult to counter.

It was to preserve their own marriage that Thornton Blackburn and his bride would make their own break for freedom in the summer of 1831; the year was significant, for 1831 was the watershed for abolitionism in the northern United States. Originally, the antislavery movement, a factor in both the South and the North in the Revolutionary era, had proposed that slaveholders support the gradual emancipation of African American slaves. Some hoped slavery as an institution would die a natural death. Those who believed black people should "return" to the African continent, incidentally ridding the United States of quantities of free blacks, sponsored an ambitious and ultimately ruinously expensive colonization scheme that resulted in the founding of Liberia. But by the 1830s, with increasing pressure to extend cotton-growing and the slavery that made it so profitable into the American West, it had become evident to antislavery advocates, both black and white, that the practice was not going to end anytime soon. More radical elements began to campaign for the immediate liberation of the nation's more than two million enslaved African Americans.

The first black antislavery convention had been held in Philadelphia in September 1830, as African Americans of the urban North worked to create mechanisms to both combat Southern slavery and ameliorate the conditions of their own lives, for even as free people they were subjected to unrelenting racial discrimination. Then, in concert with black abolitionist leaders, a white printer from Newburyport, Massachusetts, named William Lloyd Garrison published the first issue of the antislavery paper *The Liberator* on January 1, 1831. A year later Garrison helped to found the New England Anti-Slavery Society, a precursor to the American Anti-Slavery Society, formed in 1833. As the antebellum years progressed, there was a measurable increase in both popular and political opposition to maintaining a system of human bondage in a nation founded on ideals of democracy and freedom. Nearly three decades later this elemental conflict would culminate in the bloody Civil War. But before that time, a great many brave individuals, out of conviction or simple humanity, laid their livelihoods and even their lives on the line to succor black refugees who chose to take the freedom road.

For fugitives like Lucie Blackburn and her husband, the odds against making a successful escape were staggering. Federal law facilitated the efforts of owners and the brutal slave catchers they employed to retrieve runaways throughout the United States and its territories. Local and state ordinances nearly everywhere prohibited black people from defending themselves against their white captors in courts of law. That so many of the enslaved were able to liberate themselves is astonishing. That uncounted numbers were captured and carried back to places where white men ruled with the lash is unutterably tragic.

Once I began unearthing the history of the Blackburns, it became apparent why most literature about slavery and the Underground Railroad deals with the general rather than the particular. Rescuing slaves was illegal under the federal Fugitive Slave Law and the much more punitive legislation passed in 1850, so records of Underground Railroad routes and stations are scarce. Only since the middle decades of the twentieth century have most archives and libraries, historical societies and museums begun to preserve evidence pertaining to the heritage of peoples of the African Diaspora on this continent. So much has been discarded, still more destroyed, carelessly and sometimes intentionally. Only a handful of authenticated fugitive slave stories survive, mainly in autobiographies and in narratives recorded by abolitionists.

What genealogists call the "wall of slavery" makes fugitive slave biography extremely difficult to research. Theirs was a heritage of oppression, with the vast majority of its documentation produced by slaveholders rather than slaves, most of the latter of whom were illiterate. The problem lies with names. Although soon after Africans landed in America, they adopted European-style surnames, these were rarely recognized within the slaveholding culture that governed their lives. Most whites, if they acknowledged a surname for their servants at all, assumed that the slaves took the name of their owner. This was indeed often the case in the first generation out of Africa, but slaves were sold, inherited by married daughters, given away, or even raffled off as lottery prizes, and so, within a generation or two, a great many bore names that had no relation at all to the people who now claimed their service. The fact that white culture did not use slave surnames freed black Americans to choose ones they desired, pass them down through the female line as well as the male, and take names that pleased them rather than ones that carried any connection whatsoever to a hated master or difficult mistress. Names of towns and cities were popular, as were the names of people who had been kind to them, important events or battles, and even European heroes or figures from the Revolutionary War era.

To make people even more difficult to trace through history, records kept by white slave owners and overseers only very rarely mentioned slave surnames at all. It was part of the culture of domination they maintained to address even venerable black bondspeople by only their first names, as one might with children or pets. So hundreds of thousands of African Americans were born, lived, and died with no historical notice taken of their existence except, perhaps, their first names and relative ages listed in a white family's Bible or in plantation account books as "Little Buck, aged 3" or "Suky, cook, 34." Following the history of specific enslaved African Americans is therefore an exercise in the genealogy and migratory patterns of white slaveholding families. Personal papers might reveal a chance comment about this or that bondsperson. Accounts for medical care may offer insight into a slave's age or condition. Family relationships can sometimes be inferred from sale documents, wills, or inventories. Hiring agreements help trace the movements of this or that slave over time.

The vast population movements after the American Revolution further complicate the process of fugitive slave research. As slaveholders pushed out into the American interior in the successive waves known as the Westward Movement, they carried with them their slaves. Documents directly relevant to the Blackburns' slave experience have been located in repositories in Washington, D.C., New York, Virginia, Maryland, Delaware, West Virginia, Kentucky, Missouri, Ohio, Michigan, Tennessee, Louisiana, California, and Ontario, Canada.

Quite unusually, Thornton and the other members of his immediate family used the Blackburn surname all their lives, and it was sometimes recorded by the white people with whom they dealt. Still, for my first foray into tracing the biography of runaway slaves, I found myself combing documents for mention of an enslaved man, usually referred to only as Thornton, who had successively belonged to white families named Smith and Brown.

Lucie Blackburn presented her own challenges. Married slave women often—but not always—changed their surnames. Sometimes fugitive slaves did as well, to obscure their identities or, symbolically, to honor their newfound freedom. But Mrs. Blackburn altered both of her names during the course of her lifetime. It took some considerable time to realize that the "Lucie Blackburn" of Toronto was one and the same as the Kentucky slave girl "Ruthie." Despite years of intensive research, her maiden name, and thus the story of Lucie's earliest years in slavery, remains a mystery.

Again, it was the material evidence of the Blackburns' eventful lives that provided the foundation, for archaeology is always local, and so in my obsession with the Blackburns I sought out the places that they knew. The little creek still runs by the farm where Thornton's mother, Sibby, aged sixteen in 1792, worked her Kentucky owner's fields. The gracious red-brick house where Thornton lived as a little boy is standing yet on the old Maysville Road, although the slave quarters in the yard are long gone. I have been to the place where Thornton and his wife waited, breathless and terrified, for the steamboat that would bear them away to freedom, and I have stood on the Ohio River shore where they ended the first leg of their journey. In a nice piece of historical coincidence, the spot is within view of the National Underground Railroad Freedom Center at Cincinnati.

I have driven hundreds of miles of country roads, stopping at courthouses and historical societies, roaming through graveyards musing over the lives of the pioneers whose remains lay beneath my feet, and asking countless questions. I was gifted with precious stories passed down by the enslaved to their descendants, and heard the same tales retold, from very different perspectives, by people whose family fortunes were made in the slave trade. And I met many who, like myself, possess a conflicted heritage. I have always known that I have both slaves and slave owners in my own family tree.

With incredible generosity, both genealogy buffs and professional historians have shared with me their own unpublished research. Slaveholders' descendants passed on photos and letters of their ancestors, without caveat or caution. On one memorable occasion a chivalrous hitchhiker protected me from traffic and copperheads while I investigated a graveyard beneath a busy interstate off-ramp in Nashville, Tennessee. I learned that slavery and the racism it bred are not simply historical phenomena. Visiting one community in order to research its slave past, I had my car's license plate called in over the police band. The archivist I was visiting gently explained this was to see if I had "any priors," so locals would have an excuse to demand I leave town. Slavery and its aftermath are still very sensitive topics in the rural South.

There has been for me, throughout this process, a kind of historical coalescence; I'd happen upon a village library, and five minutes later, in would walk a descendant of the man who once owned Mrs. Blackburn. A wrong turn on a rural road would lead me to a place mentioned in one of the Blackburn documents, but no longer listed on any map. Stopping for lunch in a country churchyard, I found headstones belonging to children of Thornton's Kentucky owners. These were individuals with lives that paralleled Thornton's, but whose later history I had never been able to document. On another occasion, a hunch led me to turn my car around and backtrack several miles to a county courthouse that held, as far as I knew, nothing at all related to the Blackburns. There in the torn and faded pages of an 1830s land registry book was information suggestive of why Thornton and

Lucie Blackburn fled so suddenly, and in such a bold and perilous fashion. The most stunning of the coincidences came when I was describing to my elderly mother the thrilling escape from slavery of the Lightfoot brothers in 1835, fugitives from Kentucky who were friends, or possibly relatives, of Thornton Blackburn. It turned out that my mother, brought up in the Ontario country village of Markham in the 1920s, had fond childhood memories of "Old Tom Lightfoot." A son of one of that same family of former slaves, he was a market gardener like my great-grandfather, and he used to spend the week of the annual Markham Agricultural Fair as a houseguest at our family home. Such things happened not once but repeatedly over the years, until I, a fairly hard-nosed archaeologist with a scientific bent, was half willing to believe I was being gently directed along this rocky course I had chosen.

Sadly, all the years of research into the Blackburns' lives have produced images of neither Thornton and Lucie nor of the Detroit families who rescued them during the riots of 1833. Only imagination can supply the details—and their story contains more than enough drama to fuel it.

As tiny clues to the Blackburns' experience in slavery and freedom came together, twin themes emerged: The first is resistance. Black Americans fought back, constantly, and with awe-inspiring courage, against the power of the slaveholders to govern and control them. In ways small and large, African Americans resisted slavery every day of their lives. When faced with insurmountable suffering, they fled or they died. The second theme is the immense love of enslaved African Americans for their always endangered families. Slave owners sold affectionate husbands away from their wives, aged parents from their children, and even nursing mothers from newborn infants. More than the lash and the paddle, more than hunger and ragged clothing, more than the rampant sexual abuse that the system facilitated, it was the loss of family that motivated slave flight. Resistance and love of family are at the heart of Thornton and Lucie Blackburn's story.

In the more than two decades since a Toronto archaeological

team brought the Blackburn story to light, the Blackburns have come to symbolize the courage, ingenuity, and, above all, the immense craving for freedom that characterized the fugitive slave movement.

Despite unimaginable obstacles, the Blackburns were always agents of their own destinies. Abolitionists called the flight of bondspeople "self-emancipation"; in slaveholding terminology the same action was "self-theft." What eluded the slaveocracy was the fact that black people, even those living under the harshly racist society that was the foundation and context for American slavery, had the determination, intelligence, and ability to resist its dominance in complex and sophisticated ways. The Blackburns' decision to remove themselves to a place beyond the reach of their former owners was their own first step in achieving the liberty that black Americans believed they were promised at the time of the American Revolution.

Thornton and Lucie Blackburn were designated "Persons of National Historic Significance" by the government of Canada in 1999. They are also commemorated as people of statewide importance in Kentucky. Over a very emotional weekend in April 2002, and with national television coverage in both countries, twin historical plaques in their honor were erected in Louisville, Kentucky, and in Toronto, Canada. One stands at the corner of Fourth and Main streets in downtown Louisville, where Thornton Blackburn, a slave, was once employed. The second marks the location of their Toronto home and the archaeological site that brought the story of Thornton and Lucie Blackburn, free people living in a free land, to the attention of the modern world. This constituted the first binational commemoration of any Underground Railroad journey celebrated between the United States and Canada. Even a century and more after their deaths, the Blackburns continue to break new ground.

In popular culture, the image of the Underground Railroad is all too often one where kindly Quakers (all white) assist ragged, terrified fugitive slaves who are passive victims of their own condition. There is much that will never be known about the work-ings of this secret system, but one aspect of its powerful legacy is very clear. The Underground Railroad came about because an-gry men and strong, defiant women like Thornton and Lucie Blackburn rejected what it meant to be born black in the antebel-lum United States. The heroes of the Underground Railroad were the black men, women, and children who took the first courageous steps on the paths that led to their own Promised Land.

KENTUCKY

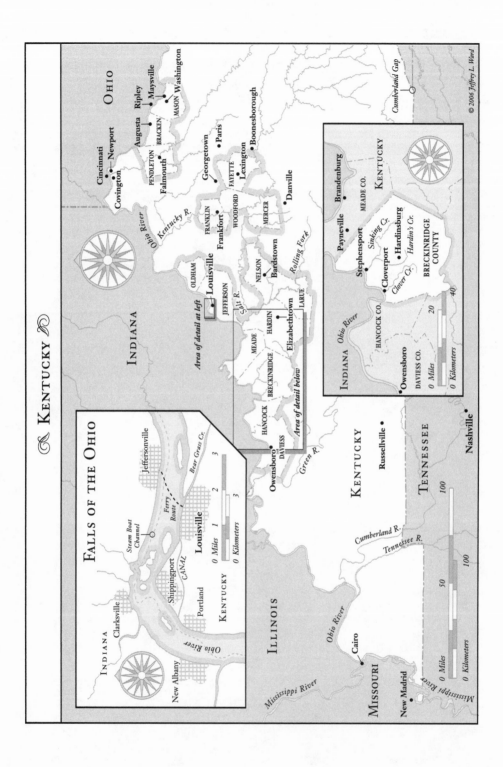

KENTUCKY

OHIO

Cincinnati
Newport
Covington
PENDLETON
Falmouth
BRACKEN
Augusta
Ripley
Maysville
MASON Washington

Georgetown
Paris
FAYETTE
Lexington
Boonesborough
WOODFORD
Danville
MERCER
FRANKLIN
Frankfort

INDIANA

Ohio River
Kentucky R.

Area of detail at left
OLDHAM
Louisville
JEFFERSON
Salt R.
Rolling Fork
Bardstown
NELSON
Elizabethtown
HARDIN
MEADE
BRECKINRIDGE
LARUE
Area of detail below
HANCOCK
DAVIESS
Owensboro
Green R.

KENTUCKY
Russellville
TENNESSEE
Nashville

ILLINOIS

Ohio River
Cumberland R.
Tennessee R.
Cairo

MISSOURI
New Madrid
Mississippi River

0 Miles 50 100
0 Kilometers 100

© 2006 Jeffrey L. Ward

KENTUCKY
Brandenburg
MEADE CO.
Payneville
Sinking Cr.
Stephensport
Cloverport
Hardinsburg
Hardin's Cr.
Clover Cr.
BRECKINRIDGE
COUNTY
HANCOCK CO.
Owensboro
DAVIESS CO.
Ohio River
INDIANA

0 Miles 20 40
0 Kilometers

FALLS OF THE OHIO

INDIANA
Clarksville
Jeffersonville
New Albany
Bear Grass Cr.
Steam Boat Channel
Ferry Route
Shippingport
CANAL
Portland
Louisville
KENTUCKY
Ohio River

0 Miles 1 2 3
0 Kilometers 3

Cumberland Gap

WADE IN THE WATER, CHILDREN

25 DOLLARS REWARD

The subscribers will give for the apprehension and return of a colored man named THORNTON, who absconded from our employ on the 3rd or 4th day of July, inst. Said Thornton is about 5 feet, 9 or 10 inches high; stout made and of a yellow complexion; light eyes, and of good address; had on when he left a blue cloth coat, and pantaloons; boots, and a black hat.

WURTS & REINHARD

—*Louisville Public Advertiser,* July 7, 1831

IT WAS JULY 3, 1831, the day before Independence Day, and Thornton Blackburn stood casually at the Louisville ferry docks at the foot of Third Street. The light-skinned slave must have been a handsome sight in his blue broadcloth coat and polished boots as he looked across the waters to the little towns and verdant countryside of the opposite shore. Beside him was his bride. Some years older than her husband, Ruthie was finely dressed in a black silk gown and carried herself modestly, as befitted the free woman one might mistake her to be.

Indiana's gentle green hills had never seemed so far away as they did on this glorious morning. The Ohio River had been the boundary between South and North since America first made these wide western lands its own. Free soil lay just on the other side of those placid waters, deceptively, tantalizingly close. The young couple was alone on the low bank above the water's edge. Behind them, above the riverbank, lay the city of Louisville. It was Sunday, and Kentucky's busiest port was quiet, for most people who worked the dockyards and warehouses were slaves and this was their one day of rest. The ferry docks were just a little way upstream from the Falls of the Ohio, with its jagged rocks and boiling, churning rapids, and the horse ferry traveling from Jeffersonville, Indiana, was making slow progress toward them against the strong current of the channel.

Though the role he was playing required him to turn a blank and affable face to the world, Thornton must have seethed within, for the least sign of uncertainty would betray him and his Ruthie as the fugitive slaves they were. At any moment they might be recognized. It was broad daylight, and both were well known along the riverfront of the city where their prominent Louisville owners lived.

Safely tucked up in Thornton's pocket were the papers that would be their passport onto the ferry and then, if all went well, a steamboat named the *Versailles*. The documents were carefully prepared, but Thornton Blackburn and his wife were entirely unable to judge their quality, for neither of them could read. One set, ostensibly made out by their indulgent masters, allowed them a day's holiday in Indiana. The second were the all-important free papers, legal documents naming the couple and describing each of them in minute detail, including physical characteristics, scars, carriage, and demeanor. These would enable them to travel up the river to Cincinnati and, God willing, liberty.

It was a desperate gamble. Their chances of discovery were very high, the consequences unthinkable. All his young life, Thornton Blackburn had seen hopeful runaways hiding in bushes by the riverside or lurking behind cotton bales on the dockyard, frightened, eager, all believing in their hearts that freedom was there, just across the river. Thornton had watched, too often, as the bleeding, whipped, and defeated were brought back by slave catchers, rough men who made their livings from retrieving fugitive slaves. Women as well as men were stripped to the waist and flogged at the post in the courthouse yard until blood pooled at their feet. Even the strongest, the most defiant who cursed their captors, their masters, and the men who wielded the lash, fainted when salt water or turpentine was poured on their horribly torn flesh so their wounds would not fester. It was not done for their sake, but lest the slave's value to his or her owner be diminished. Known runaways were then nearly always traded away, both as punishment and as a graphic example of the consequences to the "servants" left behind.

Thornton Blackburn had lived much of his life beside this same river. As a tiny child he played in its swirling shallows with crayfish and minnows, and caught fish from its banks as soon as he was old enough to hold a pole. If Thornton had loved the smooth, shining expanse of water as a boy, he'd have grown to hate it as a man. The river took people away.

"Sold down the river" is a saying first coined by Kentucky slaves, meaning the very depth of betrayal. Worth more to the great plantation owners of the Deep South than to the small farmers of more northerly Kentucky, slaves in their thousands were sent down to the auction houses at the mouth of the Lower Mississippi. There the price of American cotton, sugar, and rice on the world market dictated the value of Kentucky's "surplus" slaves. Since before Thornton was born, long lines of men, women, and children were herded onto boats or marched overland in long chained processions. They were stolen from the arms of loving wives and husbands, little ones abandoned, feeble old parents left to get along as best they could, and there was hardly an enslaved family in Kentucky that had not lost someone. And still the traders came, wheedling their way, probing the weakness of masters who drank, mistresses who feared poverty, or estate administrators wanting to rid themselves of the troublesome property that could turn so great a profit.

Should the Blackburns be apprehended in their flight on this fine July morning, there was a good possibility that both Thornton and Ruthie would be taking that slow journey down the river. They would travel south for mile upon endless mile, past the point where the Ohio River's green waters mingled with those of the muddy Mississippi, and on until they reached the market at Natchez—the "Forks of the Road," as they called it—or the many slave dealers' establishments at New Orleans, to be sold. Then Thornton would spend a few short years hoeing cotton, cutting sugarcane, or up to his knees in stinking rice paddies under the relentless lash of the overseer, before his scarred and broken body was consigned to an unmarked grave in the corner of some plantation. Kentucky slaves were well aware of the suffering in store for them in the Deep South. Blacks, both slave and free, crewed the boats that plied these inland waterways, carrying the length of the rivers' tales of the paddle and the whip, of hunger and work from "can see to can't" every blessed day, and death from cold and disease and despondency.

Ruthie, with her lovely fair skin and flashing dark eyes, faced a very different fate. Slave girls were chained, sometimes, for the riverboat voyage, to keep them from destroying themselves in the waters that churned and boiled around the great paddles of the wheel. Some did that in their misery and despair at the loss of home and family. Beautiful women like Ruthie Blackburn did it because they knew what awaited them at journey's end. Too lovely to be wasted in the fields or even as housemaids or cooks, Kentucky's light-skinned "yellow" girls were the most valuable commodity on the auction blocks of the Lower Mississippi. The prettier the girl, the higher the price.

In the infamous "fancy-girl markets" there, Ruthie Blackburn would be worth $1,000 or more to the right man. In richly decorated drawing rooms above those far-off Southern slave pens, beautiful mulatto women were displayed to a very private and specialized clientele. They were dressed in fine gowns and set to needlework to show off their accomplishments. Then chosen.

Prodded. Touched intimately. Sometimes stripped to the skin, the better to examine more private attractions. The best Thornton could hope for his wife, bitter as it was, was to be sold as a mistress, to wear fine clothes and play the courtesan for the white man who had bought absolute right to her labor, and her body. The least fortunate of the light-skinned girls sold south populated the brothels that served the gamblers and roustabouts who worked the river.

Less than two short weeks before, her master dead and his estate bankrupt, Ruthie Blackburn had been auctioned off to pay his debts. In the parlor of her old home on Green Street, the auctioneer had stood the girl high, showing her off to the crowd and crying: "A likely lass, a hard worker. Well made, too. Just right for the discerning gentleman!" Ruthie had looked so small standing there. Her skin was like coffee with the cream poured in. With her beauty and gentle, graceful manner, she had attracted several eager bidders. Judge Oldham, who managed the estate to which Thornton belonged, had been among the would-be purchasers that day. Perhaps Thornton had thought his master might be kind and buy his wife. But he did not, and finally, terribly, came the words "Sold to Virgil McKnight for $300!"

Everyone in Louisville's busy warehouse district knew that, like most Louisville commission merchants, Virgil McKnight occasionally bought and sold slaves. The city's finest merchandise was always chosen for the Mississippi trade, and its slaves were no different. Merchants like McKnight employed agents to do their selling for them, but he had purchased Ruthie cheaply and would sell her for the best price, if he could. Desperate to keep his wife with him and out of harm's way, Thornton conceived a daring plan. First, he learned sailing times of steamboats bound for Cincinnati. Then, perhaps from a literate black or an abolitionist-minded white, somehow he was able to acquire convincing sets of "free papers" made out in his and Ruthie's own names. Luckily, he possessed a good coat and hat and Ruthie an elegant silk dress to wear for their journey. These and a confident manner would be their only disguise. It could work. Traffic moved both north and south on the great Ohio. These flowing waters that had borne away tens of thousands of Kentucky's slaves might also be for them a passage north, out of this land of slavery.

A short distance down the quay, a steamboat gently rocked at its moorings. The *Versailles* rode low in the water, for black dockworkers, stripped to their waists and streaming sweat in the summer heat, had loaded her cargo the day before. She was fresh out of Wheeling, Virginia, and had just won the coveted U.S. postal route, so she carried mail along with commercial cargo and the usual complement of passengers. With a new captain and crew not yet familiar with the men and women who frequented the Louisville Landing, the *Versailles* met perfectly the Blackburns' needs that fine summer's day. By this time in the morning, a few passengers would have been making their careful way up the gangplank. The purser stood to greet them, keeping a watchful eye lest any runaway slaves try to sneak aboard. Meanwhile, the ship's officers stood on the upper deck, dapper in blue uniforms, their gilt braid glittering in the sun.

If all went according to plan, the *Versailles* would carry Thornton and Ruthie away, but not from this side of the river, where they were known as slaves. First they had to cross over to that other shore. There were no bridges over the Ohio River then, for the risk of slave escape was too great. Instead, several times a day, an old, cumbersome barge driven by six plodding horses working a great treadmill took the long diagonal trajectory that linked Louisville with the ferry docks of the town of Jeffersonville, the city's Indiana counterpart, just upstream. The vessel was to sail at eleven o'clock.

The Blackburns' escape plan was brilliant in its simplicity, but it had to be flawlessly executed. The first challenge would come when they tried to board the ferry. But Louisville was a border city with economic ties to the Indiana shore; enslaved men and women regularly passed back and forth by the ferry on their masters' business and even sometimes, if they had proven themselves trustworthy, on their own. Passes should be sufficient to allow this well-turned-out slave couple to travel over the Ohio River for a day's visit to Indiana.

Even armed with such documents, the Blackburns would not have had an easy passage. It was the Sunday of a holiday weekend, the glorious Fourth of July. Ferryboat operators were especially watchful on Sundays, for it was the one time slaveholders relaxed their surveillance, and therefore when most people made their bid for freedom, just as the Blackburns were doing themselves, and for the same reasons. Stiff penalties for even inadvertently carrying runaways encouraged viligance on the part of boat crews. Ferries running between slave and free states—in this case, Kentucky and Indiana—were required to post $3,000 bonds to ensure they would guard against slaves using their vessels to abscond. In Kentucky, heavy fines and impoundment of the vessel itself were the possible consequences for misjudging the status of an African American passenger. The proceeds were used to pay the aggrieved slaveholders the value of their lost slaves. The captain, mate, clerk, pilot, and engineer risked personal fines and imprisonment as well. If an inquiry proved that someone on the boat had *knowingly* provided assistance to a runaway, everyone involved could be charged with slave stealing and serve terms in the state penitentiary at Frankfort. No wonder every black who tried to board the ferry was questioned, and questioned again. Suspicious passengers were not even permitted to disembark at the Indiana quay, but were routinely returned to the Kentucky side of the river and turned over to the Louisville jailer.

After what must have seemed to the Blackburns an interminable delay, the old horse ferry arrived at the Louisville docks. Sailors tossed thick ropes to the dockworkers and brought the boat to the quay. Few passengers disembarked; it was early and most of the good folk on both sides of the river were readying their families for church. The sharp-eyed captain placed himself at the head of the gangway. As was expected, Thornton and Ruthie waited patiently until all the white travelers had boarded before presenting themselves to pay their fare. Careful to display no anxiety when the ship's captain demanded their documents, Thornton handed over the passes, which were subjected to meticulous examination. Their respectable attire and confident demeanor lent credence to their pretense, but in Kentucky, whatever their finery, black people were assumed to be slaves, unless they could provide evidence they were not. The Blackburns' forged documentation must have been impeccable, for at last the captain waved them aboard. Thornton helped his wife take the last long step down to the rough planking of the deck. As the unwieldy craft got under way, they stood in the bow, facing away from shore. Kentucky and their lives as slaves were behind them, and in front, green hills and a distant horizon.

The horses labored to turn the great wheel against the strong current, but finally the ferry landed above Jeffersonville. Mrs. Blackburn and her husband were again subjected to thorough scrutiny by the ferry's captain and crew before they were allowed to disembark. Then, the vessel took on a new load of passengers and goods and began its somewhat more rapid return to the Kentucky side of the river.

Just after eleven o'clock, the steamboat *Versailles* pulled away from her Louisville berth. At eighty tons, she was one of the smaller ships that plied the river. Even so, she carried between eighty and a hundred cabin passengers and as many deck-class travelers, as well as freight. Captain Monroe Quarrier was on the return leg of his maiden voyage on the *Versailles*, something Thornton Blackburn would have known since the ship carried goods for Wurts & Reinhard's, the dry-goods company to which his owner, Susan Brown, had hired his time. The captain's inexperience in this part of the river was something on which the Blackburns were counting this day.

The *Versailles* was just beginning to work up a head of steam for her journey upstream to Cincinnati when Captain Quarrier spied two waving figures standing at the Jeffersonville wharf. Pulling out of the steamboat channel and into quieter waters near the Indiana shore, he ordered the engines stopped. The pair boarded a skiff that brought them alongside the *Versailles* and the crew lowered the gangway.

Not before Thornton Bayless, the ship's clerk, put out a hand to assist Mrs. Blackburn aboard did he and the other ship's officers realize that their two passengers were black. This was the moment of truth; Ruthie and Thornton were embarking from the Indiana shore, a nominally free territory. This made their next deception—that they were free blacks lawfully seeking passage to Cincinnati on a public conveyance—slightly more credible than if they had attempted to board the boat at the Louisville docks. Clerk Bayless went forward to show their papers to Captain Quarrier. Given the stringent laws against carrying suspicious African American passengers, this was a decision only the captain could make. Now the entire plot hinged on Quarrier believing that the Blackburns were free people and not "slaves for life," as the law would have it.

Though an experienced steamboat man, the captain was anxious to remain in his new employer's good graces, and he immediately recognized the danger the Blackburns posed. He examined their papers carefully and then personally descended to the main deck, where he questioned them closely. Finally satisfied, the captain permitted his clerk to accept the money for the couple's fares. Captain Quarrier would face prosecution for his actions in respect to the Blackburns, but he would always maintain he was convinced that their manumission papers were genuine. It is, however, quite obvious that Quarrier and the youthful Bayless were utterly distracted by Ruthie Blackburn's beauty. When questioned later, neither the Captain nor the bemused ship's clerk had much recollection of Thornton at all: "One of the negroes was a genteel looking mulatto called Blackburne . . . The dress of the negro man I do not recollect but I think he wore a black coat." They could, on the other hand, describe Ruthie Blackburn in detail: "The woman was a fine looking mulatto, handsomely dressed and was called the wife of the man. She was dressed in a superior piece of black silk goods." Her manner, too, must have impressed them, for the ship's log read, "Thornton

Blackburn and Lady," surely an uncommon way for white men to describe an African American woman at the borders of the slave South in 1831.

By noon, Thornton and his wife were safely ensconced on the *Versailles*. Captain Quarrier ordered the stoking of the great boilers, and with a long blast of the ship's horn the vessel turned into the shipping channel and again got under way. Thornton and Ruthie took their places on the bottom deck. All African American passengers, slave and free, were required to travel on this uncomfortable lower level. Here the steamship crew, and the firemen and stewards, waiters and cooks passed their off hours. Free black people along with the personal servants of white passengers were forced to sit and sleep outdoors in all weathers. They shared the crowded space with fuel, baggage, and poor whites who had deck-class tickets. African Americans were not permitted to use the dining room or bar on the upper decks, although a small cabin with a stove was provided on the lowest level of some ships so those forced to remain outdoors could cook their own meals.

Mrs. Blackburn's experience aboard the *Versailles* must have been especially unpleasant. Foreign travelers on steamboats that plied America's western rivers regularly commented on the coarse nature of their companions. Even in the richly furnished dining and lounging facilities of the upper decks, the floors were in a disgraceful condition because so many people used chewing tobacco. As one regular traveler put it, "it ain't the spittin', it's the missin'" that was the problem. Frances Trollope, an intrepid Englishwoman who published a highly entertaining account of her American explorations, deplored the incessant gambling and drinking aboard the *Belvidere*, which she took from New Orleans to Memphis in 1828. She wrote, "Let no one who wishes to receive agreeable impressions of American manners, commence their travels in a Mississippi steam boat; for myself, it is with all sincerity I declare, that I would infinitely prefer sharing the apartment of a party of well-conditioned pigs to the being confined to its cabin."

It must have been very hot. When the Blackburns escaped, it was high summer and the huge boilers that powered the steamboat were located on this lower deck. The Ohio River was so shallow and its bottom so full of gravel bars, snags, and "sawyers" that boats built for its waters were constructed with the furnace above-decks. Stacks of firewood were piled everywhere, and the firemen, nearly all of them slaves, stoked the boilers that opened onto the bow of the boat day and night. Boats like the *Versailles* used enormous quantities of fuel, especially during the upstream journey against the Ohio current, and deck-class passengers were expected to help load wood at the steamboat's frequent stops. Not wishing to arouse suspicion and despite his fine clothes, Thornton would have had to assist the crew with loading the heavy fire logs and lashing them in place near the boilers.

The Blackburns must have spent their entire journey in a state of fear. Once accepted as passengers they had to maintain their masquerade, and do so perfectly, for their almost twenty-four hours aboard ship. The distance to Cincinnati was 132 river miles. The danger of being recognized was ever-present, for Ohio steamboats made frequent stops, and Thornton had worked for two years in the Louisville wholesale trade and along the city wharves, so his face was known to a large number of people who traveled and worked on the river. Ruthie was a striking woman who had also lived in downtown Louisville, not far from the waterfront. Her deceased owner was a well-known merchant who entertained frequently, so it was quite possible that someone aboard might become suspicious and start asking questions. Under Kentucky law it was incumbent on any white to take up a black he or she suspected of being a fugitive, and turn them over to the sheriff. Slave catchers lurked at every landing and transfer point, while the rewards offered for the return of runaways were often large enough to tempt the low-paid workers, black and white, who stoked the engines, washed the clothes, and catered to the tastes of the passengers of the *Versailles*. Fortunately, Ruthie and Thornton Blackburn's air of calm and their quiet refinement were evidently quite convincing. Not one person they encountered on their way up the river found in the couple's compartment or their conversation any reason to suspect them.

Sitting on the hard bench of the lower deck, Thornton Blackburn was traveling the very waters that just days before had passed his birthplace at Maysville, far to the east, where his older brother, Alfred, lived. Then it had flowed by picturesque little Augusta where Thornton's mother, Sibby Blackburn, had been living when last he knew of her whereabouts. It had been more than five years since he had seen either of them. One day he would find his way back to them again, despite all the dangerous miles that lay between.

Slave songs spoke of heaven as if it were just "across the Jordan in Canaan land." Kentucky slaves knew the land of freedom was always just across the river. For half a century, whether Thornton Blackburn was slave or free would depend on which side of one of North America's great inland waterways he resided. His passage back and forth between the two shores, with their separate realities, would shape his experience. On this day, just before Independence Day 1831, Thornton was taking his wife away to that glorious other shore. Their destination was a place they knew only in dreams. They were going to a place slaves sang about in spirituals. They were going to find a home in Glory Land.

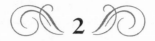

THERE IS A LAND
BEYOND THE RIVER

It grieved me to see my mother's tears at our separation. I was a heart-broken child, although too young to realize the afflictions of a tender mother, who was also a slave, the hopes of freedom for her already lost; but I was compelled to go and leave her.

—WILLIAM GRIMES, 1825

THORNTON BLACKBURN had been born within sight of free soil. Across the Ohio River's shining waters from Maysville, Kentucky, lay Ohio and the Old Northwest. The chains that were Thornton's inheritance from his slave mother could not bind this child of the river. He would one day take the freedom road.

Some places are catalysts in history, as so it was with this part of the Ohio Valley in the annals of the Underground Railroad. In 1812, as Thornton's young mother nursed her baby in one of the houses overlooking the river, buckskin clad volunteers at the landing place below mustered for war. They returned with astonishing news. On the borders of faraway Canada, they had fought black men in red coats. Word sped through the kitchens and stables of the town, out into the countryside, and down Kentucky's rushing rivers and beyond until all the slaves of the South were singing a new song: "In Canada, colored men are free."

Now there was a place to dream of. Some called it Canaan,

others the Land of the Drinking Gourd. It was said that the handle of the dipper in the sky pointed to the North Star, and by its light those who dared to burst their own bonds could reach a place where no man was a slave. At first a trickle, and then a steady stream of determined people made their way out of the South, until the shores were alive with refugees, hiding in the brush and waiting for night to fall so they could cross over the waters they called the Jordan on their way to freedom.

Legend has it, too, that it was at Maysville in 1831, just as shining steel rails were beginning to crisscross the continent, that a boy named Tice Davids fled to the riverbank and vanished from sight. Stymied in pursuit of his prey, his frustrated owner exclaimed, "There must be an underground road here somewhere!" And so the greatest social-justice system of nineteenth-century America took the language that was its hallmark and secret code from the latest technological marvel of the age. Those who hid slaves became "stationmasters," people who assisted them in their passage "conductors," and the runaways themselves became "passengers" on the "Underground Railroad."

Maysville today is a quaint riverfront town whose sleepy charm belies its historic importance. Located nearly four hundred miles below Pittsburgh, this was the pioneer gateway to the American West. All who traveled by water from the eastern seaboard passed through Maysville, the first port of entry above the treacherous Falls of the Ohio at Louisville. The town lies along a narrow strip of bottomland at the foot of an imposing limestone bluff. Some of the houses were here when Simon Kenton protected would-be settlers from Native attack, and Daniel and Jacob Boone operated twin taverns facing the river. A steep and narrow track carved by the feet of buffalo over thousands of years slashes a sharp diagonal from the bottom of the hill to its crest. This was part of the great National Road that led from Maryland to the heartland of the continent. Neat pastel cottages cling precariously to the stark green and brown of the cliff face. Here, where staircases take the place of sidewalks, live descendants of people

who were once bound for life to the folk of the lower town. Some
of their forebears watched a baby named Thornton Blackburn
learn to toddle on these cobbled streets.

Thornton's mother was just sixteen when she first came to
Maysville. She was one of more than 40,000 slaves from the eastern seaboard forcibly transported to Kentucky by their white
owners in the years following the American Revolution. It was
November 24, 1792, and Sibby Blackburn traveled in the flotilla
of flatboats carrying more than one hundred migrants from Virginia to frontier Kentucky. Sibby's owners, the elderly veteran
William Smith and his wife, Margaret, had uprooted their grown
children and their slaves to join a daughter and her husband who
had already moved west.

Sibby's voyage had begun near Blackburn's Ford, close to the
town of Manassas in Virginia's Northern Neck. There the Smith
family slaves had loaded onto a train of wagons all their owners'
possessions, tools to clear and plant new farms, and animals to
stock them. In his anxiety to maintain his own family ties,
William Smith had disregarded the bonds of blood and affection
among his slaves. One man, Francis Fedric, made the same journey as Sibby did, and at a similar age:

> I shall never forget the heart-rending scenes which I wit-
> nessed before we started. Men and women down on their
> knees begging to be purchased to go with their wives or hus-
> bands, who worked for my master, children crying and im-
> ploring not to have their parents sent away from them; but
> all their beseeching and tears were of no avail. They were
> ruthlessly separated, most of them forever. Still, after so
> many years, their wailings and lamentations and piercing
> cries sound in my ears whenever I think of Virginia.

All told, more than 200,000 white settlers made their way
across the Alleghenies in the last century. With them they
brought their slaves to create a new Virginia in the Kentucky

wilderness. Images of the West portray tough white pioneers and their equally hardy wives, chopping down trees, planting corn, skinning deer, and boiling clothes in immense vats in the front yards of neat log cabins. But, in the Kentucky Bluegrass, the fields of Missouri, the fertile Black Belt, and, later, Texas, a good many of the hands that built the American West were black, and few were willing. Yet at each stage of their own westward migration, these strong and resilient people established new families, created traditions, and made a place for themselves on land they could work but never own.

The hunger for land that drove European settlers toward an ever more distant frontier did untold damage to the other two founding peoples of North America. Native peoples were pushed from their traditional homelands, infected with European diseases, enslaved, and then herded onto reservations. Thornton Blackburn's ancestors had been chained on stinking slave ships for an Atlantic voyage so harrowing that the slaves' name for it, "Middle Passage," became imbued with fear and anguish. From the auction blocks of the Americas, they were sold to work the tobacco fields of the Tidewater, the plantations of the Carolinas, and the mines, mills, and factories of a thousand nameless towns. Without common language or heritage, stripped even of their names by white men who sought to tear Africa from them, these displaced souls melded the music, art, dance, and powerful oral traditions of a thousand scattered tribes. The American South has been called "the world they made together," and so it was, a blending of vibrant African culture with that of Europe, and the whole greater and more complex than the sum of the parts. Africans in America taught their children wisdom, age-old and half-remembered, that would help them survive in a world where white men ruled with the lash. Black women sang ancient lullabies to the white babies they nursed, and transmitted their own values to the white men who took them by force or persuasion in the slave cabins at night. In the fields men sang songs of Africa, showed "master" how to grow indigo and rice, and instituted task systems of labor that had roots on the other side of the globe.

The very cadence of African speech influenced the English of the planter class, while folktales and myths told and retold became new stories for a New World. Families shifted and changed as a father was hired out, a mother sold, or an infant given away as a gift, but the bonds they forged proved resilient, and soon networks of blood and affection spread out between plantations whose white owners were as interrelated as their slaves were. African America was born.

But the tobacco that made their owners rich also impoverished their fields, dooming the relatively stable society that had grown up in this older America. By the mid-eighteenth century, the gentry of the Old Dominion were sending sons and daughters, as well as hired overseers, to clear the unbroken land of the Virginia backcountry. In the Northern Neck, the Piedmont and the Shenandoah Valley, diversified agriculture on smaller farms would regain them the prosperity they had lost. Labor was supplied by "new Africans" purchased straight from the traders' boats but also by longtime family retainers whose skills and experience were necessary on this, America's first frontier. The next phase of the African Diaspora had begun.

Sibby was born on the eve of war in 1776 on a farm in southern Loudoun County, Virginia. Her mother gifted her with her own Senegambian name, Sibby, meaning "girl child born in strife." Sold before she reached her first birthday, Sibby would bear all her life the surname of her first owner, Colonel Thomas Blackburn. The Blackburns' Rippon Lodge by the Potomac is the oldest home in Prince William County, and remains a beloved landmark of colonial Virginia. Thomas's father, Richard, had acquired several satellite farms in Virginia's Northern Neck in the 1750s and '60s. But Thomas Blackburn was a patriot, and in the 1770s he disposed of farms and the slaves who worked them to finance revolution. A close friend and ardent supporter of General Washington, Thomas would live to see his daughters married to the brother and nephew of America's first president. They were the last two mistresses of Mount Vernon.

In April of 1777, William Smith, a captain in the Virginia troops of Colonel Nathanael Greene, purchased the farm at Blackburn's Ford. With it came several head of cattle and sheep, as well as "Will, Milley, Moses, David, Thomas, Old Will and Nell" and a mother and year-old child, both of whom were named Sibby. The Smiths, too, had a long history in Virginia. One of William's paternal ancestors was Lawrence Smith, who commanded the English forces along the Rappahannock River in the 1676 Indian War and assisted Governor William Berkeley in putting down the revolt of dissatisfied white indentured servants known as Bacon's Rebellion the same year.

As Sibby Blackburn grew, the world was changing around her. Saddled with land worn out by crop after crop of tobacco, Virginians looked across the mountains to the wide wilderness that lay beyond. American victory in the Revolutionary War nullified British treaties with their Native allies, which prohibited white settlement west of the mountains. The peoples for whom these lands were valued hunting grounds were forced back before the inexorable tide of westward expansionism.

Two of William Smith's daughters, Anne and Susan, had married brothers from the Doniphan clan. Scholarly Joseph Doniphan had already experienced frontier life, for after his own military service, he taught the children of Daniel and Rebecca Boone to read at Fort Boonsboro. He returned to Alexandria, Virginia, to wed his pretty Anne Fowke Smith, but he could not settle and in 1791 loaded his children, baggage, wife, and slaves into wagons and took the treacherous overland trails through the Cumberland Gap back to Kentucky. The Doniphans settled among friends and relations at the eastern edge of the Bluegrass. When Smith's physician son-in-law, Anderson Doniphan, announced plans to take his wife, Susan Smith Doniphan, to join his brother, the elderly William could not bear to lose another daughter. He sold off land, and sixteen-year-old Sibby Blackburn was forced to leave her mother behind. The parting, they knew, was forever.

In the fall of 1792, William Smith's party came to the place where the Monongahela River joined the waters of the Ohio. The Smith and Doniphan slaves shifted baggage and children, cows, chickens, and squealing pigs onto a flotilla of flatboats. This workhorse of the western rivers had only a rude cabin and a branch for a rudder and traveled with the current all the way to Maysville, a journey of nearly twenty days in times of low water. The girl caught her first sight of her new home as the packed vessels pulled into the mouth of Limestone Creek. It was November 24, 1792, for the family Bible records that Kentucky had already cost William Smith more than he anticipated. His daughter Susan, the doctor's wife, had died in childbirth early that morning, and was buried at the last bend in the river above their destination.

Maysville as Sibby Blackburn first knew it was a rough-and-ready place, and there were many more taverns than churches in the town. The rollicking riverport was an important transshipment point for goods entering and leaving the Kentucky interior. Bales of cotton, kegs of salt, and great hogsheads of tobacco sat on the wharf in untidy piles waiting for shipment upstream. As the weary slaves unloaded the flatboats and broke them up for building material, children of every size and color perched atop laden wagons for the long slow trudge up the Maysville hill. By nightfall, the entire party would reach the crest and the rutted road that led inland. Hemmed in by tall stands of cane and dark old-growth forest filled with enormous trees on either side, it would have been fully dark by the time Sibby and the rest reached the rippling brook known as Clark's Run. There the Smiths and Doniphans claimed three adjacent parcels of four hundred acres each. The slaves would winter in the country, preparing tools and clothing for the coming of spring when they would clear the forests and plant their owners' fields. The most trusted of the men were issued firearms, for the threat of Native attack in this part of Kentucky was far from past.

Joseph Doniphan was sheriff of Bracken County and he and his family were living at Augusta, another river town about eighteen miles downstream from Maysville. Anderson Doniphan's slaves labored at his farm while he established a flourishing practice at Germantown, treating patients in four counties and numbering both slaves and their owners among his patients. But Washington was William and Margaret Smith's own destination. The seat of Mason County, the town lay on a fertile upland plain some three and a half miles inland from the river and four miles west of their Clark's Run farmland. Established by act of the Virginia Legislature in 1786 and populated by some of the First Families of colonial Virginia, Washington, Kentucky, boasted the first church, schoolhouse, newspaper, book publishing enterprise, and post office west of the Alleghenies. Smith installed his family in the fine house he had ordered built there.

Meanwhile, Sibby Blackburn toiled with the other slaves to cut down trees and grub out the tough roots and stumps so they could plant the fields. They constructed a farmhouse so that Robert, William's unmarried son, could keep a close watch on the family slaves.

Sibby's work would have been terribly hard, as another transplanted Virginian slave remembered:

> When we arrived there we found a great deal of uncultivated land belonging to the farm. The first thing the negroes did was to clear the land of bush, and then to sow blue grass seed for the cattle to feed upon. They then fenced in the woods for what is called woodland pasture. The neighboring planters came and showed my master how to manage his new estate. They told the slaves how to tap the sugar-tree to let the liquid out, and to boil it down so as to get the sugar from it. The slaves built a great many log-huts; for my master, at the next slave-market, intended to purchase more slaves.

Sibby and the other slaves grew flax, hemp, and some cotton, although this grew only knee-high in Kentucky's cooler climate, and raised sheep for both wool and meat. Hemp was a very profitable cash crop used for cotton bagging, rope, and caulking for ships. Carding, spinning, and weaving comprised many slave women's evening duties, and textiles produced by slave women formed part of an important household economy.

Sibby Blackburn's tasks may also have included dairying, for the family made and sold cheese locally, preserving pork and beef for sale up and down the river, and putting up vegetables, pickles, fruits, and jams to last all year. The Doniphan slaves next door operated a large mill and distilling operation. Kentucky farmers had learned early on that their plentiful corn crops were best transformed into a more compact product for shipment to distant markets. Bourbon County, west of Maysville, lent its name to the fine Kentucky whiskey Dr. Doniphan had his slaves produce.

Kentucky's constitutional convention of 1792 confirmed the Commonwealth as a slave state, but Kentuckians were quick to discover that there was little profit in feeding and housing large numbers of blacks in Kentucky, whose climate and topography did not lend themselves to large-scale plantation agriculture. When Sibby Blackburn arrived, there were about 12,000 enslaved blacks living on the frontier out of a total population of about 74,000 people. Most farmers held twelve slaves or fewer, and there were only a handful of owners around Lexington and the state capital of Frankfort who possessed a hundred or more. Kentucky, too, was the northern border of the slave South. The Founding Fathers had early questioned the morality of holding nearly a million slaves in a nation founded on democratic principles. They limited its expansion by declaring all the lands north and west of the Ohio River forever free. In the North, unfree labor was waning as state after state passed gradual abolition laws. Even in the South there were abolitionists who believed that the system, bad as it was for slaves, was worse for whites because its absolute power corrupted absolutely.

In 1793, three important events radically altered the future of African America, and shifted the course Sibby Blackburn's life would take. The first was the passage of the Fugitive Slave Law by Congress in 1793. This enabled slaveholders to seek out run-aways anywhere in the United States and its territories, and accorded state governors widespread powers to apprehend and extradite slaves back to their original homes. The second was the invention of a machine—an engine, or "gin"—to separate the sticky seeds from cotton fibers. Eli Whitney's discovery revolutionized the American economy.

The cotton gin transformed cotton into the staple agricultural product of the South. It immeasurably increased not only the textile crop's profitability but the market value of the slaves believed essential for its cultivation. In 1803, Thomas Jefferson's Louisiana Purchase effectively doubled the size of the United States and opened vast new lands in the west and southwest for cotton agriculture. Under British pressure, the overseas slave trade ended in 1807, limiting supply to the domestic market and dramatically increasing the value of individual workers. Soon the slave owners of the Upper South, and especially those in Kentucky, found that their human property was worth more in the markets of the Lower Mississippi than was their labor in their own fields. They began to sell their surplus slaves to traders who marched them overland in long, chained "coffles" or loaded them onto boats to be sold down the river, in the thousands, to feed King Cotton's unquenchable appetite for labor.

But there was hope yet for the beleaguered slaves of the American South. Far to the north, in 1791, the Constitutional Act divided Britain's former province of Quebec into Upper Canada (which would come to be known as Ontario) and Lower Canada (Quebec). Antislavery-minded John Graves Simcoe, Upper Canada's first Lieutenant Governor, pushed through his reluctant provincial parliament "An Act to Prevent the Further Introduction of Slaves and to Limit the Term of Contracts for Servitude Within This Province." What is now Ontario thus became the first part of the British Empire to rule against slavery, and that by four full decades. It took time for the momentous implications of Simcoe's act to filter south of the Mason-Dixon Line, but when they did, Upper Canada was transformed into the Promised Land and the main terminus of the Underground Railroad.

In 1795, when she was nineteen, Sibby Blackburn proved her value to her owner's family when she gave birth to a little boy she named John. His father cannot be identified, for as Frederick Douglass wrote, slavery "did away with fathers." However, all Sibby's children were listed as mulatto, a term borrowed from the Portuguese meaning "of mixed blood," so it is probable that John was fathered by a white man. Sibby's little boy may have been "afflicted" in some way, for, when William Smith passed away in 1802, Sibby and her son were valued at only £70 in the old British currency. Other mother-child pairs had an appraised value of £100, while the most expensive were worth £120. George Morton, an elderly relative of William's, drew up the inventory of Smith's estate. Sibby Blackburn and her little boy fell to the lot of William's son, Robert.

A descendant of the Smiths had childhood memories of Sibby's new owner:

> I remember [Robert Smith] as a tall man, six feet or over I would think, erect and rather slender . . . He for a time wrote in the Clerk's office at Washington, and afterwards moved to Augusta, Bracken County, where he engaged in business with Frank Wells and Thomas Nelson Sr., as partners. He represented Bracken County in the Kentucky Legislature in 1815. He did some surveying in the West, and located some lands for himself, which afterwards became quite valuable . . . he was a man of energy and enterprise, and enjoyed considerable popularity.

Baby John disappeared from the Smith family records in 1806. Child mortality was very high among slaves because of inadequate nutrition, clothing, and medical attention, as well as the constant workload to which even small children were subjected. However, Sibby already had given birth to another little boy. She named him Alfred Blackburn. But little children were regularly sold, bartered, and mortgaged, so soon after, Robert Smith "put Alfred in his pocket," a favorite saying meaning he sold the child for cash. Francis Fedric observed the separation of mothers and children on the Mason County farm where he lived after his elderly master passed away:

> Aunt Aggy was the first slave sold; she had a little boy eight or nine years of age, and when she was driven to the chained gang on the road he ran after her, crying, "Mother— mother; oh my mother." My master ordered one of the slaves to fetch him the waggon whip. He took it and lashed the poor little fellow, round the neck and legs until he fell down, then he flogged him until he got up again, and still my master cut at him until the boy shrieked out dreadfully, writhing in agony, the blood streaming down his little legs. His mother was driven off with the gang, and her little boy never saw her more.

Such scenes contrast sharply with the benign image of slavery presented by contemporary white Kentuckians. An easy camaraderie had grown up in Kentucky's pioneer era; a more egalitarian air prevailed between slaves and their masters because of the exigencies of frontier conditions, and a few slaves had earned their freedom for their brave defense of their owners' families. However, by 1800, the relative equality of the frontier years was eroded by fear and hostility. Slaveholders, often greatly outnumbered by their slaves, feared nothing so much as the possibility of servile rebellion. Near Richmond, Virginia, a well-educated African American blacksmith named Gabriel Prosser and his band, rumored to be more than one thousand strong, planned revolution. Poor weather and betrayal from within foiled the plot, and the rebels were rounded up. Gabriel and his lieutenants were executed without revealing the true extent of their plans, but this and a series of lesser rebellions emphasized to slaveholders across the South the danger such evident discontent posed to themselves and their families.

Kentucky had passed its own slave code in 1798. Now patrols with wide powers of arrest and punishment were instituted, as they were in Virginia. It was the task of the dreaded "paterollers" (patrollers) to roam the roads by night seeking slaves traveling without written permission of their owners. Slave mothers like Sibby used the fearsome creatures to make their children behave, singing, "Run, nigger, run, run, nigger, run, the 'pat-er-rollers will get you if you don't look out." Other rules, stiffened over time, limited the rights of African Americans, slave and free, to gather in groups without white supervision, forbade them to carry arms, and set forth punishments for people charged with assisting slaves to escape their masters. As black life became progressively more restricted in the early years of the nineteenth century, enslaved African Americans were indeed seeking avenues of escape.

The process that brought about Sibby's separation from her own little boy began with the appointment of her owner in the fall of 1809 to be deputy sheriff of Mason County. According to the census, Robert Smith was in possession of eight slaves at that time. While improved circumstances usually boded well for slaves, since they were less likely to be sold in times of financial stability, in Sibby's case it meant that Robert became less dependent on farming. He therefore began divesting himself of land and workers. Then the War of 1812 broke out, and Robert and his brother-in-law, Dr. Doniphan, enlisted with the troops to fight on the western frontier. This may have been what prompted Robert Smith to hire out Sibby, one of his former farm workers, for the wages she would bring. In 1812, Sibby's eleven-year-old son, Alfred, was sent alone to Washington, Kentucky, probably to live with Robert's mother, Margaret.

Alfred's grieving mother was sent to live by the landing at Maysville. By this time Maysville boasted a number of factories, a ropewalk, and a glassworks, as well as tobacco warehouses, inspection stations, and cigar-rolling plants, the last of which were usually staffed with enslaved women and children. Because of the river traffic, there were also hotels and taverns that hired slaves as cooks, cleaning staff, and waiters. Under the normal terms of slave-hiring contracts, Sibby Blackburn would be entitled to food, a specified amount of clothing, and perhaps medical care, while her earnings would be paid to Robert Smith. Such arrangements were often annual, with Christmas being the time at which agreements regarding slave hiring were normally made.

Shortly after Sibby went to Maysville, she gave birth to her third child, also a son. He was quite fair-skinned, a "yellow boy" with "light" eyes, either hazel or gray. She named him Thornton Blackburn.

Who was little Thornton's father? A likely candidate was Robert Smith himself. As one former slave said in 1937, "One of the saddest, darkest and most pathetic conditions that existed during the period of slavery was the intimate mingling of slave owners, in fact many white men, with negro women . . . Very often a slave was sold who was the direct offspring of his or her owner." Robert, who was of an age with Sibby, managed the family's isolated farm on the Charles Run Road, and did not marry until 1804, about the time of Alfred's birth. Slave owners had almost total power over the women in their slave quarters, so even wives and mothers had no recourse for rejecting their advances. As for the white wives of the philandering men, as Mary Boykin Chesnut, the eloquent diarist who was wife to Senator James Chesnut of South Carolina, wrote, "Any lady is ready to tell who is the father of all the mulatto children in everybody's household but their own. Those she seems to think drop from the clouds." Perhaps, however, Robert's wife, Susan, took exception to such irregularities. The timing of Thornton's birth begs the question as to whether Sibby was sent off to Maysville because of her pregnancy.

When she learned that black people were free in Canada, did Sibby Blackburn dream of stealing away across the river with her baby? She had already lost two sons and she was again a mother. What dreams Sibby may have had for her newest son are lost to history. But when Sibby went to work in Maysville, she could see the men, women, and children arriving in droves at the landing place on the Ohio River, all making their way to Kentucky and the West. With them were hundreds upon hundreds of enslaved African Americans. She could see, too, the far shore on the other side of that broad green expanse of water. Sibby Blackburn could not touch free soil, but she and little Thornton could look upon it every day that they lived on the Ohio River.

William Wells Brown had, as a young man, worked on Ohio River steamboats that carried slaves going south for sale. He wrote: "The slaves were kept, men and women, promiscuously— all chained two and two, and a strict watch kept that they did not get loose . . . with all our care, we lost one woman who had been taken from her husband and children, and having no desire to live without them, in the agony of her soul jumped overboard, and drowned herself."

At age three, Thornton was taken from his mother's arms and carried away up the Maysville hill to live at Washington. No witnesses made note of how Robert Smith chose to inform Sibby Blackburn, a woman he had known all his life, that he had disposed of her youngest child, but Sibby knew his new owner, George Morton, for he was related to the Smiths and had evaluated Sibby along with the rest of the slaves when William Smith died in 1802. A noted local character, he was one of the last people in Mason County to sport the "short breeches and knee buckles" in vogue before the American Revolution. He had purchased Thornton not for his own use but as a present for his grandson. George Morton Murphy, called Morton, was nine years old and his widowed father was on the verge of remarrying. Perhaps it was to ease his grandson's distress at his changing family circumstances that on June 17, 1815, three days before the wedding, George Morton signed and registered this deed of gift at the Mason County Courthouse:

I, George Morton of Mason County, in consideration of love
and affection I bear my grandson, George Morton Murphy,
and in consideration of $1 paid me by George Morton Mur-
phy, now grant him two male slaves, a yellow boy named
Thornton and a black boy named Henson, both in the possession of William Murphy, the father of said George Morton Murphy, (who will be 21 years of age on December 26,
1827).

Thornton's new and very youthful owner was the son of
William Murphy, the postmaster at Washington whose strategi-
cally placed post office handled all the mail for what today are
Minnesota, Wisconsin, Indiana, Iowa, and Missouri. Murphy's
wooden post office building stood at the corner of his property,
right on the Maysville-Lexington Road. There was endless excitement for Morton and his little slave boys, for when post riders thundered into Kentucky towns on lathered horses, blowing
their long horns and full of news and stories for the adults, all the
children, white and black, ran to greet them. Later, stagecoaches
replaced the post riders. Long after slavery ended, a black Kentuckian told her interviewer, "De stage coach day war big days,
wen de stage coach war a comin thru why us little niggers would
try tet keep up wid de horses en run erlong side de coach en
sometimes a man or woman would drop us a penny den dar was
sho a scramble."

Washington was the hub of early transportation and communication by river for the state. The road between the Maysville
Landing and Lexington, some sixty-five miles into the Kentucky
interior, was so important that it later became the subject of
dispute when President Andrew Jackson refused to fund the
Maysville Road Bill as part of his anti-federalist approach to
government. Composed of three streets lined with homes of
log, brick, and stone, the town was a commercial center as well
as an agricultural marketplace and a seat of local government.
People came from miles around to shop at the seventeen

stores on the main street, and by 1824, when Thornton was
eleven or twelve years old, Washington, Kentucky, had at least
two taverns, three ropewalks, a cotton factory, and ten mechanics' shops.

The elegant brick mansion where Thornton spent his childhood remains a showpiece of Washington's gracious past. A construction date of 1805 is embossed near the top of a downspout.
Skilled slaves did the carving, plasterwork, masonry, and fine
metalwork of the gutters, although the cabins they once occupied
in the yard behind the house are long gone. A local historian described the house property in 1936:

> The home is a colonial red brick, the square porch most
> inviting. The doorway is perfect, reeded columns on each
> side and a beautiful fanlight above. This porch and its lovely
> doorway are admired by every passerby. In the rear of the
> house is an old-fashioned garden. It was originally laid out
> in squares, hundreds of Madonna lilies bordered its walks,
> lilac bushes here and there, snowballs, hundred leaf roses,
> the York and the lacquimot, rows of sage and thyme. Yellow
> jonquils in the springtime and the air perfumed with the fra-
> grance of purple violets and lilies-of-the-valley.

Items on the inventory of William Murphy's estate, made out
on July 6, 1829, would not have been out of place in the finest
homes of Virginia. They included a "dozen large Silver spoons,"
a quantity of silver plate, fine china and glassware, linens, sheets
and "2 Marseilles Counterpanes," carpets, bedsteads, and carved
wooden furniture. Murphy also had a substantial library, including a map of Kentucky, copies of the Southern periodical *Niles'
Weekly Register*, and a full encyclopedia set. As a companion to
Morton Murphy, Thornton grew up surrounded by art and literature, although he was never taught to read.

When Thornton went to live with him, Murphy owned ten
adult slaves and an uncounted number of children. Most worked

at his mill and distillery on the Licking River. His household servants included "1 negro man, Adam; one negro woman, Kitt; one negro woman Esther."

Thornton's mother was not left to mourn the loss of her youngest son in peace. When Robert Smith moved his family to live near the state capital at Frankfort, he left Sibby behind at Augusta with his widowed sister, Anne Fowke Doniphan, and her eight children. A traveler in the district in 1816 described Augusta as "one of the handsomest towns on the river." The Doniphan house stands there yet on Fourth Street with the original log cabin Joseph had constructed in 1791 at the rear.

The distance from Augusta to Washington was about eighteen miles. Only when her mistress gave her a written pass could Sibby walk there to spend time with her children. Who but their mother would tell Thornton and Alfred the trickster tales? Parents drew on African folklore to teach little ones how to survive in slavery. The clever animal fables showed how a wily person could triumph over someone stronger and more powerful than they. Someone had to warn her children to safeguard the secrets of the slave quarter, instruct them on how to keep a bland face to hide their thoughts, and teach them the degree of deference whites demanded as well as the amount of resistance to abuse and overwork that a boy, and then a man, could risk without being beaten. These were lessons slave children learned at their mothers' knees.

Lewis Clarke, who also fled Kentucky slavery, said that his mother, who lived thirty miles away with his brothers and sisters, "occasionally found an opportunity to send me some token of remembrance and affection, a sugar plum or an apple, but I scarcely ever ate them—they were laid up and handled and wept over till they wasted away in my hand. My thoughts continually by day and my dreams by night were of mother and home." Frederick Douglass spoke of how his own exhausted mother would walk twelve miles after her hours in the fields to be with her little one as he slept: "I do not ever remember seeing my mother by the light of day . . . she would lie down with me, and get me to sleep, but long before I wakened she was gone." Thornton and Alfred retained all their lives the deepest love for their mother, so she must have taken the road from Augusta at least occasionally to be with her boys or Thornton, a child of three, might have forgotten her.

She may also have shared with them her faith, for many authors of slave narratives attributed their own religious beliefs to their mothers' teachings. Josiah Henson, who knew Thornton in his later life in Canada, had also been sold away as a child. In his autobiography, Henson attributed his profound Christian faith to his mother's instruction: "Of all earthly blessings there is none can approach to a good mother. I remember her prayers to God for me . . . I remember well the feeling that those prayers wrought upon my heart, though I was but a boy." Sibby and her sons were all Baptists. Kentucky was central to the Second Great Awakening, with the landmark revival having taken place only a few miles from Washington at Cane Ridge in 1801. Between twenty and thirty thousand people participated, including a great many slaves, so it is even possible that Sibby had been allowed to attend. William Murphy was a member of Washington's Baptist church, and one boy who lived near Washington remembered his master requiring his slaves to go to chapel, sitting in the "galleries, apart from white people." Blacks were often skeptical of the messages they received in white churches and conducted their own secret outdoor services— not surprisingly, for Washington's minister once delighted in telling his mixed congregation from the pulpit that he had given his own slaves "each eighty lashes, in order to teach them their duty."

Thornton was very small when he was separated from his mother but he had the consolation that Alfred was also living in the town, and the two would form a supportive relationship that would endure all their lives. He also had new friends, for in the slave quarters behind the home owned by the county clerk, Francis Taylor, lived a large family of boys and girls. They shared a surname with the mother of their mistress, who was a Lightfoot of Virginia, and for reasons that still remain mysterious, Thornton would over the years have repeated associations with people by the name of Lightfoot, both black and white.

When Thornton was still a little boy, Kentucky's most famous statesman, Henry Clay, who often passed the Murphy house on his way back and forth to Washington, D.C., earned his title "The Great Compromiser" when his skillful negotiations saved the Union from possible rupture over the South's "peculiar institution," which was threatening to tear the nation apart. Southern cotton-growing lands had been steadily expanding through the Black Belt of the Lower Mississippi, and with them the power of slaveholding states in Congress. Ohio (free) had joined the Union in 1803, Louisiana (slave) in 1812, Indiana (free) in 1816, Mississippi (slave) in 1817, Illinois (free) in 1818, and Alabama (slave) in 1819. But it was the application of Missouri to join as a slave state that demonstrated how seriously the balance of power had shifted in the House. An aging Thomas Jefferson expressed his dismay in a letter, "like a firebell in the night awakened and filled me with terror. I considered it at once the death of the Union." Henry Clay averted the "Missouri Crisis" by presenting a bill to limit further spread of slavery to lands below the 36° 30' line of latitude in the Louisiana Territory, and saw Maine, previously part of Massachusetts, enter the Union as a free state to match the new slave one, Missouri.

While human bondage was becoming ever more tightly woven into the fabric of the nation, young Thornton Blackburn was learning to be a slave.

One recent book on the life of black children in the slave South calls theirs a "stolen childhood," and details how little ones were often expected to work from the age of four. One former slave recalled taking turns with another child to remain awake all night to rock the cradle of his owner's child, on pain of brutal punishment. Another wrote that at the age of eight he was "taken to the 'great house,' or the family mansion of my master, to serve as an errand boy, where I had to stand in the presence of my master's family all the day, and a part of the night, ready to do any thing which they commanded me to perform." House servants like Morton's two little boys would begin by brushing flies from the dinner table, sitting by Morton's mother to fetch and carry as needed, or watching her toddlers in the yard. As soon as they were tall enough, children wove, made candles and soap, polished silver and brass, chopped and stacked wood, and turned the spit over the kitchen fire.

Although serving as companion to young master Morton placed Thornton's behavior under continual scrutiny, the good manners, pleasant, confident demeanor, and refined speech Thornton acquired in the Murphy household were to stand him in good stead in his later years. Francis Fedric, the slave boy who lived near Washington at about the same time Thornton did, explained:

> My mistress took a fancy to me, and began to teach me some English words and phrases, for I only knew how to say "dis" and "dat," "den" and "dere," and a few such monosyllables . . . "Now, Francis," she said, "I want to make you quite a ladies' man. You must always be very polite to the ladies. You must say, 'I will go and tell the ladies.'" I repeated some hundreds of times, "I will go and tell the ladies" . . . But the most debasing ignorance is systematically kept up amongst the outdoor hands, any one manifesting superior intelligence being weeded out of the working gang, lest he should spoil the other slaves.

Although teaching slaves was not illegal in Kentucky as it was nearly everywhere in the South, most slave owners considered literacy highly undesirable, a sentiment Morton's father, William, seems to have shared. Benjamin Drew, a Quaker abolitionist who interviewed former fugitives in Canada in 1855, learned why when one man told him how he managed to escape: "I wrote for myself a pass—it was not spelled correctly, but nobody there supposed that a slave could write at all." Most important for his future choice of careers, Thornton learned to care for horses and maintain all their appurtenances, from horse leathers to fine carriages. As he grew into his teens, he might also have trained as a driver, for the Murphys kept both a carriage and a barouche. Postmaster William Murphy also bred horses. He was considered so fine a judge of horseflesh that he was appointed to the prestigious post of president of the Maysville Jockey Club in 1825. The club was noted throughout Kentucky and beyond, with advertisements for its races published in newspapers all up and down the Ohio and Mississippi valleys.

Morton Murphy had his own lessons, for it was part of a Southern boyhood in his social class to learn how to instruct and discipline his slaves. James Curry of North Carolina wrote for *The Liberator*, on June 10, 1840, that: "I played with my master's children, and we loved one another like brothers. This is often the case in childhood, but when the young masters and misses get older . . . they soon learn that slaves are not companions for them . . . the love of power is cultivated in their hearts by their parents, the whip is put into their hands, and they soon regard the negro in no other light than as a slave."

Experienced slave owners like the Murphys generally used rewards and praise, as well as the threat of punishment, to "train up little children in the way they should go." American slavery was, like all labor systems, as much negotiation as coercion. Nonetheless, many slaves complained of ill treatment when they were little, particularly at the hands of cruel mistresses. John Andrew Jackson said, "My earliest recollection was of my mistress, whom I feared above all persons." Israel Campbell recounted how the slave children rejoiced at the death of their sadistic mistress: "In her treatment of the slave children was her disposition still further unmasked. She fed them like so many pigs, and her presence was to them like a hawk flying over a hen with a young brood.

She delighted to be considered a 'bully'—fearing neither man nor spirit." William Grimes, taken by the Thornton family to be a house servant, recounted how he, as a young child, was punished when a jealous housemaid set out to discredit him: "First, [my master] caused me to be what they call horsed up, by being raised upon the shoulders of another slave, and the slave to confine my hands around his breast; in this situation they gave me about forty or fifty lashes; they whipped me until I hardly had any feeling in me."

Lewis Clarke complained in his 1845 autobiography that domestic servants were subjected to more regular scrutiny than field hands were and were expected to be at the beck and call of the white family they served, day and night. On the other hand, house slaves like Thornton did have better diets than outdoor workers. Inadequate food was one of the most common complaints in slave narratives. Many children were fed cornmeal mush, sometimes with a little bacon mixed in; those who ate communally on larger plantations struggled with one another to get enough food. Josiah Henson, who came to Kentucky from his owner's Maryland farm in 1825, wrote years later, "Sufficiency of food is an important item in any man's account of life; it is tenfold more so in that of the slave, whose appetite is always stimulated by his arduous labour, and whose mind is little occupied by thought on subjects of deeper interest."

Former slaves described how they "found" pigs, chickens, and other livestock, or "borrowed" flour and sugar from the larder. If Thornton was deprived of nourishment he learned early to "take" food, there being a well-understood distinction between "taking" that which was needful from a miserly owner and "stealing" from other slaves, which was wrong. One enslaved minister, born in 1840, recounted, "After I became seven or eight years old I was made a dining-room boy. I remember how Brother Henry and I used to steal the biscuits off the plates while carrying them into the dining-room, and how they would burn us while hot in our pockets."

Even if he were caught in mischief, truly brutal punishment was generally not a feature of life for the town slave. William Murphy would not have wanted a reputation as a "bad" master. Still, the fear of the cowhide whip was a continual goad to good behavior. Insolence or disobedience might earn a little boy like Thornton a beating. As the boy grew older, civil law also played a role in containing a slave lad's natural enthusiasms. State regulations governing the behavior and punishment of slaves had been much augmented in 1811, the year before Thornton's birth, and four capital crimes had been assigned the death penalty: conspiracy and rebellion, administering poison with intent to kill, manslaughter, and rape of a white woman. Other serious charges could earn the miscreant up to a hundred lashes. In addition, Mason County passed its own laws pertaining to slavery. Teens and adults who broke local ordinances against purchasing food or drink without written permission of their owners, traveling without a pass, racing horses in the streets, or allowing their owners' livestock to roam free could be sentenced to public flogging. The number of lashes depended on the severity of the crime. Children who witnessed slaves being whipped remembered it all their lives, which was of course the intent. The whipping post stood at the rear of the stone courthouse that graced Washington's Main Street. This was only a few yards away from the Murphy house, so Thornton would have been more than aware of the punishment that severe infractions might bring.

Slave owners like William Murphy were quite experienced in the management of their reluctant human property. They were aware of the need to allow people to "let off steam," lest their discontent with poor working conditions, insufficient food and clothing, and harsh punishments turn to something more dangerous. Quilting bees, cider-making parties, and celebrations of planting and harvest were an opportunity to pool labor resources, but they also permitted an overworked and oppressed people to forget their condition for a little while, and to do so within a highly structured environment controlled by their owners. Accounts survive from the Mason County farms where slave owners arranged contests, provided food and drink, and sometimes borrowed a talented slave musician from his local owner to provide entertainment. Very likely Thornton participated along with the other slaves living in the area. Saturday night dances were sometimes permitted, and the slaves were given passes by their owners to allow them to be absent for a set period of time. All slave gatherings had to be supervised by whites, including church and prayer meetings.

Music was always integral to the Kentucky culture, black and white. People made banjos, in actual fact an old African instrument, from hollow gourds, and drums were easily produced. The fiddle came from Virginia with the slaves, and no party was complete without its joyful sound. In the absence of any other music, the African traditional hand clapping and patting rhythms—called "patting juba"—were enough to set everyone's feet tapping. Christmas was the slaves' favorite time of year, for most of them were given at least part of the week off. Extra food and drink were passed around. Gifts of clothing or small amounts of money, sometimes a ribbon or bandanna for the women's hair or a penknife for a boy, were all doled out by the owners as part of the rituals needed to maintain the illusions of kindness and paternalism on which the institution of slavery rested. One woman had a few happy memories of her Kentucky childhood: "At Christmas and New Years we did have big times, and General Gano and Miss Mat would buy us candy, popcorn, and firecrackers and all the good things just like the white folks." Frederick Douglass took a more cynical view, believing that such celebrations and the accompanying alcohol were used to pacify slaves and prevent insurrection.

A bloody slave revolt sparked by a religious visionary named Denmark Vesey in 1822 emphasized to slaveholders across the South the danger that servile discontent posed to themselves and to their families. A whole series of restrictions were instituted to prevent slaves gathering without white supervision, to close schools that taught black children, and, in Virginia and particularly onerous for those whose families remained enslaved, to require emancipated blacks to remove themselves from the state within a set period of time.

Free blacks were considered dangerous. Anomalies within a slave culture, any success they achieved in business or family life appeared to contradict the comforting mythology of white supremacy that slaveholders had developed to justify living off the labor of so many unwilling and unwaged workers. Maysville had a branch of the Kentucky Colonization Society, part of a national organization largely operated by slaveholders (although there were indeed altruistic souls among them) whose purpose it was to send free African Americans "back" to Africa. Emancipated black people were integral to helping slaves escape the South entirely, as many slaveholders suspected. Thornton and Alfred Blackburn would have known "Doctor" Perkins of Washington, Kentucky. This slave, skilled in the medicinal use of herbs and plants, was regularly hired out to slaveholders to tend their ailing servants. On January 10, 1824, "Doctor, a man of color, formerly the property and slave of Constant Perkins, deceased," managed to purchase his own freedom. He then went on to buy, and later the same year emancipate, his wife and daughters. By the 1850s, Doctor Perkins was helping slaves escape from adjacent Bracken County. He died in 1854, aged seventy-six, a prisoner at the state penitentiary at Frankfort for the crime of "slave stealing."

Thornton and his brother Alfred would also have often seen "soul drivers" like the notorious Edward Stone of Bourbon County, who regularly marched long coffles of chained men, sorrowing women, and frightened children down the Maysville Road to the Landing Place. Robert Wickliffe, the largest slaveholder in Kentucky, estimated in a speech to the Legislature in 1840 that some 60,000 Kentucky slaves had been sold to the Deep South in the past seven years. Sometimes, with a refined sort of cruelty, Stone employed a fiddler to play joyful tunes to speed them on their way. A clergyman traveling in 1822 observed one of Stone's coffles:

> Having passed through Paris, in Bourbon County, Kentucky, the sound of music, (beyond a little rising of ground) attracted my attention; I looked forward and saw the flag of my country waving. Supposing I was about to meet a military parade, I drove hastily to the side of the road; and, having gained the top of the ascent, I discovered, I suppose, about forty black men, all chained together after the following manner: Each of them was handcuffed, and they were arranged in rank and file. A chain perhaps forty feet long, the size of a fifth-horse chain, was stretched between the two ranks, to which short chains were joined which connected with the handcuffs. Behind them were about thirty women, in double rank, the couples tied hand to hand. A solemn sadness sat on every countenance, and the dismal silence of this march of despair was interrupted only by the sound of two violins; yes, as if to add insult to injury, the foremost couple were furnished with a violin apiece; the second couple were ornamented with cockades, while near the center waved the Republican flag, carried by a hand, *literally in chains.*

At Germantown, Dr. Doniphan's cousin John W. Anderson was a trader with a reputation for dishonesty. In 1830, he would build his own log slave jail to house his human merchandise, chained to a row of rings in the floor, in the manner as their ancestors had been in the holds of slave ships on the Atlantic. This structure has survived the ravages of time. After a meticulous archaeological investigation, it has been taken down, log by log, and reconstructed in Cincinnati. There, its very fabric redolent of human misery, it now serves as the stunningly effective centerpiece of the new National Underground Railroad Freedom Center.

There is no question that an active Underground Railroad route ran through Washington and Maysville to the Ohio River. When Francis Fedric, who was about the same age as Thornton's brother Alfred, sought to escape, a local planter secretly took him to Maysville where a white family kindly harbored him and then rowed him across the river to Ohio. There he met "ten or twelve young men" who set him on his way north to Canada. Today, Washington's Paxton Inn proudly displays the hidden cupboard under the stairs where fugitives were concealed. In the process of restoring the Bierbower House, constructed by a Pennsylvanian who opened a carriage factory at Maysville in 1837, a "hidey hole" for concealing runaways was discovered under the front porch.

Kentucky slaves were well aware that they could find freedom north of the Canadian border. Slave owners countered with propaganda, spreading rumors that in Canada it was cold all the time, there was nothing to eat, and soldiers ate black babies. Vigilance committees were established by slaveholders in Mason County to try to stem the tide, but the number of fugitive slave notices in local papers escalated throughout the antebellum years. William Henry Singleton, enslaved on a plantation in North Carolina, said, "We learned little about the outside world. We did learn, however, that a man named Wendell Phillips and a man named Garrison were getting slaves into Canada and we were told that once you got into Canada they could not get you back again, that you were free."

Located a few miles downriver at Ripley, high on Liberty Hill, the Reverend John Rankin raised a lantern every night to guide slaves on the other side of the river to the place where the freedom road began. With strong support for his activities on the part of local free blacks, Rankin made his home a beacon of liberty for Kentucky slaves who managed to cross onto free soil. In 1826, his own brother's purchase of some slaves spurred Rankin to write *Letters on American Slavery, Addressed to Mr. Thomas Rankin*, which was one of the most influential early books on antislavery, and had a profound effect on the earnest young man who would be a leader of white abolitionists for most of the ante-bellum period, William Lloyd Garrison.

An incident John Rankin witnessed not far from Maysville was one of the most poignant scenes in the novel *Uncle Tom's Cabin*. When she learned her baby was about to be sold away to the traders, a young mother named (as in the novel) Eliza Harris jumped from floe to floe to cross the breaking ice of the Ohio River to save the child. So moving was her courage that when the girl sank, exhausted and half-frozen, in the shallows of the ice-bound riverfront on the Ohio shore, she was rescued by a slave catcher named Chancey Shaw. He exclaimed, "Woman, you have earned your freedom!" It was to Rankin's home that Shaw half carried the exhausted young woman and her child, and it was John Rankin who recounted the tale to Harriet Beecher Stowe, the novel's author. When it was made into a fabulously popular play, the scene of Eliza crossing the ice always made audiences cry.

In fact, the town where Thornton lived as a child was intimately bound up with the writing of *Uncle Tom's Cabin*. At the fine stone courthouse in Washington, a young New England schoolteacher witnessed her first slave auction. Almost thirty years after she came to Washington, Harriet Beecher Stowe wrote *Uncle Tom's Cabin* to describe in graphic and painful detail the horrors of the slave system. Translated into dozens of languages and with millions of copies sold worldwide, it has never been out of print. So influential was her book that, as legend has it, when Abraham Lincoln greeted Mrs. Stowe at a White House reception in 1862, he said, "So you're the little lady that has started this great war!"

Even though she once wrote, "The mildest form of the system of slavery is to be seen in the State of Kentucky," she set the harrowing auction where Tom was sold at the Mason County courthouse. The auction block on the courthouse lawn where the slaves were "cried off" to the highest bidder was still in evidence as late as 1939. Stowe might have been speaking of Sibby Blackburn when she wrote:

> The woman who had been advertised by the name of Hagar
> was a regular African in feature and figure . . . By her side
> stood her only remaining son, Albert, a bright-looking little
> fellow of fourteen years. The boy was the only survivor of a
> large family, who had been successively sold away from her
> to a southern market. The mother held on to him with both
> her shaking hands, and eyed with intense trepidation every
> one who walked up to examine him.

But there is another Mason County connection with *Uncle Tom's Cabin*. It comes through the Lightfoot family, thanks to Josiah Henson, whose life story provided Harriet Beecher Stowe with a model for her "Uncle Tom." The tale is an interesting one, for it links people Thornton Blackburn would have known well with one of the best-known tales of the Underground Railroad.

James Lightfoot escaped from Washington, Kentucky, to Canada in 1828 or 1829. He met Henson about five years later and convinced him to travel to Mason County, Kentucky, and rescue his sisters and brothers and their elderly parents. A lay preacher of considerable power as well as personal charm, Henson was a wanted man, for in 1830 he himself had fled a plantation in Owensboro, Kentucky, with his wife and four small children. Despite the danger, Josiah Henson traveled south to bring out the rest of the Lightfoot family. The age of their parents made them reluctant to leave, but the brothers promised that if Henson would return one year later, they would travel north with him. According to his own account, Henson then stole secretly into the interior of the state to bring out thirty more slaves. He took them safely to Canada. Making good on his promise, Josiah Henson returned to Washington a year later to carry the Lightfoot brothers and one of their nephews to freedom. The date of his journey can be closely estimated, for Josiah passed through Lancaster on "the night the stars fell," which was the great Leonid meteor shower of November 12 to 13, 1833. Josiah Henson in his autobiography closes the account of his Maysville adventures with the following:

> Mr. Frank [Francis] Taylor, the owner of the Lightfoots . . . soon after he missed his slaves, fell ill, and became quite deranged; on recovering, he was persuaded by his friends to free the remainder of the family of the Lightfoots, which he at length did, and after a short lapse of time, they all met each other in Canada, where they are now living.

Thornton Blackburn was long gone from Kentucky at the time of Stowe and Henson's visits. Morton Murphy was a delicate youth, and he died when Thornton was about twelve. In August 1824, William Murphy wanted a fresh start. He decided to sell his Washington house and move to Maysville to take up a new appointment as the town's first postmaster. For about a year, Thornton is believed to have been "bound out," or apprenticed, to a local stonemason, perhaps the same one for whom Alfred worked, since both he and his brother worked in the trade as adults. The former slave James W. C. Pennington was similarly "bound out" by his Maryland owner, and there is more than one parallel between his experience and that of the Blackburn brothers:

> The slaveholders in that state often hire the children of their slaves out to non-slaveholders, not only because they save themselves the expense of taking care of them, but in this way they get among their slaves useful trades. They put a bright slave-boy with a tradesman, until he gets such knowledge of the trade as to be able to do his own work, and then he takes him home. I remained with the stonemason until I was eleven years of age: at this time I was taken home . . . I was separated from my older brother, to whom I was much

attached . . . , our separation was permanent, as we never lived nearer after, than six miles . . . When I returned home at the age of eleven, I was set about assisting to do the mason-work of a new smith's shop.

One of Thornton's last duties at Maysville might have been to roll out a long red carpet from the docks to the steps of the Eagle Tavern, to welcome the Marquis de Lafayette and his son, George Washington Lafayette, when they made their grand tour of the United States on May 21, 1825, for William Murphy was a marshal for the day's events. The next day, Murphy was again on hand to greet the steamboat *Pennsylvania* bearing Henry Clay.

In 1825, Thornton left his Ohio River home forever. Like all slaves in the valley of the Ohio, Thornton Blackburn had lived his life in the awareness that he or someone he dearly loved might one day be sold down the river. He had watched as people he knew were loaded like cattle, first on flatboats and barges and now on the dozens of steamers that plied America's western waterways, destined for the markets of the Cotton Kingdom. Now Thornton was sent off on his own odyssey, away from the people and places that were dear to him. He would next be found at Hardinsburg, a town in central Kentucky about 250 miles west of Maysville.

3

ON JORDAN'S BANK

They hunt no more for the 'possum and the coon,
On meadow, the hill, and the shore,
They sing no more by the glimmer of the moon,
On the bench by that old cabin door;
The day goes by like a shadow o'er the heart,
With sorrow where all was delight;
The time has come when the darkies have to part,
Then my old Kentucky home, good night.
—STEPHEN COLLINS FOSTER,
"My Old Kentucky Home, Good Night," 1853

AT NOON ON November 29, 1826, a large crowd stood before the courthouse in Hardinsburg, Breckinridge County, Kentucky. On this day five nooses were lined up along the top beam of the tall gallows that had been erected in the courthouse square especially for the purpose. Even though it was a particularly chilly Wednesday, people came from miles around. There were many apprehensive black faces in the crowd. Practically all the slave owners in the district had brought along their people to watch *this* hanging. They wanted them to see firsthand what happened to niggers who killed white people. Very likely, Thornton Blackburn was there, for a year earlier he had been brought to Hardinsburg from Washington. He was just fourteen and his new home was a long way from the river.

The men standing before the courthouse were the ringleaders of the Stone massacre, the bloodiest slave revolt Kentucky had ever seen. Out of all the people in Hardinsburg that afternoon, Thornton may have been alone in knowing some of its victims. No one who ever saw the Stone brothers, long whips stuck in their saddles and rifles lying at the ready across their knees, driving their clanking, despondent coffles down to the riverfront for transport to southern markets, ever forgot the sight.

But the Stone brothers had made their last voyage. Four days out of Maysville en route to the notorious Forks of the Road market at Natchez, Mississippi, with a flatboat loaded with seventy-five slaves, their unwilling passengers mutinied. Although Edward Stone's valet had fought desperately to save his master, the Stones and three other men who had joined them for the journeys had been bludgeoned to death. The event had taken place on one night in mid-September, 1826, at the little river town of Stephensport, at the northern boundary of Breckinridge County. Although the slaves scuttled the boat on the Indiana side of the river and fled in all directions, most were rounded up and brought to the Breckinridge County Courthouse at Hardinsburg for trial. *The Maysville Eagle* of September 21, 1826, reported, "Fifty-six of these poor, deluded and desperate beings, were apprehended and lodged in a jail of Breckinridge County." The *Village Register* of West Union, Ohio, published the outcome of the case on November 14, 1826:

> THE NEGRO TRIAL:—The Paris Citizen of October 26 sayd, "the trial of the Negroes confined in the jail at Hardinsburg, for the murder of Messrs. Stones, Cobb, and Davis commenced on the 16th inst.; the result of which was the five of them were found guilty and sentenced to be hanged on the 29th day of November next, seven others strongly suspected of being guilty were tried and cleared, among whom was a noted fellow designated by the name of Roseberry's Jim. The whole of the Negroes that were on

that boat, where the murder was committed, have been apprehended except one or two and have been disposed of as follows: five of them were condemned to be hung as stated above, forty-seven of them sold, and the remainder brought to this county [that is, back to the Stone plantation in Paris, Kentucky]."

Five men filed up that steep staircase to the top of the tall wooden gallows in the Hardinsburg square, the nooses swaying in the chilly breeze. One after another, the ropes were placed around their necks and tightened. Then the trapdoor opened, and the bodies dropped down to thrash and kick, unless they were lucky enough to have their necks broken by the fall. Dr. Gideon Brown, Thornton's master, was the physician normally charged by the county with performing official duties, so it was probably he who was called on to pronounce the rebels thoroughly lifeless and see that their bodies were carted away for burial. Then the crowd dispersed. Doubtless many a shaken slave man or woman received a stern lecture on the way home based on his or her owner's interpretation of the biblical passage "Servants, obey your masters."

Edward Stone's "bright mulatto boy" who fought so hard for his master's life was freed the following January by Stone's widow. The murdered whites were interred in the little cemetery by the Baptist church in Stephensport, where they remain to this day. One grave marker reads, "Memory of Edward Stone, who departed this life September 15, 1826, in the 44th year of his age." Nearly forty years later the cemetery would be used as a campsite for Civil War soldiers. Just a few feet away from Edward Stone's grave lies Elijah Stobe, a member of the U.S. Colored Troops, one of the thousands of black men who fought in the Union Army. One imagines that these companions in death do not lie easily with one another.

There is no record of how Thornton Blackburn came to be living in Hardinsburg at the time of the Stone massacre. Perhaps he had been sold to one of the slave traders at the Maysville Landing. With their boatloads of human merchandise, they all passed by tiny Stephensport on their way to the Southern markets. Hardinsburg, Breckinridge County's administrative center and largest town, had no ready source of slaves of its own. Most local farmers and professional men traveled the sixteen miles to Stephensport to purchase labor. If so, Thornton was fortunate to have been sold before the boat on which he voyaged reached the Mississippi. At least he was still in Kentucky.

Abraham Lincoln, who was born not far from Hardinsburg in what is now LaRue County, recalled seeing slaves being transported on an Ohio River steamboat:

> A fine example was presented on board the boat for contemplating the effect of condition on human happiness. A gentleman had purchased twelve negroes in different parts of Kentucky and was taking them to a farm in the South. They were chained six and six together. A small iron clevis was around the left wrist of each, and this fastened to the main chain by a shorter one at a convenient distance from the others; so that the negroes were strung together precisely like so many fish upon a trot line.
>
> In this condition they were being separated forever from the scenes of their childhood, their friends, their fathers and mothers, and brothers and sisters, and many of them, from their wives and children, and going into perpetual slavery where the lash of the master is proverbially more ruthless and unrelenting than any other . . . One, whose offence for which he had been sold was an over-fondness for his wife, played the fiddle almost continually.

No sales agreement for Thornton can be located, so it is equally possible he was carried into central Kentucky with a migrating family. The mass population movement that brought frontiersmen and farmers, tradesmen and would-be aristocrats from the eastern seaboard to Kentucky in the last years of the eighteenth century had, by the first quarter of the nineteenth, given way to a second wave. The restless children of the pioneers now sought better farms and futures in the interior reaches of the continent. They carried with them their slaves to clear and work the land, as their parents had done before them. One Breckinridge County family whose name threads through the Blackburn story from the beginning had close blood ties in the earlier-settled river districts of the eastern part of the state. This was Dr. Gideon Brown's closest friend and near neighbor, Philip Lightfoot, who had a local tannery as well as a farming operation. Lightfoot's cousin operated an inn at Falmouth, in Pendleton County, just a few miles from Maysville, and one can readily imagine Dr. Brown asking Philip to keep an eye out for a "likely" boy to purchase when he passed through the Maysville Landing.

Although he had been sold away from his mother as a tiny child, Thornton's most enduring wish was to bring his family together again. Fugitive slave notices placed in antebellum newspapers show that newly sold slaves not infrequently tried to return to their families, even over great distances. But the penalties for escaping one's master or mistress might well have deterred a lad like Thornton, for Kentucky law was blunt: "Any slave, for rambling in the night, or riding horseback without leave, or running away, may be punished by whipping, cropping, and branding in the cheek, or otherwise, not rendering him unfit for labor." A boy of twelve or thirteen like Thornton was worth about $250 or $300 in 1825, and slaveholders went to much trouble and expense to protect their investments.

THORNTON'S NEW HOME was a far cry from sophisticated little Washington. Breckinridge County was on the eastern edge of the Pennyroyal district and to this day remains very sparsely settled. The less affluent pioneers who settled Breckinridge County came from Pennsylvania, Catholic Maryland, and the back counties of Virginia. They followed in the footsteps of Daniel Boone and crossed into Kentucky through the treacherous Cumberland Gap that was the overland route through the mountains. Migrating families generally brought with them only one or two bondspeople. Still, by 1825, more than 20 percent of the people living in Breckinridge County were black, and nearly all of them were slaves. By contrast, the overall proportion of slaves in the Bluegrass counties was more than 30 percent in these years, and Franklin County, where the capital of Frankfort was located, was nearly 40 percent African American.

Today, Hardinsburg is a small, friendly city surrounded by neatly cultivated fields. It has a population of just over 2,400 people, of whom about 200 are African American. Some are the great-great-great-grandchildren of people who were slaves here in 1825, when a lonely young boy from Mason County first arrived. They occupy tidy frame houses in an area some older white folk still call "Smoketown." The downtown retains its antebellum charm. The town mayor runs a print shop in one of the quaint storefronts facing the square, and another shop serves as a museum with antique display cases that are filled to bursting with everything from prehistoric hand axes through Second World War uniforms, Depression-era quilts from a nationally sponsored make-work project, and a nineteenth-century doctor's traveling saddlebag, complete with an intimidating array of surgical instruments and medicine bottles. In the center of the square is the courthouse. This is not the one that Thornton knew. Town residents today recount the heroic lengths to which their parents went to save county records in the 1958 fire. It is thanks to their efforts that the outline of Thornton Blackburn's teenage years in Breckinridge County can be traced.

Slave life in Hardinsburg in the 1820s is not well documented, but, in microcosm, it reflects Kentucky's conflicted attitudes toward slavery. One local tale recounts how loyal Unionists in the population defended Hardinsburg from a Confederate attack, while another recalls how, many years before the Civil War, the black cook of a local family, a woman named Minerva, saw hunger in the faces of a white boy and girl trudging alongside their family wagon out on the road. Running to get some milk and fresh buttered bread, she sat the children down on the porch to feed them. Then the family moved on, en route that day in 1816 from their old home near Hodgenville, Kentucky, to a new place in Indiana. Her owner would have occasion to remind old Minerva of the day she was good to the little boy with the big name of Abraham "Linkhorn," or Lincoln.

Thornton was just thirteen when he came to live at Hardinsburg, but under the slave regime that governed his life, he had passed the years of childhood. According to local tax records, when they acquired Thornton, Dr. Brown and his wife, Susan Talbot Brown, already owned a man between the ages of thirty-five and forty-five, two adult females, a young girl, and one elderly woman. There was one family group, for the man, Bob, was the husband of one of the women, whose name was Malinda, and their daughter was the girl, Serena. Thornton, as the new addition, is recorded in the local tax records as a single male slave, aged less than sixteen years. His arrival coincided with Dr. Brown's lease of a 59.5-acre farm located along Hardin's Creek, a few miles from the family homestead that occupied two acres of ground just outside the town limits of Hardinsburg. Soon after, Bob and Malinda were sent to live at the farm property, and young Thornton, as Dr. Brown's newest acquisition, became the only male slave residing in the slave quarters behind the family home.

Although the Brown house on the outskirts of Hardinsburg is long gone, Breckinridge County slave quarters were usually located in the rear yard behind the house, near the smokehouse and stable. The quality of servant housing depended on both the wealth and the disposition of the slave owner, but in this part of Kentucky slaves usually lived in small log cabins, sometimes weatherboarded, with a single door and an unglazed window that closed with shutters. Each cabin had a chimney, either made of stone or built of sticks coated with clay. Chimney fires were understandably common. Characteristically, there was often an earth or brick-lined pit or cellar dug into the soil in front of the hearth area. This was used for the storage of foodstuffs such as milk, butter, and meat, either legitimately obtained by the residents or purloined from their owners' stores. One man recalling his childhood in adjacent Hardin County said of the cabins: "[They] were very uncomfortable, generally without floors, other than the earth . . . Their bed-clothes were tattered rags, thrown into a corner by day, and drawn before the fire by night. 'The only thing,' said he, 'to which I can compare them, in winter, is *stock without a shelter.*'"

However modest Thornton's accommodation, it is probable that the Brown family slaves had enough to eat. They were owned by an up-and-coming family, and they occupied homes on the outskirts of a small farming town, which meant that ill treatment or outright neglect would be noted by the townsfolk. Josiah Henson commented on life in the 1820s in nearby Daviess County, saying that he had more food in Kentucky than had ever been available on his owner's Maryland farm.

By the 1820s, Thornton's new master was a man making a way for himself on several fronts—economically, socially, and politically. His early years in the district had been less auspicious. Like nearly all of his local contemporaries, Gideon Brown was born not in Kentucky but in the hill country of Culpeper County in Piedmont, Virginia. Migrating to Kentucky in 1785, his father, James, settled his family on a farm on the Rolling Fork of the Salt River. The Browns held few slaves, although James had been bequeathed one man he brought with him from Virginia, a slave named Reuben, by the terms of his father's will, on October 19, 1786. In 1806, Gideon Brown was apprenticed to a local physician, a highly respected medical man named Dr. John Goodlett who lived at Bardstown. Gideon's preceptor had taken his own training at Philadelphia, and had an extensive practice. There is no evidence that Gideon attended classes at any of the existing medical schools of the day. The untimely death of Gideon's father, the rapid remarriage of his stepmother to her deceased husband's executor, and difficulties surrounding the disposition of James Brown's meager estate apparently caused a rift in the family that never healed. As soon as young Gideon completed his medical apprenticeship, he set out to make his own way in the world. In 1810, he chose to travel north, to Hardinsburg, where the newly minted physician hung out his shingle as the only local doctor. Town records show that all he owned at the time was the horse on which he rode into town.

Gideon Brown, however, soon gained a reputation as a dependable professional man. He befriended the few families of wealth and power in Breckinridge and adjacent counties. Among these was the family of Big Bill Hardin, the founder of Hardinsburg, and locally famous for his exploits in repelling Native attacks on the pioneer settlement. The Hardin family occupied the original fortified homestead after which the town derived its name, and Bill Hardin rented and later sold to Dr. Brown a two-acre plot of ground on the edge of Hardinsburg, on which he built a comfortable home. Even more profitably, as it turned out, Gideon Brown became acquainted with John Pope Oldham and his wife, Malinda Talbot Oldham. Oldham was appointed circuit court judge in Breckinridge and Hardin counties and was also authorized to preside in the courts of Jefferson County, where Louisville was located and where his family had extensive landholdings. Although the Oldhams were to move to Louisville soon after Thornton came to live at Hardinsburg, the judge was to have a profound influence on Thornton's life. The family, which included two sons and two daughters, visited frequently, for they retained their Hardinsburg property for several years, and the presence of domestic servants in the household over the course of that time suggests John Pope and Malinda maintained the Hardinsburg property as a summer home. The Browns and Oldhams were very close, as later events proved, and Thornton Blackburn would have come to know the crusty judge and his pretty, gently spoken wife well over the years.

Judge Oldham was probably the richest man and the largest slaveholder in Breckinridge County. He was related to two of the most prominent pioneer families in the state, the Popes and the Oldhams, and his widowed mother as well as his sister had married into the extremely well-to-do Churchill clan at Louisville. The Churchills included horse breeding among their many activities, and a descendant would turn some of the family property into the site of the Kentucky Derby, Churchill Downs. The Oldham children, including John's brother, Richard, and sister, Abigail, were raised in the household of their step-father, Henry Churchill. When Abigail Oldham turned four-teen, she became the wife of her stepfather's younger brother, Samuel Churchill, and the mother of his sixteen children, thereby hopelessly complicating the Churchill family tree. Abigail and Samuel Churchill were high Louisville society in a town that prided itself on its aristocratic Virginian roots, and their home at Spring Grove and horse-breeding operations were re-gional showpieces.

Malinda Talbot Oldham was also very well connected. She was the eldest of three daughters of Clayton Merriwether Talbot, who with his brother, Thomas, were among the first settlers of Fort Nashville. For a time Clayton and his wife, "Pretty Polly" Crewes, resided north of Nashville at the border town of Russell-ville, Kentucky. In 1790, the Talbot home there served as Logan County's courthouse, producing documents whose quaint impri-matur of authenticity was that they were signed "on Clayton Tal-bot's billiard table." Prominent among the attorneys who argued cases there were Oldham himself and the rather rough-hewn but brilliant young future president Andrew Jackson. The Talbots eventually returned to Nashville to see to the education of their little girls. Clayton Talbot opened a tavern on the square and op-erated a successful construction company while his daughters attended prestigious private academies.

Sweet-faced Susan Talbot was on a visit to her sister, Malinda, when she met and, after a whirlwind courtship, married Gideon

Brown, on November 8, 1812, to her parents' evident annoyance. The match was hardly an equal one, and it was some years before Susan's father relented in his displeasure. This was manifest in tangible ways; Susan Talbot, the pampered Southern belle, brought with her to her new Hardinsburg household only a single capital asset, her old slave nurse, Rose. However, by the time Thornton Blackburn joined the Brown household thirteen years later, the family was much more comfortably situated; Gideon and Susan Brown were determinedly upwardly mobile. Soon after their marriage, the Browns had begun to acquire the three keys to Kentucky financial and social success: land, slaves, and horses.

Thornton's early training with horses while living with William Murphy at Washington would have been particularly useful when the Brown family acquired a carriage and team in 1827. Young Thornton would have found himself in much the same position as the slave Henry Watson, whose autobiography was published in 1848: "My mistress had two favorite slaves; an old nurse about sixty years of age, and a maid-servant about fifteen. On our arrival, we were installed in our new offices: the nurse was to cook; the girl was to attend to the light duty of the house; I was to take care of the horse and carriage, chop wood, and, any out-door work about the yard."

Thornton would have served in the dining room as needed, but also would have been expected to do heavy lifting and to chop firewood. He may also have assisted with his master's medical practice, working in the apothecary in his brick "doctor's shop" in the town square, and in the garden where he grew his medicinal plants and herbs. Thornton may well have helped restrain patients, whose surgery was, of course, conducted without benefit of anesthetic, or have traveled with his physician owner as he made his rounds, for Dr. Brown had a practice that extended over four counties. One slave owned by a physician acquired sufficient skill in the use of herbs and medications that after he was sold out of a doctor's family, his new owner assigned him the medical care of his plantation slaves.

Southern physicians were not particularly noted for being kind masters, although most treated slaves as well as members of white slaveholding families. Some took advantage of the availability of patients who could not complain of poor treatment, and advertised for the owners of slaves suffering from scrofula (a hideous form of tuberculosis affecting the glands in the neck), syphilis, and other illnesses to bring them forward for the purposes of testing medical treatments before they prescribed them for whites. It is sobering to realize that after Kentucky's "Father of the Ovariotomy," Dr. Ephraim McDowell, performed his first such successful surgery on a purely emergency basis, he carried out as many as nine more on slave women before trying his hand on a white patient again.

Slaves on smallholdings such as the Browns had were generally kept very close to home. They lived in intimate circumstances with their owners' families and enjoyed almost no privacy or autonomy. The objective, of course, was to extract the maximum amount of labor from each worker while maintaining as much control as possible over their personal lives. On the other hand, because there was daily contact between the slaves and their owners, black Americans in such circumstances tended to be better treated than those on large plantations, where hired overseers were responsible for making large profits for their employers.

The female slaves primarily worked in the house with Susan Brown, caring for her children, cleaning, cooking, and managing the kitchen garden and whatever chickens and other small livestock were kept about the home place. Women of the era did prodigious amounts of laundry that had to be boiled in huge kettles and wrung out by hand before being line dried, made soap and candles, and produced much of the clothing from fabric they produced themselves for household consumption. The Browns would have worn clothes made of purchased goods, but they owned both large and small looms, as well as equipment for spinning cotton, carding wool, and making thread of cotton, woolen, and flaxen fibers. The latter, mixed with wool, would have made up the ubiquitous linsey-woolsey that was the staple winter clothing of children, slaves, and even the poorer of the white farmers throughout Kentucky. Thornton may also have worn coarse clothing manufactured specifically for slave wear. Ads for "Negro cloth" and "Negro denim" appeared regularly in Kentucky newspapers. After freedom came, previously enslaved Kentuckians described their clothing as generally having been miserably inadequate for the cooler climate of this border state. Noted author and former Kentucky slave William Wells Brown wrote:

> On "Poplar Farm," the hands drew their share of clothing on Christmas day for the year. The clothing for both men and women was made up by women kept for general sewing and housework. One pair of pants, and two shirts, made the entire stock for a male field hand. The women's garments were manufactured from the same goods that the men received. Many of the men worked at night for themselves, making splint and corn brooms, baskets, shuck mats, and axe-handles, which they would sell in the city during Christmas week.

Christmas presents from their owners, too, sometimes took the form of fabric for making pretty dresses or a few hair ribbons or bright bandannas to relieve the monotony of the durable brown, gray, and butternut clothing most wore. Since Thornton lived right on the edge of town and was owned by a man who by all accounts seems to have been aspiring to move up in society, he was likely better clad than field hands on local farms, especially if he was expected to drive the family carriage.

Thornton and the slave girls would have worked alongside Gideon and Susan Brown's sons in the seasonal round of duties at the farm property as well. Plowing, planting, and harvesting all required additional hands, and on a smallholding everyone would have been expected to do his or her share. Rural farmers also helped one another as needed, and since most of the hard labor in a slave society was done by slaves, it was through the provision of slave workers for special duties that such assistance was usually rendered. As at Washington, Thornton and the other slaves in the district would have attended barn raisings, quilting bees, and planting and harvest activities such as cider pressing or winnowing the wheat crop, all of which brought together slaves from local farms. Corn shucking, tobacco harvesting, and hemp breaking were times when slaves from several families' properties cooperated to get the job done. Another former slave explained the advantages to owners:

> A husking-match is where a farmer gets say eight or ten hundred bushels of corn; he sends round to his neighbors to have their servants come such a night to help his servants husk corn, and they generally have something of a supper, and plenty of cider, and sometimes something else after supper. They commence to husk corn, and not unfrequently they keep it up till long after midnight, singing songs and telling stories; and I have often known from five to six hundred bushels to be husked in one night.

Contests of strength, endurance, or speed kept such events interesting and moved the work along as well.

These celebratory occasions came at the end of hard, long days of work for the slaves. Dances and music, as well as the liberal application of whiskey to lubricate such festivities, together with the inevitable romantic entanglements that resulted, were much anticipated by Kentucky's rural slave population, especially by young people like Thornton Blackburn.

Food was used as incentive rather than reward. One Maryland slave commented on this in his autobiography: "The slaves had no butter, coffee, tea, or sugar; occasionally they were allowed milk, but not statedly; the only exception to this statement was the 'harvest provisions.' In harvest, when cutting the grain, which lasted from two to three weeks in the heat of summer, they were allowed some fresh meat, rice, sugar, and coffee; and also their allowance of whiskey."

Young Thornton probably danced to the fiddler, kissed the girls, and perhaps imbibed a bit too freely of the whiskey. But it would be a mistake to misunderstand the fundamentally brutal, exploitative nature of the slave system under which Thornton Blackburn lived. Punishments for any form of resistance or negligence tended to be swift and vicious. Whipping was a common form of punishment for infractions of the many rules slaveholders imposed on "their people." Insolence, oversleeping, being off the property without a written pass, or inattention to duty might all bring on physical punishment. The dangers from these two ever-present forms of surveillance were fearsome, and it is unlikely that a boy like Thornton entirely escaped the whip. It is tempting to envision him, a high-spirited youth with an itch to go dancing, as another slave of a similar era recalled years later:

I took one of my master's horses to go to a negro dance, and on my return the patrols were so numerous on the road that I was unable to return home without observation, and it being past usual hour for being at home, I was so afraid that when two of them observed me I left the horse and took to my feet, and made my way to the woods, where I remained all day, afraid to go home for fear of the consequences.

Slave narratives and autobiographies are replete with accounts of people being paddled with a wooden board kept for the purpose:

A board about two feet in length and one inch in thickness, having fourteen holes bored through it, about an inch in circumference. This instrument of torture he would apply, until the slave was exhausted, on parts which the purchaser would not be likely to examine. This mode of punishment is considered one of the most cruel ever invented, as the flesh protrudes through these holes at every blow, and forms bunches and blisters the size of each hole, causing much lameness and soreness to the person receiving them.

By day, Thornton would have been kept busy under the watchful eye of the family, while by night the feared "paterollers" ranged on horseback through the countryside. These coarse men, generally employed by the county to ensure that slaves all remained safely in their own beds after dark, meted out rough justice to those found sneaking out of the quarters to meet a girl, attend a clandestine dance, or perhaps pinch a chicken or two from a neighborhood coop. Sometimes the patrollers left a slave they flogged tied up all night to a tree, as a warning to others. It was not unknown for someone who defied these men to be whipped until the blood ran or even to death. One enslaved young man about Thornton's age recalled in later years that sometimes the black folk retaliated as well:

> The laws were very strict on the slaves . . . [They] would slip off to church and frolics and the patrollers were continually after them, but the slaves would play all kinds of tricks on them . . . I went to a dance in the woods; the music consisted of tambourine, banjo and bones, but before the dance began they tied grapevines across the road, just high enough to catch a man riding horse back across the face or neck. When they heard the patrollers coming they ran, and the patrollers right after them; many of them were crippled, but not a slave was hurt or caught.

However, wise slaveholders turned a blind eye to minor infractions, if only because they were aware that too harsh treatment might encourage a young man like Thornton to abscond. Slaves frequently resisted abuse by absenting themselves for a few hours or even several days at a time. But Thornton Blackburn while he lived at Hardinsburg was in just the right age group and situation to consider leaving his chains behind altogether. The vast majority of successful runaways who made it all the way to Canada were young men, particularly those who were unmarried and did not yet have children. Coming from the Maysville area, Thornton had more cause than most to know what possibilities lay on the other side of the Ohio River.

Breckinridge County had its own active fugitive slave routes. One ran from Nashville and points south through Russellville, in Logan County, and up through Hardinsburg on the way to the Ohio shore. Another route went north to the town of Brandenburg on the river, while a third curved to the north and west of Hardinsburg toward Owensboro on the river.

There is no evidence to suggest Thornton ever tried to run away, which implies that his treatment at the Brown family's hands was probably relatively mild. He lived in Breckinridge County for almost five years, until he was about seventeen. The quality of his connection with the other slaves in the Brown family cannot be surmised. But he was much of an age with Gideon and Susan Brown's own sons and also with their first cousins the Oldham boys, Talbot and William. One can readily imagine Thornton being charged with the duty of keeping the teenage sons of the families he served safe as they stalked game in the forests or fished in the local streams. Dr. Brown owned, according to the inventory of his estate, a number of fine rifles and a shotgun, and the verse of "My Old Kentucky Home" that opens this chapter is witness to hunting as a favorite pastime for enslaved men. Archaeological evidence proves that Thornton enjoyed hunting and fishing well into his old age, so perhaps it was in the fields and streams of Breckinridge County that he acquired his skill.

How Thornton was treated by Susan and Gideon Brown is unknown, but Susan spent far more time with the household slaves than did her itinerant husband. She was unused to physical labor and with so large a family must regularly have found herself with too much to do and too few hands to accomplish essential tasks. If she occasionally took out her temper on her domestic servants or the yard boy—in this case, Thornton—it would not have been an unusual by-product of slaveholding. What little can be discerned of Gideon Brown's character suggests that he was a proud man, much concerned with keeping up appearances and with both material and social advancement.

Thornton Blackburn was a resourceful man in his later life, and there is no reason to believe he was not so from an early age. Slaves like young Thornton had little control over their owners, but a good deal of power over how their own demeanor and behavior affected the people who dictated the conditions of their lives. Brought up in slavery, he was aware that appearing willing and establishing a good relationship with Dr. and Mrs. Brown were essential, else his own life would be a misery. The manipulation of personal relationships with masters, mistresses, and other whites with whom they came into contact was both a survival skill and perhaps the subtlest form of resistance available to enslaved African Americans. As one historian eloquently put it, "Blacks and whites struggled unceasingly within the slave system, with each race endeavoring to extend its control to maximum possible limits. Each group defined its unity in large part by its contentious relationship with the other. Neither existed in autonomy. Each was defined by its opposition to the other." Dr. Brown, for his part, had to negotiate to some extent the degree of control he would have over his slave Thornton Blackburn. One of the ways this was done was by paying slaves for small services, or "Sunday work," outside their usual duties.

Dr. Brown's will shows that he paid Thornton such fees. While most enslaved African Americans used the money to provide themselves and their families with a few creature comforts, others had more long-term goals in mind. Is it possible that even as a lad Thornton was dreaming of purchasing his own freedom? Enslaved men and women regularly worked out contracts with their owners to buy themselves, often at full-market price, and sometimes were able to purchase their entire families out of slavery in this way. A prime adult house slave in the 1830s was worth between $500 and $700. Using the Consumer Price Index as a basis of comparison, this would be between $10,000 and $14,000 in today's currency.

By the time Thornton Blackburn had reached his teens, it had become apparent that the South's "peculiar institution" was clearly not going to die a natural death, as the earliest abolitionists had hoped. Clayton Talbot's old friend, Andrew Jackson, was elected to the White House in late 1828, and slavery was becoming ever more firmly entrenched, both in the economy and in the distinctive culture that flourished south of the Mason-Dixon Line. Northerners genuinely concerned about black welfare turned away from the impractical and very expensive solution offered by the American Colonization Society to "repatriate" America's two million slaves to the western coast of Africa, Henry Clay's pet project and one in which he sincerely believed. They began instead to consider immediate abolition as the solution for the nation's ills. In the meantime, dedicated reformers like William Wilberforce and Thomas Clarkson were hounding British parliamentarians toward ending slavery in the West Indies, and women across the British Isles launched a massive assault on the bastions of male-dominated capitalism. The antislavery movement offered British, American, and Canadian women a unique opportunity to become active in the political realm. For the time, they spoke out in public, even before mixed audiences, although this innovation caused fissures in the ranks of the male-dominated abolitionist movement. Many of the women who organized the bazaars, sewing clubs, reading rooms, and fund-raising drives aimed at ameliorating the condition of enslaved African Americans later went on to become leaders in other reform efforts, especially the struggle for female suffrage.

In the face of increasing criticism both from the Northern states and abroad, proslavery apologists devised complex and strident justification for slavery's continued existence, based on the Bible, history, science, and "natural law." The story of Ham was trotted out to show human bondage was the manifestation of divine will. A former slave and the greatest of all the black abolitionists, Frederick Douglass was pithy on the subject: "If the lineal descendants of Ham are alone to be scripturally enslaved, it is certain that slavery at the south must soon become unscriptural; for thousands are ushered into the world, annually, who, like myself, owe their existence to white fathers, and those fathers most frequently their own masters."

The "democratization of America" that was ushered in by Jackson's election benefited white men. It did not include Native Americans and African Americans, nor did it extend the few civil liberties enjoyed by women in the first decades of the 1800s. Although many felt a breath of fresh western air wafting through Washington, President Jackson was served by slaves in the White House and on a large plantation, the Hermitage, near Nashville. The period of Jacksonian Democracy was also characterized by a rise in sectarian feeling; this was the era of nullification. Jackson's former ally John C. Calhoun of South Carolina abandoned his former federalist stance along with his vice presidency, and promoted states' rights over the demands of the Union. What the crisis did on the larger stage was demonstrate that the rule permitting each slave to be counted for "three-fifths" of a man when determining population for election to the House of Representatives in the slaveholding states, coupled with the expansion of slavery into newly annexed territories, was giving the agrarian South a competitive edge that the industrializing North would not long endure. Tensions that had precipitated the Missouri Crisis of 1819 deepened, only finally to be resolved with the coming of the Civil War.

Whatever external problems were brewing, Thornton's own situation seemed quite stable, although he must have thought often of his mother and brother so far away on the banks of the Ohio. But the fortunes of the enslaved ever rose and fell with those who claimed their service, and in the spring of 1829, tragedy struck the Brown household. Dr. Gideon Brown died, along with at least two of his children. Brown's illness was quite short and evidently completely unexpected, because at the time the doctor was engaged in a series of complex land transfers.

Thornton Blackburn's life was thrown into turmoil. Whether he genuinely grieved for the doctor is impossible to guess, but he would have been distressed at the uncertainty in the slave quarters that invariably accompanied the death of a master or mistress. Gideon Brown and his children were buried in the private cemetery beside his house. The family slaves, even as they attended the graveside ceremony, surely wondered what was to become of them. Despite the exploitation inherent in the system under which they labored, genuine bonds of affection could and did exist between slave owners and "their people." But the chief concern of Dr. Brown's servants would have been for their own families, friendships, and homes. Were they to be sold? Divided among heirs? Sent down the river from Kentucky, never to return?

Benjamin Drew, a Quaker abolitionist, transcribed one bondsman's feelings on the death of his master:

> I look upon slavery as a disgrace, and as breaking the laws of God: that no man can keep the laws of God and hold to slavery. I believe my own master was as good a man as there is in the whole South: I loved him in health, and I loved him in death,—but I can read the Bible, and I do not see any thing there by which he could be justified in holding slaves: and I know not where he has gone to.

The last will and testament of Gideon Brown was written on April 6, 1829, and proven on May 18, 1829. Dr. Brown's illness was evident; the will was written in smooth legalese by his lawyer brother-in-law, Judge Oldham, and the physician's signature was added in a very shaky hand. Gideon Brown named two executors, his father-in-law, Clayton Talbot, now living at Huntsville,

Alabama, and John Pope Oldham of Louisville. Clear instructions were provided for the disposal of Gideon's assets and the payment of any outstanding debts against his estate. Among the many bills settled by his executors was the outstanding account of $6.00 owed to "the black man Thornton."

Brown's will required that his executors turn over to his wife, Susan, all the household goods, as well as one-third of Dr. Brown's real and personal estate, "for and during her natural life." The Browns' children were minors, so the doctor's estate was set up in such a way as to protect their interests. Probate documents at the Breckinridge County Courthouse prove that Brown was owed a great deal of money, mostly by patients. His capital assets comprised land, livestock, and, of course, slaves. The doctor was very specific about how his assets were to be invested. The executors were, at their discretion, "to purchase slaves or real estate for the use & benefit of my said children, the proceeds of the hire of such slaves and the rents of such real estate to be appropriated by my said executors for the support & education of my said children until they shall respectively marry or attain the age of 21 years." The executors were also empowered to bind out Dr. Brown's sons to some suitable trade or profession, as long as his wife agreed to the transaction. Curiously, there is no mention in the will of Gideon Brown's medical tools or his practice, nor of any of his slaves by name.

John Pope Oldham seems to have undertaken the entire management of the Brown estate. Indeed, it would be with Judge Oldham that Thornton and the other slaves would deal for years to come. The sale of Dr. Brown's effects took place on November 20, 1829. The main Brown property, comprised of the house of one of Hardinsburg's better-off families, outbuildings, slave quarters, and all the improvements, as well as two lots that together totaled almost five acres, went for $855. The initial sale of household goods, farm equipment, and livestock netted $551. Retained by Susan Talbot Brown was the fine wooden furniture, including a "set of madison tables," a sideboard, five bedsteads, and a "trundle bed and stead," plus cooking pots, tableware, curtains, carpets, bed, bath, and table linens, and silverware, including a dozen silver spoons, a cream spoon, and tongs, as well as fine "tea ware and plates," glassware, and some "old books." The only other item sold was the "loom and weaving apparatus" priced at $10.

The total value of the household and farm goods, including livestock, was appraised at $2,924.50, while the family slaves were evaluated at $1,876.00. Gideon Brown also owed $1,083.93, $13.50 of which was for "Jno Brown accts. for schooling," $4.00 to "Jno Anderson accts for Tuition," and $13.50, which was "W. Davison's accts for coffins." Judge Oldham proceeded to assist his sister-in-law with the collection of her husband's debts. It perhaps offers some insight into the character of this methodical and scrupulously honest man that he rendered his account of funds raised by the farm sale and debt collection as $2,160.39¼. He would demonstrate both his tenacity and his propensity for detail in a later case involving Thornton.

Thornton Blackburn was the most expensive of all the family slaves, evaluated at $400. Bob, the older man who had been in the service of the Browns since at least 1820, was priced at $350. The four female slaves were priced as follows, the lower value of Rose and Serena reflecting their positions as the oldest and the youngest of the Brown family slaves:

Jenny	$275
Eliza	$300
Rose	$125
Malinda	$250
Serena	$175

A year later, the census taken on September 18, 1830, shows that there were only three young women and a single man left at the Hardinsburg property. Rose had likely passed away or become sufficiently infirm that she was exempted from Susan

Brown's taxable assets. Bob was the one remaining male slave left working for the Brown family at Hardinsburg, for Thornton Blackburn was no longer living there. John Pope Oldham had found him a job. Thornton was going to Louisville, the great city at the Falls of the Ohio.

4

TROUBLING THE WATERS

If there is no struggle, there is no progress. Those who profess to favor Freedom, and yet depreciate agitation are men who want crops without plowing up the ground. They want rain without thunder and lightning. They want the ocean without the awful roar of its many waters. This struggle may be a moral one, or it may be a physical one; or it may be both moral and physical, but it must be a struggle. Power concedes nothing without demand. It never did and it never will.

—FREDERICK DOUGLASS, 1849

LATE IN THE fall of 1829, the steamboat bearing Thornton Blackburn and John Pope Oldham landed at the busy docks a few miles downriver from the Falls of the Ohio. Thornton was just seventeen years old. Whatever trepidation he may have felt regarding his change in circumstances, the youth on the verge of manhood was likely quite excited to be going to live in Kentucky's most important port city. Judge Oldham would have hired one of the dozens of hack drivers who noisily competed at the Portland docks to carry them the short distance into Louisville. Riding on the box beside the driver as they rumbled along the Portland Turnpike, Thornton was entering a whole new world. Nothing in his years at gracious Washington or at sleepy little Hardinsburg had prepared him for the bustle and activity of Kentucky's busiest port city on the Ohio River. He was also embarking on the first stage of the longest journey he would ever take. He did not know it, but this was the beginning of Thornton's journey to freedom.

The road from Portland to the city ran east along Water Street as far as the Louisville Landing. Caleb Atwater, who also traveled to Louisville in 1829, described the sights and sounds that greeted the visitor:

> Main Street, for the distance of about one mile, presents a proud display of wealth and grandeur. Houses of two and three lofty stories in height, standing upon solid stone foundations, exceed any thing of the kind in the Western States. The stores filled with the commodities and manufactures of every clime, and every art, dazzle the eye. The ringing of the bells and the roaring of the guns, belonging to the numerous steam boats in the harbor, the cracking of the coachman's whip, and the sound of the stage driver's horn, salute the ear.

In the harbor, watercraft of every size and description came and went. Fashionably dressed ladies and their gentlemen waited to board gaily painted steamboats, with their several decks and elegant drawing and dining rooms. The parasols and mustachios of the passengers contrasted sharply with the coarse clothing of the riverboat men who loitered near the wharves, smoking cigars as they waited for cargoes to clear the inspection station. Scattered here and there groups of pioneers and their bewildered children stood guard over bundles of clothes, bedding, and cookware, all hopeful their flatboats were transporting them to a better future in Missouri or Illinois. Everywhere there were burly black porters, their sweat-slicked skin gleaming as they loaded the waiting steamboats with bales, huge wooden hogsheads of good Kentucky tobacco, and crates full of exotic goods from Europe and Asia.

Louisville owed its considerable prosperity to its strategic position above the Falls of the Ohio River, the only barrier to shipping between Pittsburgh and the Mississippi. Although a canal to bypass the long limestone shelf and its treacherous rapids was under construction when Thornton arrived in the city, its completion would only enhance the control Louisville maintained over Ohio River shipping. All exports from the upper Ohio River Valley passed through the Louisville port on their way to New Orleans and the sea.

Unless the water levels were high, as they sometimes were in spring and fall, every boat headed upstream had to be unloaded below the falls and its cargo taken overland to the port of Louisville. The boats were taken over the falls empty to reduce damage from the submerged limestone ridge, and then reloaded and sent on their way. A very lucrative transshipment and carriage business had grown up around the City at the Falls. Every impoverished pioneer moving west and every wealthy planter transporting slaves and household goods downriver to try his luck in the cotton belt passed by Louisville. Most stopped for a night or a week in one of the town's hotels or boardinghouses. They bought supplies and goods, sometimes traded the piano or fine dinnerware that had seemed so essential back in Pittsburgh, did their banking, or purchased insurance for the rest of their trip. All the mercantile goods needed to supply the opening of the West were to be had at Louisville, for a price.

Louisville's urban status was formalized only in 1828, and a year later, when Thornton first knew it, the city was a compact grid of streets spread out along the riverfront. Caleb Atwater stopped at Louisville on his 1831 tour to Prairie du Chien and found about twelve hundred houses, mainly of brick, most of modest style, but with a few mansions located in the main business district and on the side streets. Thornton's new home was characterized, wrote its first historian, Henry McMurtrie, by "frugality, attention to business and an extraordinary attachment to money." In truth, Louisville looked both north and south, for it was both a center of industry and was partly dependent on a plantation economy. Visiting the district in the fall of 1829, during Thornton's time there, traveler Charles Sealsfield described this other side of the city's complex personality: "Behind Louisville the countryside is delightful: the houses and plantations vying with each other in point of elegance and cultivation. The woods have disappeared, and for the distance of twenty miles, the roads are lined in every direction with plantations."

Louisville was, however, not a healthy place to live. The ground was low-lying and marshy, and there were many pools of standing water that bred mosquitoes and other ills. They were eventually drained but in the early decades of the nineteenth century were the cause of epidemics and seasonal fevers. Yellow fever and typhus decimated the population on more than one occasion, earning Louisville the unpleasant epithet of "the Graveyard of the West." Charles Dickens was horrified to note on his 1842 visit that pigs were allowed to roam freely to consume the garbage that lay strewn about. Horse manure choked the city streets, and sanitary facilities were primitive; disease had ample opportunity to grow and spread. Asiatic cholera had not yet reached Kentucky, but it would seriously deplete the city's population in 1832.

Louisville boasted a population of about ten thousand, not including the large number of transients that regularly swelled the numbers. According to census figures, there were 2,406 slaves over the age of sixteen and an uncounted number of children, as well as some 232 free blacks. African Americans thus made up more than 25 percent of the city's residents. The bulk of the city's slaves lived and worked within the first few blocks bordering the river in the establishments of commission merchants, warehouses, public works operations, factories, and lumberyards.

Rather coincidentally, Thornton again found himself living with the family of a regional postmaster. The *Louisville Public Advertiser* of May 27, 1829, announced that "John P. Oldham, Esq., has been appointed Post Master, at Louisville, in the place of John T. Gray, Esq. . . . . [He] has given very general satisfaction to the city and county. His uniform and amiable deportment, industry, talents, and unquestioned integrity, constitute an ample guaranty that the duties of his office will be faithfully and satisfactorily performed." Since Jefferson County had not yet built an official post office, the Oldhams purchased a three-story terraced house for the purpose on Market Street between Third and Fourth streets, just two streets below the dockyards. The ground floor served as the office, while the family occupied the upper floors. Nearby stood the Jefferson County Courthouse, the jail, and other county and municipal buildings. The Oldham sons, William, aged twenty, and Talbot, eighteen, both worked at the post office. The elder daughter, Sophia, had married the prominent local attorney William Fontaine Bullock in 1829, but little Susan was still at home with her parents and going to school.

High walls surrounded the backyard of the Oldham house. Against the rear enclosure were the stables that housed the family's carriage and horses, accessed from a lane. The yard was devoted to slave housing, as well as privies and a small garden. Fire insurance maps of a later date show that most slave "quarters" in the city were long two-story wooden ells attached to the rear of the owners' dwellings. Personal servants—the nursemaid, cook, and valet—often lived in rooms in the attic of the main house, or off the kitchen.

Thornton's new home must have been both crowded and uncomfortable. The Oldhams had brought at least seven adult slaves with them when they moved from Hardinsburg, and several children were also living in the house and in the quarters to the rear. The situation was temporary: the Oldhams were selling their Hardinsburg property, for they had purchased a comfortable home south and east of Louisville, on the Bardstown Road, and intended to move there with most of their servants within the next few months. Called Fair Hope, the picturesque country villa was only a few miles from the city center, giving Judge Oldham ready access to the Jefferson County Courthouse. Set in a grove of trees, the property was much loved by the family, and until

John Pope Oldham passed away, all of his grandchildren were born in the house.

Thornton had been brought to Louisville so he could be hired out for wages. Moneys he earned would be paid to Judge Oldham on behalf of Susan Brown, and go toward supporting her and her children. Although the practice was much frowned upon because it was believed to break down the tightly woven web of controls that harnessed black labor to the slave system, hiring out one's slaves to other masters was both convenient and profitable. It was also a usual means for supporting bereft dependents, such as Susan Brown and her children. They were thus relieved of providing food, housing, and medical care for the slaves they inherited while collecting wages for their labor that were pure profit. Some slaves were even permitted by their owners to "hire their own time," that is, to find themselves a position and pay their master or mistress a set fee per week. Slaves often preferred to be hired out for the same reasons pundits disliked the practice: because it gave them an opportunity to separate themselves from their owners' constant surveillance and experience a situation somewhat similar to that of a wage laborer. Holding a job apart from one's owner often provided the enslaved with a chance to earn a little money for themselves by working overtime or taking odd jobs with other employers.

It was a usual practice for hired slaves to stay at the premises of their employers, or even to "live out," that is, find their own accommodation. Judge Oldham was a cautious man, by all accounts, and preferred to keep Thornton under his own watchful eye and that of his two sons, William and Talbot. Oldham arranged for Thornton to stay in the quarters behind his own house. The young man was his widowed sister-in-law's most valuable slave, and the judge undoubtedly was aware that the temptation for slaves to abscond was far greater in an urban setting than in the country. Slaves in a city rubbed shoulders with a greater variety and number of people than they did in a rural context. Thornton's new home lay immediately opposite Indiana, a free state that, while not a safe place for a fugitive slave to stay, did have an active Underground Railroad. Escapes by water were much more frequent than local slave owners would have liked to admit. Many advertisements appeared over the years in the local papers, such as the *Louisville Public Advertiser,* offering rewards for the return of slaves who had escaped through Louisville from places as distant as Louisiana, Alabama, Mississippi, and Tennessee. Intriguing in the detail they reveal, such notices are bleakly suggestive of the cruelty that might have prompted "a likely negro woman, of middle size, dark complexion, about 26 years of age, far advanced in pregnancy," to abscond. Her owner, who published his notice in the *Louisville Public Advertiser* of June 8, 1831, offered a paltry $5 reward for her return. Fugitives on their way north from the Kentucky interior and from more southerly states also found the city a convenient place to blend in with the crowd, at least temporarily, as they arranged further passage.

Judge Oldham had leased Thornton as a porter to one of the many dry-goods companies whose storefronts and warehouses lined Main Street. In a court record dated November 3, 1831, John Pope Oldham confirmed that he had been acting in his capacity of administrator of the estate of the deceased Dr. Gideon Brown when he hired out his sister-in-law's young slave: "[She] was possessed of a negro man slave called Thornton Blackburn aged about twenty years . . . and being so possessed of said negro man slave your orator hired him to Charles Wurts & John Reinhard of the firm of Wurts & Reinhard's until the 16th day of the present month of November at the rate of one hundred & ten dollars per year."

Wurts & Reinhard's owned facing retail and wholesale establishments on the northeast and southeast corners of Main at Fourth Street. The stores were just a block from the Oldham house. Charles Wurts and John Reinhard were the sons of two local commission merchants, and they had only recently entered into partnership. Their fathers, Daniel Wurts, Sr., and Paul

Reinhard, were elders at First Presbyterian Church, which the Oldham family attended, so it was likely through their acquaintance with Judge Oldham that the deal was struck. Thornton's service began in November rather than the more usual Christmas week, for his mistress, the widowed Mrs. Brown, was anxious for him to start earning the money on which the family depended. Susan was having considerable difficulty disposing of the Breckinridge County properties left by her husband, and the estate was embroiled in legal disputes relating to both collection of debts owed the estate and the dissolution of trusts in which Gideon Brown had engaged.

So on Monday, November 16, 1829, Thornton Blackburn presented himself at the Wurts & Reinhard's store for the first time. As the firm's porter, he worked under the supervision of the company clerk, Thomas Rogers. Rogers was almost Thornton's own age and very well connected. He was related to the city's founder, General George Rogers Clark, who had fortified Louisville as a base for his battles against the Native allies of the British in 1778. His military prowess earned him the sobriquet the "Hannibal of the West." William Clark, the general's brother, was even better known. Following Thomas Jefferson's purchase of the Louisiana Territory, Clark and Jefferson's secretary, Meriwether Lewis, had been dispatched on their monumental expedition to explore the extent of America's new acquisition and beyond. Having a clerk related to a family of such repute would have been a real asset to Wurts & Reinhard's.

Thornton was awakened every morning by the Day Bell ringing out the dawn from the belfry of the Jefferson County Courthouse. The boy was one of hundreds of black slaves hurrying to work along the streets of Louisville each morning. Visitors to Louisville in these years commented that all the labor of the city was done by enslaved African Americans, who undertook every conceivable role and task in the local economy. Tobacco factories were almost entirely operated with slave labor, while public works such as road building and the draining of the swamps on which the city had been founded were the province of teams of slaves both owned and hired by the city. African American carpenters, plasterers, bricklayers, and masons were busily putting up buildings, doing renovations, and carrying out repairs. White laborers in Louisville complained that there was little room for their skills when all the "mechanics" and artisans were owned or hired from other masters by members of the city's wealthy quasi-aristocracy. The average working day for employed slaves was fourteen hours, the same as it was for white workers.

As had been the case in Hardinsburg, the well-spoken Thornton had probably been hired by Wurts & Reinhard's both for his manners and for his way with horses. Louisville must have seemed a world away from Breckinridge County and his duties as a doctor's slave. At Louisville, Thornton acquired important skills he would find most useful in his later life. Wurts & Reinhard's not only shipped goods to shops and commission merchants in Vincennes, Indiana; Nashville, Tennessee; and other distant locations, as evidenced by regular advertisements placed in the *Louisville Public Advertiser*, but also had a healthy retail grocery and dry-goods business serving a largely local clientele.

Thomas Rogers directed Thornton in his daily duties. These included driving the company's drays down to the docks to pick up crates of oranges from the West Indies; boxes of tea from India and China; hosiery, feathered hats, and silk ribbons from France; and a host of luxury goods from other parts of Europe. These were imported by way of New Orleans and available even on the far western frontier, by virtue of the Mississippi trade.

As he drove the wagon back and forth along the paved bank below Water Street from the landing place at the river's edge, Thornton passed row upon row of hacks. Operated by local livery stables, these carriages for hire appeared whenever a steamboat was expected, their drivers chatting idly as they waited for yet another group of passengers to disembark. Thornton might well have admired their freedom. They were allowed to keep the tips they earned. The independence they enjoyed must have had much to recommend it, especially from the point of view of a slave lad just finding his feet in a new city.

In addition to drayage and portering duties, Thornton was required to deliver purchases to the homes of the elite families of Louisville who were the favored customers of Wurts & Reinhard's. The richest residents were heirs to original Kentucky pioneers, and most, as had been the case in Thornton's earliest home of Mason County, were of Virginian stock. Families related to the Oldhams like the Popes and Churchills claimed tens of thousands of acres of land worked by slave labor that, since Kentucky was by this time more or less settled, were rapidly escalating in value.

Thornton's employers, John Reinhard and Charles Wurts, did not participate in this genteel plantation society. Immigrants of Swiss and German descent, they formed part of a large and economically very important class of entrepreneurs, businessmen, and factory owners who dominated the mercantile life of the river port. Such men and their families tended to live in the commercial district near their places of employment, although the more successful among them soon acquired country properties and aspired to a more elevated position in local society. Apart from the factory owners, who generally possessed large numbers of slaves and hired others, most local businessmen had only one or two slaves who worked in their stores and warehouses and a similar number in their households to manage cooking, cleaning, and child care. Of the two men who employed Thornton in these years, Charles Wurts was still living at home, where his father, in defiance of his neighbors and local custom, employed only free blacks as domestic servants. Daniel Wurts, Sr., was a leading member of the Louisville branch of the Kentucky Colonization Society. John Reinhard, who lived two blocks from work on Fourth Street between Market and Jefferson, evidently had little objection to slavery, and owned both a maid and a nurse for his children.

The commission merchants, wholesalers, and larger retail merchants all knew each other well, married into one another's families, and established a society that centered on the acquisition of wealth. The merchants of Louisville dabbled in a variety of ventures, including the sale of livestock and real estate. Since the large slave-trading firms that the city would later boast had not yet been established, commission merchants also bought and sold slaves. Many advertisements posted by individual shops, wholesalers, and auctioneers appeared in the *Louisville Public Advertiser* offering a "likely girl, a reasonable cook," or "Wanted. Boys and girls aged 12 to 15 for tobacco work." The ad by "Joshua Lee, Auc'r," at "the Louisville Horse Market and Auction and Livery Stable," informed the public that his firm boarded horses and would "sell on commission, at public or private sale, horses, slaves, carriages, wagons, &c." While some slaves were traded locally, mainly as domestic and factory workers, as had been the case at Thornton's birthplace at Maysville, a great many were shipped on steamboats and flatboats downriver to the ports of the Lower Mississippi, where they could command higher prices. It was not unknown for promising young slaves like Thornton to be kidnapped for sale in Southern markets, so Judge Oldham, his wife, and their sons probably kept a close eye on young Thornton.

Louisville was a port city with a rough underside, and there were lots of other ways for a young man, slave or free, to get into trouble. Grogshops, eateries, and houses of entertainment of various unwholesome types lined the alleyways near the river. Black stevedores and stewards worked the riverboats, so some of these establishments catered exclusively to blacks and others, illegally, to a mixed clientele. Here slaves mingled with free blacks and working-class whites. But the conditions of urban life meant it was impossible for the Oldhams to control all of Thornton's movements and associations. The market was but a few doors west of the Oldhams' home, and there, twice a week, domestic servants and free blacks from the city met and conversed with slaves from rural plantations who came hawking their masters' wares. Thornton walked the streets of a city where most of the black people employed in the downtown core would, at least, have known one another by sight. He had the opportunity to banter with the stevedores on the docks and chat up pretty serving girls carrying lunches to their masters in their stores and offices. As Frederick Douglass wrote, "A city slave is almost a free man compared with the slave on the plantation. He is much better fed and clothed . . . Now that you're in the city, you have opportunity for education, the opportunity for freedom of movement, and you're relatively better off." Slave owners rightly feared the influence of the city on their bondspeople. In the *Louisville Public Advertiser* of November 30, 1835, the editor, Shadrach Penn, complained: "Negroes scarcely realize the fact that they are slaves . . . After being exposed to city virtues [they become] insolent, intractable, and in many instances wholly worthless. They make free negroes their associates, and imbibe feelings and imitate their conduct, and are active in prompting others to neglect their duty and to commit crimes."

The proslavery *Louisville Daily Journal* of February 22, 1848, made an interesting admission: "Slavery exists in Louisville and St. Louis only in name . . . there are two things that always, and under all circumstances, abrogates slavery. The first is a dense population . . . the next the intelligence of the slaves. Both of these are silently and imperceptibly working their legitimate results."

Most dangerous still, from Judge Oldham's point of view, was the fact that, in the city, Thornton inevitably came into contact with African Americans not under the supervision of any whites. Free people had businesses that served the commercial core; barbers and caterers, restaurateurs and seamstresses all lived and worked within a few blocks of Judge Oldham's house on Market Street. It was difficult to monitor the activities of Louisville's emancipated blacks, since they had no defined residential area; mandatory residential segregation was common only after the Civil War in many Southern towns. During slavery times, owners housed their servants in close proximity to themselves, both for convenience and to ensure their ongoing subjugation. Free blacks and hired-out slaves lived where they could: in shacks built

in alleyways, in rough housing constructed south of the city limits below Broadway, and in tenements, basements, and outbuildings throughout the downtown core. Those working in the hotels
and taverns along the waterfront sometimes slept in the hallways
or, as one traveler discovered, on the bare ground under the front
porch of his hotel. Louisville experienced an ongoing struggle to
monitor slave behavior and associations. The City Council instituted a series of regulations and gave the Night Watch, a motley
crew of rough men employed by the city, the same powers as the
"paterollers" of the countryside. Until quite recently, Louisville's
First Presbyterian Church continued to toll the ten o'clock bell,
although the reason for the familiar sound had long been forgotten. In Thornton's day, this was the signal for all slaves to return
to their homes. The penalty for breaking curfew was "35 lashes
well laid on the bare back," meted out by the city jailer, Richard
Oldham, who happened to be Judge Oldham's brother.

Slaves in Louisville, as everywhere in the South, were required
to present passes written by their owners to permit them to travel
very far from their home or place of work, while, according to a
law passed in 1823, free blacks had to carry with them at all times
their "free papers," the legal documents attesting to their emancipation. Otherwise they risked being taken up as runaways and
housed in the Louisville jail until their owners could be found.
Thornton, like all the slaves living in the business district, must
have shivered at the thought of running afoul of Richard Oldham, a former military man. His prison opposite the courthouse
housed the runaways, the miscreants, and the criminals among
the city's population, black and white. Some were assigned to city
work gangs as punishment. These might include free blacks from
other states who had moved into Kentucky. Since 1818, they had
been required to post a $500 bond for their good behavior.
Those suspected of being runaway slaves were sent to Jailer Oldham for safekeeping. In Kentucky any white, be he an official or
an ordinary citizen, had the right and responsibility to arrest
blacks suspected of wrongdoing. Upon their presentation to the
courts, a certificate was issued, and those found to be fugitive

slaves were returned to their owners, or else jailed pending sale. Anyone capturing a fugitive was entitled to a reward with extra remuneration for every mile of travel back and forth to the Jefferson County Courthouse. Runaways whose owners could not be identified were advertised for a year in the local press, after which they were sold for the price of their upkeep. For slaveholders squeamish about meting out their own punishments, Richard Oldham also could be employed to whip recalcitrant or obstreperous slaves. Town-dwelling owners often preferred not to dirty their hands with such tasks, or upset their neighbors by applying the lash in their own yards.

Charles Dickens wrote while traveling in America in 1842:

> They say the slaves are fond of their masters . . . men, looking in your face, told you such tales with the newspaper lying on the table. In all the slave districts, advertisements for runaways are as much matters of course as the announcement of the play for the evening with us. The poor creatures themselves fairly worship English people: they would do anything for them. They are perfectly acquainted with all that takes place in reference to emancipation; and of course their attachment to us grows out of their deep devotion to their owners.

Thornton Blackburn probably first learned that there was an active abolitionist movement in the Northern states while at Louisville. He had lived all but five years of his life on the Ohio River, the highway used by the ever more elaborate steamboats. Since almost all the firemen and stewards, cabin boys and waiters who staffed these floating palaces were black, some slave and others free, information relevant to African Americans was transmitted quickly up and down the length of America's inland river systems. Fugitive slaves from distant farms and towns mingled with the city's blacks in an attempt to avoid capture, and these were seen by slaveholders as a very dangerous influence on

Louisville's own enslaved population. Abolitionists were drawn to the conflict. Because of Louisville's position on the Ohio and Mississippi steamboat routes, news of developments in the burgeoning fight against slavery reached the city with extreme rapidity. Even in the plantation South, some information filtered through. William Henry Singleton, who lived at New Bern, North Carolina, in the 1850s, said that "poor white people naturally sympathized with us and the plantation owners were afraid that because of this they might teach us to read or might give us some information about what the North was trying to do." By 1829, when Thornton arrived in Louisville, there would have been plenty of literature available and a considerable degree of knowledge about antislavery activities that John Pope Oldham would have considered most unwholesome. In alley restaurants and bars catering to a largely black clientele, those who were literate could read to their friends who were not. (There were educated people among the free black population and at least some of Kentucky's slaves could read.) There African Americans could complain about their treatment at the hands of whites. Slaveholders knew that such places bred discontent, for, as was said of like establishments in New Orleans, "should a servile outbreak ever occur . . . we shall have to thank the keepers of these Negro cabarets and club houses for it, within the precincts of whose damned halls . . . heaven knows what plots are hatched against our peace."

The year Thornton turned eighteen, 1830, was a watershed in the rise of abolitionism in the United States. In 1829, the highly inflammatory *Walker's Appeal, in Four Articles; Together with a Preamble, to the Coloured Citizens of the World, but in Particular, and Very Expressly, to Those of the United States of America* was published in Boston. David Walker was a former slave, a used-clothing dealer, and a well traveled and educated man. The strongest condemnation by black America of the slave system to date, *Walker's Appeal* burst like a rocket into the debates on slavery and antislavery at every level of American society. Banned everywhere, it was nonetheless readily available, arriving in Savannah and parts of Louisiana, for instance, within months of publication, and likely in Louisville by means of the river as well. Then Philadelphia hosted the first national convention of black abolitionists on September 15, 1830. The delegates rejected the premise of the American Colonization Society that blacks and whites could not live together in harmony as citizens of the United States. Resolutions included plans for creating fugitive slave colonies north of the American border in the British Province of Upper Canada. Several of the forty participants later moved north to assume leading roles in the development of the Canadian black antislavery movement.

Abolitionist newspapers had been circulating for some time, including the *Genius of Universal Emancipation* by the New Jersey–born Quaker Benjamin Lundy and *Freedom's Journal*, the first black abolitionist paper in the United States. Abolitionists of an earlier time had believed that slavery would gradually die out, but by the 1830s it was becoming apparent that this was not the trend. The expansion of cotton-growing territories into the West and Southwest and the proposed removal of the Indians from still more lands under President Andrew Jackson's administration meant that more slaves would be needed and their prices would rise. Accordingly, reformers who had earlier subscribed to the "gradualist" school turned to a more "immediatist" stance; that is, they believed slavery should be abolished throughout the American South, and as soon as possible. Benjamin Lundy had since 1819 been traveling the length and breadth of North America seeking a safe place where African Americans could form colonies. With him for a time was a Louisville builder who had purchased his own freedom, James Charles Brown. Brown moved to Cincinnati in 1829 but regularly traveled back and forth to Louisville to visit his mother and, very likely, to help move runaways upriver. In 1829, he chaired a Cincinnati-based committee for the development of a fugitive slave colony in the British Province of Upper Canada. Named after the great British abolitionist William Wilberforce, it was located in what is now

Southwestern Ontario near the city of London. It is not known whether Brown and Thornton Blackburn were acquainted during Thornton's sojourn in Louisville, but the two men were certainly active in the same circles in later years.

Lundy went to Canada in 1831 to visit with Brown and to observe colonizing efforts among the fugitive slaves living at Wilberforce and elsewhere. Through articles in the *Genius* and his own itinerant work on behalf of abolition, Lundy spread the word that Canada was a place of refuge for bondspeople who had the courage to break their own chains. But, brought into the antislavery fold through Lundy's influence, one white reformer was to far surpass his mentor in his devotion to the antislavery cause. This was William Lloyd Garrison, the leading light of American abolitionism throughout the antebellum period. In January 1831, he would launch *The Liberator*, the most influential antislavery paper of the era. Garrison announced in his first issue: "I shall contend for the immediate enfranchisement of our slave population—I will be as harsh as truth and as uncompromising as justice on this subject—I do not wish to think, or speak, or write with moderation—I am in earnest—I will not equivocate—I will not retreat a single inch, and I will be heard."

All of this antislavery agitation has an impact on slaves like Thornton Blackburn. Although never numbering more than about 200,000 and regarded in most places, North and South, as troublemakers and fanatics, abolitionists had far greater influence than their numbers would suggest. Their constant, unrelenting criticism of the South's "peculiar institution" forced slaveholders into a progressively more defensive stance and brought the tensions over the expansion of slaveholding into the new territories of the West and Southwest to fever pitch. Slave owners accused them of enticing slaves to run away and of inciting revolt. One of the ways in which Southerners dealt with such fears was through ridicule. It was during Thornton Blackburn's time at Louisville that the famous actor Thomas D. Rice, acting as "Sambo (a Negro boy)," presented, at Samuel Drake's City Theatre on May 21, 1830, for the first time "the comic Negro song of Jim Crow." In the *Louisville Public Advertiser* of June 12, 1830, the City Hotel placed an ad:

> JIM CROW'S BENEFIT. Jim Crow respectfully informs the Ladies and Gentlemen of Louisville and its vicinity, that by the request of a number of his friends, he will offer his name by way of a BENEFIT, and he trusts the entertainment will meet general satisfaction; and the way he will sing and jump Jim Crow "will be nothing to nobody."

The story of how the term "Jim Crow" was coined is fascinating. A few days before his blackface comic debut at Louisville, Rice had observed the antics of a slave disabled by arthritis who worked at Crowe's Livery Stables. The old man sang a little song and did a shuffling dance to amuse himself. Rice wrote a song based on his tune, published it that same year, and went on to become famous as the father of American minstrelsy. By 1836, he had taken his racially demeaning blackface show to Great Britain, where, despite the great popularity of abolitionism within a certain segment of society, there was still strong color prejudice among the rank and file. The entertainment spread throughout the English-speaking world, where it continued through much of the twentieth century. Rice's original lyrics went: "Wheel about, turn about, do jes so, An' ebry time I wheel about, I jump Jim Crowe." With the rise of legislated segregation, the old Louisville slave Jim Crowe's name would become synonymous with the South's racially discriminatory laws, especially in the 1890s, although the process had begun much earlier.

While Louisvillians enjoyed minstrel shows that portrayed blacks as fools, Thornton Blackburn, for the first time in his life, was seeing what African Americans could achieve, given a degree of freedom and even limited opportunity. There had been a few emancipated blacks in Mason County when Thornton was a child, and two freed women in Hardinsburg, but most freed people gravitated to the cities and towns of the South. Their presence at Louisville gave Thornton his first exposure to a dynamic, urban, free black society, centered on church and the shared goals of mutual assistance, material progress, and community development. It was a lesson the youth would never forget. In his day, Louisville's free black population officially comprised almost 250 people, although these numbers were far from certain. The *Louisville Public Advertiser* of November 30, 1835, expressed alarm at the growth of the free black population, stating:

> We are overrun with free negroes. In certain parts of our town throngs of them may be seen at any time—and most of them have no ostensible means of obtaining a living. They lounge about through the day, and most subsist by stealing, or receiving stolen articles from slaves at night. Frequently, they are so bold as to occupy the sidewalks in groups, and compel passengers to turn out and walk around them. Their impudence naturally attracts the attention of slaves, and necessarily becomes contagious.

The liberties available to emancipated African Americans, as well as their participation in any important way in the society dominated by whites, were severely restricted. Despite this, black culture thrived in Louisville. There were hairdressers, grocers, confectioners, carpenters and other members of the building trades, a "mantua maker" (dressmaker), a number of women who sold produce at the marketplace, and some working for wages in domestic service. They socialized with one another, intermarried and established less formal liaisons, attended church, and organized celebrations under the leadership of both ministers and the most successful of the businessmen of the black community. In the absence of other avenues of political and social mobility, black men and women who had both ambition and intelligence concentrated their efforts within their own sphere. These individuals formed fraternal and benevolent societies and moved up in their ranks, entered the clergy, and served as community organizers.

Meanwhile, white Louisvillians responded with anger and occasionally with violence to any evidence of black success. Jane Swisshelm, a Pennsylvania abolitionist, newspaper publisher, and feminist who resided in Louisville for a time beginning in June 1838, rented the front part of a house from a free black who had accumulated some property:

> Jerry Wade, the Gault House barber, was a mulatto, who had bought himself and family, and acquired considerable real estate. In the back of one of his houses, lived his son with a wife and little daughter. We rented the front, and mother sent me furniture. This was highly genteel, for it gave us the appearance of owning slaves, and Olivia, young Wade's wife, represented herself as my slave, to bring her and her child security. As a free negro, she labored under many disadvantages, so begged me to claim her.

When the woman opened a little school to teach black children to read, however, Wade pleaded with her to close it, for fear his house would be burned to the ground by angry whites.

The most serious—and sometimes justified—of the charges white Kentuckians laid at the door of free blacks was that they helped fugitive slaves escape. Louisville and adjacent sections of the Ohio River corridor were major transfer points for runaways throughout the antebellum period. However, the clandestine nature of fugitive slave routes and the harsh penalties for helping slaves get away precluded much record keeping. Very little historical documentation survives today to attest to the operation of the Underground Railroad inside slave states. However, a resourceful man or woman who really wanted to obtain his or her freedom could probably find someone in Louisville who would assist him or her. A favored method of helping fugitives was through the provision of forged free papers and by assisting them in gaining steamboat passage to some Northern location, usually Cincinnati. Although the penalty for forging free papers, or providing a pass purportedly from a slave owner permitting a slave to

go from one place to another, was five years at hard labor in the
state penitentiary, it was done.

Washington Spradling was a free black barber living in Louisville at the time Thornton was working at Wurts & Reinhard's.
In fact, Spradling owned a barbershop only a few doors south
of the establishment where Thornton was employed. Spradling
was the freed offspring of a white overseer and a slave woman.
Intelligent and civic-minded, he quickly rose to a position of
prominence within the city's black community. The literate and
very capable Spradling operated a construction company as well
as two barbering establishments. He also invested in property,
and his son later became an important dealer in real estate. Spradling admitted in an 1863 interview with the Freedmen's Inquiry
Commission that he had a hand in many slave escapes over a
more than thirty-year period. Spradling knew much of what went
on in Louisville from the conversations that took place in his bar-
bershops, and undoubtedly put what he learned to good use. The
Spradling family also lent money for the liberation of slaves as
well; the old man said that he had assisted not only members of
his own family but also thirty-three other men, women, and children in purchasing their freedom.

Evidently, suspicions that Washington Spradling was assisting
slaves in making their escapes were sufficiently strong that he was
forced to employ diversionary tactics to "prove" his innocence.
In 1895, the historian Wilbur Siebert spoke with a former slave
who had fled his Oldham County master, just east of Louisville,
at the age of nineteen. John Evans made his home in Windsor,
Canada, at the time of the interview.

> Evans had known Wash Spradley, who lived on 9th Street in
> Louisville. Spradley was an Underground Railroader and
> sent fugitives northward. Chief of Police Brewster and other
> officials suspected Spradley. Lawyer Guthrie lost his slave
> and said he would give anything to get him back. This was
> Spradley's chance to allay suspicion against him. He went to

Cincinnati by the Cambria mail boat and brought the runaway back. He did this several times.

Another community leader with whom Thornton must have been acquainted was also in a position to help those seeking their freedom. Many African Americans turned to the Reverend Henry Adams, since 1829 the minister to black congregants at First Baptist Church, for guidance and information. The church had been founded in 1815 and from 1822 on had included blacks in its congregation. Adams was an interesting man. Born a slave in Franklin County, Georgia, Adams was light-skinned and moved readily between black and white congregations in his early career. A fine scholar with a knowledge of "biblical languages," probably Hebrew, Greek, and perhaps Aramaic, Adams was adept at walking the fine line between what might be perceived as arrogance on the part of a well-educated black man and the self-assertion necessary to provide leadership to a combined slave and free congregation. He would maintain this role for more than twenty-five years. Thornton Blackburn probably attended this church while he lived in Louisville, for he had close associations with the Baptist faith long after he departed from Kentucky. Although Louisville had two churches that served its slave and free black communities, one Baptist and one Methodist, slaves like Thornton Blackburn generally were permitted to attend only Baptist services. These were administered by the erudite African American pastor but remained under the direction and close control of the white First Baptist Church, while the Methodists operated under fewer restrictions.

Thornton had been living in Louisville for over a year by the time his owner, Susan Brown, moved to the city. Her children were John, seventeen; Clayton T., fifteen; Richard, thirteen; Thomas, ten; and little Mary Crewes Talbot Brown, eight. For a while, the Browns lived in the house at the post office building. John Pope and Malinda Oldham were now enjoying country life at Fair Hope outside Louisville, and only William and Talbot Oldham occupied the upstairs apartments on Market Street. Re-

united with his widowed owner and her family, Thornton continued to reside in the quarters behind the Oldham house. He
had plenty of supervision, for temporarily sharing the house with
the Oldham brothers were Susan and Malinda's father, Clayton
Talbot, and their younger sister, Sophia. The Talbots had moved
from Nashville to Huntsville, Alabama, where Clayton entered
the construction business, but Polly Talbot had passed away, and
in 1830 Clayton and Sophia came to Louisville to be close to
his children and grandchildren. Since Clayton Talbot was co-
executor of Gideon Brown's estate, Thornton was now serving
yet another master.

While it is difficult to assess interpersonal relations on the basis of such scanty evidence, it would seem that Thornton had
built up a good relationship with the Oldham brothers and with
his employers at Wurts & Reinhard's. For one thing, he had a
considerable degree of autonomy, as subsequent events would
prove, suggesting he was trusted by those monitoring his daily
movements. The partners at Wurts & Reinhard's must have
been well satisfied with Thornton's services, for on November 16,
1830, they renewed the hiring arrangements they had made with
John Pope Oldham the year before. Later events would indicate
that Thomas Rogers, Thornton's supervisor at Wurts & Reinhard's, was something of a sympathetic character, but in 1830, he
left the firm for a time to travel in the Northern states. The Jefferson County tax rolls do not show the addition of another employee in Rogers's place, suggesting that Charles Wurts and John
Reinhard chose not to replace their clerk. Some of Rogers's responsibilities may have fallen on Thornton. Although he never
learned to read, the young man displayed considerable business
acumen in his later life, and the partners who employed him at
Louisville had probably benefited from and perhaps even fos-
tered this quality in him. All in all, by the spring of 1831 Thornton's day-to-day activities were less intensely scrutinized than
they had been when he first came to Louisville. The timing was
fortunate, for Thornton Blackburn had fallen in love.

5

I'M BOUND TO GO

Why does the slave ever love? Why allow the tendrils of the heart to twine around objects which may at any moment be wrenched away by the hand of violence? . . . I did not reason thus when I was a young girl. Youth will be youth. I loved, and I indulged the hope that the dark clouds around me would turn out a bright lining. I forgot that in the land of my birth the shadows are too dense for light to penetrate.

—HARRIET JACOBS, 1861

THE WOMAN WHO caught Thornton's eye was a children's nursemaid who lived close to Louisville's First Baptist Church on Green Street, about four blocks south of the Oldham house. Ruthie, a beautiful light-skinned mulatto woman, was some years his senior. While Thornton's feelings upon meeting his beautiful Ruthie have not been recorded, the steps he would prove willing to take to protect her speak volumes.

Ruthie was the slave of George and Charlotte Backus. Her special charges were their two young children, a girl of about two and a nine-year-old boy. George Backus, a young man originally from Pomfret, Connecticut, was a commission merchant and partner in the dry-goods firm of Bell & Backus. He and his partner, Robert Bell, of Covington, Kentucky, were, like Thornton's employers, members of the close-knit mercantile community that occupied the warehousing and wholesale establishments along Main and Market streets, the two avenues that paralleled the Ohio River in the center of town. They did business with Wurts & Rein-hard's on occasion; the various local firms regularly exchanged goods, to greater or lesser satisfaction, as a long series of court disputes between Louisville merchants attest. The Bell & Backus warehouse and dry-goods establishment occupied rented quarters on Main Street within yards of the store where Thornton worked.

Thornton must have been fascinated with Ruthie. She was very attractive, with an air of refinement about her, both of which qualities were the subject of comment in later years. Her origins remain something of a mystery because, unfortunately, her maiden name has not been discovered, but Ruthie herself told Detroit journalists in 1833 that she was a "full blooded Creole from the West Indies." If so, she may have been brought to Louisville from New Orleans. George Backus and his wife had passed through the city two years earlier with seven-year-old Henry in tow, en route from Connecticut to Tennessee. Traveling by sea around the coast to New Orleans in 1827, they had then moved on up the river and lived for a time in Nashville, where George entered into business with other Backus relatives before migrating to Kentucky in 1829.

In the first part of the nineteenth century, the term "Creole" was used to refer to individuals born in the New World, most often of mixed French and/or Spanish and African heritage. The word was commonly employed in Southern Louisiana to describe members of the *gens de coleur*, the native-born children of mixed white and black parentage. Slaves and free blacks who entered the United States fleeing the bloody Haitian Revolution that began in 1791 were considered Creoles as well.

Thousands of French-speaking planters and their slaves flooded into the ports of the American South, fleeing the bloody Haitian Revolution of 1804, the largest number settling in the congenial French-speaking atmosphere of Louisiana. The state prohibited importation of Haitian slaves after the initial influx because of fears they would foment revolt, but this ban was lifted in 1803. Ruthie, born in about 1804, could easily have been brought into the United States from the French Sainte Domingue as an infant, or perhaps later in her childhood with a second wave of Haitian émigrés who, having initially fled to Cuba, moved on to the United States in 1809 and 1810.

In addition to Ruthie, the Backus family had use of another slave, a young man named Blair. He had been purchased in Nashville and was the property of Bell & Backus. Blair did duty as porter, warehouseman, and deliveryman for their mercantile operations as well as driving the Backus family barouche, an elegant four-wheeled carriage, and serving as hostler for the family's two fine riding horses. He did not live at the Backus family home but boarded out with Brown Cozzens, a former partner of Bell & Backus. While there is no evidence that the Bell & Backus dry-goods firm sold slaves along with their other merchandise, their former partner certainly had no scruples about doing so. On July 5, 1828, the *Louisville Public Advertiser* carried an advertisement on behalf of the firm Cozzens & Scott: "A family of likely Negroes for sale by the subscribers; and consisting of one man, his wife and two female children, one a girl about twelve years old, all warranted sound and healthy, and good house servants." There was no caveat, as there sometimes was with local sales, that the family should be kept together. By the fall of 1829, Brown Cozzens was in business with Robert Bell and George Backus in a company that dealt in "Dry Goods, Groceries and Hardware," although the partnership soon dissolved in a welter of mutual recriminations and expensive lawsuits.

The Bell & Backus firm was still recovering from this setback when Thornton and Ruthie met. Robert Bell seems to have been something of a silent partner, for the day-to-day business was operated by George Backus with the help, or hindrance, of his younger brother, Charles W. Backus. Charles was a gambler. His long-suffering older brother had on several occasions been forced to replace money that had gone missing from companies that had employed Charles. And there were other scandals as

well. Given his character, it was as well for Ruthie that Charles
Backus did not live with his brother and sister-in-law but had
rooms elsewhere in Louisville.

Charles's behavior must have been particularly galling, for the
Backus brothers came from a long line of famous clergymen and
educators from Windham County, Connecticut. This side of the
family produced several abolitionists, including an Ohio family
who were actively involved with the noted Quaker antislavery
worker Lucretia Mott in the operation of Underground Railroad
lines. However, another branch of the Backus family had a decided propensity for making money. In New England in the colonial era, they owned extensive farms, mills, and distilleries, as
well as shipping interests in the West Indian trade. Fueled with
money from the eastern seaboard, Backus family businesses
spread to upstate New York, Maryland, and Virginia and throughout the American West. Several members were slaveholders, and
George Backus seems to have been comfortable with his decision
to purchase Ruthie and the slave man Blair.

Of the enslaved African Americans associated with the Backus
family, only Ruthie lived at the house they rented on Green
Street. Occupied with the children, she was spared the worst of
the household chores. The Backus family leased another woman,
Anacha, who lived out, at her owner's quarters. She did the
housecleaning in the Backus home, as well as the cooking.
Ruthie, however, as the only slave living on the premises, had
a position of considerable responsibility. Charlotte Backus did
not have a ladies' maid, and Ruthie probably fulfilled some of
these personal duties for her mistress. Household slaves served
their owners day and night and, as had been the case during
Thornton's childhood in the Murphy household, had little free
time and were under constant surveillance. One former slave
wrote that domestic servants "are better fed and wear better
clothing, because the master and his family always expect to have
strangers visit them, and they want their servants to look well . . .
but you may examine their persons, and find many a lash upon

their flesh. They are sure of their whippings, and are sold the same as others."

Ruthie would have passed a great deal of time in the company of her mistress, for George Backus traveled extensively. A substantial portion of his firm's business was the warehousing and transport of Kentucky products to New Orleans. Bell & Backus also had business connections in New York, Baltimore, and Boston as well as in the cities along the Mississippi and to the west, in the older former French fur-trading settlement at Vincennes, Indiana. On April 1, 1830, the newly constituted company of Bell & Backus placed this ad in the *Louisville Public Advertiser*:

FOR SALE: 300 Kegs Boston nails, 100 lbs. ea, 20 boxes Staughton's bitters, 1 doz. Each, 25 barrels No. 3 mackerel, 100 barrels New Orleans Sugar House molasses, 25 [barrels] Fresh Ohio flour.

IN STORE: Havanna and St. Jago coffee; N. Orleans sugars; crates of queensware, assorted; boxes of China tea sets; German madder; Salt Petre; Indigo . . . Young Huson, Imperial and Gunpowder teas; fresh Turkey figs; Cognac brandy, Holland gin; Port and Madeira wines; Day & Marin's blacking; an assortment of Castings; trace chins, table and alum salt; Fools cap and superroyal printing paper; wrapping [paper]; Whittemore's cotton cards, No. 10; Window glass, assorted sizes.

A constant supply of Warfield, Brand & Co.'s Cotton Yarn— with a general stock of Dry Goods and Hardware.

The Backus family did not own their house in Louisville, but lived in rented accommodations. Comparisons between estate inventories of the era show Ruthie's owners to have been typical of prosperous, if not truly wealthy, merchant families in 1831 urban Kentucky. In their case, the appraisers clearly progressed through the house in order, recording as they went. First came the public spaces; the parlor furnishings including a mahogany sofa and three dining tables, with a full complement of fine linen and cotton tablecloths. For entertaining, Charlotte Backus had tableware for elegant dinner parties, complete with ivory-handled cutlery. Behind the scenes, the kitchen was well equipped while the bedrooms were supplied with mahogany wardrobes, a "toilet table," bedsteads, one with calico bed curtains, and a trundle bed, probably for the little girl. The description of washstands equipped with basins and ewers, wooden library shelving, glass-fronted cabinets, a rocking chair, and a variety of knickknacks completes the image of a finely furnished household. However, the last room examined for the inventory held goods that were much more utilitarian than what one would expect to find in a family bedroom. The two pairs of sheets, listed separately from those in the family linen closet, one counterpane, and one blanket, plus a couple of mattresses, probably represent the contents of the nursemaid Ruthie's bedroom. Given the sequence indicated by the inventory, it was most likely in the attic. A good many household servants had no private space at all, sleeping on the kitchen hearth or at the doorway of a child's bedroom, but the most fortunate lived inside the family home in "servants' rooms." According to real estate listings from Louisville newspapers, such rooms were generally off the kitchen or on the top floor of the house.

There is no way of telling how long Thornton and Ruthie knew each other before he asked her to marry him. It must have been in the spring of 1831 that Thornton approached John Pope Oldham and perhaps Susan Brown, his actual owner, for permission to wed his beloved. Later documents indicate that the Brown and Oldham families had been unaware of the relationship between Ruthie and Thornton until that time. Although John Pope Oldham knew of Thornton's attachment to Ruthie, no one in the family had ever met his bride. Yet it was likely Judge Oldham who had negotiated with George and Charlotte Backus regarding the logistics of the match. Since Louisville families did not keep many slaves, city-dwelling servants like

Ruthie and her intended were usually forced to seek partners outside their own households. "Abroad" marriages—that is, marriages between people owned by different masters—were therefore quite common.

Some owners, like the mistress of Harriet Jacobs whose autobiography of life in slavery is so informative, actively discouraged marriage on the part of their female domestics, preferring them to remain available to the family at all times. Forced marriages also occurred within households, but this was usually a rural phenomenon. But the Backus family seem to have been more kindly disposed. They certainly stood to gain. After all, any children of the marriage would belong to Ruthie's owners, and the Backus family turned out to be in a rather precarious financial position. Slave owners also assumed that married slaves were less likely to run away than single people, especially once children came along.

Weddings between slaves were rarely very elaborate. Sometimes there was no ceremony at all, for their marriages were not legally binding, since slaves could not enter into contracts. As one former slave wrote:

> There is no legal marriage among the slaves of the South; I never saw nor heard of such a thing in my life, and I have been through seven of the slave states. A slave marrying according to law, is a thing unknown in the history of American Slavery . . . [But] as soon as they get free from slavery they go before some anti-slavery clergyman, and have the solemn ceremony of marriage performed according to the laws of the country. And if they profess religion, and have been baptized by a slaveholding minister, they repudiate it after becoming free, and are re-baptized by a man who is worthy of doing it according to the gospel rule.

At the other end of the spectrum from those who simply told their slaves with whom to couple and when, or made them "jump the broom" as a symbol of their union, were slaveholders, fond of their servants, who made rather elaborate preparations for the event and even engaged ordained ministers for the purpose. Elizabeth Keckley, the dressmaker to both Mrs. Lincoln and Varina Davis, Jefferson Davis's wife, had a warm relationship with her owners, and wrote to her mother while still in slavery, "Give my love to all the family, both white and black." The Burwells in St. Louis, whom she supported with her needle, gave her a splendid wedding "in the parlor, in the presence of the family and a number of guests." The Backus family seems to have been exceptionally close, so it was perhaps on the occasion of her marriage that Charlotte Backus gave Ruthie a fine black silk dress.

It may even have been the Reverend Henry Adams, the black minister at the Louisville First Baptist Church, who married the Blackburns. Certainly, Thornton's owners recognized his relationship with Ruthie, for she was regularly referred to as Thornton's wife in legal documents prepared by John Pope Oldham. Therefore the union must have been sanctioned by him.

Married or single, a slave's first duty was to his or her owner. In Louisville, as in the rest of Kentucky, slaves who belonged to different masters typically resided apart. Conjugal visitations were arranged, but at their owners' convenience rather than their own. Laws pertaining to Kentucky slavery suggest that it was Thornton who traveled between households. Louisville's nightly curfew of ten o'clock specifically exempted slave men on their way to see their wives from being taken up by the Night Watch. One former slave explained to an interviewer after the Civil War:

> The new husband had to return to his own master after the wedding but it was understood by all that the new husband could visit his wife every Saturday night and stay until Monday morning. He would return every Monday to his master and work as usual indefinitely unless by chance one or the other of the two masters would buy the husband or wife, in such event they would live together as man and wife. Unless this purchase did occur it was the rule in slavery days that any children born to the slave wife would be the property of the girl's master.

As such, Ruthie's little room at the top of the stairs in her master's house would have been the only home the Blackburns had together. Travelers in the South regularly commented on the colorful and attractive attire of slaves on visiting Saturdays, and Thornton and his bride probably made the most of every minute they could have together. Their later regular church attendance suggests they may have taken the opportunity to do so from the earliest days of their marriage. Frederick Douglass later commented that church was the one place where slaves forgot the sorrow and pain of their daily lives. He wrote, "We were at times remarkably buoyant, singing hymns and making joyous exclamations, almost as triumphant in their tone as if we had already reached a land of freedom and safety." One can readily imagine the loving couple attending services together, perhaps walking by the riverside, or visiting with other enslaved or free blacks of their acquaintance in the city while George and Charlotte Backus passed their own day of rest in the company of their children.

But the Blackburns' happiness was to be cut short. In April 1831, Charlotte Backus and her little girl were carried off by one of the intermittent fevers so frequently fatal to newcomers to Louisville. George Backus was devastated by the loss of his wife and daughter. For a month he tried to continue his business, but Bell & Backus had a great deal of outstanding debt, and George was simply not equal to the task. Robert Bell was absent, for he maintained a house in Newport, Kentucky, a day's journey upstream from Louisville on the way to Cincinnati. To make matters worse, George's brother Charles was again up to his old tricks and had incurred substantial gambling debts. All in all, the death of his wife and child proved completely overwhelming to George. On May 15, 1831, during a business trip to New Orleans, George Backus died.

Upon hearing the news, Charles W. Backus immediately broke into his brother's desk and removed George's gold watch, some money, and an unknown amount of business correspondence. By all accounts, he demonstrated no concern for his orphaned nephew, little Henry, who was not yet ten and had only his nurse, Ruthie, to care for him. She was now technically his property. But her situation was very insecure. Legal claims made against Bell & Backus in the days immediately following George's death show that it was no secret in Louisville's tight little business community that the firm was overextended. That meant Ruthie stood a fair chance of being sold off to settle her former master's debts. Whatever was going to happen now, Ruthie would likely be separated from Thornton. Slave owners had little respect for the ties that bound enslaved men, women, and children, and Ruthie Blackburn would have known it.

Thornton must have been frantic. Despite the fine appurtenances of the house, the Backus family owned only two items of real value—Ruthie Blackburn and the male slave named Blair. It was their fate hanging in the balance while creditors and the executor squabbled on. Ruthie and the child Henry were both probably relieved when Robert Bell arrived to take charge, but there was little George Backus's former partner could actually do. Bell later testified that he came to Louisville to arrange for George's body to be returned to the city for burial beside his wife and daughter. He found that the courts had already, on June 7, 1831, turned the administration of the estate over to a local merchant, Frederick B. Ernest, and that Ernest was charging substantial amounts to the estate. He paid $289.31 for a New Orleans funeral, and a medical bill ($148.50) for the care of Charlotte Backus and her unnamed daughter, an account George apparently had not settled with the family physician before he died. The outstanding accounts rendered to the estate also included, poignantly, $39.00, "J. Reade's Bill for Coffins for Mrs. Backus and Child." Also of note was the cost of transporting George's corpse to Louisville from New Orleans. The thought of such a journey makes one shudder, considering that the journey upriver took twelve days or more, and it was already full summer in the Lower Mississippi.

Three local men were appointed to inventory the household and personal goods of the Backus family, with the estate sale scheduled for later in June. Robert Bell was left out of the proceedings. He also discovered that Ernest had taken upon himself the management of Bell & Backus. This was highly irregular, especially since Caldwell & Ernest, a grocery-importing firm of which Ernest was half owner, had underwritten nearly $3,000 in costs for Bell & Backus before George's demise. This hardly made Ernest an impartial administrator for what turned out to be a ruined estate. Throughout this period, Ernest must have entrusted little Henry to Ruthie's care, for his accounts show expenditures over which she had control. They included cash for a "pair of shoes for Henry Backus," at $0.82, and "making Cloathes [sic] for Henry," $2.75.

The settlement of George Backus's estate is well documented because Bell & Backus was sued by so many of the firms to which it owed money. These were located in Nashville, New York, Baltimore, and New Orleans. The litigation would produce thirty-six lawsuits filed in 1831 and 1832 against Backus's personal estate. Several were launched directly against George and Charlotte's only living child, Henry Charles Backus. The proceedings would go on for years.

Charles W. Backus, always with an eye to the main chance, also sued his brother's estate. His purported object was to gain control of their father's legacy. This had once amounted to about $3,000 and would have been turned over to Charles when he turned twenty-one on August 23, 1831. It was two years before the suit was finally settled, and that was only to pay off the legal bills incurred, some months following Charles's own premature death in 1833.

In the meantime, Frederick B. Ernest was accused of improper conduct in his management of the estate, and especially of taking undue liberties with the two Backus slaves. Ernest had hired out Blair, along with the Bell & Backus dray and team. He kept some of the monies so earned to cover his own expenses as executor. His appropriation of the funds earned by Blair, however, positioned Ernest as a favored creditor, something to which the Jefferson County Guardian Court objected. The combination of the court cases left little Henry Backus completely penniless, and the child was sent off to live with relatives in Detroit. A series of advertisements in the *Louisville Public Advertiser* running through November 1831 show that Robert Bell attempted for a few months to maintain Bell & Backus as a viable merchant house in order to pay off the creditors, but it was obvious to everyone that the firm was insolvent.

More ominously, attorneys for Charles W. Backus also inferred that Ernest had kept Ruthie Blackburn for his own use rather than hiring her out to make money for the estate. There was an unpleasantly lewd tone to his inferences. Ernest insisted he had only retained Ruthie's services as a nursemaid. It does seem that Ernest had personal reasons for reserving Ruthie Blackburn's services, a charge the court seems to have regarded as frivolous. If Ruthie were being subjected to unwanted advances from the executor of her deceased master's estate, there was absolutely nothing she could have done to defend herself. She was alone in the house on Green Street with little Henry, and Frederick B. Ernest was the court-appointed administrator of the estate to which she belonged.

Ruthie's young husband was powerless to defend her in the face of the laws and customs of the slave system. White slaveholders brooked no interference in their "right" to make free with the women under their control. Henry Bibb, describing his own marriage to a beautiful slave girl, wrote that her owner placed a condition on their wedding that "was too vulgar to be written in this book"; Mrs. Bibb's owner had reserved the right to continue to sleep with the girl, even following her marriage. Many years after the fact, Bibb was still incensed:

> And be it known to the disgrace of our country that every slaveholder, who is the keeper of a number of slaves of both sexes, is also the keeper of a house or houses of ill-fame. Licentious white men, can and do, enter at night or day the lodging places of slaves; break up the bonds of affection in

families; destroy all their domestic and social union for life; and the laws of the country afford them no protection. Will any man count, if they can be counted, the churches of Maryland, Kentucky, and Virginia, which have slaves connected with them, living in an open state of adultery, never having been married according to the laws of the State, and yet regular members of these various denominations, but more especially the Baptist and Methodist churches?

Though he was under a cloud, Ernest nonetheless arranged for the sale of George and Charlotte's personal effects. Meanwhile, Blair, perhaps thinking that no one would notice his absence in the turmoil, took the opportunity to abscond. Away more than three weeks, he was not auctioned at the sale of the Backuses' household goods, including their clothing and other slave, Ruthie. Blair was finally captured in Nashville, where he had gone, as so many runaways did, to rejoin family members. A professional slave catcher named McConnell charged $25 for apprehending the young man and putting him in the Nashville slave pen until he could be taken back to Louisville. Estate documents show that Blair's passage to Louisville on the steamboat *Vicksburg* cost $10. His reception by Ernest can only be imagined. But happily for Blair, before the end of the summer he again boarded a steamboat at the Louisville Landing. The courts had ordered him turned over to the Nashville company of Wood & Crutcher. The amount of the note they held on Bell & Backus was $1,235; Blair was worth considerably less, perhaps $600, but Wood accepted the slave and wrote off the rest of the account. At least one of the participants was happy. Blair was being reunited with his loved ones in Nashville, not that this was at all a consideration in the decision to send him there.

At the end of May 1831, Louisville attorney and leading citizen James Guthrie had been appointed Henry Backus's guardian until the estate could be settled. Guthrie, who would also become Charles W. Backus's attorney, proceeded to administer what remained of the estate. As for Ernest, some of the mud slung by Charles W. Backus stuck. He was eventually required to pay Charles's estate $1,812. Ernest was ruined by the affair. He left Louisville for a fresh start in Mississippi.

Ruthie Blackburn's fate had been decided much earlier, however. She was auctioned off to the highest bidder. The estate sale at the Backus family's former residence on Green Street was announced in the *Louisville Public Advertiser* for the morning of June 22, 1831. Handbills were printed and distributed, and an auctioneer was engaged. Accounts for the Backus estate show it was charged both for the auctioneer's fees and the keg of whiskey that customarily lubricated such occasions. Thornton Blackburn could not have known whether Ruthie would be sold to a slave trader or a local family, a kind master or a harsh one, even taken out of Louisville entirely or sent south on a riverboat to the Lower Mississippi. It was the dilemma that every slave in Kentucky faced whenever an owner died, or was bankrupted, or simply decided to rid himself of some of his "extra" labor. The black family, especially the marriage of the enslaved like Thornton and his Ruthie, was always under threat.

The men who attended the Backus sale at George and Charlotte's old home on Green Street represented a cross section of the neighboring families, most of them businessmen, although there were also boardinghouse operators, shopkeepers, and at least one important local official, Judge John Pope Oldham. Thornton may well have entertained hopes that Oldham would buy his wife, as owners sometimes did to preserve family relationships among their valued slaves. But he was destined to be disappointed. Oldham was apparently unaware of—or simply not concerned about—the danger to Thornton's wife. He went away, presumably satisfied, with his purchase of "12 cut plates press glass" and "8 common chairs." Very few of the items sold that day went for the price set on them by court-appointed appraisers two weeks earlier. What was surely Charlotte Backus's pride and joy, her gilt-edged china, brought only $18, and her pretty lacquered-wood "Japan Waiters," $2. Mr. J. Blair, whose boardinghouse stood on the south side of Main Street about a block west of Wurts & Reinhard's warehouse, purchased the dray and horses for the bargain-basement price of $100. The barouche was sold for $250, and the carriage horses to match for about $120. Their purchaser operated a brickyard at the eastern end of the Louisville riverfront. When questioned later in court about the low price accepted for so valuable an article, Ernest replied that it had been necessary to sell off items quickly in order to settle the Backus family's debts.

As the most valuable of the Backus family's assets, Ruthie was kept to the last. Many descriptions of slave auctions survive, and it is easy to picture the scene in the old Backus parlor, now bereft of the furniture, art, and ornaments that had once made the house a home. It was nearing noon that June day, the room hot and crowded with would-be purchasers, sweat soaking through the woolen jackets of the men. Standing on a crate or perhaps a chair, Ruthie was displayed to the roomful of would-be purchasers, her fear palpable, eliciting pity in only a few. The sight of a slight, lovely woman may well have aroused a salacious anticipation in the male spectators. After all, she was property.

But when Ruthie Blackburn was finally "knocked down" by the auctioneer to a local businessman named Virgil McKnight, she went for the unusually low price of $300. Was it her shy and retiring manner that finally discouraged or even shamed other purchasers? Or did the auctioneer have a prior arrangement of some kind with Frederick B. Ernest? House servants of Ruthie's caliber would ordinarily sell for about $400 on the Louisville market. She was, however, worth much more in the markets at the mouth of the Mississippi, where cotton profits swelled the value of slaves and where there was an active trade in beautiful young women as well.

The man who bought Ruthie Blackburn was a well-known commission merchant and a respected citizen who sat on several boards, according to Louisville's first city directory, published in 1834. A good deal is known about his public face, although he had not yet embarked upon the career that would bring him both fame and much approbation from Kentucky's leading citizens. In 1831, Virgil McKnight was considered a fine businessman and trustworthy colleague and a man very much on his way up. Only thirty-three, he already owned a thriving commission house and retail store and had business interests up and down the Ohio and Mississippi valleys. McKnight & Company's Drygoods Store would have been a familiar sight to Thornton and probably to Ruthie as well, for it stood just a half block west of Wurts & Reinhard's. There the proprietor advertised for sale in the *Louisville Public Advertiser* of April 10, 1828, under the title "New Store," "a general assortment of British, French and American dry goods, hardware, queensware, groceries, &c., all of which will be sold, wholesale and retail, at very low prices for cash or such produce as may suit." McKnight was in correspondence with merchants from St. Louis to New Orleans, and continued his lucrative trade under the management of his son, even though he himself had moved on to other endeavors. McKnight had also married very well. His wife was Anne Logan, the granddaughter of the frontiersman Ben Logan, who brought some of the first slaves into Kentucky in 1775, and after whom Logan County is named.

McKnight, according to one source, was "of medium height, of bulky frame; his head was large, his forehead broad and high, with a prominent brow; his hair was sandy, complexion ruddy . . . his eyes deep set, small, very dark, bright and watchful, and at times twinkled with fun." Already a director of the Bank of the United States at the time he purchased Ruthie, McKnight would soon be a beneficiary of Andrew Jackson's meddling in the national banking system. In 1833, he would be appointed the first president of the Bank of Kentucky. It was a post he would retain for more than thirty-five years. As smaller banks collapsed under the weight of unsecured credit and a massive oversupply of paper money in the Panic of 1837, McKnight was credited with saving the institution and paying off all its debtors. This feat earned him an enviable reputation for integrity.

However, none of this indicates the kind of master Virgil

McKnight might have been to the children's nursemaid he purchased in June 1831. McKnight had grown up in a slave-holding family that had moved to Kentucky from the valley of Virginia, but were originally Scots-Irish from Pennsylvania. The McKnights' new home in Woodford County was in the heart of the Bluegrass, which had the highest percentage of slaveholders in Kentucky. McKnight's father had half a dozen slaves in his household while Virgil was still living at home. In Louisville, Virgil and his wife held five slaves, all probably domestic servants, plus a coach- and yardman.

Only a single personal account provided by an emancipated African American mentions McKnight in his capacity as a slave owner. Allen Allensworth had served with distinction in the Civil War and continued his army service as a chaplain. More than half a century later, as a lieutenant colonel of the U.S. Army, he shared this anecdote of his past relations with Virgil McKnight:

> "Marse" Jim did business with the Bank of Kentucky, in Louisville. Virgil McKnight, its president, asked him if he had a likely boy who could be had for house service. "Marse" Jim answered in the affirmative. The next time he went to town he took Allen with him and turned him over to Virgil McKnight, who in turn, turned him over to Mrs. McKnight. This new home pleased the boy, as it was near the city of Louisville, where he could see his mother and sister often. Besides, he had opportunities to meet the city boys. And, too, he had opportunities to wear fine clothes. These fine clothes, however, were "Marse" Virgil's castaways. "Marse" Virgil was of great avoirdupois, so there was considerable unworn material in his clothes, which could be used for Allen. This outfit made him a regular dandy among the boys.

At the beginning of the hostilities, Allensworth was asked to join the Forty-fourth Illinois Regiment as a nurse. He jumped at the chance. On his way out of town, they marched to Louisville on the Salt River Road and up Main Street, passing the Bank of Kentucky, of which McKnight was president. To avoid being seen by McKnight he disguised himself. To do this, he dressed in an old suit of soldier blue, plastered mud over his face, put an iron camp kettle on his head for a hat, and marched boldly up the street and right by the bank. This was Allen's third start for Canada, the land of freedom.

Allensworth was lucky; he saw Virgil McKnight, but McKnight did not see him. It was to be the end of their association:

On the porch of the Bank of Kentucky stood "Marse" Virgil, and the attaches of the bank, and in front Uncle Billy, the janitor. Allen's head was up and to the front, while his eyes were to the left. About five o'clock they went into camp a short distance above Louisville. While in camp, he concluded to write "Marse" Virgil a letter, giving him information of his whereabouts.

From the rather cheeky tone of this account, McKnight does not seem to have been particularly cruel. But perhaps his treatment of slaves within his own household was not the issue. Profits were much, much higher in the Deep South, especially for attractive "yellow" girls like Thornton's wife.

Whether Virgil McKnight was actually planning to sell Ruthie Blackburn as a fancy girl, or use her to his own ends, can never be proven. But Thornton and his new bride certainly believed something dreadful was in store for her, for they immediately set about arranging their audacious escape. Less than two weeks after Ruthie was sold to Virgil McKnight, the Blackburns were on the steamboat *Versailles* steaming upriver toward Cincinnati and freedom.

What was it that had alarmed them so? On the face of it, neither their own relationship nor their living situation would be very much threatened if Ruthie were to live in the quarters behind the McKnight home. It was located on Fifth Street, between Green and Market, just a few blocks away from the Oldham house where Thornton lived, and around the corner from Ruthie's old home. But household servants knew a great deal about the private as well as the public lives of the merchant families whose fortunes were being made and lost along Louisville's Main Street. They cared for their homes and knew every intimate detail of the whites' marital—and extramarital—relationships. What's more, enslaved men and women in the commercial district also dealt with their owners' customers and overheard conversations with business partners, lawyers, and bookkeepers. Given that they could be sold at any time, it was a matter of survival for slaves to be aware of how other slaves were treated. They knew which master or mistress was kindly or cruel, capricious or consistent, which was generous with food and other necessities, and which was particularly given to harsh punishment. And every slave in the vicinity would be cognizant of whether this one or that among the white slaveholders had an eye for the women under his control.

Slaveholding propaganda maintained that black people lacked the "finer feelings" of white people, and thus were less concerned about the loss of spouses or children than a white person would be. The notice for an estate sale printed in the *Louisville Public Advertiser* on April 9, 1828, had an odd juxtaposition of items:

> 30 shares of stock of the Louisville Insurance Company; 2 town lots in the flourishing village of Jackson, Illinois; 1 undivided half lot in Mount Vernon, Bullitt County, Kentucky; Pew No. 44 in the Presbyterian Meeting House; Also a NEGRO WOMAN 30 years of age, honest, of good habits, a good washer, and without incumbrance.

"Without incumbrance" meant the woman did not have children or a husband. However, the fact that removing people from spouses and children caused them grief, thereby reducing their effectiveness as slaves, was at least tacitly acknowledged. Many owners preferred to purchase or hire slaves where such matters were not at issue.

Although it was some years before the slave trade in Louisville grew into the profitable specialist business it would become, some Louisville merchants were already engaged in slave trading on a somewhat larger scale than the ad above would suggest. Some purchased men, women, and children for immediate resale at a healthy markup to professional slave traders operating in other parts of the state. Others, possibly including McKnight, gathered groups of the choicest articles, hired agents or overseers to supervise their transport, and then paid their passage south to the markets of the Cotton Kingdom. There, Kentucky slaves were worth so much more than they were in their home state that the investor could easily recoup his funds.

The timing of Ruthie's sale lends credence to the theory that she was intended to be swiftly resold. Most Kentucky slaves were purchased in June, July, and August, and then taken down the Mississippi or walked overland to Southern markets. This was because slave auction houses in the Lower Mississippi were most active between November and April, when cotton and sugarcane planters were flush with cash following the harvest and preparing for the next season's planting. In later years, traders in the domestic slave business maintained branch offices in Kentucky, Virginia, or Maryland, as well as showrooms and slave jails in Natchez or New Orleans. So lucrative was the commerce that by the 1850s slave dealers openly roamed the Kentucky countryside buying up "surplus" slaves from rural farms and advertising in local newspapers, offering top dollar for "bucks" and "wenches" for the New Orleans market.

Whatever air of respectability it might gain later, in 1831 slave trading was considered among the lowliest occupations, with the possible exception of slave catching, which was even worse. Kentucky society preferred to maintain the myth that slavery there was more humane than in any other state, except perhaps for Virginia. Indeed, Kentuckians will tell you so today. But there was a great deal of money to be made in the market, and even respectable citizens were tempted. Frederic Bancroft, the historian who investigated the state's slave trade, found that wealthy families in Louisville and Lexington often financed privately the transport and sale of slave coffles down the river. He also discovered that merchants in downtown Louisville facilitated the trade, assembling slaves quietly on their investors' behalf and then, when there were enough to warrant a trip, hiring men to take them down the river.

A chance discovery in the land registry records for Meade County, just a few hours' steamboat ride downstream from Louisville, supports McKnight's engagement in the Mississippi River slave trade. In 1833, he would purchase at Brandenburg several slaves belonging to a local estate. There is no further record of what became of these people. They never appear in the tax records for the McKnight landholdings in any part of the state, nor does the census reflect a corresponding increase in Anne and Virgil McKnight's own household. Indeed, hiring records show that when McKnight needed additional labor, he normally leased, rather than purchased, slaves from other Louisville owners. Abram Hasbrook of Jefferson County added a codicil to his will on January 18, 1823, asking that his wife retain "the negro woman Sally and her three children, and the negro boy now living with Virgil McKnight." In the case of the Brandenburg slaves, they were not disposed of in Meade, Jefferson, or adjacent counties. They simply vanish from the records. The suspicion might be that they found themselves working in the cane fields or the cotton plantations of some far-off land. The fact that the Brandenburg slaves whom Virgil McKnight purchased were neither retained by him nor sold off locally suggests that McKnight, along with so many of his contemporaries, sold slaves "down the river" to Southern markets.

Thornton Blackburn had been forced to part with his mother at the age of three. His brother, Alfred, had been lost to him when Thornton took his own trip down the river in 1825. Now he was about to lose his wife forever, and it took little imagination to picture the life she would lead; the sale of young women into what effectively was the sex trade was no secret. A remarkable series of letters written in 1831 by traders operating between Richmond, Virginia, and Natchez at the time Ruthie Blackburn was sold, survives. The terms in which their female merchandise was described, and the obvious sexual abuse to which they were subjected even before being sold, leave no doubt that Thornton and Ruthie's fears were extremely well grounded in fact. One particularly coarse missive details how one trader gave a hapless girl a "good dose of the one-eyed man" before sending her on south to be sold. The meaning of the term is graphic and authentically contemporary.

The Clarke brothers of Kentucky had a pretty sister whose virginity was a salable asset:

> Sister was chained to a gang of a hundred and sixty slaves . . . [and] carried down the river to New Orleans, kept three or four weeks, and then put up for sale. The day before the sale, she was taken to the barber's, her hair dressed, and she was furnished with a new silk gown, and gold watch, and every thing done to set off her personal attractions, previous to the time of the bidding. The first bid was $500; then $800. The auctioneer began to extol her virtues. Then $1000 was bid. The auctioneer says, "If you only knew the *reason* why she is sold, you would give any sum for her. She is a *pious*, good girl, member of the Baptist church, *warranted* to be a virtuous girl." The bidding grew brisk. "Twelve!" "thirteen," "fourteen," "fifteen," "sixteen hundred," was at length bid, and she was knocked off to a Frenchman, named Coval. He wanted her to live with him as his housekeeper and mistress.

James W. C. Pennington, who published an account of his own life in slavery in 1849, talked of what became of women sent from Kentucky to the slave markets of New Orleans:

It is under the mildest form of slavery, as it exists in Maryland, Virginia, and Kentucky, that the finest specimens of colored females are reared. There are no mothers who rear, and educate in the natural graces, finer daughters than the Ethiopian women, who have the least chance to give scope to their maternal affections. But what is generally the fate of such female slaves? When they are not raised for the express purpose of supplying the market of a class of economical Louisiana and Mississippi gentlemen, who do not wish to incur the expense of rearing legitimate families, they are, nevertheless, on account of their attractions, exposed to the most shameful degradation, by the young masters in the families where it is claimed they are so well off.

We cannot, then, wonder that Thornton and Ruthie chose to risk whipping, certain separation, and even death, to keep her from the degradation of a sexual servitude.

6

NOW LET ME FLY

Sometimes standing on the Ohio River bluff, looking
over on a free State, and as far north as my eyes could
see, I have eagerly gazed upon the blue sky of the free
North . . . and I thought of the fishes of the water, the
fowls of the air, the wild beasts of the forest, all appeared to be free, to go just where they pleased, and I
was an unhappy slave!

—HENRY BIBB, 1849

THE MANNER OF the Blackburns' flight from Louisville was very
bold. Their daylight escape depended on their ability to deceive
a considerable number of people, and to maintain their pretense
for more than a day, under intense scrutiny. So far, it had worked.
They had managed to cross the Ohio River to Indiana without
incident, and their hailing of the *Versailles* was a masterful touch.
What Louisville slave would have the courage to do so, in full
view of the Kentucky shore, and on a sunny summer's morning?
The only tense moments had come on the two occasions when
their forged documents were examined. However, it had all
passed off smoothly. They had crossed safely to Jeffersonville on
the ferry, and then Captain Quarrier of the *Versailles* had allowed
them passage as far as Cincinnati.

Riding along on the calm waters of the river on that fine Sunday afternoon, they could begin to take stock of their situation. Tomorrow was the Fourth of July, and the symbolism of that date surely was not lost on this astute young couple. Traveling upstream, they watched as the *Versailles* chugged past wharves where stevedores hefted crates of good Kentucky whiskey, hogsheads of tobacco, and barrels of preserved pork, the bread and butter, as it were, of the river trade; neatly cultivated fields of tobacco plants and wheat, corn, flax, and hemp; the gracious estates of the rich, and the rude log cabins of the very poor. But on the Indiana side of the river visible from the port, or left, side of the vessel, the hands that loaded the riverboats, hoed the crops, took care of the babies, and made the meals were free, whether they were black or white. Off the starboard, or right-hand, side of the *Versailles*, lay Kentucky, where all the workers doing the hardest tasks, the filthy work of hempbreaking and mucking the stalls and scrubbing the chamberpots, were black and slaves. It must have been a stunning experience for this couple to travel up the Ohio River for a day and a night between those two starkly contrasting realities, with their own past and future laid out before them on parallel but very different shores.

The crew was going about its business, and the other passengers seemed to find nothing remarkable in either the Blackburns' appearance or their demeanor. No one aboard believed them to be anything other than who they pretended to be, a free black couple on a pleasant journey to Ohio. The *Versailles* stopped several times along the overnight voyage to refuel and take on passengers and goods, arriving at the Cincinnati docks early on Monday morning.

The lower part of the city was built on the floodplain of the Ohio, beautifully ringed about by tall limestone hills. British traveler Frances Trollope described her first sight of Cincinnati from the river when she arrived in February 1828, a little more than three years before the Blackburns did: "[It is] finely situated on the south side of a hill that rises gently from the water's edge; yet it is by no means a city of striking appearance; it wants domes, towers, and steeples; but its landing-place is noble, extending for more than a quarter of a mile."

As was customary for free blacks even in nominally free Ohio, Thornton and Ruthie had to wait until all the white passengers on the upper deck disembarked before descending the gangway. Nodding politely to Captain Quarrier, they left the vessel and were soon lost from view in the Cincinnati crowds. This pair of runaway slaves reached free soil on the day white Americans were celebrating their own release from Britain's imperial yoke. It was the Fourth of July, and there were already revelers out in the streets, affording the Blackburns an extra degree of anonymity. The English abolitionist Joseph Sturge wrote disapprovingly of his observations on his 1841 travels: "The fourth of July, the anniversary of the independence of the United States . . . is still marked by extravagant demonstrations of joy, and often disgraced by scenes of intemperance and demoralization." As he later testified, Monroe Quarrier and the *Versailles* crew thought no more about their former passengers as they made their own preparations to enjoy the holiday.

At the Cincinnati stagecoach offices on East Front Street, Thornton and Ruthie Blackburn purchased two tickets for Sandusky, in northern Ohio. All the time they were in southern Ohio they were in the gravest danger. Slave catchers lurked around the steamboat docks and on street corners, ever watchful for any black person who might be a runaway slave. So many of the fugitives from points south passed through Cincinnati that slave catching there was a very lucrative business. Although some local residents hated their activities and the Cincinnati branch of what would soon be called the Underground Railroad was already under way, many people in southern Ohio did not disapprove of slavery. Some settlers in the lower part of the state were originally from the Carolinas and Virginia, while the north was mainly the province of New Englanders and, by the 1830s, some German immigrants. The latter two groups disapproved of slavery, but the former did not.

This made Cincinnati a sometimes turbulent place. Although trade linked Cincinnati with Wheeling, in what is now West Virginia, and also with Pittsburgh, both upriver, its closest commercial ties were with Southern markets, to which it shipped most of its products, including prodigious amounts of preserved pork. Cincinnati had economic ties with its rival city on the river, Louisville, and even tighter links with Covington, Kentucky, just across the Ohio. Because of its proximity to Kentucky as well as the riverboats that served its port, Cincinnati had by the 1820s become something of a haven for black immigrants from other states, with about 10 percent of the urban population composed of free blacks by 1827. Increased white immigration resulted in competition between blacks and whites for employment. This was always tinder to the spark of racial animosity in American cities, and in 1829 and 1830 serious racial riots in Pittsburgh, New York, and Cincinnati demonstrated how deeply incoming workers resented their black competition. One African American who moved to Cincinnati said, "I thought upon coming to a free state like Ohio I would find every door thrown open to receive me, but from the treatment I received by the people generally, I found it little better than Virginia . . . I found every door was closed against the colored man in a free state, excepting the jails and penitentiaries."

Given the regular traffic between Cincinnati and Louisville, Thornton and Ruthie would have known what kind of treatment to expect there. Two years earlier, the municipal government had tried to crack down on the black populace by enforcing repressive Ohio Black Codes, the dreaded Code Noir, put in place years earlier (in 1804 and 1807). Apart from strictures against black people testifying against whites in court, these had been generally ignored until Cincinnati's mayor and council bowed to citizen complaints. On June 29, 1829, African Americans were suddenly put on notice that all blacks had to post a $500 bond and have their behavior guaranteed by two white men of respectable station. They were required to observe a curfew, and although many were skilled workers, certain types of employment were henceforth reserved for white craftsmen and artisans. The 1829 ordinance also reinforced the provisions of the 1793 federal Fugitive Slave Law as reported in the *Cincinnati Gazette*, July 27, 1829:

> If any person being a resident of this state shall employ, harbor, conceal any . . . negro or mulatto person . . . any person so offending shall forfeit and pay . . . a sum not exceeding one hundred dollars, one half to the informer, and the other half for the use of the poor of the township . . . and moreover to be liable for the maintenance and support of such negro or mulatto, provided he, she or they, shall become unable to support themselves.

On August 22, feelings against blacks reached fever pitch and a riot broke out; more than three hundred whites attacked the homes of the city's blacks. Officers of the law refused to involve themselves, but the African Americans responded with gunfire and dispersed the mob. The result of this ordinance and the violence that followed in its wake was the exodus of a significant portion of the black elite. More than one thousand people left the city, about six hundred moving to the Wilberforce settlement. This first African American colonizing effort in Upper Canada was created with the support of the British Lieutenant Governor of the province, Sir John Colborne, at the request of the leader of the colonization committee at Cincinnati, James Charles Brown.

It was not long before the Black Codes were loosened again. Cincinnati-area businessmen, steamboat operators, hotel keepers, and factory owners protested the loss of their best source of cheap labor.

Free though it might be, Cincinnati was no place to linger. On the same morning they landed, the Blackburns took the northbound stage out of Cincinnati. Mail coaches left daily, the direct route passing through Xenia and Springfield on the way to Sandusky. Their journey would have been neither pleasant nor swift.

The coaches ran about ten miles per hour, with coaching stations for changing the horses at similar intervals. Traveling to the shores of Lake Erie took three or four days over very rough roads. One elderly man from Lebanon, Ohio, recalled the stage-coach travel of his youth on this line: "Many classes of people were crowded into a stagecoach . . . a dozen men and women, usually men, would be packed together for an all night ride. Those facing each other would have their knees interlocked." He also tells us what the Blackburns' tickets would have cost: "The fares in the Northern States were usually about six cents a mile, in the Southern States, about ten cents." In fact, the Blackburns do not seem to have suffered from want of funds while making their escape. This begs several questions: Had they managed to accumulate some savings while still enslaved? Or did they have the help of an Underground Railroad operator in Louisville, as their knowledge of steamboat and stage schedules, as well as their possession of both money and excellent forged identification papers, suggests?

The Blackburns' passage lay in parts between deep woods and great mud holes that swallowed up the wheels. Sometimes passengers were forced to walk, carrying rails taken from nearby fences to pry the wheels free from the muck. A travelogue of the same journey by no less a personage than Charles Dickens is described in his *American Notes* of 1842:

It is impossible to convey an adequate idea to you of the kind of road over which we traveled. I can only say that it was, at the best, but a track through the wild forest, and among the swamps, bogs, and morasses of the withered bush. A great portion of it was what is called a "corduroy road": which is made by throwing round logs or whole trees into a swamp, and leaving them to settle there. Good Heaven! if you only felt one of the least of the jolts with which the coach falls from log to log! It is like nothing but going up a steep flight of stairs in an omnibus. Now the coach flung us in a heap on its floor, and now crushed our heads against its roof. Now one side of it was deep in the mire, and we were holding on to the other. Now it was lying on the horses' tails, and now again upon its back. But it never, never, was in any position, attitude, or kind of motion, to which we are accustomed in coaches; or made the smallest approach to our experience of the proceedings of any sort of vehicle that goes on wheels.

Ruthie and Thornton traveled first to the port of Sandusky, on Lake Erie, 186 miles north of Cincinnati. In the close confines of the carriage they would have had to be especially careful not to betray their motives in making their way north. But while people in southern Ohio, with their commercial and often familial links to slaveholding states, tended to be less than enthusiastic about abolitionism, the Erie shore had been settled by New Englanders who took a very dim view of the South's labor system. Help would probably have been available at Sandusky had the Blackburns found themselves in trouble. There was a wonderful natural harbor, and the town was an important transshipment point for goods and passengers. Sandusky was throughout the antebellum period a crossing point for runaway slaves.

The Blackburns' coach reached Sandusky Wednesday evening, July 6. Thornton and his wife immediately changed stagecoaches for Detroit, their final destination being the free Michigan Territory. Doubtless rumpled and very tired from the strain of their deception, they boarded the stagecoach. There they found themselves in the company of another black man. He introduced himself as James Slaughter of Detroit. Friendly and apparently very kind, Slaughter made conversation with the Blackburns all the way to the end of the trip. Ruthie seems to have been particularly relieved to meet a kindred soul and was perhaps less discreet than she ought to have been in what she disclosed. Slaughter's real objectives in making the Kentucky couple's acquaintance would not be revealed for some time.

Given that they were within sight of Canada for much of the last leg of their journey, it seems puzzling that Thornton and Ruthie did not immediately seek passage for the British colony. Some boats crossing Lake Erie regularly carried fugitives to safety, and at reduced fares or no fare at all.

There are several possible explanations for the Blackburns' choice of Detroit, rather than Canada, as their new home in freedom. One is that there may already have been an Underground Railroad route leading from Louisville to the city on the Detroit River. If so, the link may have been either Washington Spradling or the Reverend Henry Adams of Louisville's First Baptist Church, or both. Despite an odd article in *Frederick Douglass' Paper* dated April 1, 1853, where Adams was castigated for sermonizing that helping fugitive slaves was "man stealing" and therefore sinful, Adams was very much in a position to have provided both papers and information to the Blackburns. However opposed he might be to the removal of slaves from their "rightful" owners, as a man of the cloth he could hardly have condoned the future that Virgil McKnight apparently had planned for Mrs. Blackburn. While Spradling would openly discuss his assistance to runaways in later years, there seems never to have been any real suspicion of Underground Railroad activism surrounding Adams. This does not mean he wasn't involved in such efforts; only that he may have been successful at concealing his activities. Detroit would shortly become a leading center for Underground Railroad activities; a number of the black people already residing in the community would be recognized as leading lights of antislavery in the next decade. However, the Blackburns' own choice of Detroit as the place to begin new lives in freedom was one that they, in the not-too-distant future, would have cause to regret.

Meanwhile, back in Louisville, the game was already up. Somehow, John Pope Oldham had discovered that Thornton had absconded from the city. Upon further investigation it was found that Ruthie Blackburn was also not where she was supposed to be. Judge Oldham immediately contacted Virgil McKnight, with whom he was acquainted as a fellow member of the Presbyterian Church. Assuming that the runaway pair was making their way to Canada, McKnight and Oldham dispatched the judge's eldest son, William Oldham, in pursuit. The next steamboat bound for Cincinnati did not depart until the day following the holiday, so William could not leave Louisville until Tuesday, July 5. William had strict orders to search out the captain of the *Versailles* personally and learn what had become of Thornton Blackburn and his wife.

William Oldham was well acquainted with his uncle Gideon and aunt Susan Brown's slaves. Three years Thornton's senior, he had known Thornton since they were both boys in Hardinsburg. After the Oldhams moved to Louisville, William had worked for his father at the post office. Following his parents' removal to their country estate, William had been responsible for overseeing the slaves who continued to live in the quarters behind the post office, including Thornton himself. William would later swear that he "knew that Thornton had a wife the property of Virgil McKnight, but he did not know her personally."

While William was on his way to Cincinnati, John Pope Oldham discussed with Susan Brown the steps he was taking to retrieve her absconding property and obtained her power of attorney to pursue Thornton. He also met with Virgil McKnight to discuss their legal strategy for the recovery of the Blackburns. McKnight's rage at Ruthie's flight is evident even in the dry legal documents relating to the Blackburns' escape; however, there was little he could do until William Oldham returned to Louisville with news of their whereabouts.

The steamboat bearing William reached the Cincinnati wharves on July 7. He found the *Versailles* still in port, and closely questioned Captain Quarrier and his crew about the "free" black couple who had sailed to Cincinnati on their steamboat. Monroe Quarrier must have been horrified. He was not a wealthy man, and the penalties for transporting bondspeople from slave to free territory were crippling. The *Versailles* captain also knew that the ship's owner's—his employers—would bear the brunt of the

Fugitive Slave Law because he had chosen to carry the Black-burns. Quarrier was more than happy to assist young Oldham in his search for the runaways. He sent the members of his crew out to scour the city and investigate possible avenues of escape. Eventually, it was William Oldham who located the stagecoach company offices. He "found that the names of [the] negroes Thornton and Ruthy were entered on the books of the Stage office . . . and [were] destined as it appeared by the entry on said books for the City of Sandusky, Ohio." The trail was days old. There was little doubt in William's mind that Thornton was taking his bride to Canada. To his father's evident fury, William took the matter no further. Giving up the chase at Cincinnati he returned to Louisville to report what had transpired. The owners of the *Versailles* were to regret that their new captain, Monroe Quarrier, had been so trusting. The court case mounted against them by McKnight and Oldham would last fifteen years.

When William Oldham returned to Louisville, his father first discussed the matter with McKnight and then informed Charles Wurts and John Reinhard of what had happened. Under Kentucky law, Wurts & Reinhard's was not legally liable for Thornton's escape. Furthermore, he had absconded on a weekend when he was not even under their supervision. However, the partners did feel somewhat responsible, for it was they who advertised for Thornton's return in the *Louisville Public Advertiser* beginning July 7, 1831, and offered a $25 reward. No advertisement was placed for Ruthie, presumably because it was known she had left with her husband and they were likely to remain together.

Charles Wurts's brother, Edward, who was apprenticing with Wurts & Reinhard's, was called upon to testify to Mrs. Blackburn's connection with Thornton. His statement is the most detailed account of their flight and its aftermath:

> Said negro made his escape from the possession of . . .
> Wurts and Reinhard on the 3rd day of July 1831, which was
> the Sabbath day . . . [the] negro man was frequently in the

company of and associated with a mulatto woman named Ruthe, the property of Virgil McKnight, and some time previous the property of Mr. Backus then of this city, which said negro woman made her escape at the same time that the negro man Thornton Blackburn did.

McKnight and Oldham then hired lawyers and launched separate suits against the owners and the captain of the *Versailles*. Monroe Quarrier sailed to Wheeling to meet with the vessel's owners and discuss their options. The Jefferson County Chancery Court found on behalf of Oldham and McKnight, and ordered the *Versailles* to be brought back to Louisville for impoundment. On November 3, 1831, the *Versailles* was seized by the sheriff of Jefferson County.

When the *Versailles* tied up at the Louisville docks a few days later, Virgil McKnight boarded her:

> . . . and ascertained from the books of said boat that she had left the Port of Louisville on the 3rd day of July, 1831, about 10 or 11 o'clock a.m., and among the list of Deck passengers to Cincinnati of that date he saw the names of "Mr. Blackburn & Lady," who the clerk of said boat informed him were mulattoes . . . the said negroes have not been recovered, and are now probably in Canada.

When he was questioned, it was obvious that the clerk of the *Versailles*, Thornton Bayless, remembered Ruthie Blackburn but almost nothing about her husband. Captain Quarrier recalled the couple well because the Blackburns were the only free African American passengers on the trip. But their papers had seemed entirely correct, and he swore he had not realized there was reason to question the couple further. Besides, he protested, he was from Wheeling, in Virginia, where the *Versailles* was registered, and had been going about his lawful business of carrying goods and passengers on a common waterway. By this, Quarrier was implying that the *Versailles*, its officers, and its owners were out-side the jurisdiction of the sheriff of Jefferson County. Also mentioned was the fact that the couple had boarded from the Jeffersonville, Indiana, side of the river. Technically, Quarrier had not transported slaves from a slave state to a free one; the ferry captain (who was never charged in the case) had done that. A similar case had come before the Jefferson County courts in April 1830. In *Edwards v. Vail* the judge ruled that the captain was not culpable because "the negro came voluntarily on board from another state and left the boat voluntarily, and went into another state, the boat remaining all the time in Kentucky."

Captain Quarrier was about to discover how wrong he was on all counts. McKnight's and Oldham's complaints, the latter on behalf of "Gideon Brown's Heirs," were filed in the Jefferson County Circuit Court, and the sheriff of Louisville was requested to impound the *Versailles* for "safe keeping." The indemnity for the release of the *Versailles* was a very substantial $1,000, representing the estimated value of Thornton and Ruthie if they could not be recovered, plus anticipated court costs to be awarded to the successful party in the lawsuit. Quarrier raised the funds himself by mortgaging a piece of Louisville property he owned. He then hired the firm of Guthrie and Bullock. James Guthrie was the same man acting as guardian of young Henry Backus; he and William F. Bullock had the most prominent law firm in all Louisville. It was, however, perhaps an unfortunate choice on Quarrier's part. Not only was Guthrie related to John Pope Oldham through his connection with the Churchill family, but William Fontaine Bullock had been married to the Oldhams' elder daughter, Sophia, now deceased.

Leaving his fortunes in the hands of his lawyers, Captain Quarrier traveled back to Wheeling to consult with the senior partner in the steamboat company, John McFarland, on how best to proceed. When he reached the Virginia city, he discovered that Andrew Kirkpatrick, who also held shares in the boat, had died. The remaining partners responded to the suit by producing affidavits that echoed the points made by Quarrier in his own defense. These were, specifically, that the waters of the Ohio were an open and legal waterway; that the *Versailles* had rightfully been engaged in commerce between Louisville and Cincinnati; and that no one on the boat had suspected Thornton and Ruthie of being fugitive slaves.

The immense amount of detail available about Thornton and Ruthie Blackburn's escape on the *Versailles* comes from the court case against the steamboat owners and Captain Quarrier launched by Virgil McKnight and John Pope Oldham, the latter acting in his capacity as executor for Gideon Brown's estate. The tone regarding the Blackburns themselves is interesting. The manner of the couple's escape did not occasion much comment; the proceedings focused to a large extent on what happened in the first five minutes after Thornton and Ruthie boarded the *Versailles*. At issue in the protracted prosecution of the case were whether Quarrier had knowingly carried runaway slaves to free soil, and whether the Ohio River between Louisville and Cincinnati was under Kentucky jurisdiction. If the first were true, the captain could be jailed for aiding and abetting slaves who were absconding from their owners. According to Quarrier's legal defense, he found nothing to question in the identification papers presented by the Blackburns: "The negro man who came on board from Indiana presented him with papers, which he called his free papers, which papers [Captain Quarrier] examined and supposing them correct permitted the negro to go on." The matter of who owned the Ohio River was more complex. In the end this became a debate regarding the constitutionality of agreements made in the eighteenth century by the U.S. government and the state of Virginia, of which Kentucky had originally been a part.

The court battle between the Blackburns' owners and the proprietors and captain of the *Versailles* dragged on, moving through various Jefferson County courts with glacial slowness. In the meantime, the *Versailles* continued to operate the packet trade between Cincinnati and Louisville, and also occasionally traveled farther upriver. On October 20, 1831, the *Louisville Public Advertiser* announced that the ship had arrived in port from Pittsburgh bearing the owners of the *Versailles*. There were evidently no hard feelings between Quarrier and Wurts and Reinhard, for the steamboat had freight aboard destined for their warehouses. Quarrier married on November 26, 1833, at Louisville and remained in the city for a time to further his defense against the Oldham and McKnight lawsuit, but he was eventually forced to take up command of another ship, for he was much in need of funds.

In the meantime, John Pope Oldham became seriously ill. In the Bodley Family Papers at the Filson Historical Society in Louisville is a letter to William S. Bodley in Vicksburg, Mississippi, from his sister at Stockdale, Shelby County, dated June 7, 1836:

> You have doubtless heard before this of Judge Oldham's attempt to destroy himself by taking a quantity of Laudanum. Mrs. O. discovered it accidentally and immediately called in Physicians. But he refused all medicine. By the exertions of three men he was dragged about the floor (in order to prevent sleep)—and icy water was thrown over him, and so his life was saved, although he said that no friend of his would wish to have his life . . . Ann Chary was there during his illness (being a next neighbor)—I am told that he is very much ashamed of himself—She said he was insane.—The cause is, as yet, unknown.

Oldham was fifty-one at the time. He was actively pursuing several lawsuits, including the one against the owners and captain of the *Versailles*. The judge, however, seems to have suffered from long-term depression, possibly relating to his epilepsy and exacerbated by the death of his daughter Sophia, who had lived only three years following her marriage to Bullock. Both of his sons had also recently departed Louisville en route to fight in the struggle to wrest Texas from Mexico. Ironically, it was Oldham's slaves who walked the floor with him and might be credited with working so hard to save his life. Oldham and his wife eventually moved in with their married daughter, Susan Oldham Hill, and lived with her and her husband, Horace Buckner Hill, who was the cashier of the Bank of Kentucky.

Susan Brown and her children do not seem to have taken any personal interest in the suit against the *Versailles*. Thornton's mistress was content to let her litigious brother-in-law prosecute the case on her behalf; indeed, Susan Brown remained conspicuously absent in all later proceedings relating to the Blackburns. This is curious because her eldest son was only a year younger than Talbot Clayton Oldham, and presumably well able to participate in attempts to retrieve Susan's fugitive slave. Yet at no point did the Brown family engage in active pursuit of Thornton Blackburn; rather, it was the Oldham family who took umbrage at his flight, and Judge Oldham who orchestrated all attempts to discover Thornton's whereabouts and bring him back to Louisville.

The case dragged on until, in December of 1842, the Jefferson County Chancery Court awarded $400 to McKnight for the value of Ruthie Blackburn, but this was appealed. On December 7, 1843, Monroe Quarrier filed his response:

> Monroe Quarrier states on oath that he is not able to pay the decrees in the cases of McKnight vs him and others, and Brown's heirs vs him and others in the Louisville Chancery Court. He is engaged on a steamboat called the "James Hewitt," and is endeavoring to make his living by hard work and attention to the arduous duties of the hard life of a river man, and if he should be put in prison he must starve or undergo great hardship as he has no other way of making his living but by following his business on the river.

The Kentucky Court of Appeals, Spring Term of 1846, again confirmed the lower court decisions that the steamboat company and captain were responsible for the loss of Thornton and Ruthie

Blackburn. Quarrier and the others were ordered to pay both the value of the slaves and McKnight's and Oldham's court costs to date. By this time, two partners in the *Versailles* had died. Quarrier and the three living partners then appealed the case, this time asking for a federal court decision on the constitutionality of the law that gave Kentucky ownership of the river, which dated to the period when Kentucky was still part of Virginia. A slave state, Kentucky shared 664 miles of borderland with the free states of Ohio, Indiana, and Illinois. In the antebellum period, it had to retain ownership of the river in order to retain control of Kentucky's slaves. The state's claims to the Ohio River were upheld in a series of lawsuits; they were challenged, for instance, in 1820 in the case of *Handly's Lessee v. Anthony et al.*, where Chief Justice John Marshall brought down the Supreme Court decision: "When a great river is the boundary line between two nations or States, if the original property is in neither, and there be no convention respecting it, each holds to the middle of the stream. But when, as in this case, one State is the original proprietor, and grants the territory on one side only, it retains the river within its own domains, and the newly created State extends to the river only." To this day the northern border of Kentucky is the low-water mark on the opposite shore.

Although Ohio passed a law in 1799 claiming the right to apprehend criminals from boats on the waterway, Kentucky consistently refused to recognize this. In both 1822 and 1828, lawsuits instituted against ships' captains who had inadvertently carried runaway slaves on the Ohio River judged the river to be Kentucky property, and their actions therefore culpable as providing slaves with assistance in escaping. In the case against the captain of the *Magnolia* in 1828, the defense presented their view: "The slaves were not taken from Kentucky, not being . . . in this State when they were taken on board; and, if they were then in this State, not being out of it when they disembarked." In June 1846, in the case of *McFarland v. McKnight*, the federal court in Kentucky ruled that the state did in fact own the Ohio River where it touched on its territories. Therefore, the captain and owners of the *Versailles* were liable for the value of Thornton Blackburn, $600, and of Ruthie Blackburn, $400, and court costs amounting to more than $350. Quarrier and the remaining owners of the *Versailles*, with no further recourse, paid the fines.

There is little information about the character of Monroe Quarrier, the man whose mistake regarding the Blackburns' legal status cost everyone so much time and money. One contemporary account says he was "universally loved for his genial nature and unbounded generosity." The author cites one of Quarrier's adventures: On January 8, 1847, he arrived at Mobile, Alabama, decks loaded down with a huge cargo of cotton, to see a neighboring ship in flames. Despite the danger to himself and his vessel, and the refusal of less dangerously laden vessels to assist, he and his crew rescued more than one hundred people aboard the burning *Tuscaloosa*. For this feat, the grateful people of Mobile presented him with a gold-headed cane and a silver service, the "Monroe Quarrier coffee urn," which survives today.

Monroe Quarrier's later activities raise questions about ownership of slaves in the 1840s and '50s, some with modern implications. Corporations whose antebellum owners made money from their involvement in slavery are presently under investigation, and lawsuits launched against them by African Americans are demanding enormous reparations. This particularly affects companies that insured skilled and valuable slaves on behalf of their owners. Since the year 2000, the state of California has been examining the profits made by American life insurance firms founded before the Civil War. The state legislature passed a bill that included the statement:

> [I]nsurance policies from the slavery era have been discovered in the archives of several insurance companies, documenting insurance coverage for slaveholders for damage to or death of their slaves, issued by a predecessor insurance firm. These documents provide the first evidence of ill-

gotten profits from slavery, which profits in part capitalized insurers whose successors remain in existence today. [Bill No.] SB2199 Sec. 1(a).

It is alleged that companies such as New York Life and Aetna profited from slavery in this way. The ledgers of the Nautilus Insurance Company, predecessor to New York Life, have Captain Monroe Quarrier of Louisville, Kentucky, on record. Rather surprisingly he had a new partner, Robert Bell, formerly of Bell & Backus, who jointly with him owned several male slaves. Policies on their lives were purchased in 1845 and renewed for two years. All the slaves were employed in working on steamboats. The value of each was appraised at a uniform $500, regardless of skills or age. Premiums, paid in advance, cost $20 per annum. The policies specified that the insured were to travel only on the inland waterways of Alabama, and north of thirty-three degrees of latitude on the Mississippi and Ohio. Two were listed as cabin boys. Allen, Nat, Lex, and Ned were all firemen who stoked the fires that kept the steamboat boilers operating.

In addition to the six he owned jointly with Bell, Captain Quarrier insured several more slaves in his own right. These included two cabin boys, a pair of firemen, and the ship's barber named James. One man, Scott, did not have a task specified in his policy. All the men were employed on the steamboat *James Hewitt*, the same vessel Quarrier was commanding in 1847 while he was trying to avoid paying the costs in the Blackburn case. The boat had been sailing the waters of the Tombigbee River since at least 1837. When one of the slaves, a man named Zack, died at Louisville in June 1848 on board the steamboat, Nautilus Insurance paid Quarrier, the legal owner of Zack, $500.

The fact that both Bell and Quarrier were acquainted with runaway slaves named Ruthie and Thornton Blackburn before they entered into this later business partnership raises intriguing questions. Louisville was a relatively small place in the 1830s and '40s, and the merchant and shipping communities were smaller still. Did they meet in the course of the prosecution of the Blackburn fugitive slave case in the Jefferson County courts? It is curious that neither Bell nor any of the other individuals who knew Ruthie prior to her sale to McKnight were ever called upon to identify her in later legal proceedings pertaining to the Blackburns that arose in Detroit, matters on which her freedom hinged. However, Quarrier's later insurance of so many slave workers for his own benefit rather militates against hints made in the course of his prosecution by McKnight and Oldham that he turned a blind eye toward the Blackburns' escape or was somehow complicit in their flight.

For their part, Thornton and Ruthie Blackburn had voyaged far from their Louisville owners. Within a week of their escape they were living on the free soil of Michigan. The Blackburns' flight took place early in the history of the Underground Railroad. For their passage, there was no "conductor," safe house, or "station" where they could spend the night along the way. Whatever help they may have had, the success of their escape depended on their own resourcefulness. Now they were ready to take the next important step—living independent lives as free African Americans.

DETROIT

SOUTHWESTERN UPPER CANADA/CANADA WEST AND THE DETROIT RIVER FRONTIER

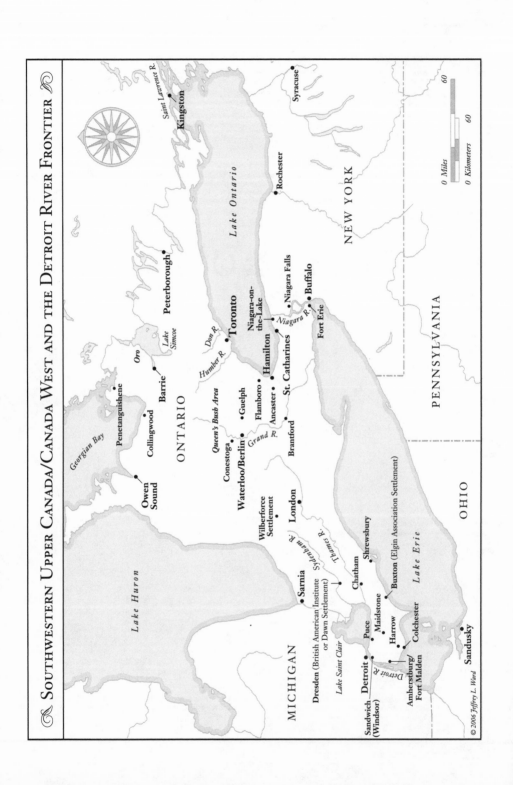

© 2006 Jeffrey L. Ward

7

STEAL AWAY, STEAL AWAY, I AIN'T GOT LONG TO STAY HERE

> I grew up like a neglected weed,—ignorant of liberty, having no experience of it . . . Now I've been free, I know what a dreadful condition slavery is. I have seen hundreds of escaped slaves, but I never saw one who was willing to go back and be a slave.
>
> —HARRIET TUBMAN, 1856

WHEN THORNTON AND RUTHIE alighted from the stagecoach at Detroit's Steamboat Hotel on the afternoon of Wednesday, July 6, 1831, they must have been exhausted. They would have been living on nerves since they had boarded the ferry at the Louisville docks early Sunday morning. The Blackburns were therefore easily persuaded to take up accommodations at the home of their new friend, James Slaughter. He lived with his wife and four children on the upper reaches of Randolph Street, which ran through the heart of the town from the steamboat docks at the Detroit River.

Arising on the morning of their first real day of freedom, the Blackburns could begin to come to terms with their new circumstances. Kentucky was far behind them, and they had left there the chains that had bound them all their lives. Detroit was a free city in a free territory. This was their first real taste of liberty, and they must have found it very sweet. Just across the Detroit River and within easy view of the shore lay the towns and villages of Upper Canada.

The Blackburns came to Michigan when the Westward Movement was in full swing. Detroit's streets were filled with would-be farmers ready to try their luck on the frontier. The city was considered the gateway to the Northwest and was the last intensively settled area before the western wilderness. It was a little more than one-fifth the size of Louisville, having a population of only 2,222 people according to the 1830 census. Although Detroit on the surface lacked amenities when compared with refined Louisville, there was actually a good deal to remind Thornton and his wife of their previous hometown. First established by the French in 1701, Le Detroit—"the Narrows"—was located at a strategic point on the Detroit River between Lake St. Clair to the north and Lake Erie to the south. Although the fortifications along the Canadian-U.S. border were supposed to have been handed over to the Americans after the Revolution, Detroit actually remained in British hands until Jay's Treaty was ratified on November 19, 1794. On July 11, 1796, Michigan Territory was finally turned over to American rule and was severed from the British Province of Upper Canada on the opposite side of the Detroit River. By the time the Blackburns made their home there, streets near the docks were dominated by trading houses, commercial enterprises, grocery stores, and dry-goods wholesalers serving the western trade. Since 1825, the area had been connected with the eastern seaboard by means of the Erie Canal. *Niles' Weekly Register* reported that each steamer crossing Lake Erie in 1831 brought "men, women and children, bed, cradles, kettles and frying pans." Steamboats that stopped at Cleveland, Sandusky, Grand Rapids, and Buffalo left every other day.

In the 1830s, the area along the river still retained some of its French colonial flavor. Ruthie Blackburn, who probably came to Kentucky by way of New Orleans, may have found herself quite at home with the lilting accents and the many French names she heard in the Detroit marketplace. Alexis de Tocqueville, the young French nobleman who traveled through the United States examining the results of democracy on the populace, arrived in

Detroit on the steamboat *Ohio* only days after the Blackburns did, and observed French Canadian farmers' wives "in coarse straw hats and carrying heavy baskets of fruit" traversing the river on market days to peddle the produce of their gardens and chicken coops. On the edges of town were neat cottages on narrow farmsteads fronting on the river, "built in the French style, large, one story high, with very steep roofs, and dormer windows." Voyageurs, the mainstay of the fur trade that had been Detroit's lifeblood for so long, were still a familiar sight on the city streets, as were Native hunters, trappers, and guides. These latter in their blankets and buckskins traveled through Detroit on their way to the annual British gift giving at Fort Malden in Upper Canada.

The town showed great promise. In 1831, Detroit was just recovering from a disastrous fire, and many of the buildings in the downtown core were new. One of the few remaining log homes was the comfortable residence of the former governor of Michigan Territory, Lewis Cass, now secretary of war in President Jackson's Cabinet. Travelers complained of the open sewers that paralleled the muddy, unpaved roadways, but a more optimistic British visitor remarked on the "rows of large and handsome brick houses; the others are generally wood, painted white, with bright green doors and windows . . . there are some excellent shops in the town, a theatre, and a great number of taverns and gaming houses." In 1834, a German immigrant named Karl Neidhard noted that the Michigan territorial capital boasted "a meeting house for the Indians, a courthouse, an academy, and two banks. The Catholics, Episcopalians, Presbyterians, Baptists, and Methodists already have fine-looking churches."

Thornton again found himself living on the banks of a great river. Here the waters served as the boundary not between slave soil and free but between American territory and the British colony of Upper Canada. There remained a strong military presence at Detroit even in the Blackburns' day; Fort Gratiot, which commanded the entrance to Lake Huron, was only a few miles north and east of the city, and the soldiers could be called upon in event of disturbance or disaster.

Slavery had been a feature of Detroit life since earliest times. Both Native Americans—called *panis*—and African Americans had been bought and sold there. The slave trade having been especially brisk during the Revolutionary War when the British occupied Detroit, warriors from allied tribes sold captives taken in Pennsylvania, Ohio, and New York as well as in raids on Kentucky's fortified pioneer stations. After the war, some of Detroit's townsfolk remained loyal to the Crown and crossed the river into Upper Canada where they—and their slaves—settled mainly in the districts of Sandwich and Amherstburg, near the British Fort Malden. Slaveholding families who stayed in Michigan interpreted the Northwest Ordinance of 1787 that forbade slavery north of the Ohio River to mean that they could retain their existing servants but that no further enslaved African Americans could be imported for sale. Thus a few of the black people whom Ruthie and Thornton encountered in Detroit in 1831 were still technically enslaved.

Upper Canada's first Lieutenant Governor had prohibited slave importation (but not slavery itself) in 1793; thus for a few years, the absurd situation obtained whereby slaves escaped from Upper Canada into Michigan, while Michigan slaves crossed over into Upper Canada to find freedom. Isaac Weld, in his *Travels Through the States of North America*, observed an attempted escape of two Canadian slaves from the British Fort Malden area into the United States. Native men were employed in retrieving the fugitives, who were fleeing by boat. Slave flight was a problem all along the border, for a letter to Lieutenant Governor Sir Francis Gore from the New York resident David M. Erskine dated May 26, 1807, mentions complaints by "Proprietors of Slaves in the Western District of the Province of Upper Canada" regarding the "Inconvenience which his Majesty's subjects . . . experience from the Desertion of their slaves into the Territory of the United States." The letter says that there is no hope of having the U.S. government return either the fugitives, indentured servants, or "His Majesty's soldiers and sailors" who had abandoned their posts by moving into the United States. By 1806, there had been so many former British slaves in Detroit that they made up a black militia company of their own. Importation of enslaved people supposedly ceased after 1807, when Judge Augustus Woodward of the Territorial Supreme Court ruled to that effect.

Many Canadian blacks, fearful that American victory might mean re-enslavement for themselves and their children, served in the British forces during the War of 1812. Their loyalty and courage won them posts in border defense, effectively freeing those who were still enslaved and opening the doors to their enfranchisement as British subjects. News of their enhanced status spread quickly. Returning American troops brought the news first to Maysville while Thornton was still a baby. After that time, the traffic in runaways along the Detroit shore generally traveled from the United States into Canada.

Michigan achieved territorial status in 1805 and thereafter was governed first by judges and then by the Territorial Secretary appointed by the federal government. The character of the new secretary, Stevens Thomson Mason, who came into office only weeks after the Blackburns' arrival in Detroit, would prove particularly important to their future security. A relative of George Mason of Gunston Hall and therefore of Thornton Blackburn's owner at the time of his birth, Robert Smith, Mason was a transplanted Virginian from Loudoun County who had been educated at Transylvania University in Lexington, Kentucky. His father, John Thomson Mason, was a friend of Andrew Jackson's and had preceded his son in the Michigan office, arriving at Detroit in 1830. Nineteen years old and too young even to vote when President Jackson's patronage brought him to the post, Michigan's "Boy Governor" took over from his father on July 12, 1831. The youthful Mason would go on to cover himself with glory prosecuting Jackson's Indian removal policies in the Black Hawk War of 1832. Since Governor George B. Porter spent long periods away from Detroit, the younger Mason served as acting governor in his stead and would later be appointed governor himself in 1834 in time to guide the Michigan Territory into statehood in 1837. His own feelings about slavery were characteristic of the Southern gentry; the Masons had imported their household slaves into Michigan from Kentucky in 1830, in complete disregard of the Northwest Ordinance.

Detroit's location on the river directly opposite the free soil of Upper Canada destined Thornton and Ruthie's adoptive home to become the most important Underground Railroad transit point in the whole western border, and substantial support for the colonization of fugitive slaves in the British province across the river would one day be provided by Michigan benefactors. But this was not the case when the Blackburns first came. Detroit's white population in the summer of 1831 was largely made up of relative newcomers, a majority of whom hailed from New England. Lacking the genteel overlay of the transplanted Virginians who dominated Louisville, Detroit's leadership came from professional men. The mayor and the town council were doctors and attorneys, merchants, and military veterans. Vaguely antislavery in sentiment, in contrast to the attitudes of earlier French and British colonials and fur traders, most of Detroit's white American residents still were far more concerned with moneymaking than with morals. The rising tide of abolitionism evident in other parts of the North had yet to gain real acceptance. Southerners had business interests that caused them to travel in the Detroit River region, and there were pro-slavery Northerners among the urban elite. A few people with strong convictions were already quietly working with the city's small black community to devise protective strategies for fugitive slaves who reached the city, but they generally kept a low profile until later in the 1830s.

Soon after his arrival in Michigan, Thornton Blackburn went to work for a local stonemason named Thomas Coquillard. Thornton is believed to have trained as a stonemason in his boyhood in

Washington, Kentucky, and this skill gained in slavery he would put to his own good use over the next few years. He was fortunate in being able to ply his trade, for in centers with large black populations where labor was not at such a premium, African American tradesmen were often forced to abandon skilled positions and take lower-paying jobs. But in 1831 there was plenty of work to be had, for Detroit was booming and there was a shortage of residential and commercial space: "Houses cannot be built here as quickly as in the eastern states because of a lack of skilled workers, especially of bricklayers. A skilled workman, particularly a mason or carpenter, earns $1.50 a day." Charles Fenno Hoffman, who visited both Louisville and Detroit in 1833, continued:

> The dwelling-houses are generally of wood, but there are a great many stores now building, or already erected, of brick, with stone basements . . . the stone, which is brought from Cleveland, Ohio, is a remarkably fine material for building purposes. It is a kind of yellow freestone, which is easily worked when first taken from the quarry, and hardens subsequently upon exposure to the air. There are at this moment many four-story stores erecting, as well as other substantial buildings, which speak for the flourishing condition of the place.

Not only was Thornton now supporting himself by virtue of his own labor, but for the first time he was also able to provide for his wife. In fact, living in Detroit gave Ruthie and Thornton their first real taste of married life. They had never lived together before, and the reality of having their own home and perhaps starting a family who would be brought up in freedom must have been very pleasing to them both. Frederick Douglass, who fled Talbot County, Maryland, in 1843, wrote that when he found employment in New Bedford, Massachusetts:

> I went at it with a glad heart and a willing hand. I was now my own master. It was a happy moment, the rapture of

which can be understood only by those who have been slaves. It was the first work, the reward of which was to be entirely my own. There was no Master Hugh standing ready, the moment I earned the money, to rob me of it. I worked that day with a pleasure I had never before experienced. I was at work for myself and my newly-married wife. It was to me the starting point of a new existence.

Ruthie Blackburn may also have worked for a time. Black women in Detroit, as everywhere else in the urban North, were an important part of the family economy. In slavery, the traditional gender roles did not apply, of course, and slaveholders required women to work alongside male slaves no matter what the task. Employment of African American women in Northern cities was often an economic necessity, a norm rather than the exception that women working outside the home was in antebellum white society. The most accomplished began dressmaking or millinery businesses, did fine laundry and ironing, or engaged in personal service, such as hairdressing or child care. Others took domestic positions in the homes of the city's white elite. The untrained and women with small children too young to be left at home took in washing, a service always in demand in frontier districts, where men tended to outnumber the female population.

Having lived in daily contact with George and Charlotte Backus, Ruthie was perhaps aware that her Connecticut-born former owners had relatives at the Detroit garrison. Rather coincidentally, little Henry Backus, their orphaned son, was sent to live there, with the family of Lieutenant Electus Backus, son-in-law of General Hugh Brady, who commanded Fort Gratiot. One wonders if Ruthie knew that the little boy she had cared for was at Detroit, and if they ever saw each other. Even if she had been especially fond of the child, she may well have been discouraged from seeking him out. Despite their distance from Louisville and the illusion of safety that such proximity to the Canadian border afforded, the Blackburns still needed to be careful. There were far fewer people of African ancestry in the streets of Detroit than the Blackburns were used to seeing, so fading into the black population, as they might have done at Boston or New York, was out of the question. Only 126 free blacks were listed in Detroit's 1830 census, and Michigan Territory's African American population, at 293, was scarcely larger. In all of Michigan Territory, African Americans made up less than 1 percent of the population. In fact, court documents indicate that while in Michigan Territory, Thornton adopted the alias "John Smith." In truth, he had a fair claim to the Smith surname. Robert Smith had owned his mother, Sibby, at the time of Thornton's birth and might even have been his father. However, the Blackburns' real surname seems to have been something of an open secret; Detroit's small black community and even some Detroit whites knew it.

In the manner of displaced people everywhere, Ruthie and Thornton gravitated toward those with whom they shared bonds of culture and experience. The 1830 census lists only fifteen families of "free coloreds," a total of 75 people, but nineteenth-century enumeration of African Americans and other marginalized groups tends to be inaccurate. Some had been slaves under the successive French, British, and American regimes, and some thirty people in Michigan were still identified as slaves. A fugitive slave notice appeared in the *Detroit Gazette* as late as 1827. Other black residents of the city were Canadians who had crossed the river as runaways after Lieutenant Governor Simcoe passed his 1793 anti-importation bill. A good many members of the community, though, were immigrants, including those who had once been enslaved in Kentucky, Virginia, and points farther south. A proportion of these were free blacks from eastern states out to make their fortunes on the frontier. Michigan Territory also had a small but growing rural black population, particularly in Cass County, where there was long-term Quaker support for black settlement. There, an efficient Underground Railroad network dated back to the War of 1812.

Free people from the American South seeking a better life for themselves and their children moved north, releasing themselves from the restrictions of living in the Southern states as what historian Ira Berlin so eloquently called "slaves without masters." They usually migrated to the cities, and there became part of the rich African American urban culture in places like Philadelphia, New York, Boston, and, somewhat later, Detroit. Free black communities not only grew in population but also gained in maturity over the course of the late eighteenth and early nineteenth centuries. Escalating Northern opposition to black immigration meant that opportunities for upward mobility, education, and involvement in civic affairs became more limited as the antebellum years progressed, but community cohesion and a strong determination to succeed were becoming hallmarks of African American urban life. Black antislavery activities during the 1830s ranged from rare instances of outright violence through more restrained and constructive developments in the fields of journalism, antislavery lecturing throughout North America and Britain, and the establishment of fugitive slave assistance organizations and of vigilance committees. Resistance was the watchword of the era, not only against slavery itself, but also in response to the misguided and self-serving white-led efforts of the American Colonization Society. Rising collective opposition to such direct threats contributed materially to the growing political and social self-consciousness of black Americans. It was into this atmosphere of evolving urban culture and antislavery resistance that the Blackburns had entered when they moved to Detroit in 1831.

The town did not yet possess the separate black institutions that provided the springboard for black intellectual and political development in other Northern centers. But it must still have seemed a deliverance. The Blackburns would have benefited from the fact that there were no slaves and slaveholders in their immediate sphere. They were not constantly under suspicion of trying to help slaves escape, and they were not forced into the quasi-servile role of free African Americans who lived in close proximity to the still enslaved. Michigan blacks had the right of protest and of petition, if not the right to vote. Free people in the northern United States also had more legal protection than free blacks in the South, although Michigan Territory was nowhere nearly as progressive as New England in this regard. Thus, in coming to Detroit, the Blackburns could aspire to economic comfort if not wealth. At the same time, blacks living in Michigan were still subject to the ideology of white supremacy that existed everywhere in North America. They were considered irredeemably inferior, and generally excluded from public education and services. It would be decades before they acquired the right to either.

The small black community that greeted the Blackburns in the summer of 1831 was relatively prosperous, and Thornton Blackburn was far from unique in having a skilled trade. While some of Detroit's African Americans worked as laborers, whitewashers, and bill stickers (people who mounted posters on trees and buildings) and held other low-paying jobs, there were carpenters, bricklayers, and other tradesmen, as well as those who owned their own businesses. The city's first directory was not published until 1837, but it lists several occupations for the nine blacks recorded: Phillip Lewis, Ephraim Clark, and Nero Lucifer were boatmen; M. Burnett was a hairdresser and G. W. Tucker a hairdresser and perfumer; William Bush and Robert Allen were barbers; Peter Copper, a teamster who had been in business for some years by the 1840s, became a cabman. Only one woman was listed as the head of a household. This was Ann Butler, a laundress, probably the widow of William Butler, who had a barbering business during the Blackburns' time in Detroit. Other African Americans were employed in the service industry in hotels and on the lake steamers that carried both passengers and goods. Although not cited in the directories, other blacks living in Detroit at this time included Robert Banks, who sold used clothing; the French and Lightfoot families; and the wealthiest member of the community, Benjamin Willoughby, who owned a lumberyard and a great deal of real estate.

By all accounts, the Blackburns were model settlers. In difficult times to come, the *Detroit Courier* of June 19, 1833, would vouch for Thornton as a "respectable, honest and industrious man and considerably superior to the common class of Negroes." Whether or not the couple had an introduction to the Detroit contacts of their unnamed Louisville benefactor cannot be proven, but it is evident that the couple soon came to be both well liked and well regarded by the African Americans of the town. Their newfound friends would quickly have apprised them of the character of their landlord, the infamous James Slaughter. The man who had seemed so kind on the Sandusky stage was actually a charming reprobate who lived off the proceeds of a notorious brothel. This he operated with an eccentric white partner named Elizabeth Welch as Slaughter, Peg Welch & Company. Thornton and Ruthie moved to new accommodations in September 1831.

Although the Blackburns' Detroit address has never been discovered, most members of the black community lived near the eastern dockyards and in the area to the north and east of the main business district. There was little tension between the tiny African American community and the local white populace; the population had not yet grown to a size where black labor might be considered a threat to white employment. The community was still scattered and unformed, although local African Americans had already undertaken at least one spectacular rescue of a fugitive from the hands of slave catchers.

As everywhere, black Detroiters made the best of their situation and created their own world that intersected with but did not attempt to duplicate the dominant white culture. Social life revolved around church and family visits, and it is believed that the Blackburns attended First Baptist Church along with the leaders of Detroit's fledgling African American community. This was an integrated congregation, but only in 1832 would William Butler, a local barber, become the first black to gain full membership. He was rejected two years later for "failure to attend services, his intemperance and indifference to church appeals." Other black congregants included George W. French and his wife, Caroline, and Madison J. and Tabitha Lightfoot. Benjamin

Willoughby attended with his wife, Deborah, and daughters, Frances and Julia. These three families were the people responsible for founding Detroit's first independent black institutions. For a generation their names headed the rosters of benevolent societies and vigilance committees, as well as petitions for the extension of the franchise and other civil rights and, most particularly, for the assistance of runaway slaves like the Blackburns.

While blacks were permitted to attend services at the white First Baptist Church, it galled these intelligent, forward-thinking people that African Americans were excluded from church offices and made to sit in a specially designated part of the building during service. The relegation to "Nigger Heaven," as galleries for black congregants were sometimes called, smacked too much of Southern practices for them to tolerate. One note in the church minutes shows how strongly Southern racial attitudes prevailed even in this distant Northern outpost: "Bro. William Scott (col.) who was for some time in bondage in a southern state was induced to leave his master and consequently has no letter but was received into the church from the testimony of brethren familiar with him." The concept that slaves were happy in their condition until "induced" to flee was part of the Southern diatribe against abolitionist agitation.

In 1836, a number of Detroit's black Baptists would formally repudiate their memberships in the white church. Subsequently services would be held at the French and Willoughby homes until such time as a small frame church could be constructed. From this humble beginning arose Detroit's Second Baptist Church, which was a major station on the Underground Railroad, and still serves an inner-city congregation to this day. Its first pastor was William C. Monroe, who would provide leadership in the fields of education, abolitionism, and church unity for decades. George W. French and Madison J. Lightfoot were the church's first deacon and clerk, respectively. A major station on the Underground Railroad, Second Baptist Church would assist more than five thousand slaves on their way to Canada.

Three of the founding families of Second Baptist Church were

Thornton and Ruthie's closest friends at Detroit. Madison J. Lightfoot bore a surname that appears far too often in the Blackburns' story for mere coincidence. His Virginia birthplace does not preclude him having lived for a time in Kentucky, for a great many of the state's slaves had been born east of the Alleghenies. Although no clue as to the precise relationship between the Lightfoots, both white and black, and Thornton Blackburn has ever been found, the presence of Lightfoots at Washington and Hardinsburg, Kentucky, and now in Detroit hints of a long-term connection between them and the Blackburn family. Perhaps knowing that Madison Lightfoot lived in Detroit had convinced Thornton to settle there in the first place? Neither the names of all the slaves in the Lightfoot family of Mason County nor of those owned by Philip Lightfoot of Hardinsburg have been recorded, so it is possible Thornton knew Madison from his earlier life. Lightfoot was well educated, wrote a beautiful hand, and played a pivotal role in promoting church union between Michigan and those of the Baptist faith living on the Upper Canadian side of the river. In 1846, he would serve the black congregation at Sandwich, Canada West, and in 1853 he would be ordained as a pastor. Lightfoot was prominent in Detroit's African American community organizations, vigilance committees, and antislavery societies throughout the period before the Civil War.

George W. French and Madison J. Lightfoot were both employed at the city's popular Steamboat Hotel, the "most celebrated hostelry west of Buffalo." Here, as one contemporary observer noted, "all the stage lines centered, and it was here that all the gay balls and social functions were given." George French, like Thornton, was from Kentucky. In fact, both he and Benjamin Willoughby came from the immediate area where Thornton had passed his boyhood, and so it is tempting to posit a long-term connection between all three men who befriended Thornton at Detroit. The French name is known to this day in Maysville, and according to the 1830 census there was a free black family with a son named George living a short way south of

Washington, on the Maysville-Lexington Road. George French, a cook, would provide the land and the building on Fort Street that, renamed Liberty Hall, was the foundation of the black Baptist church in Detroit. He served as a deacon in Second Baptist for many years and would in later years be engaged with Lightfoot in fostering relations between Michigan and Canadian churches. He was also an officer of the Detroit Vigilant Committee, founded in 1842 to protect runaway slaves and to wage "moral and political warfare" for the right to public services, education, and universal black male suffrage.

The much-respected Benjamin Willoughby had been a slave at Falmouth, in Pendleton County, just a few miles to the north and west of Maysville, where Thornton Blackburn was born. His free papers survive:

STATE OF KENTUCKY, PENDLETON COUNTY
COURT CLERK'S OFFICE SCT.

I, William C. Kennett, Clerk of the County Court Aforesaid, do hereby certify that at the December term of said Court . . . at the court-house in the town of Falmouth on Monday the 16th day of December 1816 Charles Sterne came into court and acknowledged a deed of Manumission by which he emancipated, manumitted and set free his Negro slave, Willoughby, then aged about thirty-eight or thirty-nine years and said Sterne has since agreeably to the direction of said Court entered into Bond, with security, in my Office, in the penalty of $500 conditioned to prevent said Willoughby from becoming a county charge in case of age [or] infirmity which Deed of Manumission is now of record in my office.

Charles Sterne was a veteran of the American Revolution and had served under Captain Thomas Mountjoy, who later settled at Washington, Kentucky. The Mountjoys were related to Thornton Blackburn's former owners, the Morton and Murphy families, and so Benjamin Willoughby may well have known Thornton when he was growing up.

Willoughby evidently married before leaving Kentucky, for the U.S. Census of 1850 shows that his daughter, Frances, aged forty, was born before he was freed. The birthplace of Benjamin's wife, Devon, or Deborah, Willoughby, was listed as South Carolina. There is no record of how Deborah and their elder child gained their freedom, but the family may have resided in Ohio for a time, for their second daughter, Julia, was born there about 1824. Shortly after her birth, Willoughby moved his family to Detroit. There, the foundation of his fortune was a successful lumberyard. He also owned several properties, loaned money at interest to both blacks and whites, and held mortgages on numerous homes in the city. He quietly organized fugitive slave assistance and black self-help efforts, something that became a family tradition. Julia Willoughby would one day marry William Lambert, a used-clothing dealer and abolitionist from New Jersey who had come to Detroit in 1840. He would become the "President" of the Michigan Underground Railroad and an outspoken, brilliant leader of black Detroit's fight for education, suffrage, and civil rights through the 1880s. Through Lambert's friendship with both Frederick Douglass and the hard-line white abolitionist John Brown, Benjamin Willoughby's daughter Julia would in 1859, on the eve of Brown's raid on Harpers Ferry, receive in her home some of the most vociferous and radical representatives of black abolitionism in the United States. The family tradition continued, for William and Julia's son, Benjamin Willoughby Lambert, was a founder of Detroit's NAACP chapter in 1912.

In the company of their Detroit friends, Thornton and Ruthie probably visited the Upper Canadian communities of Sandwich and Amherstburg from time to time, for the black families on both sides of the Detroit River enjoyed close relations. There was a regular ferry schedule during the warm months, while in the winter the river iced to a depth of up to twenty inches. People traveled by sleigh across what historian Afua Cooper calls the "fluid frontier" for social events, church and other celebrations, and political meetings. There were particularly close friendships between people of the Baptist faith, as the later creation of the Amherstburg Baptist Association that unified black churches of this denomination on both sides of the border proved. The two groups also operated in tandem for mutual protection, something that would soon stand Thornton and Ruthie Blackburn in good stead.

A year almost to the day after the Blackburns came to live in Detroit, the frontier town experienced its first major epidemic. There is no record of how the Blackburns and the rest of African American Detroit fared during the first visitation of Asiatic cholera to Detroit in the summer of 1832. Newspapers had followed closely its march across the United States, its westward progress shadowing the lines of transportation routes, including the Erie Canal. Soldiers sent to fight the Black Hawk War in Illinois landed in Detroit harbor already infected with the disease on July 4, 1832, and about a hundred people died. The town was growing extremely rapidly, so crowded conditions and a shortage of housing contributed to the death rate. The closure of hotels and businesses as well as the suspension of public works projects during the epidemic would have had a severe impact on the black community, since many African Americans in Detroit subsisted on meager wages. The danger passed when the cold weather came, and, mourning their own dead, black and white Detroiters returned to work.

Apart from the dangers of illness, Thornton and Ruthie enjoyed relative safety, but there was one significant threat to their security. They and the thousands of other fugitive slaves living in the northern United States were still subject to the Fugitive Slave Law. Passed by Congress in 1793, this had been strengthened through amendment in 1818. It required that runaway slaves discovered anywhere in the United States and its territories be returned to their owners. The person who claimed them had only

to obtain a certificate from a judge of his or her home state or territory and present it to one in the place where the alleged runaway was discovered. The local magistrate was to "grant a
warrant authorizing any marshal, sheriff, sergeant, constable, or
public bailiff of the state or territory . . . to apprehend such fugitive and bring him or her before such judge." If after reviewing
the case the judge was satisfied that the individual really was the
slave named in the certificate, then he would authorize the officer of the law to deliver the runaway to the claimant. Since blacks
were prohibited nearly everywhere from testifying against whites,
abuses were rampant. The Northwest Ordinance of 1787 had its
own ominous clause regarding fugitive slaves:

> Article Sixth: There shall be neither Slavery nor involuntary
> Servitude in the said territory otherwise than in the punish-
> ment of crimes, whereof the party shall have been duly con-
> victed; provided always that any person escaping into the
> same, from whom labor or service is lawfully claimed in any
> one of the original States, such fugitive may be lawfully re-
> claimed and conveyed to the person claiming his or her la-
> bor or service as aforesaid.

During the early decades of the nineteenth century, several
states, particularly those of abolitionist New England, passed
personal liberty laws intended to prevent slave owners and their
agents from using local courts and officials to help them retrieve
runaways. However, Michigan Territory was not one of them. Instead, together with Illinois, Ohio, and Indiana, Michigan passed
its own version of the Code Noir or "Black Laws." These were
intended to limit, if not entirely prevent, black settlement and
black migration. They reinforced the requirements of the federal
Fugitive Slave Law of 1793, in that "no person held to service or
labor in one state, under the laws thereof, escaping into another,
shall, in consequence of any law or regulation therein, be discharged from such service or labor, but shall be delivered up on
claim of the party to whom such service or labor may be due."

On April 13, 1827, Michigan passed the Act to Regulate Blacks and Mulattoes, and to Punish the Kidnapping of Such Persons. The Fugitive Slave Law of 1793 was acknowledged in the Michigan legislation, which established formal mechanisms for extraditing proven runaways back to their home states, and for fining those who harbored fugitives or gave them aid. Michigan gave local blacks until May 1 to register their names in the county clerk's office, and thereafter all African Americans were required to produce legal certificates attesting to their free status. The territorial law did offer legal defense for alleged fugitives to ensure that they were not falsely accused. It also instituted safeguards, including a ten-year prison term at hard labor, against the kidnapping of free blacks residing in the state for sale into slavery. This was a problem everywhere and would become more so as the value of slaves went up along with the price of cotton in the antebellum decades. The main offenders seem to have been Kentucky slave catchers, bounty hunters paid to capture slaves and return them to their owners.

Having to present free papers militated against fugitive slaves' settlement, but the next clause was aimed at discouraging *any* black settlement: as in Cincinnati, they were required to post exorbitant bonds to guarantee their good behavior.

The *Detroit Gazette* of September 11, 1828, carried a notice "To Blacks and Mulattoes," reinforcing the terms of the law. It all smacks somewhat of paranoia, since a Detroit magistrate had conducted an enumeration of Michigan blacks in 1827 and only come up with seventy-six people. A $500 bond represented a staggering amount of money to members of so oppressed a minority, especially for those who had just recently been freed—or had freed themselves—from bondage. Fines were also put in place for people who assisted fugitive slaves in escaping from their lawful owners. Although the term "Underground Railroad" was not employed until about 1831, officials were obviously aware that Michigan had its own antislavery faction and that people were willing to assist and harbor runaway bondspeople. Since there seems to have been little attempt to comply with the 1827 act, it was amended in 1828 to require judges to monitor its execution before the grand jury of any county or circuit court in Michigan.

There is no evidence that the Blackburns were required to post a bond; the legislation intended to discourage black settlement was almost never enforced. But that the laws were on the books at all was a signal to white immigrants that African Americans were less than welcome in the nominally Free Michigan Territory and, therefore, Europeans and other whites need not be concerned about competing with low-waged blacks for employment.

Despite legislation, a growing number of blacks was seeking new homes on the nation's western frontier. A significant proportion of them were fugitive slaves from the American South. Slave catchers were, of course, aware of Detroit's importance as a stopping place on the way to Canada. Blacks on the Canadian shore stood poised to receive the fugitives and assisted in their passage to free soil. The Detroit black community, relatively disorganized as it was, had already mounted a coordinated effort to rescue a pair of fugitive slaves passing through the city on the way to Upper Canada in 1828. Ben and David evaded the clutches of a slave catcher named Ezekiel K. Hudnell only when the black community threatened to storm the ship on which the runaways were being removed from the town. The men were taken swiftly across the river into Canada, and Hudnell was never able to collect his bounty. The involvement of blacks on either side of the Detroit River in the rescue was noted in the account by the sheriff of Wayne County, Thomas Sheldon, who wrote:

> There existed great excitement in Detroit in consequence of the arrest of said slaves, which excitement extended itself to the Canada shore opposite, where great numbers of runaway slaves had collected & armed themselves for the purpose of boarding the vessel & rescuing the slaves . . . both slaves made their escape from the possession of said Hudnell; whether through the inattention of said Hudnell or by the assistance of any person I have never been able to satisfy myself.

The sheriff suggested white collusion in the rescue: "To my certain knowledge large rewards were offered to any person or persons who would set at liberty said slaves." Hudnell later accused Territorial Secretary Benjamin F. H. Witherell of delaying signing the appropriate certificate approving the transfer of the fugitives just long enough for them to be spirited away. Witherell would in 1830 lose his position as Territorial Secretary to John Thomson Mason as a result of his complicity in Ben and David's escape.

After their rescue, Benjamin Witherell followed up with a letter to future President Martin Van Buren, then the U.S. secretary of state. Interestingly, he cited the New Orleans markets as the destination of free blacks kidnapped and sold into slavery:

> The people of Michigan, aware of their obligation to their fellow citizens in Kentucky, interpose no obstacle to the removal of fugitive slaves when lawfully reclaimed; but are desirous that agents claiming slaves for their owners, should furnish well authenticated evidence of their agency, as kidnapping for the New Orleans market had been often attempted, by which the lawful owners are immediately deprived of their property.

The Blackburns had settled in Detroit in hope that their troubles were behind them, but two disturbing events had occurred within their first few months in the city. First came the news that a bloody slave uprising had been launched in Southampton County, Virginia. Originally planned for the same weekend as Thornton and Ruthie's flight from Louisville, July 4, 1831, it had been delayed until August 22 because of the illness on the part of the riots' organizer. This was an educated and deeply religious slave named Nat Turner, a visionary with a gift for oratory. The uprising left fifty-five whites dead and ended with the hanging of at least sixteen slaves, including Turner. Hundreds more blacks were suspected in the plot, and in the resulting hysteria there were dozens of lynchings, beatings, and other examples of mob violence. Now more than ever, slaveholders dreaded the joint power of education and Christian faith to arouse the desire for freedom in the hearts of the enslaved. Thornton may well have feared for his mother and the brother he had left behind in Kentucky when the news came to Detroit that, first in Virginia and then across the South, slave patrols were increased and local ordinances passed that further limited and controlled the lives of blacks, both slave and free. In Virginia, the moral and practical value of continuing the slave system in the state was debated, with a vote of 58 for abolition to 73 against, taken January 25, 1832. Thomas R. Dew, the President of William and Mary University, made the strongest defense of slavery yet, citing biblical justifications as well as economic and social ones, the latter based on his belief in the inherent inferiority of blacks. New laws prohibited teaching slaves to read, prevented bondspeople from holding gatherings without whites present, even for religious purposes, and in some states followed Virginia's lead from the time of the Gabriel Prosser rebellion and required that blacks emigrate if they were manumitted, usually within the period of one year. The latter divided families where one or another member remained in slavery. Worsening conditions of black life caused an unprecedented increase in the number of emigrants to the northern states and territories, some traveling as far as Upper Canada.

The second incident had very serious personal implications for the Blackburns, although they would not realize it for some time. Walking down a city street one day, Thornton was accosted by Thomas Rogers. The former clerk of Wurts & Reinhard's in Louisville was passing through Michigan. Rogers, of course, recognized Thornton immediately. He had supervised the young man in his duties at the store and warehouses for almost a year before going off on his own travels in the fall of 1830. The surprised Thornton greeted Rogers and was, by all accounts, genuinely glad to see the white clerk. Unconscious of any danger, Thornton spoke cheerfully of his wife, his home, and the fine job he had found since he had arrived in Michigan. With at least some regard for his precarious status, Blackburn apparently maintained the fiction that he had been manumitted, as witnessed by the free papers he and Ruthie still had in their possession. The two men parted cordially.

If Thornton and Ruthie were initially concerned about this chance meeting, they seem to have all but forgotten their danger as the months passed without incident. But in June 1833, disaster struck.

As it turned out, Thomas Rogers did not complete his travels until early in 1832. Returning to Louisville, he again took up a position at Wurts & Reinhard's. Inexplicably, he withheld information about his discovery of the Blackburns from their Louisville owners for some time, and we cannot know why he eventually chose to tell Oldham what he had seen. The subject might have come up inadvertently; however, Kentucky law required that any white suspecting a black person of being a fugitive was required to report it. When he did, he swore out the following statement:

> Thomas J. Rogers residing in the City of Louisville, Kentucky, states that he was acquainted with Thornton, a mulatto man who was hired to Wurts and Reinhard, that the said Rogers had left Louisville in the fall of 1830, and was in the fall of 1831 in Detroit, Michigan Territory, while there he saw and conversed with Thornton and knew him to be the same person who was in the employment of Wurts and Reinhard as a hired Slave, that Thornton told him he had his wife in Detroit with him.

Whatever Rogers's motivation was, it would have the effect of unraveling what Thornton and Ruthie had worked so hard to achieve. Virgil McKnight and John Pope Oldham moved swiftly and in concert when they realized that the Blackburns were not in Canada after all but had remained within a jurisdiction where the Fugitive Slave Law applied. All that was required of a slaveholder or his agent was a sworn statement in court that such and such a black person was a "fugitive from labor" and a judge's decision in their favor to recover a runaway. Probably at Judge Oldham's behest, Susan Brown signed over power of attorney to a lawyer named Benjamin G. Weir so he could act on her behalf before the Michigan courts. Neither she nor her own sons took any further action, and she made no formal statement at this or any subsequent time. Her nephew, Talbot Clayton Oldham, Judge Oldham's younger son, was dispatched to Detroit with Weir so he could identify Thornton. Talbot, much of an age with Thornton, had practically grown up with the Browns' slave in his early years at Hardinsburg. Virgil McKnight, Ruthie's owner, also engaged Weir to act for him.

On Friday, June 14, 1833, Weir and young Talbot Oldham arrived by steamer at the port of Detroit. The case for apprehending the Blackburns as fugitive slaves was made immediately before Judge Henry Chipman of the Wayne County Circuit Court. The Kentuckians demanded that the Blackburns be apprehended as runaways.

On June 14, 1833, John M. Wilson, the sheriff of Detroit, presented himself at the Blackburns' door. He had been ordered to arrest Thornton Blackburn, aged twenty-one, as a runaway slave. Thornton was forthwith taken to the Detroit jail to await trial. The Michigan officials were wasting no time: on Saturday he would be presented before Judge Henry Chipman. Should the trial go against him, he would be sent back to Kentucky and slavery.

8

TELL OLD PHARAOH TO
LET MY PEOPLE GO!

Brethren, the time has come when you must act for
yourselves. However you and all of us may desire it,
there is not much hope of redemption without the
shedding of blood. If you must bleed, let it all come at
once—rather die free men than live to be slaves . . .
Let your motto be resistance! Resistance! RESIS-
TANCE!

—HENRY HIGHLAND GARNET,
radical abolitionist, 1843

THE GROUNDS FOR Thornton Blackburn's arrest in June 1833
were guaranteed by the Constitution and enshrined in the Fugitive Slave Law of 1793. Michigan's own Act to Regulate Blacks
and Mulattoes that supported and elaborated upon the federal
law was rarely enforced. But, as the Blackburns were to discover,
it gave the territorial government a powerful weapon to wield
against its black residents at any time it chose to do so.

Virgil McKnight and Susan Brown's lawyer, Benjamin Weir,
was both a practicing attorney and a member of the Louisville
City Council. The latter qualification was of some assistance, for
he came armed with a letter from Louisville's mayor, John C.
Bucklin, to the mayor of Detroit, Marshall Chapin. For good
measure, Bucklin sent along testimonials to the sterling characters of Virgil McKnight and John Pope Oldham. Bucklin was a

dry-goods merchant and, in keeping with Louisville business practice, a sometime slave dealer, as a series of advertisements he placed in the *Louisville Public Advertiser* over the years attest. Weir also presented an official "copy of the twenty-eighth section of an act of the General Assembly of the Commonwealth of Kentucky, entitled 'An Act to reduce to one, the several acts respecting slaves, free Negroes, Mulattoes and Indians.'" Equipped with statements sworn out by John Pope Oldham and Virgil McKnight before Mayor Bucklin of Louisville on June 5, 1833, Benjamin Weir and Talbot Oldham confirmed that Thornton and Ruthie were legally "slaves for life." It was on the basis of this evidence that Detroit's Judge Chipman gave orders for Sheriff John M. Wilson to have Thornton Blackburn arrested. He was to be housed in the Detroit jail, which was located in the northeastern section of the city above the Campus Martius. However, the judge was less certain of his ground in Mrs. Blackburn's case.

Although affidavits signed by McKnight, Thomas Rogers, and William Oldham were offered in evidence, no proof of Ruthie's slave status was presented to the Michigan courts; indeed, as Benjamin G. Weir swore before Judge Henry Chipman "he never saw Ruthy Blackburn and cannot say whether the woman arrested by that name and here present is that person or that she is a slave or the property of Virgil McKnight." John Pope Oldham admitted in his written testimony that he himself did not know Ruthie Blackburn, but he knew that "when [Thornton] ran off, he took with him as his wife a mulatto woman, then and still the property of Virgil McKnight of this City, said woman having been purchased by him [McKnight] a short time before her escape, of the administration of George Backus, deceased." Before Judge Chipman, Talbot Oldham made the following testimony:

Talbert [*sic*] Oldham deposes and says that he has seen the person Thornton Blackburn at Hardinsburg and at Louis-

he has frequently seen the woman here produced [in court] called Ruthy Blackburn, [he] first saw her in Sandusky, [she] has lived with Thornton Blackburn as his wife since they lived in this place. Ruthy told this witness [Slaughter] that she came from Louisville in Kentucky and had lived with Mr. and Mrs. Bacchus . . . This was about the 18th or 19th of July, two years ago. She came here with Thornton Blackburn . . . that was two years ago this July coming.

Given Slaughter's reputation, his word was, of course, highly suspect. It seems most unlikely that the people who had managed so daring an escape would confide its details to a new acquaintance. Rather, it was probably James Slaughter, who, upon hearing of the Blackburns' arrest, offered his services to Weir and Talbot Oldham in return for a large bribe. During Frazier's cross-examination, Slaughter confirmed that he had first met the Blackburns while on a business trip to Sandusky, that he had traveled with them on the stage to Detroit, and that the couple had lived with him for a time when they arrived in the city. Of Ruthie he said he had "heard her often in August and September and subsequently give the same information," but he "had never heard her say to whom she belonged, or that she was the slave of Mr. McKnight."

Meanwhile, word of the Blackburns' arrest passed rapidly through the small Detroit African American community. The city's blacks rushed to the courthouse. The *Detroit Courier* of June 19, 1833, provided the reasons: "Thornton and his wife they had ever looked upon and associated with as free and free or not [the blacks of the area] were by no means disposed to see them dragged off again to servitude," and called Thornton "the kind of person that had numerous friends and few enemies among those of his own color and of course whose arrest would be most likely to cause a disturbance."

As the news spread, people from rural Michigan streamed into the city to watch the proceedings. All of them knew fugitive

ville, Kentucky, knows him to have been the slave of Dr. Gideon Brown during his lifetime and afterwards in the possession of Mrs. Susan Brown at Louisville after the death of Dr. Brown her husband. He says that he does not know Ruthy Blackburn, nor that the person arrested and here present is the person claimed as the slave of Virgil McKnight and he further says that he saw Virgil McKnight deliver the power of attorney to [the] deponent's father, John P. Oldham, for the said Weir.

Not until the next day, Saturday, June 15, 1833, did Oldham and Weir manage to convince Judge Chipman that Ruthie should also be detained. Since all that the law required for the apprehension of a suspected fugitive slave was the sworn statement of a white man, Judge Chipman finally ordered Ruthie Blackburn arrested. So read the warrant he gave to Sheriff Wilson:

> Whereas Benjamin G. Weir . . . is the legally constituted agent of the said Virgil McKnight, and that the said mulatto woman Ruthy is the property of the said Virgil McKnight and is a person held to labor in the State aforesaid—these are therefore to direct [Sheriff Wilson] to arrest the said Mulatto woman Ruthy and deliver her to the said Benjamin G. Weir in pursuance of the provisions of the Act of the Legislative Council of the Said Territory.

Alexander D. Frazier, the Detroit City Attorney, was an irascible Scot more known for his learning than his eloquence. An eccentric man, given to ironic humor and deeply committed to the cause of justice, he is considered to be one of the fathers of the Michigan bar. However, he simply hadn't much evidence with which to craft a defense.

At the trial, the case against Ruthie was bolstered by the testimony of the Blackburns' erstwhile friend and landlord. Improbably, James Slaughter swore that:

slaves. Some were fugitives themselves. The outcome of the case would test just how safe African Americans actually were in the nominally Free Territory of Michigan. By mid-afternoon, the courthouse balcony was packed with disaffected men and women. The spectators moved about restlessly during the testimony and muttered angrily among themselves. Casting nervous glances up at the balcony, Judge Chipman warned them to be quiet, but they persisted. Meanwhile, Sheriff John M. Wilson, in the courtroom below, was becoming concerned. As the case unfolded, murmurs coming from the upper levels took on a threatening tone. Journalists present in the courtroom later wrote that the blacks said they would burn Detroit to the ground unless Thornton Blackburn and his wife were set free.

The judge before whom the Blackburns were tried was actually sympathetic to their plight. Henry Chipman of the Wayne County Circuit Court was a native of Vermont, but he had lived in Jamaica, and then married in South Carolina, where he practiced law for several years. A Detroit historian who remembered Chipman described him as "of medium height, solidly built . . . his hair was thick, long, at first flaxen and then snowy white, turning inward at the ends in a massive curl; with a high, broad forehead, clear, bright, blue eyes, large nose and wide mouth . . . in speaking he was troubled with a slight impediment." His family's official genealogy explains that Chipman moved to Detroit in 1824 because of "a disgust for slavery which his wife, though a planter's daughter shared." He was, however, well familiar with federal legislation governing slavery.

Chipman actually had little leeway in the case. Unfortunately, the Northwest Ordinance of 1787 guaranteed that fugitives apprehended north of the Ohio River would be returned to their owners. The burden of proof was on the Blackburns, for people of African ancestry were considered slaves unless they could produce legal evidence to the contrary. Where were the free papers Thornton and Ruthie had shown to Captain Quarrier aboard the *Versailles* not two years before? Such documents might well have freed the couple. Yet they were never mentioned in their Detroit trial, nor in any ensuing proceedings conducted on the Michigan side of the river. They were certainly still in their possession, as later events would prove. Perhaps the Blackburns knew their forged documents would not stand up to the scrutiny of a Kentucky attorney. Talbot Oldham, John Pope Oldham's son and Susan Brown's nephew, was well aware Thornton had never been legally freed. Another possibility is that the courts adjudged the documents to be forgeries and would not admit them as evidence.

John Pope Oldham had thoughtfully provided a copy of the 1798 Kentucky legislation pertaining to slavery to Benjamin Weir:

> Sect. 28. All negro, Mulatto or Indian Slaves in all courts of Judicatum and other places within this commonwealth shall be held, taken and adjudged to be real estate; and shall descend to the heirs and widows of persons departing this life, as lands are directed to descend in and by an Act of the General Assembly Entitled "An Act Directing the Court of decants [sic]."

This was intended to prove that Susan Brown was the legal owner of Thornton, by virtue of inheritance from her deceased husband's estate. In the absence of authentic manumission papers, the Oldham and McKnight claims to Thornton and his wife met perfectly both the letter and the spirit of the law. The fact that no one present could personally identify Ruthie provided no protection:

> When a person held in labor in any of the United States, or in either of the Territories northwest or south of the river Ohio, under the laws thereof, shall escape into any other of the said States or Territories, the person to whom such labor or service may be due, his agent or attorney, is hereby empowered to seize and arrest such fugitive from labor, and to

take him or her before any judge of the Circuit or District Court of the United States . . . and upon proof to the satisfaction of such judge or magistrate to give a certificate thereof to such claimant, his agent or attorney which shall be sufficient warrant for removing the said fugitive from labor, to the state or Territory from which he or she fled.

The publisher of the *Detroit Courier* was an attorney named Charles Cleland. His long article on the court proceedings, published on June 19, 1833, suggests that at least some of the city's white populace was sympathetic to the Blackburns' plight:

In common with the whole community, our sympathies have been enlisted; and whatever may be the abstract right given by the constitution and laws of our country to traffic in human flesh, we have found it a difficult task to divest ourselves wholly of these spontaneous prepossessions in favor of natural liberty which gain a foot hold in the breasts of most men on viewing and appreciating the necessary consequences of legalized slavery.

The rest of the Detroit press were not so favorably inclined. A month after their trial the *Detroit Journal and Advertiser* defended the Blackburns' arrest: "The Michigan law of 1827 supports the above-quoted Act and requires compliance with it. It empowers the sheriff to detain blacks or mulattoes unable to produce a Certificate of Freedom," a document the bulk of Michigan's black population probably did not possess.

Neither Thornton nor Ruthie provided any evidence that they had been legally manumitted. Despite an eloquent and impassioned defense by Alexander D. Frazier, he was unable to convince the court that Thornton and Ruthie were, in fact, free. To the consternation of the black spectators in the balcony, Judge Chipman ordered Sheriff Wilson to turn the couple over to Benjamin G. Weir and Talbot C. Oldham, as their owners' authorized representatives. Wilson was reluctant to do so. The mood of the large crowd now filing out of the courthouse was ugly. Five short years earlier, these same people had rescued Ben and David from a Kentucky slave catcher and sent them off to safety in Canada. Fearing a similar outburst, Sheriff Wilson now took a highly controversial step. Although the law required him to turn over Ruthie and Thornton immediately to their owners' representatives, instead Wilson chose to hold the Blackburns in separate cells in the city jail until such time as they could be transported, in chains, to the steamboat docks at the foot of Randolph Street and begin their journey back to Kentucky.

Weir intended to book passage on the steamboat *Ohio*, bound for Buffalo. Again Sheriff Wilson intervened. Although scheduled to leave that very afternoon, the *Ohio* was held over two extra days at Sheriff Wilson's request. That delayed the sailing until Monday, when the blacks would have to be at their places of employment, much reducing the risk of violence. The departure of the *Ohio* was set for 4 p.m. on Monday, June 17.

As would become apparent from subsequent events, Sheriff Wilson had seriously underestimated the determination of black Detroit and its white sympathizers to free Thornton and Ruthie Blackburn. People were enraged. Incarcerating a well-liked local couple whose only crime was seeking their liberty was bad enough. Housing them in a public facility on behalf of a pair of Kentucky slaveholders was not only morally unacceptable, it was also well outside the realm of Wilson's responsibilities as the Wayne County sheriff. He had also left himself open to charges of corruption. It was rumored that both he and the city jailer, Lemuel Goodell, had been promised $50 by attorney Weir for the safe delivery of his prisoners to the docks. The sheriff's position was an unpaid one in the 1830s, and his income depended on fees for serving warrants and other emoluments to the position, so the charge was a plausible one. It certainly appeared to many people, and not only African Americans, that in deciding to secure fugitive slaves in the city jail and in delaying the sailing of a private vessel in legitimate pursuit of its commercial goals, the sheriff was acting privately, rather than in the interests of his constituency.

In his cell, Thornton was confronting the painful knowledge that he was about to lose his wife and his freedom. Thomas Rogers, his former supervisor at Wurts & Reinhard's in Louisville, had been the instrument of his betrayal, and Talbot C. Oldham, a man almost his own age with whom Thornton had passed part of his boyhood, was preparing to take him back to Kentucky, in chains. While it is impossible to assess what Thornton's exact feelings might have been, whatever the conditions that slavery imposed on human thought and behavior, relationships between black and white people were as varied as the people who engaged in them. Now, as so frequently happened because of the South's "peculiar institution," these relationships were irreparably ruptured owing to race. Ruthie had her own pain to bear, suffering the special fears that only female slaves knew. She was well aware that her looks and manner were salable commodities; whatever punishment Virgil McKnight had in store for her, she would never see Thornton again after they reached Louisville.

Later that same Saturday afternoon the City Attorney visited each of the Blackburns in their separate cells. The content of Frazier's private conversations with his clients would not be revealed until several days afterward.

Word of the Blackburns' sentence spread out quickly into rural Michigan and across the river into Canada. The ferry traveled back and forth all afternoon and evening, bringing people from as far away as Amherstburg and Sandwich to protest Judge Chipman's decision. The *Ohio* was docked at the foot of Randolph Street, where the quay boiled with sullen men and angry women. Most were armed. Unbeknownst to the Blackburns, a crowd of their supporters was coalescing in Detroit. The Detroit jail stood on the northern outskirts of the built-up district between Farmer and Farrar on Gratiot Street in open scrubland. Coincidentally, much of Detroit's African American population lived within the immediate vicinity, and it was here that the people coming in from the countryside stayed, visiting with relatives and friends. Anticipation filled the air. Deputy Sheriff

Alexander McArthur later testified that "there were assembled around the . . . jail a large number of blacks and mulattoes armed with sticks, clubs, knives, pistols, swords, and other unlawful weapons avowing with loud threats their determination to rescue the . . . Prisoner Thornton Blackburn then in the custody." Wilson's precautions appeared well justified, especially when the sheriff "endeavored reasoning with [the crowd] to persuade them to disperse, but without effect, they telling him that they expected some of them would be killed but that they were determined to rescue the prisoner at all hazards."

White city residents hurried about their business, apprehensive of the menacing feeling on the streets but, in the main, unaware of its cause. Some of those in the know were so shocked that their own courts would meekly acquiesce to the demands of Kentucky slaveholders that they joined the protesters. In whispered conferences antislavery-minded people of every level and background debated how best to rescue Ruthie and Thornton before they could be sent back to their masters. Then, on the evening after the trial, the leaders of black Detroit met at the home of Benjamin Willoughby. Their sentiments must have been very much like those expressed by Henry Bibb at a meeting in Detroit in 1848 to protest the capture of another fugitive slave. *The North Star* of December 29, 1848, reported:

> Mr. B[ibb] closed by calling on the colored people of this city and state to prepare themselves with the means of self defence, for said he, ye are property in the eye of the laws of this free nation, equalized with the horse and the ox, and being held in this light by the mansteakers of the south and liable to be seized as such at any moment by himself or his agents, all protection that is left you is that which nature has bestowed; therefore, as you have no other means, you must protect yourselves by whatever means you possess.

Although the events that followed have long been considered the result of a spontaneous outburst of feeling on the part of the

Blackburns' supporters, in fact the entire affair was carefully choreographed. Several people later known as leaders of the city's African American populace were present at the Willoughby house that June night. These included Madison and Tabitha Lightfoot and George French and his wife, Caroline. According to local historian Reginald Larrie, "The real leader was reported as having been a one-armed boss barber (a term which referred to a black barber who cut the hair of both blacks and whites) whose name was John Cook." Cook had a ten-chair barbershop at the corner of Griswold and West Jefferson and was one of the most successful black businessmen in the town. He, like Benjamin Willoughby, risked a great deal in his support of the Blackburns.

Not all of the people in on the plot were black. There is good reason to believe Alexander Frazier and Charles Cleland, as well as other whites whose names have not been recorded, also came to Willoughby's house to discuss rescue plans. The outspoken publisher of the *Detroit Courier*, Cleland was an old acquaintance of Benjamin Willoughby's, and as a longtime supporter of the African American community was well known to hold strong abolitionist views. Each player was assigned his or her part, with the women of the black community taking on the most dangerous role of all.

On Sunday morning, June 16, 1833, crowds of armed men again gathered in the fields and woods about the jail and at the steamboat docks to prevent Thornton and Ruthie from being removed from Detroit. A grim-faced Sheriff Wilson briefed Deputy Sheriff McArthur on how to secure the jail in the event it was attacked. He also considered drafting more deputies but decided against it, probably to avoid arousing the fears of the city's white residents. Then, after services at Detroit's First Baptist Church ended, a respectable pair of its black congregants approached Sheriff Wilson. Mrs. Lightfoot and Mrs. French entreated him to allow them to visit Mrs. Blackburn in her cell to offer the solace of friendship and prayer. Wilson likely considered the visit harmless and possibly a means for helping defuse the public tension. At any rate, he agreed to let the ladies sit with Ruthie.

They remained with her in her cell all that afternoon and into the evening.

Night was falling when Mrs. Lightfoot and Mrs. French finally made their "sorrowful departure, the tears falling like rain, and all [three women] wringing their hands in terrible anguish." The pair covered their faces with handkerchiefs and lowered their veils to hide their sorrow as they emerged from the jail and hurried home along the darkened streets.

Not until the next morning did the jailer Goodell realize that it was Mrs. French who sat in Ruthie's prison cell, wearing Mrs. Blackburn's clothes. The *Detroit Courier* of Wednesday, June 19, 1833, gave Detroit's blacks this backhanded compliment: "By a contrivance that demonstrates that Negroes are not wholly wanting in shrewdness, the female was rescued from jail on Sunday evening and made her escape to Canada where she is now." It would be some time before Alexander Frazier would admit to having counseled Ruthie to escape to Canada. Mrs. Blackburn had been conveyed across the Detroit River and was now safely in Amherstburg.

Lemuel Goodell immediately informed Weir and Talbot Oldham that Mrs. Blackburn had escaped his custody. Enraged that he had been duped, Goodell then dashed down to Detroit's popular Steamboat Hotel, where Mrs. French's husband, George, and Madison Lightfoot both held good positions. He insulted the men, saying their wives were "a parcel of hellcats" for their deception. French and Lightfoot naturally professed ignorance of the whole matter—that is, until they learned that Mrs. French was being held in Ruthie's stead and that Oldham and Weir had appeared before Judge Chipman to demand the right to carry her off to Louisville and sell her in Ruthie Blackburn's place.

The Steamboat Hotel was staffed largely by free blacks. It had the best taproom in the city, and many a ball and public dinner was held in its "long room." Charles Cleland was the toastmaster on many festive gatherings of the local barristers, and it is said that Stevens Thomson Mason acquired his legal education under the tutelage of attorneys who frequented the bar of the Steamboat Hotel. Because of their jobs, French and Lightfoot were therefore acquainted with most of the town's judges and attorneys, which was most fortunate. One was Judge Charles Larned, formerly a general under Virginian William Henry Harrison in the War of 1812. Outraged that a free woman might be removed from Michigan and sold, Larned immediately issued a writ of habeas corpus protecting Mrs. French. She was released from jail but later rearrested for her role in the next sequence of events that took place. When George French's courageous young wife was released from the Detroit jail the second time, she found it expedient to cross over into Canada. There she remained for some months, waiting for the whole affair to die down. Meanwhile, the more conservative of Detroit's residents roundly condemned the rescue of Ruthie Blackburn. The *Democratic Free Press* of June 19, 1833, reported, "On Sunday evening, a successful attempt was made by the colored people of the city, to rescue the woman; and their movements then indicated a spirit of desperation and audacity quite incompatible with the due enforcement of the law with the ordinary means."

Meanwhile, Thornton languished in prison, consoled at least that his Ruthie was safe on Canadian soil. Alexander Frazier had assured him that Mrs. Blackburn could not be brought back from Upper Canada. On the other hand, since his wife had already made a successful escape, and from inside a locked jail cell at that, Thornton's own treatment was likely to be very rough indeed on the voyage back to Louisville. Both Benjamin Weir and Talbot Oldham resolved to take no more chances. They convinced the captain of the *Ohio* to leave for Buffalo that very afternoon. While Thornton fretted in his cell, Sheriff Wilson went outside to try to calm what was rapidly developing into a mob. Entering the angry crowd alone on three separate sorties, he attempted to convince people to go home and leave Blackburn to the execution of his sentence.

There are numerous eyewitness accounts of the drama that unfolded, some mutually contradictory, all quite colorful in their language. Written many years after the event, a pamphlet published by the *Detroit Daily Post* on February 7, 1870, seems to be a synthesis of several earlier newspaper articles and is substantially correct in most details: "The entire neighborhood was alive with armed Negroes, who concealed themselves in the alleys, fields and scrub-brush . . . the jail-yard, as the park was then called, being in the suburbs of the city." The *Democratic Free Press* of June 19, 1833, cut to the heart of the action: "One lusty fellow planted himself on the steps armed with a tremendous club, and swore that the man should not be taken away." Some of the crowd was armed with pistols, some with knives and clubs, others with swords "and other unlawful weapons." The women of the city's black community had been charged with the mission of disabling Talbot Oldham's rented carriage; they removed the linchpin.

At about four o'clock on the afternoon of Monday, June 17, 1833, a not very tall, slightly stout black man with light eyes and a resigned countenance was brought to the jailhouse door. There were manacles on Thornton's feet, heavy chains and cuffs on his hands. Sheriff Wilson, Deputy McArthur, and Jailer Goodell positioned themselves on the front step on either side of Thornton Blackburn. They were to guard their prisoner on his short trip from the stoop, down the stairs, and along the path to the waiting carriage. Talbot Oldham stood a little behind, armed and watchful for any sign of danger. The coach had been hired from the local livery stable to convey Thornton and his guardian to the docks. Weir was already aboard the *Ohio* waiting for Thornton to be brought to the vessel.

At that moment, up Gratiot Street toward the door of the jail, marched a crowd of about two hundred angry men and women: "an old negress, at their head, carrying a white rag on the top of a pole, is said to have led a motley crew of negroes, under flag, through the principal streets of the city in defiance of the civil authority," reported the *Detroit Daily Post* in the memorial account written in 1870. There were several whites in the crowd as well, although the newspapers preferred to play down their participation.

Spectators recorded how at first Sheriff Wilson tried to pull his prisoner backward through the open door into the jail; then Thornton spoke out. He "promised, if suffered to do so, he would cause the crowd to disperse, and would himself go peaceably to the boat; and the request of the slave was seconded by one of the Kentuckians, who said it was necessary for them to go in the evening boat." It was Talbot Oldham who convinced Sheriff Wilson that Thornton might have some influence with the crowd, so Sheriff Wilson allowed him to address the mob. However, as soon as he stepped forward, someone tossed him a pistol (later reports say it was Madison Lightfoot), and a great cry rang out, "Shoot the rascal!"—meaning he should shoot Goodell, the Detroit jailer. The sheriff, who was between Thornton and the rascal in question, tried to wrest the gun from his prisoner. Then Thornton wheeled and aimed his pistol straight at the sheriff himself.

Wilson surely thought he was a dead man until Thornton raised his arm high and fired into the air. As his shot rang out, pandemonium broke out. The first ranks of the crowd between the jailhouse steps and the road pressed forward toward the prison and surged up the stairs, a young man named Lewis Austin among them. The men in the doorway panicked. Goodell, McArthur, and Oldham fled back inside the jail and bolted the door behind them. Sheriff Wilson was left outside to face the seething mob alone.

The eminent historian of African American Detroit who first studied the Blackburns, Dr. Norman McRae, pieced together what happened next:

> Seeing Blackburn in difficulty, members of the mob attacked Sheriff Wilson, while Lewis Austin took Blackburn into the stagecoach that was waiting to transport Blackburn,

his captor and the sheriff to the dock. Earlier several women had removed the linchpin from the vehicle in order to disable it. As a result Blackburn was kept inside the coach until two elderly blacks, Daddy Grace and Sleepy Polly, could remove him.

The sheriff fired several shots in the air in an effort to halt the violence, but he was knocked to the ground by the force of the attack. Deputy McArthur, who watched the entire proceedings from the jail window, later testified that the sheriff "was forcibly pulled . . . down the steps of the Jail while endeavoring to detain . . . Blackburn while a number of the . . . Negroes, blacks and Mulattoes pressed in between the Sheriff and the prisoner and Struck at him . . . frequent and violent blows."

McArthur offered further details: "at this moment, one of the blacks as he believes named Beatty rushed upon the said Sheriff and with a heavy club struck him in the side of the head and repeated the blow on the back part of the head." Wilson was unconsciousness for hours, and it was several days before his life was considered out of danger. He would never regain his memory of that day. In fact, it was commonly believed that Wilson's death several years later was hastened by the injuries he sustained in the Blackburn incident. Friend Palmer recalled watching the riot and its aftermath:

> Great excitement ensued; the Presbyterian Church bell rang an alarm, the cry "To Arms" was shouted through the streets and men with guns, pistols and swords were seen coming from all directions . . . I was a distant witness to the whole affair, from my window at the University school building; from it I had an unobstructed view of the crowd, the flash of a pistol and heard the report. Then all was confusion in the school, all the scholars, ignoring Mr. Crane, broke for the outside and for the jail, where we spent the remainder of the day.

Astonishing as it may seem, only Wilson and Lewis Austin sustained serious injuries. "One Negro, named Louis Austin, was shot in the breast, the ball penetrating the lung, and lodging in the shoulder blade . . . After two years of long suffering, Louis died, attributing his death to the effects of the wound," reported the *Detroit Daily Post* on February 7, 1870. The *New York Standard*, which picked up the story on June 29, 1833, was blunt: "We have heard that Sheriff Wilson was dangerously wounded, & two negroes were shot, but neither of them have yet died."

The *Detroit Daily Post* describes what happened next. (However, in all other sources, the name of the elderly driver of the getaway cart was Daddy Grace.)

> During the melee, an old colored man, named "Daddy Walker," who, with his cart and a blind horse, had been impressed into the service, backed up his vehicle to the jail steps, while an old colored woman by the name of "Sleepy Polly," and who never before nor after showed signs of activity, seized hold of Blackburn and dragged him into the cart . . . Daddy Walker, and the mob, which had been swelled to 400 or 500 persons, immediately drove, post-haste, up Gratiot road with the evident intention of turning toward the river as soon as practicable.

Charles Cleland, who was also at the jail that day, put the number of people involved in the melee at a much more reasonable forty men and women. The *Detroit Courier* article of June 19 continues, "The driver was somewhat reluctant about his task, but a Negro in the cart, holding a drawn sword over his head, urged him and his blind horse to respectable speed. The crowd continued to push up Gratiot road and in answer to inquiries whither the fugitive had been taken, pointed forward and said, 'further on.'"

On June 19, 1833, the conservative *Democratic Free Press* published a highly critical account of the events: "It is very evident that the whole plan had been concerted on the previous day; and that no resistance was expected from the citizens of Detroit, or precautions would have been taken to prevent such disreputable proceedings."

It is of note that despite the fact that Madison Lightfoot and George French, not to mention Benjamin Willoughby, were all well-known members of the city's black society, none of their names appeared in the newspaper reports as having participated directly in the rescue. It would seem they kept to the background, for it was seven young men, all but one of them also fugitive slaves, who threw Thornton into the wagon and sped off with him down the road. They were all in terrible danger, for the entire affair had been conducted in broad daylight. According to Deputy McArthur, he had recognized "Beatty, Lewis Austin, Prince Williams, Peter Sands, Alexander Butler, John Lloyd, and Madison Mason, all blacks and Mulattoes." To make matters worse, Lewis Austin, who was fleeing along with the rest of the group, had been grievously wounded. It would appear that the plot concocted to save the Blackburns had intentionally relied on people who were ready and able to leave Detroit should events of the day make it too dangerous to remain.

There was a posse at their backs. Bugles sounded and firebells were rung as the cart bearing Thornton and his rescuers traveled east on Gratiot Street and then traveled north around the city to the Rouge River, moving down through the woods toward the Detroit River. As they urged Daddy Grace and his old blind horse to even greater exertions, they could hear the sound of dogs and men on horseback, coming closer and closer. Still the party pressed on:

> The cart entered the woods on the north side of the road, about where Russell street now is, and disappeared. The fugitive was then taken from the cart, and, with the aid of a maul and sword, his chains were severed. The stronger of the party took him on their shoulders and carried him for some distance. Beginning to feel more secure, they rested

and put handkerchiefs around his ankles so that he could run along with his rescuers [without them rattling and clanking].

Arriving near the mouth of the River Rouge, the crew carried Thornton to a waiting boat. While circumstances suggest that the boatman's services had been purchased in advance (how else would Thornton's rescuers have known where to find a boat, complete with boatman, after their wild ride to the river?), he now refused to take the fugitives across to the Canadian shore without further remuneration. But no one had money to pay him, and the sound of barking dogs was getting closer and closer. Finally, one of them handed the boatman his prized gold watch. Thornton and seven other men were then conveyed across the Detroit River to Sandwich, Upper Canada.

> The woods were scoured in all directions, and several of the blacks secured, and taken back to jail. Pistols were found on some. As it was known they would make for the river, with a view of crossing to the Canada side, horsemen were dispatched up and down to prevent them. By evening a good number had been caught, and it was ascertained that some had actually succeeded in getting over. One young negress was brought back as she was waving her handkerchief from a canoe.

After a tense voyage across the river, Thornton and his party finally arrived safely in Canada. Meanwhile, back in Detroit, all was chaos. Terrified, the two officers of the law, McArthur and Goodell, remained in the jailhouse while Sheriff Wilson lay bleeding and alone on the jailhouse steps outside. Finally, the jailer ventured out to carry the unconscious Wilson indoors so his wounds could be dressed. Talbot Oldham, too, stayed safely inside the Detroit prison until after the mob had dispersed. According to one version, the youthful Kentuckian had "deemed it [more] prudent to remain within the county walls until night, than come out among the 'wild niggers of Detroit.'" This did not happen until about eight o'clock.

Immediately after the furor died down that night, Mayor Chapin and the Detroit City Council held an emergency meeting. At their order, most of the city's black residents were rounded up and imprisoned, and the jailhouse was soon bursting at its seams. By the evening of Tuesday, June 18, the day after the riot had taken place, the prison was crowded to the door with the men and women who had been detained.

Ironically, given his own part in the affair, it was Alexander Frazier in his official capacity as the Detroit City Attorney who was ordered to prosecute the rioters. The proceedings took place in the Mayor's Court of Detroit. The first round of trials was on June 21 and 22. Of the twenty-nine people who were tried, eleven were sentenced and eighteen discharged. Although both black and white rioters had been arrested, those convicted of actual complicity in the rescue were all black. Prisoners found guilty of "unlawful assembly and a riot and disturbance," but not of participating in the rescue, were jailed for between twenty and fifty-five days. Some served sentences of several months' duration on municipal repair gangs. One was the very elderly Daddy Grace, whose cart had been commandeered. Even those eventually judged innocent were forced to post bonds as a guarantee for their future good behavior before they could be set free. The more impoverished among them could not make bail and remained incarcerated for weeks.

Talbot Oldham and Benjamin Weir were among the first to testify about the events. In his statement to the Mayor's Court, Oldham's is actually the only account that clearly places whites among the participants in the riots; he swore that Thornton was "rescued by a *mob of white men and negroes*." The Kentuckians were the only people commenting who were not from Detroit; Oldham had no civic pride to uphold. He was also indisputably at the scene, if somewhat removed because he was peeking out the jailhouse windows while the riot transpired, so his account is credible. Benjamin G. Weir was unable to offer much insight into the events of that day, since he had been preparing a place on the steamboat *Ohio* for his prisoner and was therefore not a witness to the violence. Both of the men evidently made an impression on the locals, for Friend Palmer later wrote, "At that time and long after, the name 'Kentuckian' inspired the greatest dread in the hearts of the colored people . . . and indeed, among us [white] boys he was looked upon as an ogre and a walking arsenal, and as if anything and everything horrible might be expected of him."

The night after Thornton escaped, the stables attached to the jail were torched. The fire was put out, but four days later the stables mysteriously burned down and Sheriff Wilson's horse, worth $150, perished in the blaze. The mayor and his council responded by establishing a special watch to safeguard the white townsfolk. The assumption was that the African American community was setting the fires, but there was never any evidence brought forward to prove it. The militia, under the command of the War of 1812 veteran General John R. Williams, patrolled the streets. Eliza Mason, the acting governor's older sister, wrote to her niece at Emma Willard's seminary at Troy, New York: "In consequence of a threat to burn the city a guard has been kept every night, but I assure you that I do not get much sleep for the alarm has made me so nervous I have been most uncomfortable . . . as for news I suppose your mother has told you all about the negro row. It has kept the city in a constant state of fermentation for the last week."

Public feeling on the matter is preserved in newspaper accounts, contemporary letters, and later memorials by eyewitnesses recalling the events of their youth (accurately or not). By July 6, 1833, the news had reached Boston, where William Lloyd Garrison included a full account of the Detroit riot in *The Liberator*. Although abolitionism in Detroit did not flower until the foundation of the Detroit Anti-Slavery Society in 1836, and never enjoyed the popularity it did in Philadelphia, Boston, or even racially divided Cincinnati, African Americans in Michigan had a few staunch friends who would stand beside them throughout the antebellum years. At least one historian attributed the foundation of the antislavery organization to the uproar attending the Blackburn affair of 1833. The repeated "invasion" of Michigan Territory by Southern slave catchers had long outraged Michigan whites, so the Blackburn incident, had it not exploded into mayhem, might well have engendered more support than it did. Charles Cleland blamed white agitators for stirring things up: "We fear that the ignorant zeal of the blacks has received too much encouragement from the injudicious excitement felt by some of our citizens, who would have been sorry to have countenanced an open breach of laws." His rival in the newspaper business, Sheldon McKnight, was overtly critical of the white role in what had happened, editorializing in his *Democratic Free Press* of June 19, 1833:

> We would remark, however, that the conduct of a few—(a few only we are glad to say)—of our fellow citizens, who scattered the fire-brands of excitement among the mob, was in the highest degree reprehensible. Whatever might have been their feelings, the execution of the law was of paramount importance, and private sympathy should have submitted to the public good.

On the evening of Wednesday, June 19, 1833, two days after the riot, Detroit's municipal government held a public meeting and established a committee of fifteen of the city's leading whites to investigate the incident. A series of resolutions was passed confirming the right of the slaveholder to recover his property; ordering the immediate reinforcement of the existing laws requiring black residents to post a bond for their good behavior; providing for the establishment of a city watch to patrol the streets and, tellingly, "to prevent the rescue of negroes now in jail," committing the city to provide necessary food and financial support for a watch of sixteen men for as long as needed.

The "Report of the Citizens' Committee" was published in the *Detroit Journal and Advertiser* on Friday, July 19, 1833. It refers to numerous public meetings held between the actual events on June 16 and 17 and the day the committee's findings were published one month later. A major issue for all concerned was again that so many whites had taken part in the attack on the jail. To add insult to injury, these white agitators were unrepentant: They believed violence was justified in the face of federal laws that would take law-abiding Michigan residents and condemn them to a life of slavery. These the committee roundly condemned:

> If there be found among us, those who entertain different sentiments, as a matter of speculative reasoning, it must be attributed to the natural diversities in the opinion and moral temperament of men. But those who have given a practical demonstration of their principles, by deceiving the blacks with false hopes, encouraging them in pretensions inconsistent with their condition, and the safety of the community in which we live; or by inciting them to avowed opposition to the laws and constituted authorities, are entitled to unqualified reprobation as enemies, alike, to the blacks, and to the essential interests of the country.

Madison Lightfoot and George French were only briefly incarcerated. Lightfoot was jailed for three days in the vain hope that he would expose the others who had planned the rescue, while "Mrs. Lightfoot was fined $25 for being 'the prime mover of the riot'—which she never denied." It was widely believed that Madison Lightfoot had supplied Thornton with the pistol, although he seems never to have been charged with the offense. When George French was released from his cell, he thought it prudent to join his wife in Upper Canada, where they remained for several months, although the family later returned to Detroit. Benjamin Willoughby and John Cook seem to have escaped prosecution entirely, possibly because their role in the events was only later revealed.

In the wake of the riots, a curfew was maintained in Detroit for some weeks. All blacks out at night were required to carry a lit lantern to ensure their visibility. The night watch prevented any African American from approaching the Detroit River bank, but the only person they caught was a smuggler plying his clandestine trade. Following the Blackburn incident, the night watch was made a regular component of the city government. A rather amusing memoir of their activities was published in 1887:

> At the suggestion of Mayor Chapin, sentinels were placed at night at certain points with orders to "arrest any suspicious persons." The mayor was personally very attentive in hunting up delinquents, and passing up the street late at night, he came in contact with a sentinel who did not know him, and who judged from his haste, that he was certainly a "suspicious person," he accordingly arrested him, and held him in custody until the arrival of the sergeant of the guard. This was exceedingly annoying as it detained him, and prevented him from making other arrests which were important to the security of the public tranquillity.

Matters were far from resolved in July 1833, when the more militant elements in the Michigan black community held a protest parade to demand the release of people who had not actually been charged. Seeing dozens of blacks marching in the streets stirred up white fears and turned against them many who had previously been supportive or at least neutral in the matter. Next it was rumored that African Canadians from Fort Malden were planning to traverse the river and set fire to Detroit. The mayor's committee laid the blame for what happened next on the black communities on either side of the Detroit River:

> The committee think it their duty further, to state that the information has reached them, of threats being made, by the negroes at Malden, to set fire to our city, and that on the night of the 11th instant, a fire was actually set to the gaol,

which, but for the timely exertion of the fire companies, would have been consumed; and there is no doubt on the mind of any one, that the act was committed by the blacks, for the double purpose of revenge, and the liberation of their brethren confined there, under the sentence of the mayor's court.

White Detroit was kept in a continual state of turmoil over fears that another riot was imminent. Describing a theatrical performance she had attended in July, Eliza Mason wrote that "the discomfort of the crowded theatre was aggravated by fears of fire which had been threatened by the negroes who had been rioting because of the attempt of some Southern slave owners to recover an escaped slave who had been in Detroit for some time." Merchant Charles M. Bull wrote to his father on July 20, 1833:

We all got in an uncomfortable state owing to fears of fire from the negroes, who had set fire only two or three nights before to a *large* barn near the jail and burned it down, containing a horse, cow and other property—we have had two fires recently and now never go to bed without expecting an alarm—they have threatened to burn the city unless the prisoners are set at liberty—and however willingly the inhabitants may be to do it, the example would be so bad that they are prevented—it is really very uncomfortable to be kept in continual dread, for we do not know where they mean to stop their depredations.

The same man overlaid racism with his own terror of civil unrest when he wrote, "I never did like negroes and this has given me a horrible idea of them—the children on going from school are as much afraid of them as we used to be of the Indians." As the rumors spread and expanded, white mobs began attacking blacks as they walked the city streets. Assaults on their homes resulted in over forty black dwellings being burned to the ground. The mayor finally put in a formal request for military protection with

Lewis Cass, the United States secretary of war who had been visiting Detroit when the Blackburn Riots broke out. Through his intervention, martial law was declared, and troops were called out from Fort Gratiot.

Mayor's Office, City of Detroit, July 25, 1833

SIR:—The recent excesses committed in this city by the Black population within its limits, and particularly the repeated attempts to fire the town, have so far excited the apprehensions of our citizens for their property and lives, that I am instructed by the common council of the city, to ask that a detachment of the United States troops may be stationed at this place, to act under the directions of the municipal authority until the excitement had subsided and tranquillity is restored.

Very Respectfully &c.,
[signed M. CHAPIN]

Cass would hardly be neutral to the situation; in fact, he was tugged in several directions. When he had been governor of Michigan Territory, he had been furious with the British government for permitting runaways to take refuge in Upper Canada. A former slaveholder himself, he did not consider slavery a moral issue, but shared Thomas Jefferson's belief that slavery was dangerous because it was a corrupting force in white society. In a letter to a Kentucky friend in 1828 he had written, "Where this evil, which threatens so much injury to the holders of this species of property in Kentucky, is to end, I cannot see—it has increased to an alarming extent."

In a letter dated July 30, 1833, Lieutenant W. W. Morris of Fort Gratiot informed Mayor Chapin that he and his troops had arrived. His soldiers, along with the militia and the night patrol, guarded the streets from the threat posed by the fifty-odd blacks who remained in the city at that point. It all seems rather hysterical, but Brigadier General Hugh Brady (who was Electus Backus's father-in-law) was instructed by Cass to keep his soldiers at their posts until all danger was past.

A majority of Detroit's white citizenry remained markedly hostile to African Americans for months after the event. The *Detroit Daily Post* articles of January 1 and February 7, 1870, recalled that "an intense hatred was engendered against them. No one would employ them and there was a general exodus of the colored people from the city." As had been the case with the Cincinnati race riots two years earlier, people were forced to abandon their homes and businesses; they "sold them for nominal sums, to get away from the persecution. Some left their property and never returned." Eventually Mayor Chapin ordered all the African Americans who could not post a $500 bond to leave the city. Most went to Canada. Detroit lost all but the most entrenched of its black citizenry. A coldhearted journalist writing in the *Detroit Daily Post* on February 7, 1870, later lamented the lasting inconvenience this caused—for whites! "There remained city lots that could not be sold with a clear title because the properties had been assumed, but never actually purchased from their previous, African American, owners." Detroit's black population did not again increase in size until after 1837, when Michigan became a state and the constitution abolishing slavery and safeguarding personal liberty was ratified.

So many blacks had left that when General Brady returned from a tour of the Upper Great Lakes on August 7, 1833, he recalled his troops, finding that, as Lieutenant Morris wrote, "the negroes had, with few exceptions, evacuated the city and fled to Canada." When the report of the committee that investigated the riots was published, its official position was that while it was unfortunate that the laws of the land required Judge Chipman to turn the Blackburns over to Southern slaveholding interests, there was no justification for so violent a response. Public peace was paramount. The first three resolutions of the group read as follows:

Resolved. That as freemen who duly appreciate liberty, and believing that true liberty can alone be guaranteed by wholesome laws, we deprecate the recent violation of those laws.

Resolved. That however we may deprecate the existence of slavery in our free and happy country; yet so long as it is sanctioned by the supreme law of the land, it becomes the duty of every good citizen to support the constitution by his aid in giving effect to its provisions, in this as well as in other respects.

Resolved. That while we hold personal liberty to be a sacred and inalienable right, <u>yet when the property of the master is clearly proven in the slave</u>, it becomes our duty to see that the laws be maintained, and that no riotous mob is allowed to violate them.

The issue was thus reduced to a confirmation of the right of American citizens to maintain their personal *property*, and that included slaves. On the other hand, the committee's lengthy report offers an interesting clue to what the more popular attitude toward Judge Chipman's decision may really have been:

If any portion of our citizens have represented to the governor of Upper Canada that the requisitions for the delivery of the perpetrators of these acts [the Blackburn rescue], arrested by the authorities of that government, is only a pretense to regain possession of the slaves; can they reconcile such a representation with the facts of the case, or the duty they owe to the violated laws of their country? If they are right, what must the world think of the sentiments expressed at the meeting of the citizens, what of the Executive who made the requisition, what of the Mayor's court that convicted a part of the rioters?

What indeed?

CANADA

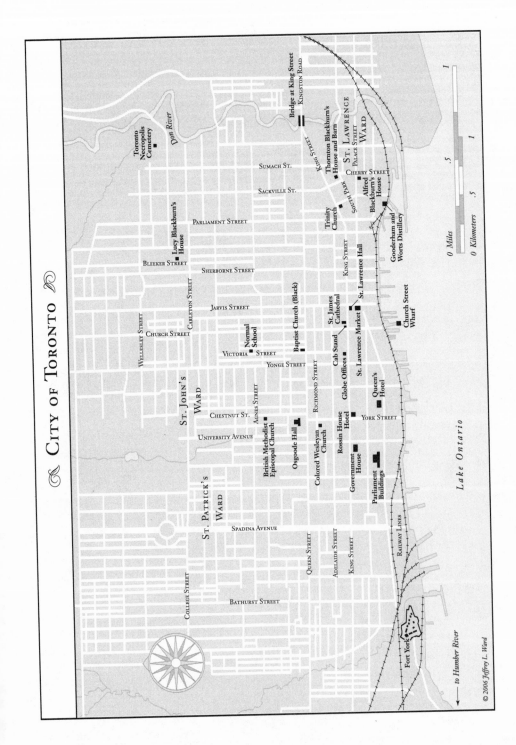

CITY OF TORONTO

Toronto Necropolis Cemetery

Don River

Bridge at King Street

KINGSTON ROAD

KING STREET

Thornton Blackburn's House and Barn

ST. LAWRENCE WARD

PLACE STREET

SUMACH ST.

CHERRY STREET

SACKVILLE ST.

Lucy Blackburn's House

SOUTH PARK

Alfred Blackburn's House

PARLIAMENT STREET

Trinity Church

Gooderham and Worts Distillery

BLEEKER STREET

SHERBORNE STREET

KING STREET

CARLETON STREET

JARVIS STREET

St. Lawrence Hall

Baptist Church (Black)

Church Street Wharf

WELLESLEY STREET

CHURCH STREET

Normal School

St. James Cathedral

St. Lawrence Market

ST. JOHN'S WARD

VICTORIA STREET

Cab Stand

RICHMOND STREET

YONGE STREET

Globe Offices

AGNES STREET

Queen's Hotel

CHESTNUT ST.

Rossin House Hotel

YORK STREET

British Methodist Episcopal Church

UNIVERSITY AVENUE

Osgoode Hall

Colored Wesleyan Church

ST. PATRICK'S WARD

Government House

SPADINA AVENUE

Parliament Buildings

QUEEN STREET

ADELAIDE STREET

KING STREET

COLLEGE STREET

RAILWAY LINES

BATHURST STREET

Lake Ontario

Fort York

to Humber River

0 Miles .5 1

0 Kilometers .5 1

© 2006 Jeffrey L. Ward

9

OH, FREEDOM!

Tell the Republicans on your side of the line we Royalists do not know men by their color. Should you come to us you will be entitled to all the privileges of the rest of His Majesty's subjects.

—LIEUTENANT GOVERNOR SIR JOHN COLBORNE, 1829

ONCE SAFELY IN Upper Canada, Thornton Blackburn was reunited with his wife. They met on the banks of the Detroit River in the little town of Sandwich, the seat of the province's Western District. The boundaries between the Blackburns' old life and their new one would be established here. In honor of her new liberty, Mrs. Blackburn took a new name. A free woman in a free land, for the rest of her life she would be *Lucie* Blackburn.

There were eight men, all African Americans, who came safely across the Detroit River into Upper Canada on the evening of Monday, June 17, 1833. These were Thornton Blackburn, Peter Sands, John Lloyd, Prince Williams, Lewis Austin, Madison J. Mason, Alexander Butler, and the man known only as Beatty. It was about six in the evening. The Blackburns and their friends had found refuge, but they were not safe—not yet. Although they did not know it, the long arm of the Fugitive Slave Law was reaching out for them.

Thornton's emotions when he arrived on Canadian soil are not recorded. When his contemporary Josiah Henson had finally reached Canada with his wife and children three years earlier, he kissed the ground and then ran around, crying out and jumping for joy, to the amusement of onlookers, until a customs officer who happened to be standing by asked him if he were mad. Another Kentucky fugitive, Lewis Clarke, expressed his own feelings:

> When I stepped ashore here, I said, sure enough, I AM FREE. Good heaven! what a sensation, when it first visits the bosom of a full-grown man; one *born* to bondage—one who had been taught, from early infancy, that this was his inevitable lot for life. Not till then did I dare to cherish, for a moment, the feeling that one of the limbs of my body was my own. The slaves often say, when cut in the hand or foot, "Plague on the old foot" or "the old hand; it is master's—let him take care of it. Nigger don't care, if he never get well." My hands, my feet, were now my own. But what to do with them, was the next question.

Undoubtedly some of the Blackburns' Canadian friends were on hand to welcome Thornton and his rescuers at the Sandwich shore. Of immediate concern to Thornton and Lucie was the fate of the Detroit friends who had so carefully planned their escape. Retribution against Detroit blacks would be, they knew, swift and sure; it was only a matter of what form the government's retaliation would take. The newly christened Lucie Blackburn had no way of knowing what had happened to Mrs. French. The last she had seen of her friend was when Mrs. Blackburn slipped out of the Detroit jail, wearing her clothes and hidden behind her veil.

Thornton and Lucie Blackburn had left their old lives behind, but the future was bright. Upper Canada was by the 1830s the destination of choice for runaway slaves. Visiting abolitionists returned with glowing reports of the opportunities that awaited African American immigrants, and the British colony had both proximity and familiarity of culture in its favor. Local communi-

ties along the Detroit riverfront had significant black populations, many of them former American slaves, with close ties to
blacks living in Michigan. Lucie Blackburn had already found
safe haven in Amherstburg, about eighteen miles south of Sandwich, on the night of her rescue from the Detroit jail.

Upper Canada had its own history of slavery dating back to the
period of the French regime, when both Native peoples and a
few Africans were imported for the purpose. The practice had
been continued under British rule. United Empire Loyalists
from the United States seeking refuge after the American Revolution were permitted to bring their movable property, including
livestock and slaves, and these same people made up a significant
proportion of Upper Canada's white elite. However, in 1793,
Upper Canada had become the first of England's colonies to rule
against slavery.

That it did so some forty years before the rest of the British
Empire was very much due to the efforts of one man. Lieutenant
Governor John Graves Simcoe had served with distinction as
commander of the New York Loyalist regiment, the Queen's
Rangers, during the Revolution, and acquired a deep distaste for
slavery. Returning to England, he spent nine years in the British
Parliament, enthusiastically supporting William Wilberforce in
his campaign to end Britain's role in the Atlantic slave trade.
When Upper and Lower Canada were created in 1791, Simcoe
was appointed the first Lieutenant Governor of Upper Canada,
which included much of what is now Ontario. Simcoe came to
his first parliament at Niagara with a plan for the immediate abolition of slavery. The nine members of his Executive Council
who owned some of the province's few slaves defeated his bill, but
soon a shocking incident turned the tide of political opinion in
Simcoe's favor. Near Queenston on the shores of Lake Erie a
slave woman named Chloe Cooley was observed being forced,
bound and gagged, into a boat. Her owner, fearing the loss of his
asset in the face of Simcoe's known opposition to slavery, had
sold her away into New York State. The girl's fate was reported

to the Lieutenant Governor and Chief Justice William Osgood. The Attorney General of Upper Canada, John White, was ordered to devise a means for ending Upper Canadian slavery once and for all.

The result was An Act to Prevent the Further Introduction of Slaves, and to Limit the Term of Contracts for Servitude Within This Province. Effectively, it was a gradual abolition bill. This compromise legislation protected existing slaveholder property rights, but only for the current generation. The children of slaves were henceforth to be considered free after the age of twenty-five, and their own children were legally born free. The new law, passed on July 9, 1793, made slaveholding unattractive, for owners were wholly responsible, without much benefit to themselves, for the welfare and upkeep of two generations of slave offspring. According to the diary of John White, whose political career was ruined by his presentation of Simcoe's antislavery bill in the House, this act was passed "with much opposition but little argument."

All this boded well for the Blackburns' future security. By the time they arrived, slavery had all but died out in the province, hastened in its passage by the implacable nerve with which Upper Canada's black defenders had fought during the War of 1812. Terrified at the idea that American victory would reintroduce slavery into Canada, they had flocked to enlist. These were the "black men in red coats" the Kentucky Volunteers had encountered at Lundy's Lane, Queenston, and Stoney Creek and guarding the Detroit and Niagara frontiers. News of their freedom was carried with the Kentucky soldiers to Maysville in the year of Thornton's birth, sparking the first real wave of Underground Railroad refugees who came to Upper Canada in search of liberty.

For years before the Blackburns arrived, Upper Canada had been a place where slavery was legal but where American fugitive slaves were welcomed, at least on an official level, as settlers. The province had since earliest times experienced a desperate shortage of workers, and former bondspeople and the skills they had learned in slavery on either side of the American border were welcome additions. The main conduits for their arrival were the Detroit and Niagara River frontiers, and their numbers increased as conditions of Southern servitude worsened over the first decades of the nineteenth century. Communities along the Detroit River and the Lake Erie shore had significant black populations by this time, and their numbers would be greatly augmented over the next few decades. A town-dwelling population had taken hold in Toronto, Kingston, and the Niagara region.

The new Lieutenant Governor in 1819 established an African Canadian military colony in the vast uncleared lands of Oro Township north of Lake Simcoe. His settlers were veterans of the War of 1812, and his move was both kindly and strategic: homes of these intensely loyal veterans lined the Wilberforce road that led south from the Upper Great Lakes and formed a first line of defense should hostilities break out with the United States at some future date.

> Sir Peregrine Maitland has granted land in several instances to Blacks and persons of Color, all in the same settlement, which is on a line parallel to the Road running from Lake Simcoe to Gloucester Bay on Lake Huron, generally known by the name of the Paratargaskene [Penetanguishene] Road. Those already settled have proved industrious and steady, and the Lt. Governor proposes to himself considerable advantages from the measure both in the view of the policy, and particularly in that of Humanity.

Another group, this time from Cincinnati, was establishing itself north of London in the western part of Upper Canada. This settlement was also named Wilberforce in honor of the great British abolitionist leader.

Sandwich, where the boat bearing Thornton and his rescuers landed that summer's evening in 1833, was the capital of the

Western District and the seat of government for a large part of the province. Sandwich was located across the river from Detroit and two miles south of the landing place known simply as "The Ferry," which would one day become the city of Windsor. Originally settled by French fur-trading families from Michigan and by British Loyalists on lands bought from local Native bands, it had its own small black population, some of them descendants of Upper Canadian slaves and others more recent immigrants from the United States. A short distance to the south was Amherstburg, a town that had grown up around the British Fort Malden. It had a larger African Canadian population, some of whom were instrumental in the Blackburn rescue from the Detroit jail. In time Amherstburg was to gain a reputation as one of the most important fugitive slave reception areas along the entire U.S.-Canadian border.

At about the same time Thornton and his rescuers landed on the shore on the evening of June 17, 1833, the sheriff of the Western District, William Hands, received a message from the mayor of Detroit. Marshall Chapin requested that the entire Blackburn party, including Thornton's wife, be detained until formal extradition documents could be prepared. In citing the grounds for their detention, Chapin carefully avoided mentioning the Blackburns' fugitive slave status; rather, he asked Sheriff Hands to hold the couple and their associates for crimes allegedly committed in Detroit over the two preceding days. Most serious was the charge of attempting to murder Sheriff John M. Wilson. It was an accusation certain to elicit Sheriff Hands's best efforts; a former resident of Detroit himself, he had previously joined with Sheriff Wilson in cross-border efforts to bring criminals to justice.

Quite late that same night, Sheriff Hands finally reached François Bâby, one of three local justices of the peace. Bâby was the son of a well-to-do slaveholder who had come to Canada after Detroit was turned over to the Americans. The charges brought by Mayor Chapin were grave and, if well founded, might merit a return of the Blackburns and their rescuers to Detroit to stand trial. Bâby asked a second judge, George Jacob, to work with him to issue a warrant for the Blackburn party's arrest. Judge Jacob was reluctant; at issue was whether the Blackburns were "fugitives from slavery" or "fugitives from justice." Jacob was personally of the opinion that the charges against Lucie Blackburn and the men had been trumped up in order to facilitate the return of runaway slaves to their owners. It was something of which he wanted no part. Bâby convinced Jacob that the Blackburn party should be held at least until the government at the Town of York (modern Toronto) could be consulted.

A new piece of provincial legislation had been written largely because of previous irregularities in the transfer of accused criminals back and forth across the border with the United States. The Fugitive Offenders Act formalized extradition protocols between Canada and the United States for the first time. Only in play since the previous February, it had not yet been put to the test. The Chief Justice of Upper Canada, Sir John Beverley Robinson, reported some years later that the law had been passed in response to the fact that Michigan and New York states had "long had Statutes expressly directing the surrender of fugitives from foreign countries in certain cases, while in this Province there was no positive law of any kind," even though extraditions had customarily been reciprocal, if rather informally handled, up to that time.

Given Upper Canada's reputation as a haven for refugee American blacks, it must have come as a shock when Thornton Blackburn, Peter Sands, Prince Williams, and all the other men were arrested somewhere along the road to Amherstburg on the very night of their arrival in Upper Canada. Lucie Blackburn was also taken into custody. The prisoners were housed in the Sandwich jail, with Mrs. Blackburn incarcerated separately from her husband. All that was lacking was a formal extradition request from Michigan's territorial government. As the Blackburns and the rest of their party filed into the Sandwich jail that evening, they could see the lights of Detroit across the river. It must have seemed very near.

A charcoal sketch done during the summer of Thornton and Lucie's incarceration from Springwells, Michigan, directly across the river, shows a village with only a dozen or so houses, only one of them of brick with double chimneys. Farmers' fields stretched down to the waterfront as late as 1833. The town was anchored at the southern end by Western District Grammar School (foreground) and the Anglican church of St. John, built in 1819 to replace one burned during the War of 1812. By odd coincidence, both Robert Smith, Thornton's former owner, and Smith's brother-in-law, Dr. Anderson Doniphan, had been with the soldiers who occupied Upper Canada. The Kentucky Volunteers stabled their horses in this church, and torched it when they left in September 1813 to disband at Maysville.

The large house in the drawing belonged to the Bâbys, whose roots stretched back from Detroit to old Quebec. Before he was killed at the Battle of the Thames, Jacques Bâby was closely allied with the Natives because of his commercial interests, and had entertained the Shawnee Chief Tecumseh in his home. Tecumseh was the nemesis of the Kentuckians along the Ohio River shore long before Thornton was born. The Bâby house was commandeered for the headquarters of General William Henry Harrison, future president of the United States, when his troops occupied the district. The children of the local elite intermarried, of course, so between them the Hands and Bâbys were related to most of the families that made up the infrastructure of society and government.

Beside St. John's Church in the drawing is the stolid weight of the Western District courthouse and jail. It had been constructed in 1800 and within its walls conditions were grim. By 1833, jailer Abraham Unsworth was already requesting monies to make improvements, although the four-square, two-story brick structure continued to house prisoners through 1850, when it was replaced with the present stone structure. The minister at the Anglican church next door served as prison chaplain, and there was a local physician who provided medical services as well. With the prisoners all safely in their cells, Abraham Unsworth called on the services of Dr. P. McMullins. Both Unsworth and McMullins would prove good friends to the Blackburns. Lewis Austin needed immediate attention, for his chest wound was serious. The doctor may have had more than one patient, for Detroit newspaper accounts suggest that another of Thornton's rescuers, perhaps the man named John Lloyd, had also been shot. The captives undoubtedly spent a very uneasy night in the stone cells of the Sandwich jail.

The next day Talbot Oldham crossed over to the Canadian side of the river. Hoping to salvage something from Monday's fiasco, John Pope Oldham's son visited the Western District Courthouse to demand that Thornton and his wife be turned over to him. The Oldham-McKnight campaign to recover Thornton and Lucie went well beyond their monetary value. In common with many slaveholders, he probably felt that the flight of blacks—and Canada's acceptance of the fugitives—was both an affront and a threat to the whole slaveocracy. The young man must have been completely nonplussed, for Canadian officials refused to recognize his proofs of legal ownership of the Blackburns; his credentials as a representative of a slaveholder were worthless in the British colony. In fact, Oldham's arrogant manner caused such offense as to engender sympathy for the Blackburns on the part of Western District authorities.

Upper Canadians were already touchy on the subject of their sovereignty. The tenets of American expansionism had been articulated in the 1823 Monroe Doctrine, and people in the province anxiously looked southward for the invasion that might come. Anyone over thirty could also remember the War of 1812, when Kentucky's own War Hawk Henry Clay had said, "I verily believe that the militia of Kentucky are alone competent to place Montreal and Upper Canada at your feet." A great many residents of the Western District were Americans, either Loyalists or more recent immigrants who had come in search of land.

The Sandwich-Amherstburg corridor had been the scene of much fighting. People well remembered that the young Lewis Cass, now secretary of war, had been the first to step ashore when

American forces invaded this part of Upper Canada, as well as the later depredations wrought by troops under William Henry Harrison. His largely Kentucky-bred force had occupied the district, harassing settlers, appropriating livestock, and burning the Anglican church of St. John's to the ground.

More recently, Kentucky-based slave catchers had taken to crossing over into Upper Canada, and there had been several known cases where free people were kidnapped from the Detroit River district and sold into Southern slavery. No one in the Sandwich area appreciated violent invasions of Canadian homes and businesses, and on at least one occasion a local family had saved American refugees from their captors.

On Tuesday, June 18, Justices Bâby and Jacob were surprised by another visitor. Charles Cleland, attorney and the publisher of the *Detroit Courier*, took the ferry to Sandwich to offer his own services and those of Alexander D. Frazier, City Attorney for Detroit, to help the Canadian government in crafting the case for the Blackburns' defense. It was an extraordinary move. Frazier, who had advised Lucie prior to her escape, was on that very day serving in his official capacity and preparing to prosecute the Detroit African Americans arrested for helping the Blackburns flee. Now two Detroit lawyers were offering their legal expertise to the British colonial government of Upper Canada on the Blackburns' behalf.

Frazier and Cleland were not alone in repudiating Michigan's actions in the Blackburn case; in fact, Cleland explained to the astonished Canadian judges, he and Frazier were backed by a contingent of prominent Detroiters who were horrified that Michigan authorities would so readily comply with the federal Fugitive Slave Law that was easily evaded in other northern jurisdictions. From their perspective, both Judge Chipman and Sheriff Wilson had acted on behalf of slave agents rather than in the public good.

Frazier would pay dearly for his assistance to the Blackburns, but his help in their defense would prove invaluable. Cleland was equally dedicated to justice, but cut from rather different cloth. He did not enjoy the law and had early moved into publishing. He was a strong abolitionist, continuing to support the Blackburns in his *Detroit Courier* even after his business partner quit the paper in protest. Cleland was to repeat his offer of legal assistance in at least one other fugitive slave suit, which was prosecuted in the Western District courts in 1841. A good-hearted man known for his personal generosity to the less fortunate, Cleland was always in a precarious financial situation, something his good friend Benjamin Willoughby had been known to help alleviate on occasion. This, too, was much in the Blackburns' favor.

Public opinion in Sandwich was decidedly on the side of the fugitives, and this was probably true in York, the provincial capital of Upper Canada, as well. The U.S. government had for some years been pressuring the Canadians to return fugitive slaves to American soil, so far to no avail. The Chief Justice of Upper Canada, John Beverley Robinson, had, in his previous capacity of Attorney General, set the province's official policy in the matter when he presented this opinion in 1819:

> Whatever may have been the condition of . . . Negroes in the Country to which they formerly belonged, here they are free—For the enjoyment of all civil rights consequent to a mere residence in the country and among them the right to personal freedom as acknowledged and protected by the Laws of England . . . [must] be extended to these Negroes as well as to others under His Majesty's Government in this Province.

Robinson was citing British case law. In 1772, a slave named James Somerset had claimed freedom because his American owner had temporarily transported him to England. An Elizabethan-era legal precedent had been cited to bolster his case that "every man who comes to England is entitled to the protection of the

English law, whatever oppression he may heretofore have suffered and whatever may be the color of his skin." Robinson chose to extend this privilege to American slaves who reached Upper Canada as well. He was away from the province at the time the Blackburn case was tried, but the safeguards he had put in place against just such a situation would be applied in Thornton and Lucie's defense.

John Beverley Robinson was the most important lawmaker in Upper Canada. He served first as Attorney General and then as Chief Justice of Upper Canada for the entire period between the War of 1812 and the outbreak of the American Civil War. The son of a Virginia Loyalist whose family had owned slaves, he was a Tory to his fingertips. But Robinson was also a stickler for the law, an extremely detailed and dedicated jurist, and a devoted Upper Canadian patriot. He consistently resisted American attempts to infringe on freedoms guaranteed under British law. His own feelings on the institution of slavery have never been entirely clear; in later years he upheld the wishes of local residents to exclude black children from the common schools, an issue that caused much friction, particularly in rural areas and especially because black taxpayers were required to support the public school system. He also more than once expressed concern that the province not provide safe haven to genuine criminals just because they happened to be black. Yet it was Robinson who drafted the Fugitive Offenders Act in such a way as to safeguard runaways who reached Canada from summary removal. It is not overstating the case to say that the Underground Railroad could not have found its main terminus in Canada had it not been for legal decisions made by John Beverley Robinson.

Thornton and his wife were the latest in a long line of Kentucky runaways who sought safety in Upper Canada. In fact, Kentucky, from which came a large proportion of Upper Canada's fugitive slave population, protested to Congress in January 1821, demanding that the United States circumvent colonial authorities and open direct negotiations with the British government to force Canada to return slaves to their "rightful" owners:

An application was made a short time ago by Mr. Quincy Adams to the British Chargé d'Affaires at Washington, to know if American slave owners could follow fugitive slaves into His Majesty's Provinces with a hope of recovering their property. Mr. Antrobus sent to Gr. P. Maitland who forwarded him in reply the opinion of the Attorney General for Upper Canada, which was decidedly negative to the proposition. This . . . was brought on by two or three slaves having been traced from the Michigan Territory to some of our most Western Settlements.

In 1826, Henry Clay was the secretary of state in President John Quincy Adams's Cabinet. He again broached the subject in the first phase of what was to be a long series of diplomatic correspondence on this difficult topic:

[Slaves] escape, principally from Virginia and Kentucky to Upper Canada, whither they are pursued by those who are lawfully entitled to their labor; and, as there is no existing regulation by which they can be surrendered, the attempt to recapture them leads to disagreeable collisions. In proportion as they are successful in their retreat from Canada, will the number of fugitive slaves increase, and the cause of collision multiply. They are generally the most worthless of their class, and far, therefore, from being an acquisition which the British Government can be anxious to make, the sooner, we should think, they are gotten rid of, the better for Canada. It may be asked why, if they are so worthless, are we desirous of getting them back? The motive is to be found in the particular interest which those have who are entitled to their service, and the desire which is generally felt to prevent the example of the fugitives becoming contagious.

In a letter dated September 26, 1827, from the U.S. minister to Britain, Clay was informed that the British government would never "depart from the principle recognized by the British courts that every man is free who reaches British ground." Another request from the House of Representatives urging the American president to intercede with the British government on the matter was similarly rebuffed in 1828. Then in 1829, the governor of Illinois requested the extradition of a fugitive slave and his rescuer, both of whom had reached Montreal. After consultation with his Executive Council, Sir James Kemp, administrator of Lower Canada, refused on the grounds that neither man had committed a crime punishable as a capital offense under Canadian law. He said, "The state of slavery is not recognized in the Law of Canada nor does the Law admit that any Man can be the proprietor of another." Ultimately the same arguments would assist Thornton and Lucie Blackburn.

The earlier history of Canadian-U.S. relations on the matter of the fugitive slave was summed up in the first African American newspaper produced in the United States. Called *Freedom's Journal*, the publication was the brainchild of two educated black men living in New York, Samuel E. Cornish, pastor of the city's first black Presbyterian church, and John B. Russwurm. The latter, refused entry to U.S. institutions on account of his color, received his preparatory school training at Montreal before becoming the first black graduate of Maine's Bowdoin College. On January 9, 1829, the paper reprinted the following from the *Hampshire Gazette*:

RUNAWAY SLAVES.

Some hundred (perhaps thousands) of slaves have escaped from Virginia and Kentucky into Upper Canada, and there being no regulation by which they can be surrendered to their masters, those states asked for the interposition of the general government with Great Britain. The British government have informed the American minister that it is utterly impossible for them to agree to a stipulation for the surrender of fugitive slaves.—They cannot, they say, depart from the principle, in their possessions where slavery is not admitted, that every man is free who reaches British ground. It was intimated to the American minister, that such was the state of public opinion in England on the subject of slavery, that no administration could or would admit in a treaty such a stipulation as we asked.

The American government's discontent with Canada's refusal to return fugitive slaves to its own soil was to find many modes of expression over the antebellum years but was never resolved to its satisfaction. It was the case of Thornton and Lucie Blackburn that would establish the legal precedents upon which all subsequent fugitive slave extradition cases would be tried. Upper Canada and later Canada West continued to receive fugitive slaves right up until the end of the Civil War, more than three decades after the Blackburn incident.

The welcome afforded to American black refugees by the government of the Canadas constituted a highly effective form of resistance to the institution of slavery. It injured American slavery both in its pocketbook and in the propaganda that supported the system. Britain had already removed from the United States thousands of slaves who had been promised their freedom if they joined the forces of the Crown during the Revolution. A few thousand Black Loyalists were given poor land in Nova Scotia and New Brunswick, with a small number moving into Upper and Lower Canada (Ontario and Quebec). They were so ill treated that a significant number of the transplanted black Americans emigrated to the colony of Sierra Leone in West Africa. A second wave of African Americans were again freed after assisting the British in the War of 1812. The so-called Black Refugees subsequently settled in the Maritime provinces. But their combined numbers paled in significance beside those of fugitive slaves who came to Canada, either alone or through the routes of the Underground Railroad between about 1813 and 1865.

To gain a sense of the impact that this had, one needs to appreciate the magnitude of the financial loss it represented to the

South. Estimates of the number of runaways who settled north of the border before the Civil War range between about 20,000 and 100,000, but most credible sources place the figure at between 30,000 and 35,000 people. This was in addition to the many times that figure who settled in the northern United States without crossing the border into Canada. There were fewer than 1 million slaves in the United States at the time of the American Revolution, and nearly 4 million enslaved African Americans by the time of Abraham Lincoln's Emancipation Proclamation in 1863, so this exodus to Canada may seem insignificant. Simple mathematics serves to illustrate that it was not. If 40,000 people arrived in Canada in total, estimating the market value of each runaway at a very average $500 (American dollars), it would mean that the South had lost more than $20,000,000 in human property by 1861. The majority of people who sought their own freedom were in the prime of life, in reasonably good health, and possessed of both enterprise and ingenuity. So they came from the highest echelons of the slavery hierarchy, with correspondingly high market value. The end of the overseas trade in 1807 had inevitably meant an increase in the per capita cost of labor. The price of slaves escalated over the antebellum period, paralleling the growth of King Cotton. Where Thornton Blackburn had been valued at $600 and his wife at $400 in the 1830s, by 1856 planters were paying as much as $1,600 for a prime male field hand—or $20,000 in today's currency. The books of one Richmond, Virginia, slave-trading company show slaves graded according to age. "No. 1 Men" were worth between $1,500 and $1,600, and "No. 1 Girls" between the ages of sixteen and twenty were priced from $1,350 to $1,400. Slave women like Lucie were also valuable because they produced, in the natural course of things, more slaves. Because a female slave's children "followed the condition of the mother," the departure from the slave states of each woman capable of bearing children meant, in real economic terms, several thousand dollars in potential loss to her owner. Each generation provided still more fodder for the auction block, so a single woman's escape could represent lost revenues with an exponential increase from one generation to the next. It is evident even from this gross overview that, for every slave who escaped to Canada, there was a great deal more at stake than the loss of the individual's sale price.

Antislavery enthusiasm was particularly high in Upper Canada at the time. In 1833, the British Parliament was in the process of abolishing slavery throughout the empire. This measure would pass the House on August 1, 1833, to take effect the following year. The slaves of the West Indies would thereby be freed and their owners compensated for their financial loss with the massive sum of £20,000,000. It is of note that there were so few people still living in legal slavery in Upper Canada that the British government set aside no compensation for the province's slaveholders. The Western District judges who had Thornton, his wife, and his friends arrested in Sandwich were more than aware of the way the wind was blowing regarding British slavery. Undoubtedly officials on the Michigan side of the border were as well, which made them even more anxious to recover the Blackburns and bring them back to face American justice.

On June 21, the Acting Governor of Michigan Territory, Stevens Thomson Mason, sent a formal extradition request to Sir John Colborne. He demanded the return of Thornton and Lucie Blackburn and the other men involved in the riot on the grounds that they had incited civic unrest and attempted to kill the sheriff of Detroit. Michigan's twenty-one-year-old "Boy Governor" had a fine legal mind. Cognizant of Upper Canada's determination to protect black refugees, Mason presented his demands on grounds acceptable under Upper Canadian law for the extradition of "fugitives from justice." Mason called Thornton "alias John Smith," although the Detroit newspapers all referred to him by his real name. The Michigan documents named the seven men who assisted Thornton in his escape and demanded their return for trial. Mason asked that the Upper Canadian authorities deliver the fugitives up at the earliest possible opportunity to Alexander

McArthur, deputy sheriff of Wayne County; Sheriff Wilson was as yet in no condition to arrest anyone.

Attached to the extradition request were supporting documents including affidavits of John Pope Oldham and Virgil McKnight claiming the Blackburns as their legal property. Mason, Virginian by birth and Kentuckian by adoption, likely was trying to show that due process had been served. Still, providing legal proof of the couple's enslavement to Upper Canada's abolitionist Lieutenant Governor was not a particularly politic move on Mason's part.

On the other hand, he had every reason to believe that the Blackburn party would be extradited. There was a long tradition of sending accused criminals back and forth over the Detroit River, although until the passage of the Fugitive Offenders Act of February 1833, such matters had been handled locally. Furthermore, in the Blackburn case an actual crime had been committed. There had been rioting in the streets of Detroit and the rescue of legally incarcerated individuals from the custody of an officer of the courts. Eyewitnesses also swore that in the course of his escape Thornton had brandished a pistol in a threatening manner, and some of his rescuers had been observed taking part in the bloody assault on the Detroit sheriff. John M. Wilson was, even now, not considered out of danger. As far as the Michigan government was concerned, it seemed like the Blackburn extradition case was going to be an open-and-shut affair.

When he was appointed to the newly created province, Simcoe as the first lieutenant governor of Upper Canada had established the new provincial government along British imperial lines: there was an Executive Council of handpicked men to advise him; a Legislative Council, also appointed; and the Legislative Assembly the only elected body. Stacked with members of the colonial elite, this was a government hardly representative of the provincial population, an inequity that would, in time, arouse the populace to rebellion. Above all was the Lieutenant Governor, the Crown's appointed man. Thornton and Lucie Blackburn were fortunate that the Lieutenant Governor of Upper Canada at the time of their arrest was Sir John Colborne. Having come to Canada in 1828, Colborne was a veteran military officer who had fought in the Crimea and taken part in the historic charge of the Light Brigade under Wellington. A Tory with High Church principles, he was yet imbued with the aura of reform wafting through the British Parliament at the time. The same man who had welcomed Cincinnati African Americans into Upper Canada to establish the Wilberforce colony in 1829 was unlikely to acquiesce to an extradition demand for runaway slaves in 1833.

The Blackburns also had a staunch ally on Colborne's Executive Council in the person of the Reverend John Strachan, one of the most powerful figures in Upper Canadian politics. Although Colborne and Strachan did not get along particularly well, Strachan was the leading churchman in the only officially recognized denomination in the province, the Church of England. He was also a teacher who had been in charge of the grammar school education of most of the members of the Family Compact, including the Chief Justice himself. When he was appointed Bishop of Toronto in 1839, Strachan ensured that the churches under his control were not segregated, nor were the educational institutions he helped to found. These included Upper Canada's first university, colleges, the preparatory school, Upper Canada College, and the Normal School for teacher education.

Colborne, for his part, was adamant that no fugitive slave would be sent back to bondage on his watch, and Strachan was behind him, but the rest of the Executive Council was not so firmly abolitionist in its principles. There was concern that refusing to extradite the Blackburns would cause the Americans to retaliate. Having recently taken up his post as Upper Canada's latest Attorney General, Robert Simpson Jameson was given the tricky task of finding a way to avoid sending the Blackburns back to Michigan while maintaining cordial relations with its territorial governor. Jameson had arrived in Canada just in time to cut his legal teeth on the thorny issue of fugitive slave extradition.

While Jameson was considering their case at York, the Blackburns needed an attorney in Sandwich to work on their behalf. Every local lawyer refused their case. It is a measure of their implacable resolve to recover the Blackburns that Benjamin Weir and Talbot Oldham had cleverly put them all on retainer to prevent the Blackburns and their rescuers from having benefit of counsel. On June 23, Charles Cleland wrote to his colleague Alexander Chewett, judge of the Western District court in Sandwich:

> Several of our worthy citizens are desirous of encouraging your devices on behalf of Smith [Blackburn], whose only offence is that of having been *born in Africa* [my emphasis] followed up by his escape from a Slave holder in Kentucky . . . They are solicitous that [Blackburn] not be given up:—having fled to your shores for protection, they hope he will find an asylum, inasmuch as liberty, the natural right of all men is as dear to him as to the heroes who have shed their blood in its defense.

Cleland went on to say that his clients were only asking Colborne to delay his decision in the matter until the "plain, unvarnished facts" could be "embodied in the testimony of disinterested and respectable witnesses." To his evident chagrin, Chewett was forced to decline, because he had already been employed "to give my legal assistance to those who consider themselves on the opposite side of the question." He did, however, help the Blackburns by personally forwarding Cleland's letter to one of the two judges directly responsible for the case, and the one most sympathetic to the Blackburns, George Jacob. Thus Jacob became aware of the depths of Oldham and Weir's chicanery and the fact that there was now no one but Frazier and Cleland to defend the Blackburns and their friends at the local level. As American attorneys they could only advise, being barred from mounting a formal defense in an Upper Canadian courtroom.

Two days later Cleland and Frazier traveled to Sandwich and

Excavations at the Thornton and Lucie Blackburn Site,
Sackville Street School, Toronto, 1985.
(Archaeological Resource Center, Toronto)

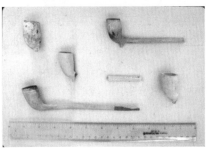

Blackburn excavations, summer 1985:
(*clockwise from top left*) Foundations of
kitchen fireplace, cutlery found in root
cellar, transfer-printed dinnerware, and
clay smoking pipes. (Christopher Koch)

THE COFFLE GANG. (*See page* 164.)

Slaves passing down the Maysville-Lexington Road from Paris,
Kentucky, to the Maysville Landing, ca. 1850s.
(Anon., *The Suppressed Book about Slavery*, New York: Carleton, Publisher, 1864,
Special Collections and Digital Programs, University of Kentucky Libraries)

Main Street, Louisville, Kentucky, ca. 1850.
(Filson Historical Society)

Mary Brown Miller, whose parents, Gideon and Susan Brown, owned Thornton Blackburn at Hardinsburg, Kentucky. (Roger and Elizabeth Chovil)

Judge John Pope Oldham (1785–1858), the brother-in-law of Thornton Blackburn's owners and superintendent of the Brown slaves after Dr. Gideon Brown's death. (Susan Curran White)

Virgil McKnight, portrait by unknown artist. McKnight purchased Mrs. Blackburn only days before she and her husband fled slavery forever. (Filson Historical Society)

Slave Market, ca. 1850–1860. Oil on canvas, 29³/₄ x 39¹/₂ inches. This painting portrays the sale of a young, beautiful light-skinned slave girl at the "fancy girl" market in New Orleans. (Carnegie Museum of Art, Gift of Mrs. Fitch Ingersoll)

Louisville seen from the Indiana shore. In the foreground is the landing place at Jeffersonville, from which the Blackburns hailed the *Versailles*. Engraving by William Wellstood from a drawing by John William Hill, published in *Ladies' Repository*, October 1854. (Kentucky Historical Society)

25 DOLLARS REWARD.

The subscribers will give for the apprehension and return of a colored man, named THORNTON, who absconded from our employ on the 3d or 4th of July, inst. Said Thornton is about 5 feet, 9 or 10 inches high; stout made, and of a yellow complexion; light eyes, and of good address; had on when he left, a blue cloth coat and pantaloons, boots, and a black hat.

july 7   WURTS & REINHARD.

Fugitive slave notice for Thornton.
Louisville Public Advertiser, July 7, 1831.
(Karolyn Smardz Frost)

Panoramic view of Cincinnati's Public Landing, where the Blackburns arrived on July 4, 1833. (Collection of The Public Library of Cincinnati and Hamilton County)

Detroit waterfront, from Sandwich, Upper Canada, 1837.
(Bentley Historical Library, University of Michigan)

Also the deposition of Thomas I Rogers taken by consent of Counsel at the same time and place and to be read in in the same causes and between the same parties The Deponent being of lawful age and first duly sworn deposes and says — That he knew Thornton Blackburn a mulatto man in the employ of Wurts and Reinhard in the year 1831, & that he afterwards met with said negro man in Detroit in the Territory of Michigan in the fall of the same year, and that he was residing in that place. He further states that the steam Boat Versailles has not been to the best of his knowledge and belief in the Port of Louisville for the last twelve months — And further this deponent saith not —

T. L. Rogers

Affidavit of Thomas Rogers describing his meeting in Detroit with Thornton Blackburn.
(Thornton Blackburn File, Michigan State Archives)

Pencil sketch of Sandwich, Upper Canada, drawn during the summer of 1833, probably while the Blackburns were incarcerated in the jail, which is the large building to the left of the church. (Windsor's Community Museum, Baby House)

Thornton Blackburn's cab beside Scadding Cabin Museum, a relic of historic Toronto, ca. 1895. (York Pioneers Historical Society)

View of King Street, Toronto, 1846, attributed to Thomas Young. Thornton Blackburn's taxi is in the center traveling along King Street toward the cab stand beside St. James Cathedral. (Royal Ontario Museum)

View of Osgoode Hall at the top of York Street, Toronto, ca. 1856, where Thornton worked as a dining room waiter in 1834. (Canadian Heritage Gallery)

Main Street, South Buxton, in the Elgin Association Settlement, ca. 1860s
(Buxton Museum and National Historic Site)

This organization was effected on the 25th of March 1852.
John M. Tensley, President.
Thorton Blackburn, Vice-President.
W. R. Abbett, Treasurer.
James Thomas Fisher, Secretary.
Board of Directors:
Rev. Wm. King, Buxton, C. W.
H. R. Thomas, Buffalo. N. Y.
A. Smith, Toronto.
George Brown, do.
F. Messour. do.
A Committee of three was appointed to select a good mill seat as soon as the weather permits travelling.
Committee: Rev. Wm. King, W. R. Abbett, John M. Tensley.
The number of shares taken up:

Rev. William King, six shares	£150
W. R. Abbett, six shares	150
H. R. Thomas, four shares	100
F. Messour, four shares	100
J. T. Fisher, three shares	75
A. Smith, two shares	50
T. Blackburh, two shares	50
John M. Tensley, two shares	50
George Brown, one share	25
	£750

Voice of the Fugitive, April 22, 1852, naming Thornton Blackburn as the vice president of the Canadian Mill & Mercantile Association.
(Karolyn Smardz Frost)

MOTHER ESCAPING WITH SEVEN CHILDREN

Ann Maria Jackson and her children, whom the Blackburns received in Toronto after the family fled Delaware slavery in 1858.
(Karolyn Smardz Frost)

Tombstone of Thornton Blackburn, Section E, Lot 100, Toronto Necropolis. The inscription reads, "In memory of Thornton Blackburn, Died February 26, 1890, age 76 years. A Native of Maysville, Kentucky, U.S.A. Blessed are the dead which die in the Lord." Other interments there include Sibby Blackburn (1855), Alfred Blackburn (1863), Ann Maria Jackson (1880), Richard M. Jackson (1885), Thornton Blackburn (1890), and Lucie Blackburn (1895). (Duncan Scherberger)

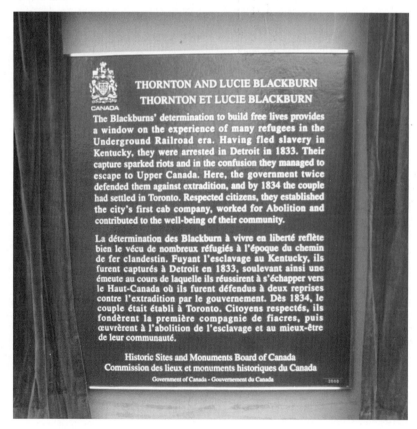

Historic plaque at the Blackburn Site in Toronto, August 29, 2002.
(Norm Frost)

swore out affidavits before Judge George Jacob. Frazier confirmed that he "was well acquainted with one Thornton Blackburn and Ruthe [*sic*] his wife, both persons of color . . . having
resided in the City of Detroit for about two years past, where
they have excellent characters, and were very much respected for
persons of their sphere in life." Cleland pointed out that it was
the "good character of Thornton, and also of his wife, both of
whom, I am informed, are connected with the Baptist Church,"
that had "enlisted the sympathies of a larger portion of the community of Detroit." Again, Cleland emphasized that Thornton
and his wife had white as well as black support on the Michigan
side of the river.

Frazier's account of events put the Blackburns and their rescuers
in the most favorable possible light. He presented the Detroit riot
of June 17, 1833, as nothing more than an impassioned and well-
meaning attempt to rescue a fugitive slave that had gotten out of
hand. He implied that in his official capacity he had entertained
particular doubts as to the validity of Judge Chipman's decision
in Mrs. Blackburn's case, since neither Talbot Oldham nor Benjamin Weir could personally identify her. Frazier even cautiously
admitted that he had given advice to Ruthie Blackburn *after* she
escaped, but before she left Detroit on the night of June 16. He
said: "In the evening of that day Ruthe [*sic*], Thornton's wife, escaped by stratagem from the Jail, and, upon the deponent's assur-
ance that she would be safe, fled to this Province." This was an
extraordinary step for the holder of a very responsible municipal
office to take.

Alexander Frazier then dropped another bombshell. He said
that it was he who had told Thornton, already in jail in Detroit
and waiting to be taken back to Kentucky, that the former slave
would be safe from further prosecution if he were to escape to
Upper Canada. He effectively admitted collusion in the Blackburn
jailbreak.

Frazier's main arguments were that first, Ruthie Blackburn
could not have been involved in the riot since she was already in
Upper Canada at the time it took place and second, that Sheriff

Wilson was not acting as the sheriff of Wayne County at the time he imprisoned the Blackburns, since he had no authority to jail them. Under the Fugitive Slave Law of 1793, Wilson was supposed to turn the Blackburns over directly to their owners or to the agent or attorney acting for their owners. Thus Frazier introduced the idea that Wilson was in effect acting as agent for John Pope Oldham and Virgil McKnight, rather than in his official capacity as the Wayne County sheriff.

A group of concerned Detroit citizens did indeed cross the river to offer their support against extraditing the Blackburns and their rescuers before the judges of the Western District, François Bâby and George Jacob. A clue is found in the "Report of the Citizens' Committee" in the *Detroit Journal and Advertiser* of July 19, 1833:

> If any portion of our citizens have represented to the governor of Upper Canada that the requisitions for the delivery of the perpetrators of these acts, arrested by the authorities of that government, is *only a pretence to regain possession of the slaves* [my emphasis]; can they reconcile such a representation with the facts of the case, or the duty they owe to the violated laws of their country?

The Detroit City Attorney demonstrated admirable political acumen with his closing salvo. He said that he had "every reason to believe that the object in demanding the delivery of Thornton and his wife [was] to turn them over to the owners so that they may carry them off into captivity and that they never will attempt to try them for any offence whatever." He made the point that the Blackburns hadn't actually done anything to warrant their initial incarceration "unless it be a mere misdemeanor, and I trust that for such an offence persons are not to be delivered up to be sent into slavery—Such would be the inevitable consequence."

Frazier's entire argument was calculated to cut the Upper Canadians to their patriotic quick. He was implying that by extraditing the Blackburns, Colborne and his Executive Council would be playing into the hands of wily American officials who cared only for supporting the South's "peculiar institution" and nothing for justice. From the Canadians' perspective, two legal and diplomatic issues were at stake. The first was Upper Canada's long-standing resistance to American pressure in the matter of the fugitive slave. The second was the need, acknowledged on both sides of the border, for formal and binding agreements governing the extradition process when the genuinely criminal sought refuge in the adjacent nation.

Meanwhile, Thornton had decided to make his own stand. He asked the prison chaplain, the Reverend William Johnson of St. John's Anglican Church, to write out a petition. Johnson was the missionary chaplain at St. John's Church, which continues to serve the faithful of Sandwich, and was chaplain to the prisoners at the Western District jail, right next to his church. Lieutenant Governor Colborne received Thornton's petition on June 27, 1833.

This is the only document that survives more or less in Thornton Blackburn's own words. Although the Reverend Johnson surely added his own embellishments—the petition has distinctly High Church overtones—Thornton's determination to win freedom and especially to protect his wife comes through even at a distance of more than 170 years. The arguments were cogent and the objectives very clear.

Surprisingly, Thornton maintained that he was freed two years prior to leaving Kentucky:

> The Petition of Thornton Blackburn on behalf of himself, and his wife Ruth Blackburn, both people of colour, at present confined in the Gaol of Sandwich, Western District, Humbly Showeth,

> That your Excellency's Petitioner was unfortunately born and brought up a Slave in the State of Kentucky, That by the generosity of his owner he received his Freedom, in testimony of which he has now in his possession an attested

Copy of his manumission . . . he resided two years in Louisville, and from there came to Detroit, Michigan Territory,
where he together with his wife has lived peaceably, and
borne a respectable character, following his employment,
that of a Stone Mason for the last two years. That some
short time since a party of People came from Kentucky to
Detroit in quest of Slaves, who had deserted from their
owners and that, from their persuasions and statements and
other influential motives, the Deputy Sheriff of Detroit arrested Your Petitioner, and his wife, and without giving them
any just or satisfactory reason, for so doing, cast Your Petitioner and his wife in to the Public Prison.

Thornton's supposed manumission, dated to the time of Dr.
Gideon Brown's death, seems to have been an invention to bolster his cause. Furthermore, while one can readily believe that a
legally manumitted slave might be retained in bondage, for there
are many such documented cases, the matter of Thornton's freedom was never discussed, then or later, in government deliberations on either side of the border. No manumission papers were
placed in evidence in the Detroit court of Judge Chipman, yet
Thornton was apparently prepared to send documentation attesting to his freedom to Upper Canada's Lieutenant Governor.
Captain Quarrier of the *Versailles* testified that Thornton and his
wife had presented free papers when they boarded his steamboat,
but all other evidence suggests that these documents were forged.
Since the case against the owners of the *Versailles* continued over
many years and was prosecuted by some of the most able attorneys in Kentucky, there seems little room for doubt that Thornton's status as a "slave for life" was unquestioned by American
authorities at any level.

Thornton's petition again highlighted the strong support he
and his wife enjoyed among white Detroiters:

Your Petitioner begs leave Humbly to say, that his unfortunate situation and that of his wife excited the general Sympa-

thy of the white Inhabitants of Detroit, and this Sympathy
could not be concealed from the people of colour of the
place, and they unknown to your Petitioner entered into an
agreement to effect his rescue. On Sunday night last, a female friend was admitted into the prison by the Prison Jailer
to visit Your Petitioner's wife, and while there exchanged
Dress with her, and thus she made her escape.

Thornton did not admit in his petition that he had held a pistol in his own hand during the riot. He also disavowed prior
knowledge of any plans for his rescue. He did mention that the
two Upper Canadian judges François Bâby and George Jacob
disagreed as to whether or not he and his wife should be arrested
in Sandwich. The document then went on to describe how neither the Blackburns nor their friends had been able to find any
lawyer who would represent them in the case. Finally, playing on
the Canadian government's sensitivities in the matter, Blackburn
proffered his trump card. There is a distinctly Anglican flavor to
this part of the petition, which strongly echoes the rhythms of
the Book of Common Prayer, probably thanks to Johnson's litur-
gical background: "Your Petitioner is convinced that the object
of the Party is to have him and his wife carried back to Hopeless
Slavery, where complaints can neither be heard, nor grievances
redressed."

Hinting that the Lieutenant Governor, his Executive Council,
and the Attorney General of Upper Canada were being manipu-
lated to serve American interests was a shrewd move, and one
calculated to arouse patriotic ire in the hearts of loyal British subjects. Thornton went on to suggest that the only reason that the
Blackburns had been charged with a crime at all was to induce
the Upper Canadian government to send them back across the
border so Michigan officials could return them to their former
owners. He ended with an eloquent plea on behalf of his wife:

Your Petitioner therefore Humbly begs that Your Excellency
will be graciously pleased to permit him to pass his days in

this Land of Freedom, and in particular that his unfortunate Wife against whom there is not the slightest shadow of crime, except her exertions to escape from Slavery, may not be delivered up from under Your Excellency's protection, to those who are only exerting themselves to accomplish their own avaricious ends.

Your Petitioner further begs leave to enclose to Your Excellency a letter wherein it is stated that several respectable Witnesses are coming to this side to give evidence upon oath, in behalf of Your Petitioner.

Your Petitioner therefore Humbly craves that Your Excellency will suspend your Decision until such depositions may arrive.

And Your Excellency's Petitioner
as in Duty bound will ever pray
his
Thornton X Blackburn
Mark

Unfortunately, the letter bearing the names of the Blackburns' Detroit supporters has not been discovered in either Michigan or Upper Canadian records. But even the judicial and penal officials in Sandwich who were responsible for keeping the Blackburns in jail were signatories to Thornton's petition to Colborne. Among those who signed were George Jacob and two of his sons-in-law, Charles Askin and John Gowie Watson. Askin was the son of John Askin, perhaps the most successful fur trader at Detroit in his day and a Loyalist who removed to Sandwich when Detroit was transferred to American hands. His father had been one of the Detroit River district's leading slaveholders. A copy of Thornton's petition survives in Charles Askin's personal papers, so he too may have had a hand in its design. Other signatories included John Alexander Wilkinson, Dr. P. McMullins, Abraham Unsworth, and the prominent local merchant John Gentle, Sr. None of these men had cause to love the Americans. Wilkinson had been a hero of the British troops in the War of 1812 along the Detroit River frontier and was married to Sheriff William Hands's daughter, though not happily. Gentle was a Scot who crossed over from Detroit at the time of Jay's Treaty and became a dry-goods merchant. Conspicuous for its absence from the document was the name François Bâby. He remained adamant in his championship of slavery, despite the fact that other members of his own family were by this time staunchly abolitionist.

At about the same time Thornton's petition would have reached Colborne at York, another document was being presented to the Lieutenant Governor of Upper Canada. This was "The Petition of Madison Mason, Lewis Austin, Prince Williams, Peter Sans [sic], and Alexander Butler." The paper gave an abbreviated account of the events leading up to the riot, but, interestingly, called Thornton "Thornton Brown," using the surname of his owner, Susan Brown. Two of Thornton's rescuers were inexplicably missing from the petition. John Lloyd's name had been crossed out, both in the initial salutation and in the list of signatures ("marks") at the end, and the man known only as Beatty was not mentioned either. Dr. P. McMullins, who also signed as a witness, drafted the second petition.

The petition provided by Thornton's rescuers reiterated that "people of colour, were not the only ones, who sympathized with the unfortunate Prisoner." It also introduced the idea that some whites were at least complicit if not actively involved in the Blackburns' rescue, since "a great number of the white population of Detroit, encouraged your Petitioners, to extricate the unfortunate man from the jaws of Slavery." Of course, Lieutenant Governor John Colborne and Attorney General Jameson were already well aware of Frazier's and Cleland's involvement in the case, so the support of white Detroiters for the Blackburns and their friends was an established fact. The participation of whites *before* the riot was asserted by Frazier himself in his affidavit to the Upper Canadian magistrates, and confirmed by the *Democratic Free Press* account of the riot on June 19, 1833.

This second petition confirms that the members of Thornton's party could not hire legal counsel, since "the lawyers of Sandwich, as well as those of Detroit, were arrayed against your Petitioners." Thornton's rescuers then pleaded with Upper Canadian officials not to send them back to stand trial in Michigan. They stated bluntly that their own freedom was at stake. The document begs for clemency in light of the danger they faced in the United States because of the color of their skin:

> Should it be the unfortunate lot of your Petitioners, to be given up, to the Governor of Michigan Territory, they know not the moment, they may be seized upon, hurried away, and disposed of, like the beasts of the field; to be subject to the tortures, and tyranny, of the unfeeling slave-driver during their existence.
>
> We our Excellency's Petitioners, humbly implore your Excellency, not to send them to that land, where a Black face can have no guarantee against slavery.

The stage was now set for a confrontation between Michigan and Upper Canada over the issue of the fugitive slave. The outcome of deliberations over the case of Thornton and Lucie Blackburn and their friends would determine not only their future liberty or bondage but also whether the Underground Railroad would continue to run to its terminus north of the border in what remained of British North America.

ONE MORE RIVER TO CROSS

Canada was a sort of land of Canaan to the Negro. He sang, sighed, and longed to get there, as did the Jews for Zion, as they wept by the rivers of Babylon. In spite of its distance from the South, nothing but physical and brute force could prevent their striving to get there. What but the Providence of God can account for the fact that Washington and his contemporaries did not extend their dominion farther north?

—S. J. CELESTINE EDWARDS, 1891

THE BLACKBURN INCIDENT brought about a genuine crisis in relations between the United States and Canada. The situation was more critical than was evident at the time for, as it turned out, the decisions made in the case would dictate how the British colonial governors of Upper Canada responded to similar American demands for the entire period before the Civil War. For weeks, officials deliberated the matter in the Executive Council chambers at York. The Executive Council carefully weighed strict adherence to Upper Canadian principles against what disagreeable results rebuffing the Americans might produce.

Everyone involved was aware that precedents were being established. The Blackburn extradition case was the first test of the new Fugitive Offenders Act, and its outcome was crucial to future relations with the United States. Crafted by Chief Justice John Beverley Robinson at the request of Sir John Colborne and passed in February 1833, just a few months before the Detroit riots, the law was based on three simple principles. First, it required that there be reasonable proof that a crime had been committed. Escaping from slavery did not in itself constitute a crime, since slaves could not steal themselves in a place that did not recognize them as slaves. Furthermore, the crime had to be of a capital nature, that is, one punishable under British law by death, flogging, or incarceration at hard labor. Again, mere flight from a slave master did not qualify unless the exodus was accompanied by a misdeed of a more serious nature, such as murder, mayhem, theft, rape, or, as was the accusation leveled at the Blackburns, inciting civil disobedience. The last clause of the Fugitive Offenders Act, moreover, contained a loophole carefully crafted to avoid this very situation—the final decision in each case was left to the discretion of the Lieutenant Governor of the Province of Upper Canada. Even if all other terms were met, Sir John Colborne could still refuse to turn over the refugee, should he deem it "inexpedient" to do so.

Throughout these deliberations it was clear that only Thornton and his wife mattered in the dispute. Michigan's demands for the return of the other men involved in the riot were halfhearted; there was no discussion of their possible guilt or innocence. This is curious since all but one of them were probably runaway slaves. It was Thornton and Lucie Blackburn whose defiance of the Southern slaveocracy, unjustified capture, and subsequent sentencing by Judge Chipman in Detroit who had aroused a whole minority population to collective violence. Now, held in an Upper Canadian jail and the subject of formal extradition proceedings between the Michigan and the Canadian governments, the Blackburns had become pivotal in a subtle tug-of-war between the United States as a slaveholding nation and Upper Canada, the first colony in the British Empire to take steps to end slavery within its borders, and the place at the end of the Underground Railroad.

In the Executive Council chambers, the presiding council-lor was the Honorable and Venerable John Strachan. Strachan brought his considerable influence to bear on the Blackburns' behalf. A political conservative to the bone, Strachan was also a patriot who had personally confronted General Henry Dearborn during the April 1813 occupation of the Town of York by Amer-ican forces. The tall, lanky former schoolmaster had so berated the military commander that he won major concessions as to how York's townsfolk and their property would be treated. In this instance, Strachan had expressed his objections to returning Thornton and Lucie Blackburn to Michigan authorities from the outset. On July 16 he summed up the council's recommen-dations to the Lieutenant Governor: "Since the Law of this Province does not recognize the giving up of prisoners guilty of such offense as that said to have been committed . . . Your Excel-lency cannot in our judgment legally deliver up the persons de-manded."

Three days later, on July 19, 1833, Attorney General Jameson wrote up the formal opinion on which the Executive Council's decision had been based. The argument centered on not the Blackburns' guilt or innocence—they admitted to having escaped the custody of Sheriff Wilson—but whether such flight, or the Blackburns' supposed involvement in the subsequent violence, could be considered a capital crime in Canada. The attack on Sheriff Wilson was ignored in favor of information presented by Charles Cleland and Alexander Frazier of Detroit. They had help-fully pointed out the appropriate passages of U.S. law that sup-ported the Blackburns' innocence. Attorney General Jameson reiterated the facts of the case, and then exonerated Lucie Black-burn. He wrote, "There appears to be an error in the Deposition accompanying the Requisition." If she had already "eluded the Gaoler in disguise" and then sought asylum in Upper Canada, how could Mrs. Blackburn be considered "one of the persons as-sisting in the Riot and Rescue?" She had not been in Detroit and did not play a part in her husband's rescue. Since escaping the custody of an officer of the law, justified or not, was a "mere" misdemeanor rather than a capital crime, Mrs. Blackburn could not be guilty of any extraditable offense, as far as Jameson was concerned.

As for Thornton, Jameson stated that he did "not attach much weight" to Frazier's contention that the Blackburns' incarceration by Sheriff Wilson had been illegal in the first place. The real matter at hand was Thornton's escape from the Detroit jail. The terms of the Fugitive Slave Law stipulated that the alleged offender could be extradited for nothing less than a capital crime, and neither jail breaking on Thornton's part nor escaping the custody of Sheriff Wilson, lawful or not, was a capital crime, even under U.S. law. Jameson pointed out that the penalty in the United States for rescuing a fugitive from a slave owner, agent, or attorney was a fine of $500. In other words, this, too, was a misdemeanor, not a crime punishable by "Death, corporal punishment, by Pillory or Whipping, or by confinement at hard labor." Certainly escaping from the agent of a slave owner could not be a crime under Canadian law and therefore could not be a consideration in the case.

Jameson informed the Lieutenant Governor that in the absence of any legal reason to retain the Blackburns in custody, the laws of the province required that they be set free. His letter to Colborne dated July 16, 1833, put this in quite strong terms:

> Sir, I take the liberty of reminding you that in consequence of the decision of the Governor in Council that the law did not warrant His Excellency in complying with the requisition of the Acting Governor of Michigan for the restoration of Thornton and other fugitives committed by M. Bâby to custody at Sandwich, it becomes necessary to apprize the Sheriff, who has only authority to detain them "until an order had been made upon such requisition," that such an order has been made and that it is against their being delivered up.

Sir John Colborne ordered the magistrates of the Western District to arrange for the Blackburns' discharge. The Blackburns and their rescuers had been incarcerated since June 17, 1833, and released following Attorney General Robert Simpson Jameson's provision of his first opinion in the matter to the Executive Council. This was read in the House on July 15, 1833, with the Reverend John Strachan in the chair. He presented Sir John Colborne with the Executive Council's recommendations on July 16. The Blackburns and their rescuers thus were probably set free about a week later, on or about July 22, 1833, allowing time for the transmission of such orders from the Lieutenant Governor's residence at York to William Hands as sheriff of the Western District at Sandwich. Thornton and his wife, Lewis Austin, Prince Williams, Peter Sands, Alexander Butler, John Lloyd, Beatty, and Madison Mason were all released from the Sandwich jail. They were free at last.

After their release the Blackburns traveled to Amherstburg to join their friends. At least one of their fellow prisoners, Prince Williams, accompanied them. In the little town on the Detroit River where they would spend the next year, the Blackburns were reunited with Mr. and Mrs. French. Despite their undoubted relief at their release, one can well imagine their distress when they learned of the harsh sentences handed down in Detroit to some of the men and women who had come to their rescue. That it was their own advocate and friend Alexander D. Frazier who was required to prosecute the dozens of Michigan blacks who had so readily leaped to their assistance was an exquisite irony that was surely not lost on Lucie or her husband.

The event that freed Thornton and Lucie from the Detroit jail would go down in Detroit history as the Blackburn Riots of 1833, the first racial riots in Detroit. In their wake, refugees from Detroit continued to move across the border into Upper Canada. Support for the Blackburn rescue was far from universal in Michigan; the majority of whites grew progressively more hostile as the summer of 1833 wore on. Some of the black Detroiters who took refuge in Canada at the time would eventually return to reclaim the homes and shops they had toiled for years to obtain. But most would remain on the other side of the river, secure in the legal protection afforded black immigrants in the British colony. Undoubtedly some joined the cadre of committed antislavery workers who ran the Underground Railroad stations along the Detroit shore. Thornton and Lucie's entry into Upper Canada approximately coincided with the second wave of American blacks who immigrated to the British Colony; in addition to growing numbers of escaping slaves, there was the exodus of free blacks from Virginia, Maryland, and other states in the wake of the Nat Turner rebellion of 1831. Tightening restrictions on everyday life, increasing violence, and the exclusion of free people from trades and crafts that they had previously practiced sent hundreds of families north. Within a few short years of the Blackburn rescue, this part of the Detroit River boundary between Canada and the United States would be known as the most heavily traveled crossing point on the Underground Railroad to Canada.

While Lucie and Thornton stayed in Amherstburg recovering from their ordeal, diplomatic correspondence between Michigan and Upper Canada continued to fly back and forth. The Blackburns were probably entirely unaware that ongoing and very complicated negotiations threatened their continued freedom. The couple's rocky path to freedom had one more obstacle.

Stevens Thomson Mason had, all along, been serving in an acting capacity on behalf of Michigan's real territorial governor, George B. Porter. Porter owned extensive farmlands in Pennsylvania and spent a good deal of his governorship away from Michigan, so he was not in town at the time of the Blackburn incident. Upon his return to Detroit in July 1833, the governor reviewed the contentious fugitive slave case that had caused such an uproar. Convinced of its merits and outraged at the Canadian response, he immediately renewed demands that Upper Canada extradite Thornton, his wife, and the others who had accompanied them to Sandwich. In his letter to Colborne, dated August 12, 1833, Governor Porter threatened retribution if Upper Canada again rebuffed Michigan's request:

> The great object of the present application is, that these Individuals may be surrendered to the proper authority for trial and if found guilty, suffer the punishment due their crimes. But independent of this consideration, I am desirous of placing the whole facts before you and obtaining the decision of your government thereon, to know what the rule of our intercourse in matters of this kind shall be. It must be reciprocal.

Porter was clearly furious. He attached a raft of supporting documentation to his letter. All the original depositions filed before Judge Chipman in the Blackburns' first trial, as well as the statements of Thomas Rogers, Benjamin Weir, Talbot Oldham, and the Blackburns' venal landlord, James Slaughter, that had been put forward in the Blackburns' original June 15 trial, were included, as were the original arrest warrants for the couple. Sheriff Wilson had sufficiently recovered by this time to make a formal statement, and although he always maintained he had no recollection of the riot itself, he nevertheless provided a detailed description of the attack he had suffered, based on descriptions provided by his deputy and the city jailer. He accepted Deputy Sheriff McArthur's account of the events and confirmed that "Thornton was present aiding and abetting in the said riot and rescue." McArthur also issued a new affidavit in which he gave a fuller and more colorful outline of the day's events. It was also more damning. In the document dated August 10, 1833, McArthur stated that Sheriff Wilson had several times gone into the crowd of people milling about the foot of the jailhouse steps to try to defuse the situation. Later, on the steps, Thornton brandished his pistol first at the jailer, Goodell, and then at Sheriff Wilson, while the crowd urged Thornton to "shoot him—shoot him—

blow him through!" The sheriff was "holding the said Prisoner Blackburn fast when a number of the said Blacks and mulattos among which the deponent was able to identify one Lewis Austin rushing forward seized upon the said prisoner Blackburn."

McArthur implicated Lucie Blackburn (calling her Ruthie), swearing she had been active in whipping up the crowd before the jailhouse, although, in rather contradictory fashion, he admitted that she had already escaped from the jail the day before the riot, and that she was in Canada at the time it occurred. Perhaps he thought she was there in spirit, for McArthur painted Thornton's wife as a vengeful Fury:

> The Deponent further declares that he verily believes that Rutha Blackburn, the wife of the Prisoner, was active in exciting the said Blacks and mulattoes to assist in the rescue of her husband, the said Thornton Blackburn, that while in custody she threatened him the said deponent, and declared that she would be revenged—that if she could not do it herself she would get others to do so—and this deponent further declares that he believes that the said Rutha was an accessory to the concealment and the harboring of the said prisoner Thornton Blackburn after his rescue as aforesaid, having previously to his rescue by artifice and fraud made her escape from the said Jail.

Governor Porter's requisition came before the Executive Council of Upper Canada at the Town of York on Tuesday, August 27, 1833. Attorney General Jameson was asked to deliver his opinion on whether the newly framed charges against the Blackburns met the criteria for criminal extradition under Upper Canadian law. Jameson submitted his brief on September 12. This time the decision was more equivocal. While the Executive Council dithered, Colborne sent an order that all the papers pertaining to the case be sent to the Lieutenant Governor's office. John Strachan, who was chairing the Executive Council, asked whether Attorney General Jameson believed "if a similar outrage had been committed in this Province, the offender or offenders would be liable to undergo any of the punishments stated in the Act passed last session." He was referring to the Fugitive Offenders Act. Jameson tabled his earlier brief of July 12, but on September 17 he responded to the specific question, reluctantly admitting "the forcible rescue from the custody of the Sheriff of this Province, attended with the aggravated circumstances detailed in the affidavits of John M. Wilson and Alexander McArthur . . . would undoubtedly subject the offender and those actively aiding and abetting him to the gravest punishment in the Act, death alone excepted."

Accordingly, the council recommended to the Lieutenant Governor, who was present in the chamber, that "such assistance as is authorized by the Law be furnished to the agents of the Governor of Michigan in apprehending and committing to secure custody, Beatty, Thornton Blackburn, Lewis Austin, Prince Williams, Peter Sands, Alexander Butler, John Lloyd and Madison Mason." This Order in Council, accepted by Colborne, did not include provision for the arrest of Mrs. Blackburn. "With respect to Rutha Blackburn, the Council do not consider the proof that she was aiding and abetting in the rescue, as sufficient to warrant her restoration to the Government of Michigan."

Upper Canada's Executive Council was careful to add a caveat alluding to the fact that the Blackburns and most of their party were fugitive slaves:

> The Council beg it to be understood that they have not in the slightest degree been influenced by the circumstances of the parties being claimed as Slaves, a condition which the Laws of this Province do not recognize and which they could not under any circumstances admit as a reason for delivering up Fugitives from the neighboring States.

The redoubtable Reverend Strachan was not satisfied with this. To preempt the Blackburns' arrest, he suggested that "as the question involves matters of great importance in our relations with a neighboring state," it should be turned over to the Chief Justice and his court for an opinion.

On September 27, Chief Justice John Beverley Robinson and Judges Levius Peters Sherwood and James Buchanan Macaulay of the Court of King's Bench gave their own response. The characters of these three men are of some interest: Robinson was known to be fair; his education at the hands of John Strachan meant he was influenced by his principles. As Chief Justice he could always be counted on to uphold the strict rule of law. Sherwood, like Robinson, came from a slaveholding family of Loyalists. The Sherwoods settled in Prescott, in the eastern part of what today is Ontario. He was staunchly conservative, supported the missionary work of the Anglican Church, and tended toward mercy in his judgments. Justice Macaulay's father was a Scot who had been regimental surgeon to Lieutenant Governor Simcoe and stationed at Fort York in 1793. Macaulay, like Robinson, had been schooled by Strachan. Although his parents had brought slaves with them after the American Revolution, he had served along the Niagara frontier in the War of 1812 alongside black troops, and at this very moment was in the process of subdividing his family's suburban Toronto estate into lots, many of which were purchased by African Canadians and African Americans. This district came to be known as Macaulay Town, and later St. John's Ward, and was, from the 1830s on, the area where most black immigrants to Toronto settled. In fact, it had been Judge Macaulay's questioning of the casual extradition arrangements between Western District and Michigan officials that had resulted in Chief Justice Robinson's drafting of the Fugitive Offenders Act in the first place. This, in turn, formalized the conditions under which extradition could take place, and severely restricted the chances of a runaway slave being sent back to his or her master by an Upper Canadian official or magistrate.

The "Report of the Judges" filed by the Court of King's Bench on September 27, 1833, began by citing the Fugitive Offenders Act and making a point of confirming the discretionary powers of

Upper Canada's Lieutenant Governor and his council in any extradition case. Robinson, Sherwood, and Macaulay thus made it known that they did not consider the material provided by Governor Porter sufficient to warrant the release of Thornton and Lucie Blackburn and the rest of their party to the tender mercies of Michigan justice. The Court of King's Bench then responded directly to Porter's veiled threats regarding the need for a mutual agreement between Michigan Territory and Upper Canada in the matter of criminal extradition: "It is evident that the conduct of this and of other Governments in respect to the delivering up of offenders can be no further reciprocal towards each other, than the laws of each will allow." Furthermore,

> it has not escaped our attention as a peculiar feature of this case that two of the persons whom the Government of this Province is requested to deliver up are persons recognized by the Government of Michigan as slaves and that it appears upon these documents that if they should be delivered up they would by the laws of the United States be forced into a state of Slavery from which they had escaped two years ago when they fled from Kentucky to Detroit; that if they should be sent to Michigan and upon trial be convicted of this Riot, and punished they would after undergoing their punishments be subject to be taken by their masters and continued in a state of Slavery for life.

The Court of King's Bench reminded the Executive Council that the prisoners had already been "apprehended and in custody in this Province upon this same charge and liberated by the decision of the Governor and Council." Since no "new and strong evidence" had been presented by Michigan's territorial governor and "by mere accident" no "official or legal formality" had been overlooked, the council questioned how would it look if the Blackburn party was again taken into custody? They also dealt with the motives of the men implicated in the attack on Sheriff

Wilson. They ruled that, since the mob's objective was clearly "the rescue of the Prisoner rather than to take the life of the Sheriff," there had at no point been an intent to kill. The whole affair had simply gotten out of hand in the heat of the moment.

The judges explicitly stated that the Blackburns' fugitive slave status had no bearing on the extradition case. Slaves or not, they would have to be extradited if they had committed a capital crime, despite Upper Canada's long history of protecting African American refugees. But neither were the three jurists insensible to what would become of the Blackburns if they were returned to Michigan. Chief Justice Robinson and his two colleagues, in delicate legalese, skewered the real point home: if the Blackburns were found guilty of a crime in an American court, following their punishment they would be placed under the control of their owners and returned to a state of slavery, but "on the other hand if they should never be prosecuted or if they should be tried and acquitted this consequence would equally follow." No matter what the evidence presented or the outcome of any trial, Thornton, his wife, and the brave young men who crossed the river with him would be slaves for life.

Robinson, Sherwood, and Macaulay closed their report with the statement that they could not advise on any course that would accord greater punishment than could be "pursued with respect to free white persons under the same circumstances." This was an argument against the extradition of fugitive slaves that would be reiterated many times over the succeeding years. The Executive Council then made its final recommendations and urged Colborne to use his discretionary power to refuse Governor Porter's demands. The very next day, September 28, 1833, Colborne wrote to Porter with his decision—he declined to return the fugitives on the grounds that if he did, their ultimate fate, whether guilty or innocent of inciting a riot, would be a return to bondage.

The Blackburns' plight may have occasioned the first runaway slave case tried under the Fugitive Offenders Act, but it was far from the last. Key arguments from the Blackburn decision were repeated in several instances over the next three decades: that the crime the runaway had allegedly committed had to be of a capital nature under Canadian law; that self-theft could not in and of itself be considered a crime in Upper Canada, where slavery did not exist; and that British colonial officials had to be fully convinced that the extradition demand was genuinely based on the desire to prosecute a fugitive for his criminal act, rather than simply to return a runaway slave to an American slave owner.

On the U.S. side of the border, the Blackburn incident also continued to have repercussions. Detroit City Attorney Alexander Frazier was attacked for his role in helping the Blackburns. A series of unpleasant articles in the press were deflected by the good offices of his friend Charles Cleland, although Frazier's reputation suffered for some time. Critical pieces appeared in the *Detroit Journal and Michigan Advertiser* on July 29, 1833, and in the *Democratic Free Press* on August 7, 1833. These, among other things, accused Frazier of making Thornton sign over his entire property to him before he would agree to undertake the runaway slave's defense. No record of landownership by the Blackburns, or the "Smiths," for that matter, in Detroit has been discovered, so this may have been simple libel. Subsequently a special committee of the city council was struck to investigate Frazier's extraordinary behavior when he offered his assistance to the Upper Canadian government in developing a defense against the Blackburns' extradition. No decision ever appeared in the printed minutes of the Detroit City Council, although the matter was deferred several times. When it came time for his reappointment, however, Frazier quietly stepped down. In later years he would serve as head of the city's water commission and he also held other public offices. But even as the most respected jurist in the city for many years, Frazier was never again entrusted with a position where he could put his own concern for the welfare of the city's black community above what the Detroit City Council considered his civic responsibilities. And although Charles Cleland continued to assist fugitive slaves seeking to avoid extradition from Canada, Alexander D. Frazier was absent from at least official efforts to do so.

Some of the Detroit blacks prosecuted by Frazier settled in Amherstburg along with Lucie and Thornton. When the Blackburns and their friends came to Amherstburg, fugitive slaves were about 10 percent of the local population. Close enough to the Michigan shore that sometimes slaves, desperate to evade pursuit, swam the great river at its narrowest point, Amherstburg would come to be called the "main terminus of the Underground Railroad." The intrepid British traveler Harriet Martineau recorded her impressions of these border lands in 1838:

> The finest harvest-field of romance perhaps in the world is the frontier between the United States and Canada . . . I remember observing to a friend in the ferry-boat, when we were crossing the Niagara from Lewistown to Queenstown, that it seemed very absurd, on looking at the opposite banks of the river, to think that, while the one belonged to the people who lived on it, the other was called the property of a nation three thousand miles off, the shores looking so much alike as they do. My friend replied with a smile, "Runaway slaves see a great difference." "That they do," cried the ferryman, in a tone of the deepest earnestness. He said that the leap ashore of an escaped slave is a sight unlike any other that can be seen.

The bonds forged so early between Canadian black settlements along the Detroit River and the communities on the American side were never broken. As time went on, the Underground Railroad advanced in structure and complexity along the Michigan shore. In Detroit, the Lightfoots, Frenches, Willoughbys, and other families the Blackburns had known while they lived there would take leading roles. Important events, such as the anniversary of West Indian emancipation, which took place on August 1 each year, were regularly celebrated in common, sometimes taking the form of festive waterborne processions on the Detroit

River. Community leaders in Amherstburg, Sandwich, and other parts of Essex County were supportive of efforts by Detroit's Second Baptist Church and Michigan's vigilance committees, established in the late 1830s to protect and assist fugitive slaves on their way to Canada. These communities received the refugees spirited across the Detroit River by their Michigan friends, providing them with clothing, food, and sometimes short-term employment so they could move farther into the interior of the province. Central to the work on both sides of the border was the black church; from that institution grew the benevolent, self-help, educational, and political protest organizations that together formed the infrastructure for African American and African Canadian society.

None of this is to say that prejudice the Blackburns encountered in their new home was not very strong in this part of Upper Canada. Benjamin Lundy, a Quaker abolitionist who visited the province in 1832 to examine the condition of resettled fugitive slaves, attributed this to American immigrants who imported their racism with them. He said:

> It may not be amiss to observe that the white emigrants from the United States retain all the prejudices here that they formerly had against coloured people in their native country . . . if our good Republicans choose to leave their "free" government where they can tyrannize over the coloured man with impunity and take up their abode among Monarchists, where all are "free and equal" they would act wisely to assume fewer airs, and submit cheerfully, like good "liege subjects" to the regulations adopted by the government of their choice.

Although racism was hardly confined to white former Americans living in the Western District, it is true that Thornton and Lucie probably got their first taste of black Canada's response to such prejudice while living there. While African Canadians were legally entitled to full civic participation with whites, on occasion they were refused for jury duty, for instance, and their children were regularly excluded from the public schools. People experienced insults and sometimes even violence when they sought accommodations in steamboats, inns, and, later, trains. Blacks living in Canada organized to protest white attempts to discriminate against them. Josiah Henson, who became a respected community leader among African Canadians, wrote in 1852:

> Not to speak of the prejudice manifested in the every day intercourse of the black and white man in Canada, let the coloured man but leave his home on business or pleasure, and let him betake himself to the public conveyances, and he will, at once, be met with a prejudice which will be open to the notice of every observer . . . it is the invariable rule to refuse [the black man's] association with the white at the dinner table, in the salon of the steam vessel.

Samuel Ringgold Ward, writing in the same year to the *Voice of the Fugitive* in an article entitled "Canadian Negro Hate," said that racism in Canada was worse than that in the United States because it was so *polite*. Partly as a result of this hostility, African Americans and African Canadians continued to settle in districts where other black families already lived, for mutual assistance and protection and in order to pool their resources for the development of churches, schools, and other amenities.

The Amherstburg black community already had its own Baptist congregation, although the church was not built until 1842. The Amherstburg Baptist Association was founded in 1841. The confirmation of their mutual interests and shared concerns, this network of black congregations in Michigan and what is now Ontario was actually initiated by Detroit's Second Baptist Church, spearheaded by the Lightfoot and French families. Not only a religious organization but also an antislavery group, it was dedicated to moral reform, including the promotion of temperance. Its creation coincided with the founding of several other activist organizations in which these same individuals were involved; the Detroit Vigilant Committee, for instance, was basically an Underground Railroad group dedicated to the assistance of fugitives trying to reach Canada. William Lambert, Benjamin Willoughby's son-in-law, was its president.

While records for this early period are scanty, tax and census documents suggest that Thornton and Lucie may have stayed with the family of another fugitive slave named Nelson Brown while they lived in Amherstburg. In 1833, Brown was a twenty-three-year-old immigrant from the United States. He had lived in Upper Canada with his wife, Ellen, since 1827. He was literate and philosophically had much in common with the Blackburns and their Detroit friends; he, too, was engaged in self-help and antislavery activities for several decades. In 1841, Brown would have known the Lightfoots and Frenches well, for he became involved in the development of the Amherstburg Baptist Association, and his name appeared several times over the years chairing local meetings and assisting in the work of fugitive slave reception. In the 1840s, he was in the forefront of a conflict in black communities across the province over the issue of "begging," that is, the solicitation in the United States and Britain of funds, clothing, and books for the benefit of "poor fugitive slaves in Canada." Some of the efforts were well intentioned, others outright fraud. All of them enraged the proud and self-sufficient farmers of the Amherstburg area. They eventually would establish an organization called the "True Band" to promote self-reliance and self-help in black Canada. Brown was corresponding secretary for the first Amherstburg True Band, formed in March 1855, and the movement spread across the southern part of the province.

Properties had been available for black settlement in the back ranges of Amherstburg since the period immediately following the War of 1812, largely through the kind offices of British half-pay officer Charles Stuart. He had divided part of his thousand-acre land grant among would-be black settlers, but left

Amherstburg in 1819 to work on behalf of antislavery in New
York State at the Oneida Institute, where he encountered the
young Theodore Dwight Weld, who would become a leading antislavery figure. Then he went to England, his intent to undermine the fund-raising efforts of the American Colonization
Society. This all took place well before the Blackburns' time in
the Western District, but Stuart's legacy lived on, and they would
come to know him when he returned to Canada in 1851 to take
up the antislavery cause once more.

The Blackburns' sojourn in Amherstburg would prove to be
short, but the community continued to succor those in need
throughout the years leading up to the Civil War.

As a river-port town, Amherstburg had plenty of employment
for newcomers, including working at the dockyards, fishing for
whitefish, an important local export, or laboring in the three limestone quarries of Anderdon Township to the north of Amherstburg. Some were also engaged in farming, the main pillar of the
local economy. It was former Virginia and Kentucky bondsmen
living on Stuart's lands who introduced the cultivation of tobacco
as a commercial crop into what is now Southwestern Ontario.
Joseph Pickering traveled in the area during the harvest of 1826,
writing home to England that "black slaves who have run away
from their masters in Kentucky, arrive in Canada almost weekly,
where they are free and work at raising tobacco; I believe they introduced the practice. One person will attend and manage the
whole process of four acres, planting, hoeing, budding, etc., during the summer."

The Anderdon quarries produced building stone in such quantities that special wharves were being constructed along the
riverfront above the town to facilitate shipping the lime and cut
stone down the Detroit River to the port cities along the Great
Lakes. Amherstburg's first reeve (a position equivalent to a
mayor in a rural district), John Sloan, and his wife were well
known in the district for their assistance to runaway blacks. The
Sloans owned limestone quarries and hired a succession of runaway slaves at the stoneworks. They also sold and leased land to

African Canadians. In fact, they and an English gentleman farmer who lived near their quarries, Rowland Wingfield, privately supported a racially integrated private school on the Sloans' Anderdon lands. Wingfield also encouraged African Canadian settlement on his extensive properties in the district. Thornton had worked for Thomas Coquillard in Detroit as a stonemason, and, since so many other American fugitives worked in the Anderdon quarries north of Amherstburg, it seems likely Thornton did so as well.

Of the men who risked their lives and freedom when they snatched Thornton from the jailhouse door and carried him off to Canada, little is known. Only Prince Williams settled at Amherstburg, where he would spend the rest of his life working as a stonemason. He rented a house in town from John Sloan and his wife and attended the Baptist church but seems not to have involved himself further in the very active antislavery and fugitive slave assistance movements operating in the area. Alexander Butler was the son of William Butler, the first black to join the Baptist church in Detroit and the only member of the group who was not a fugitive slave. He eventually returned to Detroit, where he lived with his widowed mother and worked as a barber. Butler was never tried for his part in the Blackburn Riots of 1833. Lewis Austin also returned to Detroit, but died in 1835 from the bullet wound suffered on the day of the Blackburn escape. John Lloyd, Beatty, and Madison Mason disappeared from the historical record entirely; it is possible that Lloyd died soon after his time at Sandwich, for his name was removed from the petition the other men sent to Sir John Colborne requesting clemency and he had not made his mark on the document.

What became of Peter Sands remained a mystery for nearly twenty years. Research into the history of the William and Susannah Steward Home in Niagara-on-the-Lake, near Niagara Falls, brought to light details of black life in the district before the Civil War. The restored cottage was built in the 1830s in the "colored village" on the edge of the Fort George Military Reserve. It turned out that Steward, who was a teamster, later subdivided his property. One-quarter of his lot was sold to a black barber by the name of Peter Sands, the same man involved in the Blackburn rescue. Sands operated a barbershop near the center of town and attended the local Anglican church. He built a small house on his property, which he occupied until about 1845, when he moved to the village of Thorold and provided barbering services in a shop on the town square for the benefit of Irish workers constructing the Welland Canal. According to the 1861 census of Canada, Sands was fifty years old, which would make him a contemporary of Blackburn's at the time of the Detroit riots.

Pursuing their new lives in Canada, the Blackburns could finally breathe the free air of the British province in the knowledge that their safety was assured and their liberty guaranteed by the laws of the Province and the goodwill of the Lieutenant Governor. Few slaveholders went to the trouble and expense that John Pope Oldham and Virgil McKnight were wiling to go to. But there were a number of other such cases. Not all of them ended as happily, as we will see, but there were victories for antislavery as well. The principles applied in the Blackburn case would recur in each subsequent suit, always with further refinements. Slaveholders, too, grew far more sophisticated in their attempts to convince the British colonial government of Upper Canada to hand back their absconding "property."

WRESTLING JACOB

A slave escaping bondage on his master's horse is a vicious struggle between two parties, of which the slave-owner is not only the aggressor, but the blackest criminal of the two. It is the case of the dealer in human flesh versus the stealer of horse-flesh . . . it is as much a theft in the slave walking from slavery to liberty in his master's shoes as riding on his master's horse; and yet surely a slave breaking out of his master's house is not guilty of the same burglary which a thief would commit who should force the same locks and bolts in order to break in.

—SIR FRANCIS BOND HEAD,
Lieutenant Governor of Upper Canada, 1837

THE FIRST CASE that followed the Blackburns' occurred a year later. Abraham Johnson, a runaway from Virginia, was apprehended at Sandwich on August 4, 1834. Again Stevens T. Mason, now the governor of Michigan Territory, tendered the formal extradition requisition. To justify his extradition, Johnson was accused of stealing the sorrel horse on which he escaped. Horse theft was a capital offense and therefore extraditable under Upper Canadian law. This time, it was Charles Elliot, a local justice of the peace, who acted as prosecutor.

Unlike George Jacob, Elliot had strong prejudices against the area's black settlers. In fact, it had been his summary return of two forgers—who happened to be black, but not fugitive slaves—to Michigan for trial in 1832 that prompted Judge Macaulay's call for the drafting of the Fugitive Offenders Act of 1833. Again, white antislavery factions in the Detroit community dispatched Charles Cleland to assist Upper Canada in finding grounds for their government's refusing the extradition request. Charles Elliot reported to officials at York that Cleland had already acted in such a capacity "for some blacks," and what was more, had actually thrown up in Elliot's law office while presenting his brief on Johnson's behalf. Since Cleland drank, this was possibly true, but Elliot's missive also stated, quite disingenuously, that no man as upright and respectable as his Virginian client would perjure himself to "regain a slave, a slave who, it must be known, will burst his fetters again at the very first opportunity." Despite Elliot's interference—he hosted Johnson's owner at his home during the proceedings and cared for him through an illness as well as acting as his attorney—the Executive Council decided that Johnson's only motive in stealing the horse was to facilitate his escape, and, since escaping from slavery was not illegal under British colonial law, he was set free.

The next major dispute arose over the extradition of Solomon Moseby. This was the first of two serious attempts to overturn Canada's policy of protecting former American slaves. In Moseby's case he had actually stolen the horse on which he fled. Since horse theft was indeed a capital crime under British law, he met the terms of Upper Canada's Fugitive Offenders Act for extradition to the United States. The Kentucky fugitive was discovered in 1837 living at Niagara. This time it was the governor of Kentucky who demanded his extradition. Moseby's Upper Canadian attorney maintained that David Castleman of Fayette County, Kentucky, had come to Canada to recover his lost human property, not his horse, and that the whole matter was a smoke screen to trick Upper Canada into giving up legitimate refugees and to establish a legal precedent that would favor slaveholders in the future. This was probably true: Castleman was a wealthy horse breeder from Lexington—his Castleton Farm is still famous for its saddlebred horses—and his nephew was John Cabell Breckinridge, a hard-line pro-slavery man who would one day be vice president in Buchanan's administration, and later an opponent of Abraham Lincoln for leadership of the Republican party. Effectively, Castleman and the four men who came to Canada with him represented a slaveholder assault against Canada's willingness to protect fugitive slaves. It was only one day after he had filed his claim for Moseby in the Niagara court that Castleman went to Hamilton, at the western end of Lake Ontario, to claim a second runaway. In both cases, the charge was horse theft.

Upper Canada's new Attorney General, C. A. Hagerman, had initially been inclined to turn Moseby over to Castleman. After receiving petitions from literally hundreds of people, black and white, on Moseby's behalf, Hagerman looked deeper into the case and discovered that no charges had been laid in the case in Kentucky until just a few months earlier. Yet the alleged crime was more than four years old. Moseby's Niagara attorney pointed out that it was highly unlikely a prominent Kentuckian like Castleman would employ four other men to travel all the way to Canada, at a cost of about $400, to retrieve a horse worth only $150 and punish the man who had stolen it. Sir John Colborne had departed the province by this time, and Sir Francis Bond Head, perhaps the least able Lieutenant Governor Upper Canada ever had, while sympathetic to fugitive slaves in general, was busy at the time with events leading up to what would, in December 1837, become the Upper Canadian Rebellion. Given Head's preoccupation, the Executive Council went ahead and recommended Solomon Moseby's extradition.

The decision touched off Upper Canada's first violent racial incident. In fact, the Moseby affair resembled the Blackburn rescue in several important ways. With Moseby in the Niagara jail, blacks from the area converged on Niagara and camped out around the prison. According to the Toronto-based *Colonial Advocate*, these "fine fellows . . . waited ten days and ten nights at the jailhouse door." Local whites favored Moseby and, while not daring to flout local authority directly, still offered food, lodging, and campsites for the protesters. The blacks were armed with pitchforks and shovels, sticks and stones, but not with guns. Should the constables plan to move Moseby, the women planned to block the bridge over which the group guarding the prisoner would have to pass, singing hymns.

When Moseby's jailers tried to remove him from the prison yard, a nervous sentry fired on the unarmed crowd. A brawl broke out while Moseby got away through the cornfields to safety. Robert Simpson Jameson's brilliantly literary wife, Anna Brownell Jameson, who was traveling in the district at the time, later wrote:

> It was the conduct of the women which, on this occasion excited the strongest surprise and interest . . . they had prevailed upon their husbands, brothers and lovers to use no arms, do no illegal violence, but to lose their lives rather than see their comrade taken by force across the line. One woman had seized the sheriff, and held him pinioned in her arms; another, on one of the artillery-men presenting his piece, and swearing that he would shoot her if she did not get out of his way, gave him only one glance of unutterable contempt, and with one hand knocking up his piece, and collaring him with the other, held him in such a manner as to prevent his firing.

The Niagara incident left two men dead, while as many of the blacks involved in Moseby's rescue as could be found were incarcerated. But Upper Canadian authorities had a more practical punishment for them than Detroit officials had devised in the wake of the Blackburn incident. Each male rioter was offered his freedom if he would serve in the militia that was being mustered to put down the Upper Canadian Rebellion, which had just broken out. These men would spend two years guarding the provincial borders against incursions of private militias raised on the U.S. side of the border to support the rebels over the winter of 1837–38. In American history books this conflict is known as the Patriot War. The Niagara black militia later kept the peace among the rowdy Irish workers along the Welland Canal that bisected the Niagara Peninsula. Solomon Moseby escaped to England but returned to Upper Canada some years later, where no obvious efforts were ever made to recapture him. Sir Francis Bond Head had been very much torn in the matter. He later recommended to Lord Glenelg, Britain's secretary of state for the colonies:

> Giving up a slave for trial to American laws is, in fact, giving him back to his former master; and therefore that until the republican authorities can separate trial from such unjust punishment that, however willing we may be to give up a man to the former, we are justified in refusing to give him up to the latter, unless sufficient security be entered into in this province, that the person delivered up for trial shall be brought back into Upper Canada, as soon as his trial or the punishment awarded by it shall be concluded.

This was not at all what American authorities had in mind. And there was another case in the offing. Almost at the same time as the Niagara riots, Kentucky runaway Jesse Happy was apprehended at the request of none other than David Castleman. Happy was jailed in Hamilton while the governor of Kentucky demanded his extradition, again on the grounds that the runaway slave had stolen a horse. However, it turned out that Happy was an honest man and had left his master's horse, bridle, and saddle behind in Perrysburg, Ohio, on the U.S. side of the border, before he crossed into Canada. He had even had a friend write to his owner to tell him where to find his property. The Hamilton black community mounted a protest against his arrest, and petitions were taken up and forwarded to Bond Head, who turned the matter over to the British Colonial Office.

Following the logic of Bond Head expressed above, the British Colonial Office consulted its legal advisers in the matter. Their response to the Upper Canadian request for advice was to point out that if false charges were brought in Upper Canada, the accuser would be liable for prosecution on a charge of perjury, but that this was not the case when an American slaveholder made his accusation from the safety of a U.S. courtroom. Therefore, in no case ought a runaway be returned to the United States without the charges being proven in an Upper Canadian court. Furthermore, if a slave had committed a crime in order to facilitate his escape, then it was his motive that needed to be considered: Lord Glenelg, the Colonial Secretary, confirmed that since Happy had stolen the horse in order to escape from slavery, and had neither kept the horse nor profited in any way from the theft except by achieving a successful flight, he had not committed a crime that would be considered actionable under British law. The Executive Council had already reached the same conclusion and freed Happy before the British response had been received.

The possibility of being charged with perjury would henceforth significantly increase both the cost and the risk incurred by Southern slave owners trying to get their slaves retained. There was now a very real possibility of an owner presenting a trumped-up charge as grounds for criminal extradition being charged and incarcerated in a Canadian prison. However, in 1841 the justice system was again put to the test. Upper and Lower Canada had just been joined under a single governor in the Act of Union, and Upper Canada became known as Canada West. The government was itinerant, sitting at Toronto (the old Town of York), at Kingston at the eastern end of Lake Ontario, and at Montreal. Nelson Hackett's was the landmark case where the fugitive slave was actually guilty of the crime of which he had been accused. He was also the only black refugee Canada ever returned to the United States in a formal criminal extradition procedure. The case involved a number of people familiar from the Blackburns' experience, and the whole incident again took place on the Detroit River border. It demonstrates the level of involvement in Upper Canadian affairs by African American activists living in Michigan, and also provides further clues as to the personal sentiments of members of the Sandwich white elite regarding slavery.

When Hackett escaped from Fayetteville, in northwestern Arkansas, he took not only his master's racehorse, beaver coat, and $100, but also a gold watch and a saddle stolen from two local white families. Only ten days after his arrival at Chatham, Canada West, his owner found him and had him arrested. Beaten about the head with the handle of a large whip, and accused of a number of crimes, the fugitive was taken to Sandwich and imprisoned at the slaveholder's request. Yet again, an acting governor of Michigan, now James Wright Gordon, issued a criminal extradition requisition on behalf of a Southern slaveholder. Hackett was brought before Western District judges while his owner, Alfred Wallace, engaged a prominent local attorney and traveled to Kingston to lay his case directly before the new Governor-General of Canada, Charles Bagot. Bagot, for his part, had instructions to keep the United States happy in the wake of the cross-border issues aroused by the 1837 Rebellion. Unfortunately for Hackett, he took his orders all too literally.

The stolen items were indeed found in Hackett's possession in Chatham, but, probably on the advice of Chief Justice Robinson, who had earlier expressed his concern that the Upper Canadian government use caution in setting precedents regarding fugitive slave reception, lest actual felons be welcomed into the province, Bagot hesitated before making a decision. Attorney General William H. Draper and the Upper Canadian Legislative Council were also reluctant to proceed, and the case dragged on for months. It was discovered that Hackett had not actually been indicted in Arkansas, the jurisdiction in which the offense was allegedly committed, so in November 1841, his owner obtained a requisition from the governor of Arkansas.

Several members of the Detroit Vigilant Committee attended

Nelson Hackett's trial in Sandwich before the Court of King's Bench to ensure that he would not be sent secretly back over the border without due process. Their suspicions were well founded. This time, though, there is evidence of considerable collusion on behalf of the aggrieved slave owner on the part of members of the Western District's white elite. Again, the faithful advocate of the fugitive, Charles Cleland, went to Sandwich to attempt to plead the Hackett case. Then, late one night, a local ferry owner who had lived for a time near Hackett's Arkansas home was secretly authorized to row the runaway across the river to America, and to hand him over to be incarcerated in the Detroit jail. The Detroit attorney and abolitionist Charles H. Stewart, who had been on hand to examine Hackett's case file for any flaw or loophole that might save him, wrote to the wealthy American Quaker abolitionist Lewis Tappan of the American Anti-Slavery Society on August 9, 1842:

> I have no doubt that Hackett was the victim of a conspiracy, among the Canadians and his captors. This restoration to captivity . . . was invaluable to men, so offended by the escape of slaves, and who would thus be enabled to exhibit their power as over-reaching even British protection . . . this of course paralyses all effort at escape, as proving that there is safety in no place . . .
>
> I believe . . . the frontier authorities were to use and did use their influence with Sir Charles Bagot and that they were to be well paid provided that the surrender was made. I suspect as participants in this, the Justice, the Jailor, Mr. Prince (the Queen's District Counsel), and also perhaps Mr. Bâby, the alleged counsel of the prisoner . . . I am certain Mr. Prince was active in this matter.

Once in the hands of his Arkansas master the young man was never tried for his alleged thefts. Rather, Nelson Hackett was publicly and unmercifully whipped before being sold away to Texas.

Despite the clandestine nature of his transfer to American hands, the Detroit Vigilant Committee decided no overt action should be taken in light of the terrible price that Detroit blacks paid for their role in the Blackburns' rescue nearly nine years earlier. It was Madison Lightfoot who chaired the meetings of the committee on the evenings of February 14 and 22, 1842. The Detroit-based group protested by letter to British and Upper Canadian authorities, as did Upper Canadian and British abolitionists. An inquiry was launched in the House, and such was the public pressure on both sides of the Atlantic that on June 26, 1842, a missive was received by the Executive Council from the Colonial Office in Britain, demanding the names of all those concerned in the affair and further details of how a runaway who had sought asylum on British soil had come to be sent back to slavery. Detroit antislavery advocate Charles H. Stewart commented on September 2, 1842, in a letter to the *Anti-Slavery Reporter*, "The process of recovering fugitive slaves, even from the heretofore sacred palladium of British protection, by the cunning device of alleged crime, is becoming a matter of frequent occurrence, and is stimulated to increasing perfection by every successful issue."

The Nelson Hackett affair caused the British government considerable embarrassment. Hackett was handed over to his Arkansas masters just when Lord Ashburton and Daniel Webster, secretary of state in President John Tyler's administration, were engaged in delicate negotiations to set northern borders for Maine and Minnesota and finalize arrangements for the mutual extradition of criminals between Canada and the United States. Britain had also just adamantly refused to return a shipload of American slaves who mutinied on board the *Creole* while en route from Virginia to be sold at New Orleans. The so-called *Creole* affair blew up when the mutineers sought asylum in Nassau. To make the whole Hackett case even more embarrassing to the British government, the World Anti-Slavery Convention took place in London in the same year, and a large number of important abolitionists from the United States were in attendance. The

Webster-Ashburton Treaty was delayed on account of abolitionist concerns that the extradition clauses it contained might open
the door to endangering fugitives already living in British
colonies, but finally passed into law in 1842. Still, according to
the *Anti-Slavery Reporter*, dated October 5, 1842, Charles Stuart,
who had spent time in Upper Canada, warned that the treaty
contained a "pledge to the U.S. that we will be slave-catchers for
her benefit." The British abolitionist community in the end convinced the Colonial Office that it should supervise all future extradition cases, which would henceforth be sent to London for
decision.

The Detroit Vigilant Committee was involved in another fugitive slave rescue in 1848, this time of runaways living in rural
Michigan who were about to be kidnapped by Kentucky slave
catchers. Adam Crosswhite and his family were saved at the last
moment and taken across the river to Canada. True to form,
those involved in the rescue included the Lightfoots, the
Frenches, and Willoughby's son-in-law William Lambert, along
with George De Baptiste, Lambert's closest confidant and a very
important antislavery and Underground Railroad figure in Detroit history. De Baptiste had been the personal valet to President
William Henry Harrison, hero of the Battle of Tippecanoe, during his brief time at the White House, before becoming a leader
in the Underground Railroad in Indiana and later Detroit. The
Blackburns and their Toronto friends were undoubtedly aware of
the Crosswhite case, since another Kentucky fugitive now resident in Detroit, Henry Bibb, wrote an article for Frederick Douglass's paper, *The North Star*, on December 15, 1848, discussing
the legal issues surrounding it.

In 1856, the case of runaway Archie Lanton caused a serious
deterioration between the local representative to the Legislative
Council, Colonel John Prince, and Canada's black community.
Prince had commanded black troops in the 1837 Rebellion, and
had enjoyed the community's political support in Essex County
(where Sandwich and Amherstburg were located). Lanton was

charged with stealing two horses. He was duly arrested by the Canadian authorities and taken before two Western District magistrates. However, they carelessly left Lanton in the custody of the U.S.-based slave catchers who claimed him. Lanton was forthwith smuggled back across the border. The Attorney General of the Canadas dismissed the two magistrates, to the fury of Colonel Prince, who launched a blisteringly racist attack on the province's black settlers in the House. He eventually lost his seat in Parliament as a result, for the African Canadians of his district never forgot his words and banded together to vote him out of office.

The last fugitive slave case took place on the eve of the American Civil War. It was tried in Toronto and centered on the escape of John Anderson from his Missouri master. Unfortunately, Anderson's case, since he killed a white man in making his escape, met all the criteria for extradition under the terms of the Fugitive Offenders Act of 1833, as well as under the more recently negotiated Webster-Ashburton Treaty. His trial was attended by hundreds of Toronto blacks. The three judges at the Court of Queen's Bench in Toronto's Osgoode Hall disagreed; two were in favor of extraditing Anderson and one against. The matter went to appeal, while blacks in Toronto and Montreal rallied to Anderson's cause and public meetings, debates, and open demonstrations were held against the judges' ruling. Across the ocean, the British Colonial Office became embroiled in the matter, but before its ruling to set the fugitive free could reach Canada, Anderson was released on a technicality regarding the wording of the writ.

The vast sums of money slaveholders expended in trying to recover fugitive slaves from Canada make no sense in purely economic terms. But the moral effect of Upper Canada's reception of American runaway slaves was even more important than the impact on the economies of the Southern states. Upper Canada, by accepting runaway slaves and by fostering its growing reputation as a safe haven for refugees, encouraged more fugitives to settle there. This did untold damage to American slaveholding interests. The myth of white superiority, on which American race slavery was based, was shaken to its foundations by the successful flight and even more by the productive lives fugitives built for themselves after their escape.

That fugitive slaves flourishing in Upper Canada as farmers, small-business people, family men and women, and individuals of initiative and ability who avidly sought education for themselves and their children was a form of resistance to the racial shibboleths upon which Southern slavery rested. People like the Blackburns graphically refuted Southern beliefs in the inferiority of African Americans, their incapacity for hard work, and a supposed inability to govern themselves without white control. Furthermore, the fact that thousands escaped, and thousands more attempted to do so and failed, emphatically contradicted fables about "contented slaves." The efforts to recover blacks from what remained of British North America were political maneuvers meant to demonstrate to the larger world that Americans would brook no foreign interference in the execution of their national policies. The reception that African Americans received as refugees in Canada, the Caribbean, Mexico, and Britain was a sharp rebuke to the United States and its vaunted ideals of liberty and equality, ostensibly for all men, in the court of world opinion.

Southern slaveholders falsified the numbers of slaves who escaped annually and invented stories to discourage their slaves from considering Canada as a haven. Much nonsense was touted regarding the province's freezing climate and infertile soil:

> Our master used to tell us all manner of stories about what a dreadful place [Canada] was . . . they said it was so cold there that men going mowing had to break the ice with their scythes . . . I have heard it as common talk, that the wild geese were so common in Canada, that they would scratch a man's eyes out; that corn wouldn't grow there, nor any thing else but rice; that every thing they had there was imported.

The Blackburn case had established the grounds for refusing American demands for fugitive slave extradition. It was foundational to Canadian public-policy development, and the same principles underlie the national refugee policies in practice today. Canada still generally does not return people accused of crimes to nations where their punishments would exceed in quality and degree the consequences of the same offense in Canada. Lucie Blackburn's was the first and only instance in which the extradition of a female slave was sought from Upper Canada. This was also the only instance where the return of a group of African Americans, rather than an individual, was the subject of dispute between Canadian and U.S. authorities. Colborne, Jameson, and Strachan had between them crafted the grounds for rebuffing formal extradition demands on the basis of spurious criminal charges. Reinforced with new British law and policy over the antebellum period, this set the stage for the emigration of literally tens of thousands of people from the American South to British colonies and a few to Britain herself.

AT HOME IN THE PROMISED LAND

Sir, I ask you to send the fugitives to Canada. I don't
know much of this Province but I beleaves that there is
Rome enough for the colored and whites of the United
States. We wants farmers mechanic men of all qualifi-
cations &c, if they are not made, we will make them, if
we cannot make the old we will make their children.
—JOHN HENRY HILL TO WILLIAM STILL,
October 30, 1853

ONE YEAR AFTER their release from the Sandwich jail, Thornton
and Lucie moved to Toronto. The first sight the Blackburns had
of their new home was probably from the water. As their ship
passed the mouth of the Humber River and rounded Gibraltar
Point, the entire panorama of the city of Toronto was arrayed before them. Toronto sat in a little basin the waters of Lake Ontario
had left behind as the glaciers receded some twelve thousand
years before. Lying low on the horizon between the two great
rivers of the fur trade, the Humber and the Don, Toronto was
blessed with a protected harbor, enclosed on its eastern end by
the sand spit that flowed from the Don mouth. This curved out
into the lake in a huge arc, forming what today are the Toronto
Islands. In the distance, they could see the gentle rise of farmers'
fields and uncut forests that formed Toronto's northern hinter-

land. Their ship carried them into the bay, past the blockhouse to the south and the facing palisades of Fort York that together stood sentinel at the harbor's western entrance.

It was 1834, the year Toronto became a city and shed the British colonial title given by its founder, Lieutenant Governor Simcoe, in 1793. The old Town of York again bore the name familiar to its original inhabitants. To the Mohawk, who for centuries set weirs to catch the abundant fish of the bay each spring and summer, this was Toronto, "the place where trees stand in the water." The first Toronto directory described the city as Thornton and Lucie first knew it:

> The town of York is laid out at right angles: the streets are spacious; the Main street, called King street, runs through the center of the Town, from east to west, and is 1½ miles in length . . . the Houses are partly built of wood, but many of them are of Brick and Stone: it contains the Public buildings of the Province, viz. The New Parliament buildings with the Government Offices attached, the Government House, the College of Upper Canada, the Hospital, the Upper Canada Bank, the Court House, and Gaol [and] a splendid hall called Osgoode Hall, for the Law society.

Toronto was third only to Rochester and Buffalo in size and prosperity among the Great Lakes ports of its day. It was an attractive place in many ways, a raw frontier town with a genteel colonial overlay owing to its position as seat of the provincial government. The westernmost real urban center on Canadian soil, the city had much in common with the Blackburns' previous homes of Louisville and Detroit. Toronto's legendarily muddy streets were lined with the warehouses of forwarding merchants, retail and wholesale establishments, and commission houses, and the city was poised to provide the goods and services for outbound settlers, this time for the opening of the great continental Northwest. The center had long since outgrown her original boundaries and now stretched westward along the waterfront toward Fort York, although the low-lying eastern district near the Don River would take another decade to attract much settlement. Above Lot Street (now Queen Street), the exclusive one-hundred-acre Park Lots awarded members of Simcoe's government and officer corps in 1793 retarded northward expansion for many years. Charles Dickens visited in 1842 and wrote "the town itself is full of life and motion, bustle, business and improvement" and the shops would "do no discredit to [London] itself." High praise indeed for a town a bare half century old on the frontiers of Upper Canada. Industry was already a major part of the city's economy, and the smoke of Toronto's factories could be seen on the horizon for miles.

Toronto's chronic shortage of labor was a boon to newcomers like the Blackburns, although housing was at a premium. Thornton was only twenty-two years old; he and his wife had their entire futures before them. But it was not mere economic advantage that they sought, for moving to Toronto was Thornton's first step in realizing a dream: he was reuniting his shattered family. Amazingly, wonderfully, he had found his older brother, Alfred.

The Blackburn brothers had not seen each other since Thornton was taken from his Mason County home in 1825 and sent to Hardinsburg at the age of twelve or thirteen. Alfred, several years older than he, had also chosen to follow the North Star to freedom in Canada. He had escaped to Canada alone, as so many young men found that they had to in order to avoid an upcoming sale or, just as often, in protest against the loss of a wife or children whom they could not save. It is not known if Alfred had left behind a wife in slavery, but he never married while he lived in Toronto. The manner by which he escaped his Kentucky master is not recorded, but the son of the Reverend John Rankin, who operated the busy Liberty Hill Underground Railroad station at Ripley, Ohio, told an interviewer in the 1890s a most intriguing tale. He said the first fugitive slave he could remember being harbored in their home had escaped from Maysville. The year had been 1826, and the young man's name was Alfred.

Alfred and Thornton may have learned of each other's where-abouts through Toronto's Baptist minister, the Reverend Washington Christian. In 1826, the powerful and charismatic preacher had brought together a dozen fugitive slaves for open-air worship on the shores of Toronto Bay. His integrated congregation had grown rapidly until, in 1829, the white members had broken away to form their own church. Elder Christian was a missionary as well as a minister. He traveled regularly in the province's Western District, where he was credited with founding more churches than any other pastor of his era. Alfred was part of his Toronto congregation, so it would have been a simple matter for the minister to connect Thornton and Lucie, whose rescue had occasioned the Detroit riots, with the young member of his Toronto flock who shared with Thornton both a surname and a birthplace. The reunion of the Blackburn brothers must have been a great joy to them both, although the fact that their beloved mother, Sibby, remained behind in slavery would have been a source of continuing anxiety.

When Thornton found him, Alfred was working as a carpenter and living on Toronto's eastern outskirts, near the marshes at the mouth of the Don River. Known as the Park, the district had only recently been annexed to the city and named St. Lawrence Ward. Damp and considered somewhat unhealthy, it was sparsely settled, a place where even a poor man could take up a couple of acres, keep a cow and a few chickens, and perhaps plant a vegetable garden and a few fruit trees. The swamps were rich in game. Alfred's landlord was probably also his employer. Enoch Turner, a well-to-do brewer and noted for philanthropic acts, was a likely candidate to give a young runaway slave a home and a job when he arrived in Toronto. Alfred occupied one of several workers' cottages by a pretty stream known as Vale Pleasant. There Turner's own gracious home overlooked Lake Ontario just east of the modern Parliament Street. Next door was the milling complex of Gooderham & Worts, with its landmark windmill. In time, Thornton and Lucie would become acquainted with the large, intermarried Gooderham and Worts families.

Under patriarch William Gooderham, these recent immigrants from Britain would soon turn their Toronto flour mills, which stood near Alfred's house on the shores of Toronto Bay, into one of the largest distilleries in the world. The Blackburns would find their acquaintance with the wealthy and powerful Gooderham clan very useful.

In addition to Alfred's welcome presence, Lucie Blackburn and her husband probably had other reasons for moving to the capital of Upper Canada. For one thing, the city was on the north shore of Lake Ontario, much farther from the American border than Amherstburg, so there was less danger of being kidnapped by American slave catchers who did not scruple to cross into the British colony in search of runaways. Slave owners knew that they could expect little assistance from white Torontonians, as the 1826 attempted kidnapping of Tilly, a former slave working as a servant in Toronto, demonstrated:

> Two passersby ran after the sleigh [in which the girl had been carried off], and on its halting at a tavern one hurried off for a constable while the other kept watch. Entering the tavern they demanded the girl, and under threat of arrest the fellow had to let her go. If he had not, the crowd in the barroom would have piled on him, for in Toronto Yankee slave hunters are detested.

Torontonians also generally displayed a lower degree of the deeply rooted antiblack prejudice that plagued communities along the Detroit and Niagara rivers boundaries. With its population nearing ten thousand and a tiny black presence of no more than fifty families, Toronto was unique in Upper Canada in that segregation was never practiced in its churches, schools, or places of public entertainment. While it was true that slaves were at one time sold like so many sheep or horses in the pages of the *Upper Canada Gazette*, Lieutenant Governor Simcoe's gradual emancipation bill of 1793, coupled with a strong public distaste for slavery, had effectively freed them and their children by about the time of the War of 1812. Some of Toronto's black men had fought in that war. There were a few Black Loyalists in town as well. They were African Americans who sided with the Crown in the American Revolution in return for freedom and the promise of land in Canada. The rest of Toronto's Black populace was made up of more recently arrived American immigrants, both fugitive slave and free, who sought better lives "under the paw of the British lion." Blacks seem to have been regarded with sort of an amused tolerance at this early date. The Reverend Henry Scadding, the city's most reliable early chronicler, recalled their presence in the Toronto of his youth:

> The Negro population was small. Every individual of color was recognizable at sight. Black Joe and Whistling Jack were two notabilities, both of them Negroes of African birth. In military bands a Negro drummer or cymbal-player was formerly often to be seen. The two men just named, after obtaining discharge from a regiment here, gained an honest livelihood by chance employment about the town. Joe, a well-formed, well-trained figure, was to be seen still arrayed in some old cast-off shell jacket, acting as porter or engaged about horses . . . [or] in the capacity of sheriff's assistant administering the lash to wretched culprits in the Market Place. The other, besides playing other parts, officiated occasionally as a sweep; but his most memorable accomplishment was a melodious and powerful style of whistling musical airs and a faculty for imitating the bagpipes to perfection.

When they first came, the Blackburns found Toronto a typical preindustrial walking city. Most black residents clustered around their two main churches. Washington Christian's First Calvinistic Baptist Church served the community that lived above or behind their businesses in the east end, in what had been the original Town of York. Among them were hairdressers, grocers, fishmongers, and restaurateurs, all doing well with a largely white clientele. As was true in the cities of the American North, the barbers and other small-business owners formed Toronto's urban black elite. Newcomers found homes in Toronto's first working-class suburb, known as Macaulay Town, after Judge James Buchanan Macaulay, whose family originally owned the land. The second black church was located there, the African Methodist Episcopal, although black Torontonians also attended the Anglican, Roman Catholic, and churches of other denominations. West and north of the city proper, these narrow streets and small houses would soon be renamed St. John's Ward, and annexed to the city. In this burgeoning immigrant district, a man from Glasgow or Dublin or Hamburg could find a room and hold a conversation in his native language. There, too, fugitive slaves from Lexington, Baltimore, or Nashville might rent a flat and perhaps, after a few years of hard work, purchase their first modest home. A few relatively affluent African American immigrant families occupied houses south of Macaulay Town, along York Street, which ran south to the bay. Free blacks who had come to Canada in the wake of Nat Turner's 1831 slave revolt, they were in the main comfortably off financially and had some education. These ambitious men and women added a layer of sophistication and their arrival stimulated the foundation of a real infrastructure for Toronto's small black community. It is possible the Blackburns were already acquainted with one or two local families. One was that of James Charles Brown, formerly of Louisville and Cincinnati, who had traveled on colonizing missions with the abolitionist Benjamin Lundy in the 1820s and was responsible for the founding of Upper Canada's Wilberforce Colony. He, too, was a member of Washington Christian's church and had probably attended that of the Reverend Henry Adams during Thornton and Lucie's time in Louisville.

In 1837, James G. Birney, a Kentucky slaveholder-turned-abolitionist, visited Toronto. He wrote approvingly:

> On Sunday I attended, in the morning, the "English Church" [Church of England]. I saw here several colored people sit-

ting promiscuously with the whites. In the afternoon, I went
to a Baptist Church, the pastor of which is Mr. Christian, a
colored man, a native of Virginia and formerly a Slave. The
Congregation, which was larger than the building could
well accommodate, was composed of about an equal number
of whites and colored persons. There was no distinction in
seats, nor any, the least recognition, so far as I could discern,
of a difference made by complexion or any other cause. There
is a considerable number of the members of the Church that
are whites. I never saw a better looking or more orderly
Congregation assembled. In their persons they were neat—
in their attention to the services decorous and exemplary.

In Toronto, as elsewhere, the churches were not only the soul
of the community but its heart and mind as well. The only large
buildings the African Canadians owned in common, they provided immigrants like the Blackburns with an instant entrée to
the city's black society. Meeting halls for lectures, political gatherings, and social events, they also facilitated the formation of
antislavery, benevolent, self-help, and fraternal organizations.
Children and adults learned to read in Sabbath school, although
no members of the Blackburn family seem to have availed themselves of the opportunity. The churches were served mainly by
American-trained clergymen and missionaries already experienced
both in community development and in keeping the fires of
antislavery activism burning in the hearts of their flocks. Visiting
abolitionists regularly lectured and the political meetings that
swung black community support behind this or that local candidate also took place here. In Canada, Thornton and Alfred could
vote, serve on juries, and even run for office, although it would be
some years yet before the first African Canadian politician would
take his place in Toronto's municipal government.
    Most advocates of fugitive slave resettlement in Canada ad-
vised the immigrants to acquire farms where they could own land
and live independently of white control, but the towns and cities
were particularly attractive to both free and formerly enslaved

African Americans who, like the Blackburns, had skills most readily marketed in an urban setting. Single women and older men without families could not easily support themselves in rural districts and gravitated to the African Canadian society already established at Toronto, Hamilton, London, and St. Catharines. Milliners, barbers, cabinetmakers, carpenters, builders of all kinds, dressmakers, women trained as ladies' maids who could do fine ironing and mending, and people with capital to invest in real estate all came to Toronto. A year before the Blackburns arrived in Toronto, the city's first mayor, William Lyon Mackenzie, was struck by the conditions of black life in Philadelphia as compared with Toronto:

> They speak of equality in this country, but it is in Upper Canada that it can be seen in all its glory. There is a man of colour, a barber and a hairdresser in our town of York, named Butler; he is married to a coloured woman and they are respectable, well behaved people in their line, and punctual in their dealings; they have, of course, a black family and (hear it, ye slave-trading, equal rights and independence people) they keep white men and women servants from Europe to wait on them and their black children. This is turning the table on the Sothrons [sic], and fairly balancing accounts with the ebony-hearted slave-holders.

Soon after his arrival, Thornton Blackburn found work as a waiter in the Benchers' Dining Room at Osgoode Hall, where the law courts were located. There, Thornton would have encountered for the first time the very men who had negotiated the terms of his own freedom. Chief Justice Robinson, Attorney General Jameson, and Judges Sherwood and Macaulay were regular attendees at the Court of King's Bench. Law students and attorneys from out of town boarded in the upstairs rooms. Thornton served their meals. Breakfast was at eight in the morning, dinner at 5 p.m., and tea at eight in the evening. Luncheon was a shilling, and "every member being a Barrister may call for a bottle of wine." It was a long shift; a regular day in early nineteenth-century Toronto for a working man was fourteen to sixteen hours long, with only Sundays off. Thornton was paid but £1 per month, although there were tips and his meals were included. One can better understand what that wage meant at the time by realizing that the very well housed and fed students were charged £9.20 per quarter for full room and board, or just over £2 per month. The fine brick building where Thornton worked still stands as the eastern section of Osgoode Hall, now ornamented with a colonnaded portico. Once on the extreme western end of the city surrounded by the tenements and little shops of Macaulay Town, the much expanded structure is now in the heart of Toronto's business district. Since Osgoode Hall was far from Alfred's house, the long walk back and forth each day afforded Thornton an opportunity to familiarize himself with his new surroundings.

When the Blackburns had saved enough money, they rented a large double lot only a couple of streets north of Alfred's place. The property sloped gently toward Toronto Bay. The Government Park, south of the eastern extension of King Street between the city's eastern limits and the great Don River, had originally been set aside for naval yards that Lieutenant Governor Simcoe planned but were never realized. Subsequently it was turned over to the trustees of the Toronto Hospital, a group that included the Reverend John Strachan. They laid out streets and began to lease and sell off lots to raise money to support their new building. Just slightly to the east was the bridge over the Don River. The Blackburns paid an annual rent of £5. Their two lots were not actually available for purchase until 1848, when Lucie and her husband paid £60 for them. Far from the churches and neighborhoods that were the black community's religious and social centers, the Blackburns remained for many years almost the only blacks living in the city's east end.

On the north side of South Park Street (later Eastern Avenue) near the corner of Sackville, Thornton Blackburn and his wife constructed a little frame house, probably enlisting Alfred's expert help. The Blackburn home was less than 800 square feet in size and was not, throughout the couple's fifty-year occupation of it, subjected to any additions or major alterations. John Ross Robertson, editor of the Toronto *Telegram*, described it a half-century later: "No. 54 of this street [Eastern Avenue] is a very small one storey [*sic*] frame building, painted almost black by wind and weather."

This was the very house that was the subject of the 1985 archaeological excavation that first brought their presence in Toronto to the attention of the modern public. Stylistically, it bore no resemblance to Toronto's usual buildings of the day. Thornton Blackburn had brought to freedom with him a sense of what "home" should look like; he had constructed, on Canadian soil, a classic African American "shotgun house." This form, only one room wide and with the short gable end to the street, is typical of vernacular architecture in Southern cities and towns ranging from Kentucky to Mississippi, and from coastal Georgia through Texas and on to California. Eminently suited to the long, narrow house lots of North American cities, it has a much longer history. It voyaged from West Africa in the minds of men and women on the ships of the Middle Passage, to shelter slaves of the New World. Erected first on the Caribbean island of Hispaniola, it entered America by way of New Orleans in the 1790s with refugees fleeing Toussaint-Louverture's bloody slave uprising in Haiti. Its use spread first up the Mississippi and then radiated out into all the southern United States. There are tens of thousands of standing examples in the cities of the South.

The word "shotgun" is believed to derive from "togun," the Yoruba word for "house." The corridor-like configuration of Lucie and Thornton's Toronto home, lacking hallways and with the front and back doors in direct line with each other, forms a passageway for evil spirits to pass through, so they do no harm to the occupants. This ancient belief had been forgotten in the Blackburns' day. Then, as now, it was commonly held that the name "shotgun" meant one could fire a shotgun through the front door of the house and have the shell exit the rear door without meeting any obstruction. The excavations focused on the house, barn, and yard, including the garbage dump where they incinerated their trash. The Blackburns occupied their home for more than half a century, and while the archaeological inquiry produced no startling finds, the site was a treasure trove of information about the everyday life of African Americans in nineteenth-century Toronto. By the end of the summer of 1985, the dig had exposed the fragile foundations of an old horse barn and a little frame cottage facing south toward the lake. It was built on wooden sills set right on the ground. Only a single room wide and with its gable end facing South Park Street, the modern Eastern Avenue, the building comprised only three small rooms set in a row. The parlor was the front room, and from the front window they had a wonderful view of Toronto Bay, with the Gooderham Distillery to one side. Behind was their tiny bedroom, and then came the kitchen, with its fireplace and back door to the garden and "necessary" house. In this cozy and comfortable cottage Thornton and Lucie would reside for the rest of their lives.

Under the floor of the bedroom was a deep cellar dug into the earth. The cellar's seemingly odd placement is typical of shotgun houses and a legacy of slavery; in fact, belowground storage pits are so common on plantation sites that archaeologists consider their presence indicative of which buildings were used to house slaves. In earth-lined holes concealed under beds in the slave quarters of plantations all over the American South, hungry slaves kept the food they purloined, items of pottery, cloth and metal that, bereft of possessions, some hoarded, and secret amulets and charms. These last, perhaps, might ward off the whip and keep their babies from being sold away from them.

In the Blackburns' kitchen was a hearth made of soft red brick with a chimney above. The house was demolished in 1892, and when archaeologists excavated the Blackburn home in 1985, its

bricks were discovered tipped, domino fashion, into the hand-
dug root cellar under the middle room. They were covered in a
thick layer of glass from the melting of their constituents over
the years, and it is entirely surprising that the Blackburns'
wooden home had not gone up in flames at some point. Firebrick
had been scarce and expensive in 1834 because Toronto was un-
dergoing a massive building boom, so the Blackburns had used
salvaged builders' brick instead.

In a root cellar whose rough earthen walls today still bear the
curvature of the spade used to create it, archaeologists found bits
of preserving jars, tobacco pipes, a cracked wineglass, buttons
and bobbins and rusty pins. Redolent of an all but forgotten past,
this was the detritus of frugal lives lived simply, but so very well.

Like their English, Irish, and Scots neighbors, mainly crafts-
people of various descriptions, the Blackburns lived carefully,
initially heating their three-roomed shotgun house with their
own wood, and then by means of coal stoves. They exploited the
natural sources of food in the vicinity, for bones of wild fish and
game were discovered in the ashes of the kitchen hearth. Hunting and fishing were traditional ways in which slaves supple-
mented their meager diets, and the habit translated well to the
semirural character of the district in which they now lived. Their
simple dishes and glassware, silver-plated spoons, and bits of
glass and corroded metal together paint a picture of day-to-day
living from 1834 through the 1890s. Most of the household objects recovered speak to the domestic work undertaken by Lucie
Blackburn. But the little pearl-handled pocketknife was surely
Thornton's prized possession, and the brass pocket watch and
simple jewelry the archaeologists found bear witness to the couple's increasing prosperity.

The Blackburns planted a very large vegetable garden on the
west end of their land, taking up the whole corner of South Park
Street and running some 120 feet up the side of Sackville Street.
Perhaps they intended to expand the size of their home one day,
once children came along, but in this they were destined to be
disappointed. Lucie remained childless, and eventually Thorn-

ton must have resigned himself to the fact that no additions would need to be made to their house. A wooden porch was constructed at the rear in about 1850, closing off the part of the property where an extra room might have been built.

After they were established in their new home, the Blackburns set about making plans to secure their future. As long as Thornton worked under white supervision, he was reminded of slavery. Toronto, although perhaps more tolerant than the rest of the province, was not free from racism, and there were always plenty of American businessmen and university students in the port city to reinforce the old plantation ideas. Britain had made a great deal of money in the slave trade before its abolition and for all her antislavery rhetoric, the cotton mills in Lancashire still ran on the raw materials produced by hundreds of thousands of slaves in the American South. When the British Imperial Act finally freed the slaves of the West Indies in 1834, the editor of the Toronto *Patriot* wrote, on December 2, 1834, "Everybody knows that the natives of Africa and their descendants are a lazy race. Nothing but want, which is every man's master, will make them work: and when the cravings of nature are satisfied, like other animals, they go to sleep." Black society operated separately from white in Canada as it did everywhere else in nineteenth-century North America. The two worlds intersected in employment, commerce, and occasionally religion, but otherwise occupied separate spheres.

But Thornton was an enterprising man, and his wife an excellent money manager, as later developments would show. Within only two years of their arrival in Toronto, the Blackburns hit upon an idea that would make their fortunes and ensure them a permanent place in the city's history. In 1837, they began the first taxi business in Upper Canada.

Perhaps Thornton heard talk, while waiting tables at Osgoode Hall, about a new type of public transportation called the hackney cab. Just arrived in North America from England, one was already plying the streets of Montreal. In Louisville, Thornton had regularly seen horse-drawn hacks carrying steamboat passengers and their baggage to destinations about the city, but these were rented from local livery stables. What Thornton wanted was an independently owned cab that would be hired by the trip or the hour. He could set his own hours and would no longer be subject to scheduling determined by someone else. Even more important, everything he earned would belong to himself and Lucie.

After interviewing the Blackburns in 1888 about the beginnings of their cab company for one of a series of articles about the history of early Toronto, John Ross Robertson recorded that, "Mr. Blackburn obtained the pattern of a Montreal cab and [took] it to Paul Bishop," who was considered the finest "mechanic" of his day; and "in 1837 [Bishop] delivered to him the first cab built in Upper Canada." Officially christened "The City," this cab soon became a familiar sight on Toronto streets. Its four passengers entered from the rear, with the luggage strapped to the roof. Thornton rode up top. The carriage was gaily painted in the Blackburn cab company's own colors of red and yellow. A detailed watercolor of King Street, Toronto's main shopping thoroughfare, in 1846 shows the Blackburns' taxi trundling westward in front of St. James's Cathedral. The Toronto Transit Commission uses the Blackburn logo colors of red and yellow for its streetcars and buses to this day.

Thornton and Lucie's cab company did extremely well. The couple constructed a one-and-a-half-story stable and barn on their land to house their horse and cab. Within a short time, prominent Torontonians were complaining in letters to the newspapers that their coachmen, many of whom were also runaway slaves, were leaving their employ and setting themselves up in the cab business. In 1837, a licensing system was established with set tariffs for distances. Maps of the city show these as concentric circles radiating out from the city taxi stand on Church Street, on the west side of the Anglican Church of St. James. A substantial £30 bond was required of each cab owner. According to the *Toronto Directory and Street Guide for 1843–4*, regulations were strict; when waiting for fares at the stand, horses' heads had to face toward the bay, and additional charges were set for the number of bags and packages passengers carried with them. Some cabbies were reckless, for there were fines for driving too fast and frightening both pedestrians and passengers. Drivers were strictly forbidden to "leave their vehicles, needlessly or wantonly flourish their whips, or use any abusive, obscene, or impertinent language."

With their cab company well under way, Thornton and Lucie engaged in the social, religious, and economic life of their city, and in the vibrant black culture that was evolving alongside the larger white society. By 1837, there were more than fifty black families in Toronto, and Thornton and Lucie Blackburn likely had at least a nodding acquaintance with all of them. While the city was becoming more important as a terminus of the Underground Railroad in these years, not all of the black families were fugitive slaves by any means. Free African Americans came as well, and the Blackburns formed part of a social stratum of entrepreneurial families who owned their own businesses. A few were quite well-to-do, as one chronicler observed:

> Some brought a little capital with them, as the Rosses, Sey, Wardell, Hickman, etc. The elder Ross, originally a carpenter, owns 200 acres in the Gore of Toronto, more than half under good cultivation, with extensive buildings, plenty of fine stock, besides several little houses in town. Abbot, once a tobacconist, now lives on the rents of five to six frame houses, and the interest of a capital valued at £30,000. The generallity [sic], however, came penniless to Canada. Among these, Lafferty, a carter, now owning several houses in King Street . . .

The Blackburns began purchasing investment properties, in their case on Agnes and Elizabeth streets in St. John's Ward, the old Macaulay Town. Thornton Blackburn's closest friend was

John M. Tinsley, a free-born builder who moved to Toronto from Richmond, Virginia. Trained as a carpenter and millwright, he first visited in 1831 and purchased land in Macaulay Town, but then returned to his home and prosperous business interests. After February 6, 1837, when Senator John C. Calhoun gave his speech in Congress confirming his belief that slavery—far from being the "necessary evil" that Thomas Jefferson and others of his generation believed it to be—was actually a "positive good" because it supposedly benefited blacks by providing them with the blessings of white supervision, Tinsley moved permanently to Toronto in 1842 with his wife and eight children. The family included John's artist son, John D. Tinsley, his son-in-law, William Custaloe, and numerous grandchildren. The families shared a pair of semidetached houses on Agnes Street in the recently developed north end of St. John's Ward. A pillar of Toronto's black Baptist Church, John M. Tinsley and his construction company provided a long series of fugitive slaves with their first Toronto job. Tinsley's name was mentioned in letters sent by former runaways to the secretary of the Pennsylvania Anti-Slavery Society, William Still, at Philadelphia, whose large Underground Railroad operation forwarded fugitives to what is now Ontario, Canada. The Tinsleys and Custaloes also billeted recently arrived fugitive slaves in their home, as did many of their neighbors in the years of the Underground Railroad. The 1861 census for the city of Toronto, for instance, shows a twenty-three-year-old man named Robert Smith, lately of Louisiana, living with the Tinsley family. He, too, was a Baptist, and would become an important connection of the Blackburns.

John M. Tinsley added to his real estate holdings over time by constructing a series of modest cottages and tenements in the district. In 1838, Thornton Blackburn acquired a lot adjoining Tinsley's Agnes Street property and, probably with his friend's expert assistance, built a rental house there. In the next few years, the Blackburns would acquire five more properties, four in the same district and one to the north and east of their own home.

The properties served a dual purpose as far as Thornton and Lucie were concerned. That several of their tenants were recently arrived fugitive slaves paying only nominal rents suggests that the Blackburns, like other better-off black families, gave practical assistance to newcomers by providing them with inexpensive housing. At the same time, Toronto real estate could only appreciate, and rental properties were a secure and profitable investment on which the childless Blackburns might depend in their old age.

Some of the city's finer restaurants and inns were operated by black men and women known to the Blackburns in the 1830s. J. T. Fisher owned a saloon and wrote impassioned letters counseling the use of violence to overthrow slavery. R. Beverly Snow had a restaurant on Colborne Street, and later the Tontine Coffee House and the upscale eatery, the Epicurean Recess. Snow had fled Washington, D.C., following three days and nights of rioting—the so-called Snow Riots—that destroyed his elegant oyster bar, several churches, and a black orphanage, and sparked the creation of the first U.S. National Guard. Local antiblack feeling had been aroused by the recent imprisonment of an abolitionist in Washington, as well as the attempted murder of the wife of the architect of the Capitol Building, Anna Thornton, by one of her own slaves.

The most successful of all the African American immigrants to Toronto was Wilson Ruffin Abbott. Born free in Richmond, Virginia, and a former carpenter, steamboat steward, and grocer, he arrived in Toronto by way of New York in 1837 after the burning of his grocery business in Mobile, Alabama, by jealous white competitors. His wife, Ellen Toyer, a cultured free woman from Baltimore, taught her husband to read and brought up their family of nine children. The Abbotts made a fortune in real estate and were the unquestioned leaders of Toronto's black elite, their influence felt in its intersecting abolitionist, benevolent, and social circles. Thornton's name is sometimes found associated with that of Abbott's, an officer in antislavery and fugitive-slave assistance organizations who was active in protesting black mistreatment in Toronto, and who supported politicians sympathetic to African Canadian causes. He would one day become Toronto's first black politician, while his son, Anderson, would be the first Canadian-born black doctor to graduate from King's College Medical School. Anderson Ruffin Abbott was one of the attending surgeons for the U.S. Colored Troops during the Civil War.

The Blackburns' first years in the city, the 1830s, were an important time for black Torontonians, for it was in this decade the community began to establish the strong, stable infrastructure of associations and organizations that would support its ever-changing population throughout the years before the Civil War. Although membership rolls for African Toronto's early institutional and associational life are lacking, the couple's involvement in community affairs is suggested by the occasional appearance of the Blackburn name in reference to black political, social, and economic activities. People took very seriously their responsibility to care for their families, their friends, and the community at large. African Canadians did this while maintaining alongside African Americans the relentless battle that was the struggle against slavery in the American South and the pernicious racial oppression that pervaded all parts of the continent. The hybrid African American and African Canadian society thus mounted something of a protest movement in exile, one that was highly organized. Upper Canada's first abolitionist organization, the British-American Anti-Slavery Society, was inaugurated by the black community in 1833. Among the officers of the society was the Reverend Washington Christian. There was regular intercourse between overseas and American antislavery groups, on the one hand, and African American immigrants living in Toronto, on the other, and the influence of the Canada-based antislavery movement on American slavery has only begun to be understood.

In 1837, Thornton joined Washington Christian and other prominent black Torontonians in a subtle protest to highlight the unspoken racial discrimination on the part of civil servants and legislators that prevented African American immigrants from becoming permanently naturalized in Upper Canada. Black people were entitled, under British colonial law, to all the rights and privileges of full civic participation, but could not exercise those rights without taking this important step. Thornton Blackburn's name appeared in the *Journals of the Legislative Assembly* as one of several Toronto-based blacks who were making formal application for naturalization. The bill to naturalize the applicants passed the Upper Canadian legislature on February 27, 1837, but with an amendment that excluded from the list the names of every black person who had applied. Expunged were the names of Thornton Blackburn, Washington Christian, and two Toronto barbers, William Henderson Edwoods, who had a flourishing shop on Church Street, and Newton Cary. The latter was one of several brothers from southern Virginia who had moved first to Cincinnati and then to Toronto. All were active in antislavery, self-help, and fraternal societies in the city. No grounds were given in the *Journal of the House of Assembly* to account for the omission of these very respectable men, and the substance of the preceding debate was not recorded. The circumstances certainly suggest that the applicants expected to be refused. That they applied at all could be construed as a statement of protest against the exclusion of black immigrants from their full rights as British subjects.

Despite such incidents, blacks living in Canada were most appreciative of the freedoms they did enjoy. The most important annual holiday was August 1, Emancipation Day, when black Canada celebrated the release of the West Indian slaves from bondage in 1834. Many years after the fact, Dr. Anderson Ruffin Abbott recalled an Emancipation Day parade that originated in St. John's Ward:

> They provided a banquet which was held under a pavilion erected on a vacant lot running from Elizabeth Street to Sayre Street opposite Osgoode Hall, which was then a barracks for the 92nd West Indian Regiment. The procession

was headed by the band of the Regiment. The tallest man in this Regiment was a Black man, a drummer, known as Black Charlie. The procession carried a Union Jack and a blue silk banner on which was inscribed in gilt letters, "The Abolition Society, Organized 1833." The Mayor of the City, Mr. Metcalf, made a speech on this occasion followed by several other speeches of prominent citizens. These celebrations were carried on yearly amid much enthusiasm, because it gave the refugee colonists an opportunity to express their gratitude and appreciation for the privileges they enjoyed under British rule.

In June of 1837, a seventeen-year-old girl ascended the British throne. Queen Victoria would come to symbolize the safety that fugitive slaves found in Canada. But in December of the same year, reformer William Lyon Mackenzie, who had been Toronto's first mayor, initiated his revolt against the province's governing oligarchy, the so-called Family Compact. This was the group of wealthy largely British and United Empire Loyalist families that dominated both Canadian politics and the civil service for the first half century of Upper Canada's history. For the defense of the province against Mackenzie's rebels, Toronto's black community of no more than four hundred men, women, and children mustered an astonishing fifty volunteers. These were attached to a unit of the Queen's Light Infantry and were placed under the command of John Beverley Robinson, son of the Chief Justice of the same name. The younger Robinson, who would one day be appointed Lieutenant Governor of the province, had great respect for Upper Canada's black residents, for his father had arranged for his teenage education in the arts of fencing and boxing to be provided by a striking man of enormous physique named John Charles. This was Black Charlie, the regimental drummer stationed at Fort York and the same man who beat the drum in the Emancipation Day parade so vividly described by Anderson Ruffin Abbott.

Although neither Thornton nor Alfred enlisted—they were planning another, highly personal enterprise at the time—African Canadian men they knew served intermittently for two years defending the Detroit and Niagara river borders from incursions by Mackenzie's American sympathizers. James Charles Brown fought as a gunner and Josiah Henson was a sergeant. Wilson Ruffin Abbott, in the country but two years when he enlisted, served as well. The Reverend Jehu Jones proudly boasted, "There is a regiment composed entirely of colored men—the commissioned officers are white. I have seen several of the members in this city—the corps are stationed on the Frontier. Great confidence is reposed in this regiment, and they have the most important post, in consequence of their acknowledged loyalty to the British Crown."

Although absent from the military enlistment rolls, the Blackburns did claim a role in the Upper Canadian Rebellion. On December 4, 1837, the rebels from the east attempted to cross over the Don River. Legendary in Toronto history is the tale of how one black man stood alone on the Don Bridge with a shotgun over his crossed arms. He would not let the rebels pass. Although his name has not been recorded, the only two male African Canadians living in the district of the Don Bridge in 1837 were Alfred and Thornton Blackburn. When the elderly Thornton and Lucie received John Ross Robertson at their home in 1888, they proudly pointed out the bullet hole in the doors. It was put there, they told the newspaperman, by Mackenzie's rebels.

By this time, the Blackburns were well settled into their city. Alfred was employed, the Upper Canadian Rebellion was behind them, and their taxi company was earning a comfortable living. Now they were ready to put into operation a plan they must have been preparing for some time. Thornton was going to Kentucky to rescue his mother.

The long and dangerous route Thornton took back to the slave South is nowhere documented, but he probably entered the United States by way of Michigan. What knowledge there is of his journey comes from the traditions of Detroit's black community. The *Detroit Daily Post* of February 7, 1870, ran a lengthy article entitled "Our New Voters." This included a description of the Blackburn Riots of 1833 and ended: "The two runaways, on being liberated from the Sandwich jail, went to Amherstburg, where they lived some time. They afterward went to Toronto . . . Blackburn went to Louisville, and stole his mother from slavery. Blackburn and his wife still live in Toronto, and are classed among the wealthy people of that city."

Since Detroit blacks were well aware of Thornton's clandestine southward journey, it was probably with the assistance of his old friends Madison Lightfoot, George French, and Benjamin Willoughby that Thornton crossed back over the river and again entered the land of his birth. He would have needed their help, for all the time he was in Michigan he was in danger of being recognized because of his role in the Blackburn Riots only five years before.

All that long way south through Michigan and Ohio, slave catchers were lying in wait. Thornton was a wanted man and still subject to the Fugitive Slave Law. Recaptured runaways were chased by bloodhounds and torn with the lash, branded with hot irons, and even mutilated by their owners so they could not run again. Most of those apprehended were sold away to the cotton, rice, or cane fields of the Deep South, far from family and friends or any hope for escape.

Thornton made a journey of more than one thousand miles. He had not seen his mother in twelve years and had no way of knowing if she was still alive. He probably began his search near the place where he and Alfred had last known her to be, a decade before, at the little river town of Augusta, just a few miles downriver from Maysville. It was nine miles from Ripley, Ohio, where the Reverend John Rankin still lit the lantern every night to guide runaway slaves to his safe house on Liberty Hill. From there they were sent northward through a series of safe houses to the border at Detroit and Niagara. Perhaps it was at Ripley that Thornton found someone to help him in his quest.

There is record of only one woman named Sibby living anywhere within a three-county radius of Augusta at the time, but she was not a slave nor was she using the surname Blackburn. An indenture dated January 20, 1837, and found in the Bracken County Court records shows that Sibby Davis bound out her ten-year-old son, Franky, to Henry R. Reeder of Washington, Kentucky, "to learn the art, trade and mystery of a house servant." Franky was to serve until he reached the age of twenty-one. There is no other information available about this woman, except that she was unmarried or widowed, for otherwise her husband rather than she would have signed a legal document of this nature. Were Sibby Davis and Sibby Blackburn the same person? It is, of course, possible that Thornton's mother had been freed, had remarried, and had given birth to another son after Thornton and Alfred left the district. It is perhaps of note that the free woman Sibby Davis does not appear in the next U.S. Census for Bracken County, Kentucky.

By whatever means Thornton and his mother came to be reunited, their joy at finding each other again must have been profound. No one will ever know the terror they experienced on that long perilous road north, and their final relief when they arrived safely in Canada. Alfred Blackburn, waiting in Toronto, had not seen his mother in almost a decade, and Lucie had never met her mother-in-law. As Louis Hughes, who witnessed the reunion after many years of his fugitive slave wife and her mother and sister at Cincinnati wrote, "No mortal who has not experienced it can imagine the feeling of those who meet again after long years of enforced separation and hardship and utter ignorance of one another's condition and place of habitation . . . This first evening we spent together can never be forgotten. I can see the old woman now, with bowed form and gray locks, as she gave thanks in joyful tones yet reverent manner, for such a wonderful blessing."

Sibby Blackburn had certainly arrived in Toronto by 1840 when a brilliant African Canadian theology student named Peter Gallego conducted a census of Toronto's black population. He listed householders by name, occupation, religious affiliation, and the number of family members, and determined the total population to be 525. Thornton Blackburn was noted as having a family of four, which included his wife, his brother, and his elderly mother. The 1842 Census of Canada also confirms that there were two people living in the household of Alfred Blackburn, one an older woman, and two in Thornton's home on South Park Street. By 1842, the tax assessment rolls listed Thornton as a "yeoman," a term indicative of independent land ownership and a respectable place in the community.

The 1851 Census for the Liberties of St. Lawrence Ward (the district outside the city proper) shows an elderly woman named "Mary" Blackburn, a "mulatto" born in the United States, living on Palace Street with her son Alfred Blackburn. Her name apparently an error on the part of the census taker, since in all other Toronto records she is shown as Sibby. Their home was only a block from that of Thornton and Lucie. Sibby was listed as a Baptist and likely joined her son Alfred in worship at Washington Christian's new Baptist church at the corner of Queen and Victoria Streets of a Sunday. The four members of the Blackburn family were safe, together, and free at last.

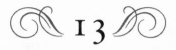

SOLDIERS IN THE
ARMY OF THE LORD

FUGITIVES IN CANADA.—The Toronto Globe of
the 15th says: "Great numbers of escaped slaves still
continue to pour into Canada from all parts of the
United States. Most of these refugees go toward the
Elgin (colored) Association, in the Western District,
and are there, we understand, purchasing land from
the Reverend Mr. King, the President of the Association, as fast as he can sell it to them.

Families are separating, leaving their homes, and
flying in all directions to seek in Canada, under the
British flag, the protection denied them in the Free
Republic!

We would not feel called upon to remark upon the
bill, were it not likely to prove injurious to ourselves,
by driving immense numbers of slaves to settle among
us. But flying from danger, it is quite natural that they
should direct their course to the nearest place of safety,
and that place is Canada.

—*THE NORTH STAR*, Rochester, New York,
October 24, 1850

THE BLACKBURNS lived and worked between the black and white
worlds that made up mid-nineteenth-century Toronto. Specifi-

cally, they engaged in the life of the larger Toronto society from which their cab business drew its patrons. In the 1840s, as St. Lawrence Ward filled with Irish immigrants, mainly Ulster Protestants, the Blackburns found themselves with new white neighbors, and the district, now dubbed "Corktown," after County Cork, soon lost its bucolic character. When a new Anglican church was constructed just a block from their home, to meet the needs of the Protestant Irish, *The Church* newspaper of Friday, April 21, 1843, reported the Blackburns as some of the first subscribers to the building fund of what quickly came to be called "Little" Trinity Church. They may have made the decision to abandon the Baptist church partly because of their relationship with Enoch Turner, Alfred's employer, and perhaps because of the wealthy distilling family of the Gooderhams and their in-laws, the Worts, for these familes largely funded the construction of the church building in 1843.

The Blackburns were to find their own connections with the Gooderham family useful in later years. However, their social and political activities would have continued to center around the events and organizations that were developed by Toronto's black churches. Dark days were coming for the African Americans who remained south of the border, and Toronto's black community would need all its strength to support a new influx of immigrants.

In 1850, the United States Congress ratified the Fugitive Slave Law. The changes included in this bill greatly strengthened the 1793 Fugitive Slave Law, which was the same one under which the Blackburns had suffered capture and trial in Detroit in 1833. Proposed by Kentucky's Henry Clay, "the Great Compromiser," the law was part of a much larger bill intended to appease the American South, which was growing progressively more dissatisfied with Northern efforts to halt the progress of slavery into the West and Southwest and furious at the increasingly vociferous antislavery protestors in the states above the Mason-Dixon Line. The Fugitive Slave Law of 1850 gave slaveholders and their agents wide-ranging powers to recover their human property in any state where they might be found. Even in the North, judicial and law enforcement officials were required to assist federal commissioners appointed for the task of recapturing and detaining accused fugitives. Special tribunals were struck to facilitate the court process, and judges required only an affidavit from a claimant to condemn an accused fugitive to a lifetime of servitude. As Frederick Douglass put it, "Under this law the oaths of any two villains (the capturer and the claimant) are sufficient to confine a free man to slavery for life." Since blacks could not testify against whites in most American courts, this opened the door to widespread abuse, but it was passed into law on September 18, 1850. On September 19, 1850, the Toronto *Globe* expressed outrage: "What would be thought in Canada, if an Imperial and Local Act were passed converting all the inhabitants of our free Canada into slavehunters?"

This new legislation was the single greatest impetus to African American migration to Canada during the antebellum period, effectively doubling the black population of what is now Ontario within a decade. The impact of this influx, which overwhelmed existing fugitive slave resettlement schemes, would also directly engage Thornton and Lucie Blackburn in political protest and self-help efforts mounted by African Canadian abolitionist groups. Underground Railroad operators, alarmed by the potential of this blanket law, threw into high gear the mechanisms for assisting blacks in their flight north to freedom in Canada. Bounty hunters roamed at will, anxious for profits gained either legally or otherwise, capturing unwary black people and turning them in for a slaveholder's reward, or selling them as merchandise. Hundreds of unfortunate captives were taken to the South without incident, although spectacular rescues of individual slaves arrested under the law were effected in some places. Shadrach Minkins, a waiter from Norfolk, Virginia, had the misfortune to be the first escapee to be captured under the Fugitive Slave Law in Boston. He was forcibly rescued in the midst of his trial by a coalition of black and white abolitionists. Spirited north to Canada, he subsequently made his home in Montreal, where he opened a restaurant. The case garnered attention from President Millard Fillmore, who demanded that those guilty of rescuing Minkins be punished, although no time was actually served by the participants. At Syracuse, in October 1851, a runaway named William McHenry, or "Jerry," was taken from the federal marshals especially appointed to execute the Fugitive Slave Law and sent to Canada with the help of two local clergymen, who later found it necessary to move north of the border themselves. Less fortunate was Anthony Burns, who, to set an example, was sent back to the South under the guard of a platoon of U.S. marshals at a cost of more than $20,000.

Some of those taken into custody under the Fugitive Slave Law were not actually slaves; free papers were easily destroyed, and individuals who had been free for generations were thus enslaved. Within months of the law's passage, Northern states passed personal liberty laws to circumvent the impact of this federal legislation. However, a number of well-educated and financially comfortable families from Boston, New York, Philadelphia, and other cities moved to Canada West in search of security and the protection of the law. *The Liberator* of October 4, 1850, the *Cleveland Daily True Democrat* of October 1 and 5, 1850, and the *Milwaukee Daily Free Democrat* of October 1 and 22, 1850, all reported mass emigration of blacks to Canada. Some four hundred left Massachusetts alone, and that by the end of May 1851. The Fugitive Slave Law had a significant impact on the way many Americans in the North felt about slavery and antislavery. Such draconian measures so outraged people in the North over the federal interference into their states' rights that many who had previously been neutral on the issue were pushed into the abolitionist fold. Horace Greeley of the *New-York Tribune* wrote that the Fugitive Slave Law was a "very bad investment for slaveholders, [producing] a wide and powerful feeling among all classes averse to the Institution itself." When *Uncle Tom's Cabin* was published a year later, the antislavery banners were unfurled across the Northern states, and they would not be put away until after Appomattox.

When Harriet Beecher Stowe wrote *Uncle Tom's Cabin*, her husband believed it might earn her enough to buy a new silk dress. The book, with its dramatic portrayal of slave conditions, alerted literally millions of readers worldwide to the plight of American bondspeople. Shortly after it appeared as a serial in 1851 in *The National Era*, two panoramas of *Uncle Tom's Cabin* were presented at Toronto's St. Lawrence Hall. Transformed into an immensely popular play, it had its first of literally hundreds of performances in the city at the Toronto Lyceum in May and June 1853, and the Blackburns might well have seen it. Thornton and Alfred, of course, knew the stone courthouse at Washington, Kentucky, the site of the famous auction where Uncle Tom was sold, and both men were undoubtedly familiar with Josiah Henson, whose autobiography reputedly provided Stowe with a model for Uncle Tom. Henson was prominent among Canadian blacks as founder of the British American Institute, a manual labor school near Chatham, and as both a lay preacher and community organizer of considerable note. He was also the rescuer of the Lightfoots, so he was doubly likely to have been known to the Blackburn family.

The rumblings of disunion were growing louder as the United States moved inexorably toward war, with the popularity of Stowe's portrayal of plantation slavery yet another irritant under the skin of the already sensitive South. Northern states were no longer safe, even as a stopping place, for fugitive slaves, and what had been a steady stream of refugees entering Canada turned into a flood.

Existing charitable and self-help organizations operated by the black community, like Toronto's Liberating Society, were strained to the limits trying to deal with the deluge of impoverished refugees. Not everyone welcomed the newcomers with open arms; Lord Elgin, Lieutenant Governor of Upper Canada and a former governor of Jamaica, expressed fears that Upper Canada would be "flooded with blackies who are rushing across the frontier to escape from the bloodhounds whom the Fugitive slave bill has let loose on their track." Lord Grey of the British Colonial Office sent a letter to Elgin dated October 25, 1850, asking if nothing could be done to "turn the current to the West Indies," where there was a shortage of labor.

Traffic on the Underground Railroad peaked in this immediate antebellum decade, and thousands more fled unaided. The Blackburns' old friends, the Lightfoots, the Frenches, and now William Lambert and a newcomer to Detroit, George De Baptiste, were busy organizing the transfer to Canada of thousands of runaways who reached Detroit in these years. Also active along the Detroit River frontier was another slave Lucie and her husband knew well. This was Henry Bibb, who had been born not far from Louisville in Shelby County, Kentucky. Escaping in 1837, Bibb had secretly returned three times in futile attempts to rescue his wife and daughter. Eventually he remarried and established himself in Detroit as one of the era's most celebrated antislavery lecturers and the author of a popular fugitive slave autobiography. Henry and his second wife, the abolitionist and teacher Mary Bibb, moved to Sandwich, Upper Canada, after the passage of the Fugitive Slave Law and launched Canada's first black antislavery newspaper. Henry Bibb's *Voice of the Fugitive* announced on August 12, 1851:

> And Still They Come. Fugitive Slaves are constantly arriving here from all parts of the south. We have just been called on by a very fine looking man from Louisiana, away below New Orleans,—several from Kentucky and Missouri and some from North Carolina, two of them arrived in Amherstburg a few weeks since, having been 101 days on their journey from the land of whips & chains, to the land "where colored men are free."

Involved both in supporting the settlements in what is now Southwestern Ontario and in arousing public indignation about the treatment of slaves in the United States were several white abolitionists who had settled in what is now Ontario, mainly in Toronto, during the 1840s. These men and women had previously been engaged in British and American antislavery work and brought with them both organizational expertise and a network of contacts among abolitionists. The Blackburns were perhaps closest to one Scottish family named Brown that was to loom large in both publishing and politics almost until the end of the Blackburns' lives. The most prominent was George Brown, founder of the Toronto *Globe* in 1844; in its pages, he would champion antislavery for decades. The *Globe* was the precursor of today's *Globe and Mail*, Canada's national newspaper. In 1851, Brown entered politics as a Reformer, once receiving a letter that promised support if he would favor the exclusion of black children from public schools and a poll tax to limit African American immigration. Brown's response, published in the *Globe*, was pithy and immediate; he confessed himself shocked that there were "150 men degraded enough to sign such a paper."

Although African Canadians were very conservative in politics, fearing the "republicanism" that in their minds enabled slavery in the United States, they threw their support behind their very vocal antislavery friend. The black vote was important to Brown throughout his political career. Known as the "Father of Confederation," George Brown would be responsible for bringing together the dissonant factions of these former British colonies to establish the new country of Canada in 1867. In the 1850s, Thornton Blackburn was to serve on at least one committee with George Brown that focused on improving conditions for fugitive slaves settling in the southwestern part of the province. Their association would come about as a result of a convention held in Toronto in September 1851. Perhaps indicative of a deeper friendship between the men is the fact that in 1855, the Blackburns purchased their family grave plot at the newly established Toronto Necropolis Cemetery, directly adjacent to one George Brown intended for his own burial.

The purpose of Brown and the Blackburns' shared work was to

enhance the economic stability of a black settlement that had just been founded in the western part of the province. While the Blackburns' adopted home of Toronto was becoming pivotal in the Anglo-American antislavery movement, the rest of the province, and particularly the old Western District, had evolved into a laboratory for fugitive slave resettlement. By the late 1840s, it had become apparent that new mechanisms to help people whose homes, families, and entire way of life had been left behind south of the Mason-Dixon Line had to be found, and soon, lest white prejudice against them be stirred up in districts receiving the largest numbers. Developments in the United States would soon make the matter even more critical.

In Dawn Township, near Chatham in Canada West, Josiah Henson and Hiram Wilson had already established the British American Institute, and a number of black families had bought farms nearby. Along the Detroit River were neat farmsteads scattered among those of white settlers, part of the Sandwich Mission established in 1846. Despite fiscal difficulties experienced by early fugitive slave settlements, more such schemes were planned. Colonizing provided incoming refugees with their own land and livelihoods, and it was hoped that successful colonies in Canada would demonstrate that people with black skin were as industrious, temperate, pious, and worthy of freedom as those with white.

The Blackburns were affluent, for all the modest lifestyle they maintained, and were solicited for funds to underwrite such ventures. The one in which they became the most involved was founded in 1849 on nine thousand acres of marshy land in Raleigh Township, south of Chatham. It was the brainchild of Scots Presbyterian minister Reverend William King. After he lost his wife and children to illness, King found himself the heir to his Louisiana-born wife's slaves. Convinced of the equality of African Americans with whites, he set about establishing a model community to demonstrate that black people, once freed and given a more or less level playing field, would make successful citizens. King came to Canada and appealed to Lord Elgin, the Governor General, for land and to the well-to-do businessmen of Toronto and Montreal for backing. Its formal title was Elgin Settlement and Buxton Mission, but it was most often known simply as Buxton, after the contemporary British abolitionist Thomas Fowell Buxton. There was much local opposition to the settlement at first, but the newcomers proved themselves model citizens.

Reverend King imposed a stringent set of rules regarding who might purchase land (fugitive slaves of good character), how long a commitment was required (ten years), the style of house that could be constructed, and even the size of the garden and type of fencing that could be erected. It was also self-governing and adhered to strict temperance principles. Despite much opposition on the part of local whites, who objected to so many former slaves living in their midst and who refused the children access to local schools, Buxton thrived. By 1860, there would be more than twelve hundred people living at the settlement and on adjacent lands. The settlers built their own school. Taught by Knox College students, this was the only grammar school for black children in the province. Students were trained in Latin and Greek, higher mathematics, music, theology, and other upper-level subjects, and a significant number attended the University of Toronto, Knox College's divinity school, and the Toronto Normal School, which was the teachers' college of the day. Families from as far away as Alabama sent their children to attend the Buxton School. The local white school soon closed its doors, parents preferring to send their children to the superior Buxton facility.

The modern village of North Buxton remains home to about two hundred descendants of the fugitive slave families who once found safe haven there. There is a persistent tradition among the oldest families that Thornton and Lucie Blackburn spent some of their retirement years at Buxton, although records show they always maintained their home in Toronto.

Moving from his involvement in the Elgin Association, George

Brown became the driving force behind the creation of the Anti-Slavery Society of Canada. This was sparked by the passage of the harsh Fugitive Slave Law in January 1851 by the U.S. Congress. The first organizational meeting inaugurated Toronto's elegant new St. Lawrence Hall, which stood on King Street nearly opposite Thornton's taxi stand by St. James Cathedral. The *Globe* of March 1, 1851, reported that this was the "largest and most enthusiastic meeting we have ever seen in Toronto . . . [and] was called to enable the citizens of Toronto to enter their protest against the manifold and unspeakable iniquities of slavery." African Canadians, African Americans, and a great many clergymen as well as the rank and file of the city's white population joined in efforts both to protest the new American legislation and to accommodate the increase in American refugees that would surely follow implementation of the revised Fugitive Slave Law.

The ASC's officers were largely clergymen, with Michael Willis, in charge of the Presbyterian Knox College, as president and George Brown's brother-in-law, Thomas Henning, as corresponding secretary. Captain Charles Stuart, the old friend of the Amherstburg black community again residing in Canada, was also appointed a society secretary. The main organizing group included two black men: Henry Bibb and A. Beckford Jones, also a fugitive slave and prosperous apothecary from London who would go on to found the London Anti-Slavery Society. Wilson Ruffin Abbott, who had just moved his family to the Chatham area so his son Anderson could be educated at the Buxton school, was a local vice president. Distance precluded much active participation by these men in the actual deliberations of the society, which may have influenced their initial appointment. White abolitionists in Toronto, like their American counterparts, were not all entirely comfortable with sitting at a table with blacks, however much they opposed slavery in the abstract. The societies in Windsor, Chatham, Amherstburg, and elsewhere were, by contrast, vibrant and active organizations under mainly black leadership.

It is frustrating not to have more information about Lucie Blackburn's role in black Canadian resistance at this juncture. Paradoxically, as a black woman she had more scope for action than did her white sisters in the antislavery movement. Slavery and poverty were both great leveling forces, and black Americans and black Canadians were quite familiar with women in leadership roles. On the American side of the border, Sojourner Truth, a fugitive slave, was a regular lecturer at U.S. conferences and widely considered one of the most eloquent speakers on the subject, male or female. Delaware-born abolitionist and educator Mary Ann Shadd attended conventions although she could not vote, gave regular lectures, and in 1849 published "Hints to the Colored People of the United States" in an attempt to encourage black self- and political awareness. Black women in Toronto lectured, administered church organizations and temperance and benevolent societies, and organized fund-raising drives. In Chatham, Canada West, women were in the forefront of the temperance crusade, an important plank in efforts to "uplift the race," while Barbara Freeman of Windsor, whose husband, Coleman Freeman, had been part of the British-American Anti-Slavery Society since the 1830s, served on the governing boards of the provincial branches of the Anti-Slavery Society of Canada.

However, if she attended the ASC meetings—and a great many women did—Mrs. Blackburn's participation would have been circumscribed by the gender conventions observed by the white male officers of the society. In Toronto, women, white or black, had no voice in official antislavery. British and Canadian abolitionists generally did not adhere to the American William Lloyd Garrison's feminism that would have allowed women into every sphere of influence. There were no female officers on the Anti-Slavery Society executive board, nor were women permitted to either lecture or vote at its meetings; yet, as was the case in Britain and the United States, Toronto women were very active in the practical side of fugitive slave reception and assistance. An auxiliary was formed, the Toronto Ladies Association for the Relief of Destitute Colored Refugees, which also included members

of Toronto's black community. This group became more politically active as time went on; an article in *Frederick Douglass' Paper*
of January 21, 1853, recorded an "address" from the Toronto
Ladies Association to the "women of the United States" that
pleaded passionately for an end to slavery, which "substitutes
concubinage for the sacred institution of marriage" and tears
"children from the arms of their parents." In a typically Victorian
elliptical reference to the power of the bedroom, the appeal
begged American women to "use [their] influence to win [their
husbands and slave owners] into the path of 'virtue.'"

The exclusion of women from the ASC is odd considering that
a member of the Windsor ASC Executive, Harriet Tubman, was
the most famous of all the Underground Railroad conductors.
She had escaped from Maryland in 1849 and was living in St.
Catharines, Upper Canada. The ASC president, Michael Willis,
became a great friend of this staunch, unstoppable woman and
helped to finance her ventures. Two years after the passage of the
Fugitive Slave Law, Willis wrote an open letter to *Frederick Douglass' Paper*:

> From 4,000 to 5,000 crossed the lines in a few months, and
> found, on British ground, that liberty which was denied to
> them in the country of their birth. Many of these refugees
> had lived for years unmolested in the Northern States, pro-
> tected by the difficulty which some of these States threw in
> the way of the slaveholders in recovering their human prop-
> erty. That difficulty, however, was at length removed by the
> Fugitive Slave Law, and no alternative remained for these
> oppressed people, but to take refuge under the British flag.
> Many of them arrived in Canada in a state of destitution,
> which was the more severely felt when they came in the fall
> of the year . . . a considerable amount of suffering has been
> the consequence.

Toronto's African Canadians, including the Blackburn family,
were very well informed about international antislavery, for lec-

tures by some of its leading lights were presented in the city. Six weeks after its inauguration, the Anti-Slavery Society of Canada welcomed three illustrious speakers to Toronto. The black abolitionist Frederick Douglass, the American Samuel J. May, and the eloquent British antislavery activist George Thompson traveled together to Upper Canada in March 1851, a journey reported in some detail in Frederick Douglass's newspaper, *The North Star*, on April 10 of that year. Douglass was impressed by the gentlemanly and courteous treatment he had received on the Canadian steamer the *Chief Justice* while en route from Lewiston, New York, to Toronto. Most talks drew large crowds of both blacks and whites, although Douglass annoyed recently arrived African Americans in one audience by saying that their leaving the United States had materially weakened the black abolitionist cause. Part of his speech was an appeal to Torontonians to do all they could to help end slavery in the United States. He said that taking arms against slave catchers was the only means by which such "human bloodhounds" could really be discouraged. This latter call to violence elicited a hysterical response from Toronto's very conservative Anglican organ, *The Church*. Usually at least tacitly supportive of the fugitive slave, the established Church of England was very opposed to any call to actually kill or injure slaveholders, "bloodhounds" or not. The *Globe* responded that the Church of England's position was more fitted to the Middle Ages than to the nineteenth century.

Because of his anti-emigrationist stance, at least at this point in his career, Douglass would not take part in the most important antislavery event ever held in Toronto, the Convention of Colored Freemen. However, a prosperous Toronto couple named Thornton and Lucie Blackburn would be there. At the conference, Thornton would be appointed to a very responsible post, one that was a recognition on the part of his peers of both his business acumen and his dedication to the cause of the fugitive slave.

In the summer of 1851, Henry Bibb put out a call for a great "North American Convention." Its purpose was to discuss issues arising from the large numbers of runaways entering Canada and to establish mechanisms for their reception. The call for delegates in the *Voice of the Fugitive* of August 13, 1851, announced: "Don't be afraid of sending too many, but be sure to send us men of good common sense. It is not necessary that they should all be orators or good public speakers . . . If ever there was a time when our people should be willing to make sacrifices for their own advancement, it is now." The same paper on August 27, 1851, named seventy-one delegates, although it was later reported that only fifty-three formally participated. John G. Bowes, the mayor of Toronto, opened the North American Convention, also called the Convention of Colored Freemen, at St. Lawrence Hall on September 11, 1851.

Thornton Blackburn was one of only five delegates appointed to represent Toronto's black community at this landmark event. Also on the committee was John D. Tinsley, an artist and "shorthand writer" transplanted from Virginia and whose father was associated with Thornton in a variety of real estate transactions. Vice president of the meeting was James Charles Brown, now living at Chatham, while other members of the Toronto group included R. Beverly Snow, the unwitting catalyst of Washington, D.C.'s Snow Riots, who had more reason than most to promote Canada as a safe haven for those who had suffered persecution. From Detroit came William Lambert, the clothing dealer Robert Banks, the tailor Alfred Derrick, the Methodist minister John W. Brooks, and the barber Thomas Freeman. These men, though active in Underground Railroad operations through Michigan, had previously shared Frederick Douglass's reservations about encouraging the emigration from the United States of those people best fitted to resist slavery and help the fugitive. Now they abandoned their stance in the face of the Fugitive Slave Law. The missionary Hiram Wilson, who had just moved from Josiah Henson's fugitive slave settlement at the modern Dresden to St. Catharines, chaired part of the conference, one of only three white men presiding.

Vermont's tiny black community could not afford to send James Theodore Holly, who had been involved with Bibb in designing the meeting, so they appointed the Toronto saloon keeper J. T. Fisher to present their inspiring written proposal for the creation of a new black North American League. Its goal was to unify the efforts of the dozens of separate black organizations that had proliferated in the United States and Canada in past years. It was proposed that the league would have its head office in Toronto, with branches all over the United States and Canada. Two-thirds of the executive was to be made up of Toronto residents in order to facilitate decision making. Objectives of the new North American League were ambitious:

first, to make a comfortable asylum for refugees from slavery: second, to encourage the removal of the free colored people from the United States to Canada; third, to have them engage in the cultivation of the soil, as the basis of all industrial operations—after agriculture becomes well developed, to erect mills and manufactories—after erection of mills and manufactories to proceed to commercial exportation.

The conference debated for three days. Finally it resolved that the "British Government is the most favorable in the civilized world to the people of color, and is thereby entitled to our entire confidence." The *Voice of the Fugitive* was lauded as the only black abolitionist newspaper in Canada West, and the conference vowed to help extend the newspaper's circulation. Delegates expressed disapproval of self-segregated schooling and churches as "contributing greatly toward the promotion of prejudice, heretofore unknown in the Canadas, and we do hereby recommend that all such organizations be abandoned as speedily as may be practicable." The most senior members of the black abolitionist movement discussed whether abolitionists and Underground Railroad operators should promote Liberia, the West Indies, Britain, or Canada as the destination of the fugitives who fled U.S. soil. All concluded Canada provided blacks with the best opportunities for landownership, economic advancement, and education, and by far the most advanced civil liberty. Canada West was thus confirmed as the approved haven for passengers on the Underground Railroad. The fact that the meetings were held in Toronto, rather than in an American city such as Boston or New York, spoke volumes: the newspapers of the day said it was because the city was the only place on the continent that so large a group of black abolitionists felt safe to congregate.

Thornton Blackburn and his wife would have been introduced to nearly all the most prominent abolitionists in the Great Lakes region at this conference, as well as several who came from farther afield. Present at the deliberations was Dr. Martin R. Delany, a free black educated in Pittsburgh who had first published an abolitionist paper of his own, *The Mystery*, and later worked as co-editor with Douglass on *The North Star*. He and three other delegates believed it was "impolitic and contrary to our professed policy in opposing the infamous Fugitive Slave Law, and schemes of American colonization," to support removal of fugitives from American soil. While he and the others had their names stricken from the record of the resolution calling for further African American immigration into Canada, Delany would himself within a few years become so disillusioned with America's embedded racism that he would first move to Canada and then begin colonizing efforts on the west coast of Africa. He is known as the father of American black nationalism.

A number of important antislavery figures moved to Canada after the conference. Abraham Doras Shadd, a free black shoemaker, had been one of only six black men appointed to the executive of the American Anti-Slavery Society when it was formed. Present at the first black antislavery convention, which was held in Philadelphia in 1830, Shadd, between 1830 and the early 1850s, was on the executive committee of the American Society of Free Persons of Color, the most vociferous opponent of the American Colonization Society. Shadd came to Toronto accompanied by his accomplished eldest daughter, Mary Ann, a school-teacher, author, and soon to be a publisher.

In 1852, Abraham Doras Shadd settled his large family on a farm on the outskirts of the Elgin Association settlement. Influential and highly principled, Shadd went on to become the first black man to achieve public office in Canada West. He was elected alderman for Kent County in 1862. Mary Ann Shadd joined the Bibbs in Sandwich and opened a school for black children in Windsor in early spring 1852. That same year she published *A Plea for Emigration; or, Notes of Canada West in Its Moral, Social, and Political Aspects*, which extolled the virtues of Canada as a place for black immigrants to settle. The outspoken Shadd would go on to found Canada West's second and highly influential abolitionist paper, *The Provincial Freeman*, after the demise of Bibbs's *Voice of the Fugitive*. Mary Ann Shadd's *Provincial Freeman* would be published under a masthead that trumpeted her feelings on accepting aid for fugitive slave resettlement to the world: "Self-Reliance Is the True Road to Independence."

The Reverend Samuel Ringgold Ward and a noted Underground Railroad operator, the Reverend Jermain Wesley Loguen, both lived in Syracuse at the time they attended the Toronto meetings. These men's personal freedom was endangered less than one month later because of their involvement in the rescue of the fugitive slave Jerry McHenry, who had been captured in New York state and was about to be sent back to the South under the terms of the Fugitive Slave Law. Ward and Loguen found this a good time to move their families to Canada, Ward settling in Toronto and becoming a traveling lecturer for the Anti-Slavery Society of Canada, and Loguen becoming pastor of a St. Catharines church and supporting Harriet Tubman in her daring personal missions to rescue slaves from the Southern states.

Thornton himself came out of the meetings with a new office that was at once a recognition of his business skills and a commentary on his personal dedication to the twin causes of antislavery and black self-help. He was appointed vice president of the

Canadian Mill and Mercantile Association. Prompted by concerns that prejudice would be engendered because of the large numbers of fugitive slaves entering Canada, all needing employment, this was a black-led initiative to create jobs for them in the area of highest black settlement, near the American border around Chatham. Dr. Anderson Ruffin Abbott, who had attended the Buxton school, wrote in "The Elgin Settlement," dated February 1, 1894, and published in the *New York Age*: "This sudden influx of a pauper population caused great alarm to the people in that section, and had it not been for the influence of the better class, who comprised the bulk of the Anti-Slavery and Abolition societies, legislation would have been invoked to put a stop to it."

The Canadian Mill and Mercantile Association was a joint-stock company supported by subscription. The *Voice of the Fugitive* of May 6, 1852, named its officers, while detailing the group's objectives and underlying philosophical stance: "The company will establish a saw mill, grist mill and good country store, believing that this is the only way for us to become independent and respectable in business transactions." The mills would provide immediate employment for incoming fugitives and secure the economic base of the Buxton community for years to come. Thornton's friend John M. Tinsley was named president, Wilson Ruffin Abbott the treasurer, and Toronto's John T. Fisher was secretary. The first stockholders were listed as the Reverend William King of Buxton, Thornton Blackburn of Toronto, John M. Tinsley, and George Brown, publisher of the Toronto *Globe*, for a total value of £750. The board of directors included Henry K. Thomas of Buffalo, who was soon to move to the Buxton settlement and whose nephew James T. Rapier, educated at the Buxton school and the Toronto Normal School, would one day be elected Alabama's first black congressman during Reconstruction.

Henry Bibb heartily approved these efforts, writing in the *Voice of the Fugitive*, "We are happy to see that our people are getting their eyes open, and are now beginning to strike for something higher than perpetual begging." This latter referred to the custom of some black abolitionists, as well as a number of charlatans out only to line their own pockets, to lecture in the northern United States and England to raise money supposedly destined for the "destitute" fugitives in Canada. The practice infuriated the independent, community-minded blacks living in Canada, who felt such fund-raising efforts not only unnecessary but damaging to the cause of black self-actualization. The same paper on April 22, 1852, reported, "A committee of three was appointed to select a good mill seat as soon as the weather permits traveling." These were Thornton's fellow officers in the organization: the Reverend William King, John M. Tinsley, and Wilson Ruffin Abbott, the latter the most prominent of the Toronto blacks.

On Emancipation Day 1854, Henry Bibb, the crusader and the publisher of the *Voice of the Fugitive*, died at the age of thirty-nine. His newspaper offices had mysteriously burned, and the loss of the paper to the community was tragic. His own passage was marked by the people who respected his lifelong dedication to the cause of freedom on both sides of the border. Given their long association with the district, it is possible Thornton and Lucie Blackburn attended the memorial to the great abolitionist and colleague. The Detroit Emancipation Day celebrations chaired by William Lambert included a waterborne vigil on the river in honor of Bibb. George De Baptiste announced the death of his old friend to the assembled multitudes. Soon after the *Voice of the Fugitive* ceased publication, Mary Ann Shadd, the first woman newspaper publisher in Canada, would found *The Provincial Freeman*, and her paper served the needs of black Canada for another five or so years. The two newspapers performed vital functions: informing Canadians of the conditions and progress of the Underground Railroad; offering advice on agricultural, business, household, and political matters, all of which were very important to the newly arrived former slaves, some of whom had never managed anything before in their lives; and haranguing both other blacks and the U.S. and Canadian governments on political and social issues. *The Provincial Freeman* warned African Canadians throughout the 1850s that slave catchers were operating in the Toronto area, and on January 20, 1854, published the following:

A PLAN TO KIDNAP FUGITIVES:

We copy this week, from the Montreal Gazette, a letter from a police officer of Maryland, directed to the Chief of Police in Montreal, requesting him to engage in a kidnapping scheme. While we know that such a proposition will be rejected with scorn by all loyal subjects, we would warn our brethren throughout the Provinces to be careful about venturing across the line, and indeed to keep a sharp look-out even within the borders. This plan, it will be seen, only contemplates getting them to the borders. Times are dull in the States, while the price of everything, the slaves included, is high, so that a reward, accompanied with a description, as this man promises, may tempt the hungry Yankees to any acts of villainy. Persons at Windsor, Niagara, and other places on the line should be doubly careful, and those more remote should not be tempted to the frontier by any letter from unknown parties, no matter how plausible they may seem.

The 1850s were a busy time both personally and professionally for Thornton and Lucie Blackburn. The work of the Canadian Mill and Mercantile Association consumed a good deal of energy and necessitated travel back and forth to Buxton, a distance of almost 200 miles. Fortunately, the Great Western Railway opened the line from Toronto as far as Windsor in January of 1854. Tracks were constructed through the north end of the Elgin Association lands and provided employment for a good many of the men who found refuge at the settlement. Railroad wages enabled them to pay off their mortgages much faster than earlier settlers had been able to do. More fugitives were arriving daily, for the advent of the railway also enhanced the abilities of the Underground Railroad to transport its passengers more swiftly north-ward. Larger numbers of women and children were now able to travel its routes, for the way was less arduous and dangerous than before. William Troy, a minister to the black community at Windsor and himself a fugitive slave, wrote in his memoirs:

> The number of fugitive slaves in Canada is now upwards of forty thousand. They are scattered through the western province singly and in settlements from Kingston, 100 miles below Toronto; to Amherstburg and Colchester, 200 miles west of Toronto; and from Toronto eastward to St. Cather-ines, Suspension Bridge and Chippewa, a further distance of 80 miles. The number of souls in these settlements varies from a few families (as at Kingston) to 200 families (as in the Elgin settlement), and 300 or 400 families (as in Col-chester). They are increasing every year by about 2,000 new accessions from the land of bondage. Some have come fif-teen hundred miles, travelling at night and hiding by day, for freedom. Coming stripped of nearly everything, many need, in the beginning, a helping hand extended to them. But, generally speaking, the fugitive slaves are pleased to ob-tain labour, and to thus become self-sustaining, so far as their physical wants are concerned. It is believed that nine-tenths of the fugitives have received no aid for their physical wants from any source whatever, but have been able, by God's blessing, to sustain themselves.

Whites alarmed by the numbers of black American refugees and the Toronto *Colonist* of April 27, 1855, voiced their concerns: "We fear that they are coming rather too fast for the good of the Province. People may talk about the horrors of slavery as much as they choose; but fugitive slaves are by no means a desirable class of immigrants for Canada, especially when they come in large numbers." In the face of vigorous protest the *Colonist* found it advisable to retract its statement, or at least soften it. *The*

Provincial Freeman of May 5, 1855, reprinted the following from a subsequent edition of the *Colonist*:

> We understand that some of our colored friends are annoyed, because we said recently that fugitive slaves were not the most desirable of settlers. Our meaning we thought was obvious enough, namely, that men of that class are usually too ignorant and too brutally trained to make good citizens. Were the fugitives men of intelligence and industrious habits, we should be glad to receive them among us, without once enquiring what was their color.

George P. Ure's *Handbook of Toronto*, published in 1858, said that many of the African American newcomers "reached our city in the greatest distress, their immediate wants had to be provided for while employment was obtained as far as possible for those who were able to labor." Toronto black families did what they could to alleviate the suffering of the newcomers, Thornton and Lucie Blackburn among them. In addition to renting their several St. John's Ward properties to a series of recently arrived refugees, they also sometimes received people in their own home. In 1858, the Blackburns made lifelong friends with Ann Maria Jackson and her family of nine children. The account of Mrs. Jackson's adventures was recorded by William Still, secretary of the Philadelphia Vigilant Committee, who kept careful notes about each fugitive his organization succored, and who after the Civil War published their stories in *The Underground Rail Road*.

Ann Maria Jackson's story is one of the most poignant in all its annals. She came to William Still's busy Underground Railroad station at Philadelphia by way of Wilmington, Delaware. Mrs. Jackson was sent on to the Pennsylvania organization for protection, and there she told Still her heartbreaking story of how she, a slave, had been married to a free man, but in the fall of 1858, "she lost her husband under most trying circumstances . . . she had been allowed to live with her husband and children, independently of her master, by supporting herself and them with the white-wash brush, wash-tub, etc."

But, as Mrs. Jackson told her benefactor,

> she had never been at ease in Slavery a day after the birth of her first-born. The desire to go to some part of the world where she could have the control and comfort of her children, had always been a prevailing idea with her. "It almost broke my heart," she said, "when he came and took my children away as soon as they were big enough to hand me a drink of water. My husband was always very kind to me, and I had often wanted him to run away with me and the children, but I could not get him in the notion; he did not feel that he could, and so he stayed, and died broken-hearted, crazy."

Grieving now for her husband and terrified for her children, she resolved to take her remaining family and make her escape.

Still forwarded Ann Maria and seven children on to Canada, where the dedicated Hiram Wilson received them at St. Catharines. Wilson wrote to Still on November 20, 1858:

> Dear Bro. Still—I am happy to inform you that Mrs. Jackson and her interesting family of children arrived safe in very good health and spirits at my house in St. Catharines. On Saturday evening last with sincere pleasure I provided them with comfortable quarters till this morning, when they left for Toronto.

Ann Maria and her family probably stayed only a short time in Thornton and Lucie's tiny home before moving to rented rooms in St. John's Ward. There, Mrs. Jackson took in washing and sent her children to school to gain the education they had been denied in slavery.

Happily, as it turned out, Mrs. Jackson's eldest son, who had been sold away from her, also escaped. Evidently Still made the connection, for he wrote in his volume *The Underground Railroad*:

> JAMES HENRY JACKSON is seventeen years of age; he testifies that he fled from Frederica, Delaware, where he had been owned by Joseph Brown. Jim does not make any serious complaint against his master, except that he had him in the market for sale. To avert this fate, Jim was moved to flee. His mother, Ann Jackson, lived nine miles from Milford . . . Of the going of her son she had no knowledge.

James had left Philadelphia at the beginning of September 1858, eventually arriving in St. Catharines, in Canada West. Sent on to Toronto to be reunited with his delighted mother, he went to work as a waiter at the elegant Queen's Hotel. Ann Maria Jackson's second son, Richard M. Jackson, finally escaped to Toronto as well. Census records show that Dick Jackson, a very popular barber, was living with his sister on Elizabeth Street by 1871. The entire Jackson family had reached freedom. His brother Albert Jackson grew up to become the first African Canadian postal worker in the city, and his appointment caused some friction because it elevated a black man over white postal workers in lesser positions such as mail sorting. Albert was kept as an inside worker, despite being hired as a postman to deliver mail, until the people of St. John's Ward launched a public inquiry. The committee included another of Ann Maria's grown sons, John. Eventually Albert was assigned to deliver mail rather than simply sort it at the post office building.

White resistance to African American settlement in Southwestern Ontario increased as the 1850s wore on, making the work of the Blackburns and their partners in the Canadian Mill and Mercantile Association all the more vital.

Thornton and the other officers of the company had as their first objective to construct a steam sawmill so Elgin settlers could profit from the beautiful stands of highly salable timber that blanketed the settlement. Most settlers, both white and black, wasted such resources by burning these trees they cleared from their land, but Blackburn and the other officers learned that the fine hardwood lumber could easily be exported, especially to Britain. Josiah Henson had just returned from participating in the Great Exhibition in London, where he presented four highly polished boards produced by former slaves in the vicinity of the British American Institute at Dawn, just a few miles from Buxton. It was likely Henson who suggested that the new venture in which Thornton was engaged should look to England to market its milled lumber. The second goal of the association was to provide for the construction of a gristmill. This way the Buxtonites could avoid transporting their grain to the mills in Chatham. This would save money and help make the settlement as self-sufficient as possible. The finely honed business skills of Tinsley, Blackburn, and Abbott came to the fore in respect to the third objective: since all goods brought into the settlement were purchased in either Chatham or surrounding villages, often at ruinous prices, the association proposed underwriting the establishment of a general store in the village.

A description of the Canadian Mill and Mercantile Association's accomplishments appeared in the *Fifth Annual Report of the Elgin Association*, announcing the completion of the sawmill was anticipated by midsummer 1855. That spring Buxton founder Reverend William King, together with Wilson Ruffin Abbott and John M. Tinsley, went to Detroit and purchased a steam sawmill engine. They also learned that a second mill, this time for grinding grain, could be operated using the same engine. The necessary attachments were ordered from their Cincinnati manufacturer, and the fifteen-horsepower engine was put to work. The mill was northeast of the crossroads at South Buxton. The economic importance of a steam sawmill to the growing community was lauded:

The value of oak timber on the Association lands is valued at $57,000, of maple, hickory, etc. is valued at $70,000. But they had no saw mill before. Now the mill is completed and will be ready by the 4th of July and a plank road is to be built to open up 2 markets for the timber . . . the road will be 8 miles long from the Great Western Rail Road to the Lake. The 2 markets are across the Lake and on the Railroad.

Wilson Ruffin Abbott contributed the land on which the mill would be built, but Thornton Blackburn did not take part in the 1855 trip to purchase the mill machinery. The Blackburns, in fact, seem to have missed most activities at Buxton that year, probably because of serious illness in the family. Thornton's mother had been in poor health for some months, and Alfred was clearly not well. He suffered from emphysema, and had not been employed since the previous year. With Thornton managing their rental properties in St. John's Ward and operating the taxi business, undoubtedly much of the work entailed in caring for her in-laws fell to Lucie. Sibby Blackburn, aged eighty, passed away on October 27, 1855. Her place of birth on the death records was listed as Virginia. The cause of her passing was simply "old age." The records of the Toronto General Burying Grounds show that Thornton purchased a family plot with room for six individuals in the summer of that same year, so his mother's death must have seemed imminent. Although Alfred was quite unwell, he continued to live alone at his own home near the southwest corner of Palace and what is now Cherry Street.

But Buxton thrived. The *Anti-Slavery Reporter* of December 1, 1855, informed its readership that since the first settler had arrived on December 3, 1849, the community had made steady and admirable progress, with nearly all of the land now taken up. There were 827 cleared acres, with 216 ready for planting. The tobacco crop in particular was of superior quality. The town with its homesteads looked "neat and attractive," and there were some 150 children attending day school on a regular basis. Both Greek and Latin were taught in the school, and some of the girls were studying piano. The article also commented on the inauguration of the new sawmill, which served as a gristmill. The *Sixth Annual Report of the Elgin Association* offered the following: "The saw mill now supplies abundance of lumber for the settlement, so that during the next year, there is a prospect of having more houses finished than during any one year since the settlement commenced." A little more than two years later, the *Anti-Slavery Reporter*, in the March 1, 1858, issue, reprinted an article from the *New-York Tribune* about Buxton. Evidently, the Canadian Mill and Mercantile Association's 1851 goals had been met, although there is no direct evidence that the general store was ever constructed as a result of that organization's efforts. It is known that some $3,000 had been raised in Toronto and Buffalo for the association's purposes.

The fact that the driving force behind the Canadian Mill and Mercantile Association was the Toronto black community, including successful businessman Thornton Blackburn, was not surprising. Black leaders were understandably concerned that no refugee African American appear indigent or engage in criminal activities out of desperation to feed his or her family; a single bad example undermined years of effort. The black abolitionist movement never wavered. In the United States, African American spokesmen and -women grew ever less patient, demanding an immediate end to slavery and some even counseling violence against slaveholders. On the Canadian side of the border, the ongoing immigration of people from the South kept the memories of bondage fresh for those who were fugitives themselves and strengthened the determination of the Blackburns and their contemporaries to fight on, until the battle to end human bondage was won.

From the safety of Toronto, the Blackburns and their friends watched as from the United States came ominous signs of war. The pages of the *Globe* were filled with the brewing dissension between North and South. In 1854, the U.S. Congress passed the Kansas-Nebraska Act, leaving the highly contentious issue of whether the newest state to join the Union would be slave or free up to local voters and creating a battlefield that became known as Bleeding Kansas. There the fanatical white abolitionist John Brown massacred five pro-slavery men at Pottawatomie Creek. In March 1857, the U.S. Supreme Court brought down its landmark Dred Scott Decision, where Chief Justice Roger Taney expressed his opinion that a slave had no rights a white man was bound to respect. Taney had effectively declared the provisions of the Missouri Compromise of 1820 unconstitutional. The great national divide over the issue of slavery widened until there was no possibility of healing the breach.

In 1858, a gangly politician from Illinois, born not far from Hardinsburg, Kentucky, where Thornton had lived as a slave of Gideon and Susan Brown, would range over the Midwest holding a series of debates in which he developed his views on slavery, nationhood, and the inviolable quality of the Union. The last speech in the series was given at Alton, Illinois, on October 15, 1858, and was perhaps the most eloquent of Abraham Lincoln's early commentaries on slavery:

> These are the two principles that have stood face to face from the beginning of time and will ever continue to struggle. The one is the common right of humanity, the other the divine right of kings. It is the same principle in whatever shape it develops itself. It is the same spirit that says, "You work and toil and earn bread, and I eat it." No matter what shape it comes, whether from the mouth of a king who seeks to bestride the people of his own nation and live by the fruit of their labor, or from one race of men as an apology for enslaving another race, it is the same tyrannical principle.

In 1859, the same John Brown who had fought in Kansas, with the backing of a segment of the black Canadian population, was almost single-handedly to bring the United States to the brink of war. Brown arrived at Detroit with fourteen fugitive slaves he had rescued from Missouri and held a landmark meeting to garner backing for his plan to establish a separate black state in the mountains of western Virginia. His arrival in the city was coordinated by William Lambert, the son-in-law of the now deceased Benjamin Willoughby, who had orchestrated Thornton and Lucie Blackburns' rescue from the city twenty-six years before. It was organized to coincide with the arrival of Frederick Douglass, who was scheduled to give a speech. The two men were entertained in the Lambert home, where the widowed Deborah Willoughby, aged eighty-five, also resided. The official meeting at the house of William Webb, an important local black abolitionist who had arrived in Detroit after the Blackburns' time there, was seminal to the development of Brown's future plans. Brown and his men passed part of the winter of 1858–59 in Chatham, Ontario. There, hosted by Isaac Shadd, Mary Ann's brother and partner in *The Provincial Freeman*, Brown sought black Canadian support for a raid on the U.S. Army arsenal at Harpers Ferry, Virginia. Harriet Tubman, still living at St. Catharines, gave her wholehearted backing to his scheme. On May 8, 1858, John Brown held a convention at Chatham chaired by the Reverend William C. Monroe of Detroit and attended by William Lambert to explain his manifesto for revolution and to devise a constitution for the new African American state. The Blackburns' names are not listed among the delegates, but they may well have been present for they had many friends in the room. In addition to Monroe and Lambert, Dr. Martin R. Delany, the dissenter against Canadian emigration from the 1851 Toronto convention now himself residing at Chatham, Canada West, was present, as were Mary Ann Shadd and her brothers. Brown believed the violence would spark a slave revolt that would spread across the nation and result in the creation of an independent African American republic in the hills of western Virginia. He was well financed by monies provided by the "Secret Six," white American abolitionists who believed in Brown's scheme. However, the Reverend William King of Buxton cautioned the people of his community that Brown's plan had no chance of success, and in the end only one Canadian black, Osborne Anderson, took part.

Brown expected slaves living around Harpers Ferry to rise up and join him in overthrowing their oppressors. Poor communications and worse planning thwarted the plot and the anticipated servile revolt never materialized. Quickly surrounded, two of his sons killed and himself wounded, Brown was forced to surrender. The failure of John Brown's raid on Harpers Ferry was announced in the Toronto *Globe* of October 19, 1859. By the next day, the paper was describing the attack as an "organized uprising of Virginia slaves" and Brown as the "hero of the rebellion at Harpers Ferry." Although the Civil War was as yet two years in the future, the publisher George Brown took the occasion to caution slaveholders: "A war with the North, which the slaveholders often threaten, will appear a rather different affair when this insurrection is properly considered. They will probably agree that it is better to let the North alone, and be content with the preservation of their States' rights." On December 6, 1859, the *Globe* announced the execution of John Brown in the most sentimental and heartfelt terms. In Toronto and Montreal, hugely attended church services were held to mourn John Brown and collections taken up to help support his impoverished widow. Here, half a century after Thomas Jefferson penned the words, was the "fireball in the night" that heralded the coming Civil War. Osborne Anderson escaped to Canada and published his own account of the incident.

Abraham Lincoln was elected president of the United States on November 6, 1860. He had once written: "Slavery is founded on the selfishness of man's nature—opposition to it on his love of justice. These principles are in eternal antagonism; and when brought into collision so fiercely as slavery extension brings them, shocks and throes and convulsions must ceaselessly follow." This would prove prophetic. His anti-expansionist stance was too strong for the inflamed Southerners to stomach. One month later, South Carolina seceded from the Union, followed by six more states, forming the Confederate States of America under their own president, the Kentucky-born Mississippi planter and politician Jefferson Davis.

Although most military bastions in the South passed readily into Confederate hands, a few, like Fort Sumter in the harbor of Charleston, South Carolina, held firm. On April 12, 1861, Southern soldiers fired on the military arsenal at Fort Sumter, and the Civil War began. The Union officer in command of the fort, Robert Anderson, was none other than the brother of the Louisville attorney who prosecuted Captain Monroe Quarrier of the steamboat *Versailles* for permitting Thornton and Lucie Blackburn to escape from slavery.

GIRD UP YOUR SWORD

> I listened to the sounds [of the bombardment at Fort
> Sumter] and though many miles away, I fancied I heard
> the cannon, in thunder tones, say, "The year of jubilee
> has come, return, you exiles, home."
>
> —JAMES T. RAPIER, 1860

WHEN THE CIVIL WAR broke out, both Britain and Canada found themselves unsure as to what side to support in the conflict. Antislavery was popular on both sides of the Atlantic, but some fair-minded people could see little difference between Americans fighting for freedom from British imperial rule in the 1776 Revolutionary War, and the Confederacy wishing to leave the Union less than a century later. Abraham Lincoln's main concern was to preserve the Union rather than abolish slavery. His repeated assertions to this effect disappointed abolitionists, dampening enthusiasm for the Northern cause and deeply affecting the American blacks who had found refuge in British North America.

Union interference in neutral shipping infuriated wealthy investors and British parliamentarians alike. British textile factories depended on imported Southern cotton, and the progress of the war caused hardship in the mill towns that dotted the English countryside, a direct effect of the American blockade of Southern ports reported regularly in the Canadian press. When the Confederate delegation to Britain was taken prisoner on the high seas in an infamous incident known as the Trent Affair, Britain considered the act piracy and weighed its role in the conflict carefully. Sympathy for the South escalated in Canada, and black Canadians must have been stunned when three cheers arose spontaneously in the House of Assembly when the news came of the Confederate victory at Bull Run in July 1861. Toronto's George Brown, however, never wavered in his support for the Northern cause, and the pages of the *Globe* crowed over every Union victory. Canada and especially its black population had long feared that Yankee ambitions to expand U.S. territory might be directed northward. Having a large standing army on its border in the event of a Union victory made Canadians wonder what Lincoln might consider, then, as America's Manifest Destiny. This was not in the least unfounded. In 1863, Secretary of State William Seward urged Lincoln to consider invading Canada to reinstill waning enthusiasm for the war effort. A popular marching song to the tune of "Yankee Doodle" went:

> Secession he would first put down
> Wholly and forever
> And afterwards from Britain's Crown,
> He Canada would sever.

Toronto blacks like Thornton, Lucie, Alfred, and Sibby Blackburn who had all suffered terribly at the hands of the slaveholding South experienced no crisis of loyalties as to which side they supported. Rallies were held to cheer on the Northern troops and many a prayer for the Union was sent heavenward from the little Baptist church at Queen and Victoria streets, the British Methodist Episcopal in St. John's Ward, and the Colored Wesleyan Methodist on Richmond Street. The African Canadian community was by this time both prosperous and proactive. A significant proportion had resources to support protest efforts, and had a long-standing commitment to antislavery. Should any of them have doubts as to the root causes of the war, the vice president of the Confederate States, Alexander Stephens, was on hand to clarify: "Our new government is founded . . . upon the great truth that the negro is not equal to the white man; that slavery—subordination to the superior race—is his natural and normal condition."

Thornton and the rest of Toronto's black community had ample opportunity to keep up with the war news. Toronto papers reported that thousands of slaves, called contraband, were flooding daily to the Union lines as the long processions of blue-clad soldiers marched into Southern states. African Canadians and expatriate African Americans hailed Union victories and wondered anxiously at what Lincoln intended when he overturned John Fremont's premature declaration of freedom for the bondspeople of the Western states. Blacks in Canada worried over the fate of loved ones and friends, both slave and free, now scattered and homeless as battles ravaged the landscapes in the chaos that was war. The names of the Confederate and Union officers and men wounded and killed filled the pages of Toronto newspapers, for the city press gave daily coverage to events transpiring during the entire war period. Some were familiar to black Torontonians from their days in slavery. In the Blackburns' case, it all must have felt rather close to home. Kentucky sided with the Union, but the hearts of Bluegrass families were with Virginia and the Southern cause, so at least as many Kentuckians rode south to join the Confederates. Generals Albert Sidney Johnston and Basil W. Duke, both of the Confederacy, grew up at the same time Thornton did in Washington, Kentucky, Johnston the son of one town doctor and Duke the other, and both had intermarried with relatives of Thornton's owner, William Murphy. The great hero of the Union and future president of the United States Ulysses S. Grant studied at the Maysville Academy high on the Maysville Hill while Sibby, Alfred, and Thornton Blackburn lived in the area. Anne and Joseph Doniphan's son and William Smith's grandson, Alexander W. Doniphan, whom Sibby Blackburn helped to bring up after she moved to Augusta, was now a senior Union officer.

Whatever Abraham Lincoln's personal and political convictions may have been, both African Americans and African Canadians had always known that the Civil War was being fought over slavery and that a Union victory was the only way to achieve universal emancipation. Here was the blood that black abolitionist David Walker had vowed so long ago would have to be shed to force the South to give up its four million slaves.

The romance of war, and the belief that the cause of the Union was a just one, attracted young Canadian men, although a few also went south to join the forces of the Confederacy. The numbers were not inconsiderable; Canada's first prime minister, Sir John Macdonald, who provided the only estimate of Canadians who fought in the American Civil War, put the figure at about forty thousand, which included an undetermined number of black soldiers. While white Canadians were welcomed into the ranks of the two warring factions, at first Lincoln resisted enlisting blacks. Canada's blacks formed secret militia units pending the day when Lincoln would realize that he would have to arm the African Americans who were so eager to fight. Thomas Cary, Mary Ann Shadd Cary's husband, secretly recruited at Toronto and Chatham, as did Osborne Anderson, Canada's sole veteran of the John Brown raid, and Josiah Henson in Southwestern Ontario. The historian James St. George Walker has noted that all this activity was illegal, since the residents of a British province could not enlist men for a foreign military venture. Henson was actually charged under the Foreign Enlistment Act, but finally acquitted when he said he had only provided information on how to go about joining the American army for men who had requested it.

In July 1862, Congress authorized President Lincoln to enlist the eager black recruits in the Union forces. However, no active call for their participation went out until February 1863, a month after Lincoln's Emancipation Proclamation went into effect on

January 1. Although actually liberating only slaves in the rebel states of the Confederacy, the Emancipation Proclamation, in loud and ringing tones, sounded the death knell for American slavery. Furthermore, Lincoln committed all the military and civil powers of his government to "recognize and maintain the freedom" of black Americans.

The proclamation galvanized the war effort. On January 3, 1863, George Brown in the *Globe* was characteristically outspoken: "From the outset we have never had a moment's doubt that the cause of the North was the cause of freedom. It was in order to perpetuate slavery that the Southern States had gone into rebellion . . . some time was required to free the Northern mind from the trammels which had fettered it; while the haughty slaveocracy ruled at Washington."

Childless, Lucie and Thornton saw the sons of their closest friends march off to fight. The flower of Buxton's youth went south—an astonishing seven hundred men—most enlisting at the Detroit recruiting center. Blacks from Canada joined state regiments such as the Fifth Massachusetts Colored Cavalry Regiment, the Fifty-fourth and Fifty-fifth Massachusetts Infantry Regiments; and the Twenty-ninth Connecticut Infantry Regiment, but most were soldiers of the U.S. Colored Troops, formed on May 22, 1863. More than 175,000 black men would see service before the end of the war. African American troops proved themselves ferocious fighters, but there were horrific incidents where captured men wearing Union blue were massacred or burned alive after a battle concluded, as they were at Fort Pillow in Tennessee on April 12, 1864. The Confederate commander in the case was Nathan Bedford Forrest, a former Tennessee slave dealer who would go on to be Grand Wizard of the Ku Klux Klan in the postwar years.

Harriet Tubman, now living in Auburn, New York, went south to help. The stellar Underground Railroad operative worked for the Union Army throughout the war as a scout, spy, and nurse, and was said to be the only woman who commanded troops during the Civil War, leading raids in Georgia. She was treated shamefully at war's end, and cheated out of her pension. Mary Ann Shadd Cary, now a widow with young children, served as the only female Union recruiting officer. She enlisted troops in Indiana and assisted Delany to do so in Connecticut, while her brother Abraham fought first in the Fifty-fourth Massachusetts and then in the U.S. Colored Troops. Dr. Martin R. Delany, who in 1858 led the first Niger Expedition with a view of setting up an American colony in Africa, abandoned his Black Nationalist platform during the American crisis and volunteered for military service. President Lincoln personally assigned him the rank of Major, making him the highest-ranking line officer in the U.S. Colored Troops. Although there were very few black officers— most served as enlisted men under whites—Wilson Ruffin and Ellen Toyer Abbott's son Anderson became an officer in the Union Army Medical Corps, and his Toronto-educated teacher Dr. Alexander T. Augusta was promoted to the rank of Major. In Baltimore, Augusta was mobbed for having the audacity to wear an officer's uniform.

There were a great many Southerners in Toronto during the war years. Both President Abraham Lincoln and President Jefferson Davis were anxious to garner Canadian support for their respective causes and sent special commissioners to Canada. They also sent spies, and spies to spy on the spies. Extensive intelligence operations at strategic border and port cities made Niagara Falls; St. Catharines; Toronto; Montreal; St. John, New Brunswick; and Halifax, Nova Scotia veritable nests of secretive visitors, receiving guests with letters sewn into their clothing and holding whispered conferences in the drawing rooms of the local hotels. Confederate spies in Toronto made the elegant Queen's Hotel their headquarters.

Because of numerous desertions from both armies, and also the escape of prisoners, especially Confederates from Union prison camps in the Northern states, thousands of Americans also came to Canada in search of asylum. Toronto's St. John's

Ward, which had inexpensive rents and was home to most of the city's black population, filled with Southern men in ragged gray uniforms and scalawags evading the draft in the Northern states. But the vast majority of people who lived, worked, and probably provided more intimate services there were former slaves from Virginia and Maryland, Kentucky and Tennessee.

Black Torontonians must have been distressed by Canada's relatively welcoming reception of the Confederates. Given the general support for Underground Railroad activities that had characterized earlier administrations, the fact that former African American slaves were at risk of encountering, on omnibuses, trains, or even on the sidewalks of their own neighborhoods, men and women who had once owned their persons was stunningly contradictory.

As former Southern officers filtered north over the border, pro-Southern Canadians also offered money and assistance to the cause. Among them was George Taylor Denison, one of the wealthiest men in Canada and the grandson of a family who had held slaves in early York. Denison was a prominent military man from a family whose record of service to the Crown was unblemished. Nonetheless, he was an ardent supporter of the Southern cause. His uncle, George Oscar Dewson, a Florida Confederate, served first as an officer and then as a spy for the South. Denison regularly entertained prominent Confederates, including General Robert E. Lee, at his Toronto home. He would remain an unreconstructed Southern sympathizer for the rest of his life. This was unfortunate for the black Torontonians who lived in St. John's Ward in the latter part of the nineteenth century. Denison would serve as Magistrate of the Police Court, where he pronounced severe sentences on African Canadians brought before his bench. These would include an old retired cabbie named Thornton Blackburn, who in his later life was known to partake of a dram or two with his Irish neighbors. Denison was also implicated in the *Georgian* Affair of November 1864, when he attempted to purchase a ship using Confederate funds so it could be outfitted as a gunboat to harass Union shipping on the Great Lakes. The matter was mysteriously revealed to Union operatives in Toronto, and the ship seized by the Canadian government. Denison was badly embarrassed and suffered heavy financial losses.

Thornton Blackburn also had personal connections with at least some of the white Southerners who took up residence in Toronto during the Civil War and were entertained at George Taylor Denison's home. Names familiar from Thornton's Kentucky years occur in the memoirs of John W. Headley, who made a circuitous trip from Virginia to Mississippi and on north to Canada by way of Kentucky, Missouri, and Michigan carrying a letter for Confederate commissioner Jacob Thompson, stationed at Toronto. He later wrote:

> The Queen's Hotel where we stopped fronted on Toronto Bay. It may be said we found Confederate headquarters here at this hotel . . . There was everything in the prospect at Toronto to make a sojourn enjoyable. The leading newspapers of Canada were published here and the South got a friendly comment on the course of events . . . Among the first Kentuckians we met were Dr. Stuart Robinson, the famous Presbyterian minister from Louisville; Dr. Luke P. Blackburn, Mrs. W.C.P. Breckinridge, with her children, her sister Miss Mollie Desha, and Miss Maria Hunt of Lexington. Within a few days we had met, perhaps, a hundred Confederates and prominent citizens of Kentucky, Missouri, West Virginia, and Maryland, who were refugees.

Issa Desha Breckinridge was the daughter of Joseph Desha of Mason County, who had fought on the borders of Canada in the War of 1812 and was governor of Kentucky from 1824 to 1828. She had been educated at the girls' academy in Washington, Kentucky, while Thornton lived in the town, and was now married to the Confederate general John Cabell Breckinridge, the former proslavery vice president of the United States under President Buchanan.

The Reverend Stuart Robinson had fled to Canada after his public prayers for the success of the Confederate forces brought the wrath of Union military commanders down on his head. He was the minister of the church attended by both John Pope and Malinda Oldham and by the Wurts and Reinhard families for whom Thornton had worked in Louisville. Robinson would be implicated in a number of the plots hatched in various Canadian intelligence networks, and was to return to Kentucky an unreconstructed pro-slavery man at the end of the war. For a time, he even occupied a pulpit at Niagara-on-the-Lake, near Niagara Falls on the Canadian side of the river, where some of the Southern officers and their families found refuge after the war was over and before amnesty was declared. The former Americans who made up the largely Loyalist populace of the town found nothing unusual, it seems, about having slaveholders in their midst, but the reaction of the former fugitive slaves living in Niagara's "colored village" has not been recorded.

Perhaps the most prominent of the clandestine operators in Canada was a Confederate physician named Luke Pryor Blackburn. His connections to the Blackburns of Toronto are not so much through his surname, although he was distantly related to Virginian Colonel Thomas Blackburn who had once owned Thornton's mother, Sibby. Thornton knew the physician's wife from his time in Louisville, for she was Julia Churchill, the niece of John Pope Oldham and the youngest daughter of Abigail and Samuel Churchill. The connection between Thornton Blackburn, Toronto's first cab company owner, and the illustrious Dr. Luke Pryor and Julia Churchill Blackburn was also a matter of public knowledge. Many years later, when Luke Pryor Blackburn was elected governor of Kentucky in 1879, an article in the Toronto *World* referred to the elderly black cabdriver who shared the doctor's surname as "Gov. Blackburn."

Dr. Blackburn was a zealous pro-slavery man. One of the most noted epidemiologists of his day, he specialized in treating yellow fever, the scourge of New Orleans and other cities of the Deep South. Too old to serve in the regular forces, he proposed to Major General Dabney H. Maury, who commanded the Department of the Gulf out of Mobile, Alabama, that he be sent to Canada. His purpose was to purchase a vessel to run the American blockades and bring a cargo of ice to the hospitals of the Gulf, returning with a load of cotton. He received his formal commission on June 23, 1863. Dr. Blackburn and his wife arrived in Toronto, and he opened what quickly became a successful medical practice on Toronto's fashionable Adelaide Street. The couple settled at the Queen's Hotel, where they proceeded to meet with potential supporters and sympathizers. In an odd twist of fate, Thornton Blackburn, the Toronto cabbie, may well have found himself in the strange position of delivering patients to Dr. Blackburn's offices and ferrying his wife to social engagements and on shopping expeditions.

It was while living in Toronto that Dr. Blackburn was implicated in the scandalous "Yellow Fever Plot." He volunteered his medical services to assist the British government when there was a yellow fever epidemic on the island of Bermuda. From there, Blackburn arranged for clothing collected from fever victims to be sent to Halifax, Nova Scotia, and then forwarded to Union troops occupying parts of the South. The shipment included a valise of fine shirts intended as a gift for President Lincoln himself. His attempt at germ warfare was unsuccessful; yellow fever can only be spread by mosquitoes. The Canadian public was shocked by the discovery of the plot, and the newspapers carried in full the proceedings against Luke Pryor Blackburn when he was indicted for this breach of Canadian sovereignty in the Montreal Police Court. Acquitted for lack of evidence in October 1865, he continued to practice medicine in Toronto, his patients apparently unconcerned with his political beliefs or the crimes of which he had been accused. A fellow conspirator, the Reverend Stuart Robinson of Louisville, also successfully defended himself against the charges. In 1872, Luke Pryor Blackburn returned to Louisville to resume his medical practice. He embarked on a political career that would take him and his wife to the Governor's Mansion in Kentucky, a position he retained from 1879 until 1883. The Toronto papers continued for many years to record details of Dr. Blackburn's career, speaking as if of an old friend. His tombstone ironically reads, "Luke Pryor Blackburn, the Good Samaritan."

There has always been a persistent belief that John Wilkes Booth met with the Confederate spy ring in Montreal prior to the shooting. He did visit Montreal several times and had a large amount on deposit at the Ontario Bank there. John Surratt, one of his co-conspirators, fled to Canada after the event, but Surratt's mother, at whose Washington boardinghouse the meetings had been held, hanged from a Washington gibbet in his stead.

It was not until more than a year after Confederate General Robert E. Lee surrendered, bringing the Civil War to an end, that another of Thornton's Kentucky connections, Mary Eliza Zane, arrived in Toronto. She was the bride of George R. R. Cockburn, an Edinburgh-born educator of considerable note and, from 1861 on, the Principal of Upper Canada College. The couple married in Toronto at St. James's Cathedral on December 27, 1866. Undoubtedly there were many members of her wealthy and prominent Louisville family present at the event. Perhaps Thornton, whose cabstand was just outside the cathedral's west entrance, drove some of them to and from the wedding. He would, in that case, have been familiar with a good many of the guests, for they included a great many relatives of Louisville's John Pope and Malinda Oldham.

Mary Eliza Zane Cockburn was the granddaughter of Abigail Oldham Churchill, John Pope Oldham's sister. She was not born until 1844 and would not have known Thornton, the fugitive slave whose whereabouts had been so avidly sought by her great-uncle John Pope Oldham, who had died in 1858. However, Thornton would have recognized Mary Eliza's mother, Emily Ann Churchill. Family letters found in the Filson Historical Society collections at Louisville attest to a close relationship, and the Louisville members of the family regularly visited back and forth between Toronto and Kentucky. Thornton probably had multiple opportunities to show off his bright red and yellow cab to the people for whom he had toiled without wages for so long.

George R. R. Cockburn, later a Conservative Party minister of Parliament from 1887 to 1896, was closely allied with Southern sympathizer and scion of one of Toronto's most prominent early families George Taylor Denison in Toronto's prestigious Empire Club, established to promote union among the disparate sections of the British Empire. Many years later, on December 28, 1916, Denison gave a stunningly racist speech at the Empire Club. The subject was Canada's lack of preparedness for the war with Germany. Denison disparaged Reconstruction and lauded its failure, cheering the fact that finally, with the rise of the New South and the imposition of Jim Crow legislation, white men of talent and ability were no longer subject to the governance of their inferiors, meaning the newly enfranchised African Americans. He said of the former president of the Confederacy, "Jefferson Davis suffered terribly in the prison; they had to let him out because they were afraid he would die. I saw him a very short time after he was discharged, and I did not think he could ever get over it; yet he was a kindly, humane man, who never committed any crime."

In the months before Lincoln's assassination, relations between his government and Canada grew warmer. For the American president, black Canada served as an example of what the future might hold for emancipated African Americans in the event of Union victory. Even before the outcome of the Civil War was decided, Lincoln had been looking toward the future and wondering how best to manage the peace. There were four million enslaved Americans. Most could not read and had no experience in dealing with business, the civil service, or, if they were to be full members of American society with the right to vote, politics. Accordingly, Lincoln looked to the thirty-five thousand people of African descent in Canada. They had all the privileges and problems of freedom, and he wanted to see how they had fared.

The May 8, 1863, edition of the New York paper *The Anglo-African* shows Toronto black Robert Phillips, who regularly received fugitive slaves sent from William Still's Philadelphia Underground Railroad station at his home, presiding over a meeting at the city's Colored Wesleyan Methodist Church on April 21, 1863. The objective was to endorse U.S. government plans to emancipate and "elevate" former slaves in an address to be delivered to the U.S. government from "The Colored Citizens of Canada." The resolution passed by the meeting included the following paragraph:

> We rejoice that we are subjects of Her Most Gracious Majesty the Queen, and that we live under a flag that has "braved a thousand years the battle and the breeze." As loyal subjects we cannot but regret that there are subjects of Her Most Gracious Queen living in Canada and England, who, by their expressions and acts, countenance and aid the fierce onslaught on human freedom and the effort to establish a Confederacy whose chief cornerstone is slavery.

The meeting coincided with the arrival in Toronto of a special commission sent by President Lincoln to examine the condition of fugitive slaves living in Canada West. In 1863, Dr. Samuel Gridley Howe, noted abolitionist, educator, and humanitarian, was appointed to head the Freedmen's Inquiry Commission established by President Lincoln. He was better known, perhaps, for his work with the deaf, blind, and insane, and for his famous wife (Julia Ward Howe, author of "Battle Hymn of the Republic"; her stirring piece of poetry was later set to the tune, fittingly, of a Union army marching song called "John Brown's Body"). Howe was an interesting choice. He was reputed to have been one of the "Secret Six" who provided the funding for John Brown's raid at Harpers Ferry. After Brown was captured, Howe had briefly sought asylum in Canada before returning to the United States.

Howe's report offers a uniquely detailed glimpse into the conditions of Thornton and Lucie Blackburn's lives in Canada in the 1860s. He and his colleagues interviewed former slaves, as well as white officials who had dealings with them. He explored the history of slavery and freedom in Canada, the refugees' physical condition and health, and the degree of "amalgamation" that had taken place. ("Amalgamation" referred, of course, to interracial marriage.) This latter, the specter of which has been raised by every white supremacist from that day to this, was something Howe found of negligible importance to the Canadians with whom he spoke. Howe's commissioners discovered among Canadian blacks a good deal of prosperity and plenty of evidence of industry. Howe recorded the following:

> It is commonly said that the Canadian refugees are "picked men"; that the very fact of their escape from slavery is proof of their superiority . . . No! the refugees in Canada earn a living, and gather property; they marry and respect women; they build churches and send their children to schools; they improve in manners and morals;—not because they are "picked men," but simply because they are free men.

As far as education was concerned, white authorities confirmed that African Canadian parents were most anxious to have their children taught, that they were well able to learn, and that had it not been for the prejudice expressed by the school system in most places, they would have progressed much more quickly. African Canadians had tidy comfortable homes, and particularly at Toronto and in the colonies like Buxton, which Howe visited, they were very prosperous. In religion they were exemplary, and the numbers of blacks in prison or in the poorhouse were smaller than the general proportion of the white population. Howe did emphasize the numbers of fugitives who intended to return to the United States after the Civil War. He said the African Americans "had not taken firm root in Canada, and . . . desire to go to the southern region of the United States, partly from love of warmth, but more from love of *home*."

The *Report to the Freedmen's Inquiry Commission* was comprehensive and generally very positive. The document does betray the racial stereotypes and beliefs of its authors, and it is clear throughout that black people are considered substantially different from whites on most levels, the persistent "other." For instance, Howe and his associates cited medical opinions that the intermarriage of black and white people had a negative effect on the health and longevity of their children. In the introductory paragraphs, the report emphasized the affection some former slaves expressed for the masters they had left behind, probably as a way of reassuring Southerners they were not about to be murdered in their beds the day after their slaves were freed. Indeed, as the horrific statistics on lynching in later years prove, it was the blacks themselves who ran that risk.

The Freedmen's Bureau grew out of the Howe commission's work and was the governing body and shield for black Americans in the South from 1865 until 1869. It continued to assist their cause on an extremely wide variety of levels until its demise in a welter of disorganization, corrupt business practices, and the failure of the Freedman's Bank, in 1876. As W.E.B. DuBois said, this was hardly surprising:

> In a time of perfect calm, amid willing neighbors and streaming wealth, the social uplifting of 4,000,000 slaves to an assured and self-sustaining place in the body politic and economic would have been an herculean task; but when to the inherent difficulties of so delicate and nice a social operation were added the spite and hate of conflict, the Hell of War; when suspicion and cruelty were rife, and gaunt Hunger wept beside Bereavement,—in such a case, the work of any instrument of social regeneration was in large part foredoomed to failure.

Canada's joyful response to Union victory in the Civil War ended abruptly when the news came of Lincoln's assassination on April 14, 1865. The great liberator was mourned deeply by the black community of Toronto, who turned out in their thousands for the memorial services at St. James's Cathedral and all the black churches. People of Thornton and Lucie's generation, with three decades in Canada behind them, were wise enough to realize that Lincoln's death might put an end to the dream of a productive peace after so terribly destructive a war. When Lincoln's body was being carried through the United States, his funeral train stopped at Buffalo, where long lines of Canadians crossed the bridge to share in the sorrow of their neighbors.

It must have been disturbing to the black population that former Confederates were given asylum in Canada in the immediately postbellum period. In June 1867, two years after the war ended, George Taylor Denison learned that his old hero, the former Confederate president Jefferson Davis, was stopping by Toronto. Denison hastily spread the word, and when the *Rothesay Castle* steamed into port, more than one thousand people turned out to cheer Davis. Newspapers in the Northern states were predictably furious, and implied that Canada's annexation to the United States could not come too soon. Davis was en route from seeing his children in Montreal to visit with his former officers, spies, and commissioners who had settled at the western end of Lake Ontario at Niagara-on-the-Lake until the coast was clear to return to the United States.

The dissolution of the Union and the years of destruction and waste that followed encouraged Canadian politicians and the public alike to think in terms of national unity. The possibility of invasion by Union troops at the end of the conflict seemed quite real, and a nation unified both militarily and economically was seen as the only protection against American territorial ambitions. George Brown, now a senior political figure in Canada West, almost miraculously in the face of French and English Canadian mutual animosity, managed to draw together the conflicting factions in the various provinces. On June 30, 1867, with great celebration, the Confederation of Canada was confirmed, and at midnight that evening British North America was transformed into a nation. Toronto's church bells pealed out their joy, and Toronto's black population joined with the whites in praying for the future of their new country called Canada.

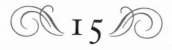

OH, WASN'T THAT
A WIDE RIVER?

I was born in Maysville, Kentucky. I got here last Tuesday evening and spent the fourth of July in Canada. I felt as big and free as any man could feel, and I worked part of the day for my own benefit; I guess my master's time is out.

—BENJAMIN BLACKBURN, 1855

THE BLACKBURNS, WHO had escaped their own bondage more than thirty years before, had lived to see the emancipation of all the slaves in the United States as an established fact. Between 1865 and 1870, the U.S. Congress passed the Thirteenth, Fourteenth, and Fifteenth amendments to the Constitution, and after years of struggle and bloody strife had finally come freedom, citizenship, equality before the law, and the guarantee that black men—but not yet women—could participate fully in the political process. All over the South thousands of people were on the move. They went in search of family members sold away years before, of new jobs that paid real wages, and of an education denied them all their lives in slavery. Universities, colleges, and manual labor institutes aimed at the education of black youth were founded; the roots of Hampton, Howard, and Fisk universities all date to this period. The Freedmen's Bureau established more than three thousand schools and set about the monumental task of turning this vast formerly enslaved labor force into participants in a democratic society. It was a heady time, redolent with possibilities and hope.

In the decade after the war, Thornton and Lucie Blackburn saw many friends leave Canada forever. Some of the black abolitionists who had migrated to Canada in the 1850s to operate their antislavery campaign in exile had never intended to be more than sojourners on Canadian soil. They immediately moved back to the United States to rejoin family and friends and to assist in the work of making a life for millions of the formerly enslaved. The Buxton school emptied. Like students at Toronto Normal School, the medical schools, and Knox College, they passed through the war-torn nation to the plantation South, some to teach, others to minister to the souls of a long-oppressed people. Dr. Anderson Ruffin Abbott, educated at Buxton and then Toronto and the first Canadian-born black physician, managed hospitals on behalf of the Freedmen's Bureau. Mary Ann Shadd Cary attended Howard University to study law, and then taught school in Washington, D.C. Her sister, Emaline Shadd, a prizewinning graduate of Toronto's Normal School, went south for a time during Reconstruction to teach those who had been slaves to read, and then became one of the first female professors at Howard University.

Black men educated in Canada involved themselves in Reconstruction politics and were elected to high office. Prominent among them were men such as James T. Rapier, the nephew of Henry K. Thomas who served with Thornton in the Canadian Mill and Mercantile Association; he became the first black congressman in Alabama. Another of Mary Ann's siblings, Isaac Shadd, who had hosted John Brown at Chatham, moved to the Deep South after the war to assist with the experiment in black plantation ownership at Davis Bend, Mississippi. He was later elected to the Mississippi House of Representatives and served as Speaker from 1874 to 1876. His brother Abraham, became a judge in Arkansas, although he lived out his latter life in Canada.

The Blackburns, however, had truly become African Canadians and so remained in the home they had made in Toronto. Thornton was fifty-three years old when the Civil War ended in the spring of 1865, and his wife was about sixty-two. What family they had managed to reunite were now all buried in Canadian soil. Alfred had passed away on June 10, 1863, and been laid to rest in the Blackburn family plot at the Toronto Necropolis beside his mother, Sibby. Alfred had never owned his home, which was, according to the tax rolls, almost falling down by the time he died, and he had been unable to work for some time. There was no will, so the possessions he and his mother had accumulated would have gone to Thornton and his wife.

One or two people named Blackburn who came to Canada over the years may have been relatives, but any proof of their relationship has been lost. Most of the Blackburns' oldest friends passed on in the next few years, and although the Buxton settlement continued, the Elgin Association's affairs were wound up in 1873, the need for fugitive slave assistance having passed with the ending of the Civil War. Every stockholder was remunerated, and the former colony continued as a fully self-sufficient farming town.

Most of Lucie and Thornton's friends were living in Toronto's west end, but the Blackburns themselves continued to occupy their little house on South Park Street. The district where they lived was now completely built up. Little houses and rows of tenements lined the crowded streets where cottages and farmhouses used to be. Photos of the period show rutted mud roads and rickety tenements crowded cheek by jowl with noisome foundries and factories. Their neighbors in St. Lawrence Ward were mainly impoverished Ulster Irish factory and mill workers, although they also included skilled tradesmen such as bricklayers, carpenters, blacksmiths, and coopers, most of whom were employed at the Gooderham & Worts distillery or at the cooperage the same company maintained a block south and east of the Blackburn house. Charles Barber, a local entrepreneur whose children intermarried with the Gooderhams, operated a soap and candle factory as well as a potashery next door to their home, and the district was becoming both loud and odoriferous, for a large pork-packing plant occupied the lands near the mouth of the Don River, while the city pound was on a lot diagonally across the street.

Beside Alfred's old home a block south of Lucie and Thornton's house, the Palace Street Public School was doubled in size to accommodate the growing number of children living in the district, although most of the Irish youngsters did not attend. Child labor was common, and the majority of households in the district needed the income provided by their offspring working as newspaper boys or factory hands in the many industrial establishments that dominated St. Lawrence Ward. The blocks between the Blackburns' house and the lake had turned into an industrial morass. Railroad tracks crisscrossed the blocks where formerly stands of trees, gardens, and marshland had been. The Toronto Rolling Mills and the Gooderham & Worts distillery employed hundreds of men and obscured the Blackburns' view of Lake Ontario, the border between their Toronto home and the United States.

As ever, Thornton and Lucie adapted. Tax records show that in 1860, Lucie and Thornton increased the size of their garden at the corner of Eastern and Sackville Streets, providing both food and a pleasant occupation for their retirement years. The Blackburns' large double lot, still treed and with a lovely yard, must have seemed an island of green in the gray world that most of the locals inhabited. Fruit trees occupied the back part of the lot, and there was the shady porch behind the house for a pleasant afternoon's rest.

An article providing some small insight into Thornton's character in his later life survives in the papers of Anderson Ruffin Abbott. It is a strange piece titled "Our Colored Citizens/Pen Pictures of Prominent Africans Resident in Toronto/Old Residents—Wealthy Citizens—White Sheep—Amazons." Published in the *New York Age* in 1875, it is attributed to Abbott himself, but its racist tone makes it highly unlikely that a black person wrote it, and how it came to be included with his papers remains a mystery:

> Toronto may fairly claim to be fortunate in her colored citizens. As a rule, they are a well-behaved, law-abiding class, and very few of the chronic crooks of the city are recruited from their ranks. There are among them, further, many who are large property holders, and who, by their thrift and quiet industry, set a good example to their Anglo-Saxon and Celtic neighbors . . .
>
> Old Blackburn is a . . . venerable fixture of Toronto. He is over 85 years of age and healthy. He resides on Eastern Ave. He used to be a hack driver, and laid by a considerable fortune. He is now retired and lives in opulence with his swarthy lady. He used to be a great "sport" at one time, and even now the old man still exhibits mashing propensities which age can hardly prevent, and he fully considers himself the Adonis he used to be.

The Blackburns' tiny cottage could hardly be considered an example of "opulence," although the couple was financially more than comfortable. Thornton had retired from the taxi business just after the Civil War. Possibly the inauguration of Toronto's first horse-drawn streetcar service in 1861 encouraged him to make the decision. Most of the cabs in the city were operated by large companies by this time; the hacks were rented out for a period of hours to individual drivers, just as they are today. Thornton was listed in the census for these years as a "Gentleman," meaning he was living on his means. These included substantial savings as well as the proceeds from the rental of the couple's several properties. The Toronto law firm of Chadwick & Beatty handled their legal affairs throughout this period. The Blackburns still attended Little Trinity Church in the company of some of Toronto's wealthiest industrialists and businessmen. Although the archaeological record demonstrates that Thornton and Lucie lived very modestly, they had, according to 1861 census records, some $6,000 invested in their home and business, and Thornton's "carriage for hire" was listed as being worth $100 for tax purposes. The connections with the Gooderham and Worts clans forged at their neighborhood Anglican church stood the Blackburns in good stead in their later lives. For instance, Thornton and Lucie patronized the lawyers at Chadwick & Beatty, a very prestigious and expensive firm started in 1863. Its partners were Gooderham connections; William Henry Beatty was married to Charlotte Louisa Worts, daughter of James Gooderham Worts. By 1901, the law firm was the largest in Canada and still survives as the founding partnership of Fasken Campbell Godfrey. The Blackburns, with their investments, rental properties, and society attorneys, had come a long way from Louisville, where Thornton had toiled as a hired slave and Lucie as a nursemaid some four decades before.

Although Samuel Gridley Howe's report to the Freedmen's Inquiry Commission quoted a local clergyman as saying that "if freedom is established in the United States, there will be one great black streak, reaching from here to the uttermost parts of the South," the anticipated exodus did not wholly materialize. While a significant proportion of Canada's black population did leave for the United States, the migrants mainly consisted of fugitives who had come in the last antebellum decade. With more recent memories of the South as home and anxious to find the loved ones they had left behind, they returned immediately. There is good evidence that some former fugitives went South to locate family members they had lost through slavery and brought them home to Toronto. Lucie and Thornton, the Abbotts, Tinsleys, Lightfoots, and other leading families formed the nucleus of a much-reduced African Canadian population in the latter part of the nineteenth century. The total black population of the country in 1871 was listed in the census as only 21,946, although such

mainstream city newspapers, including the Toronto *World*, e *Globe*, and the *Telegram*, detailed the passing of some of the ackburns' more elderly friends and associates. Wilson Ruffin bott died in 1876, after having been elected city councillor for . Patrick's Ward, beating the scion of one of the old Family mpact families, a son of Chief Justice John Beverley Robin- n, for the position. Abbott was laid to rest in the Toronto ecropolis. It is of note that the senior Abbott's ethnicity was ually omitted from tax rolls and census reports; his color was nsidered insignificant in the face of his wealth, prominence, d importance in the city. In the same year, the Blackburns' old iend and helper Madison Lightfoot passed away in Detroit. ightfoot had by the time of his death served as the Recording ecretary for the Amherstburg Baptist Association for thirty- ree years.

The next loss was closer to home for Lucie and Thornton. nn Maria Jackson died, aged seventy, on January 28, 1880. The ause was listed as "dyspepsia." She was eulogized by the Rev- rend Charles A. Washington at the British Methodist Episcopal hurch on Chestnut Street (the old Sayer Street Chapel) in St. ohn's Ward. This courageous woman, who had taken in washing p to the year before her death, went peacefully at the home of er daughter Mrs. Harry Nelson. Ann Maria was laid to rest in he plot Thornton had purchased for his own family at the Toronto Necropolis when his mother died. Also buried in the Blackburn plot is Richard M. Jackson, one of Ann Maria's sons. Other members of the large Jackson family are interred in vari- us parts of the same cemetery.

In the 1870s and early 1880s, this black man nicknamed Dick ackson was a very well-known hairdresser in Toronto. The "bar- er to the stars" of his day, he had shops on Church Street and hen on King. He worked in partnership with Reuben Custaloe, he grandson of the builder John M. Tinsley. Ads for "Dick and Rube's" well-patronized and extremely fashionable hairdressing establishment appeared in city newspapers in the 1870s. He died at the age of thirty-eight. Half of Toronto's businessmen and a

figures are generally quite unreliable and the numbe:
been as much as 20 percent higher.

By the turn of the century, Dr. Abbott had becon
resident physician at Toronto General Hospital. He c
serve as Canadian correspondent for the *New York .*
one article he described the Blackburns' elderly cont(
although not Thornton and Lucie themselves:

> The Afro-American population of Toronto is abou
> The descendants of successive colonies, principal
> Virginia, Maryland and South Carolina settled here
> the troublous period following the Nat Turner Insur.
> A considerable accession to the population took place i
> during the enforcement of the Fugitive Slave Law
> Southern State has an exiled son or daughter in this (
> the bulk of the colonists were free and intelligent m
> left Virginia rather than submit to intolerable pers
> and came to Canada bringing sufficient means with t
> purchase homes and secure for them an honorable a1
> stantial citizenship. A very few of the original settlers
> ing; but their family names frequently crop out i
> descendents. Whenever we come across a particularly
> youngster with such patronymics as Harris, Johnson
> ley, Abbott, Edmunds, Williams, Lewis, Hickman, Hu
> Mink, Judah, Harney, Davis, Hollands, Jackson, Ri(
> Burke, Drake, Berry, Coates, Crouch, Smith, Grant, '
> Warren, Watkins, Bryant, Carey, dovetail in their nam
> may know that they belong to the old stock. Pat T
> who is over 108 years old, and Elisha Edmunds, wh(
> to Toronto when it bore the pseudonym of Muddy
> York, are the nestors.

There was a clear respect for some of the older c(
leaders who had worked closely with whites to amelior:
tions for the black populace as well as to end slavery. (

good proportion of the municipal politicians turned out for the funeral of this well-liked young man. The services took place at the St. John's Ward British Methodist Episcopal Church on Chestnut Street on June 2, 1885. Long obituaries appeared in the Toronto *World* and in the *Globe*. One, on June 3, 1885, in the *World*, said that "a thousand people were at the funeral, including aldermen and military officers, former mayors of the city, and a host of the town's notables [who had] all frequented his shop, . . . while Dick deftly scraped their faces he entertained them with the latest gossip of the day—political, personal and social."

The newspaper accounts of Jackson's death said that Jackson "was well liked by both the white and colored population . . . Not a few will miss the deceased from their acquaintanceship." The procession of more than fifty carriages and hundreds of pedestrians wound its way through the city streets from the corner of Queen Street east of Bay to the Necropolis, which was about half a mile to the east. Both the publisher of the Toronto *World* and John Ross Robertson, of the Toronto *Telegram*, were in attendance. This was a remarkable tribute to a man whose value to the community clearly transcended any divisions of race or class that existed in the highly stratified late-nineteenth-century city.

Richard "Dick" Jackson was laid to rest at the Toronto Necropolis beside his mother, Ann Maria Jackson, in the plot Thornton and Lucie had purchased for themselves. His burial place bore witness to the lasting friendship that had grown up between the Blackburns and the intrepid black washerwoman who had brought her seven children out of slavery and whom the Toronto couple, fugitives themselves so many years earlier, had received in their home upon the Jacksons' arrival in Canada.

The degree of racial tolerance the Blackburns experienced in Toronto was at least in part due to the fact that black people never made up more than 2 percent of the population. In Chatham, where there was so highly developed a community that Martin R. Delany called it "the black man's Paris," the proportion was approximately 50 percent and the degree of racial discrimination on the part of the whites extreme. Samuel Gridley Howe had discovered a disturbing amount of racism in Canada: "As long as the colored people form a very small proportion of the population, and are dependent, they receive protection and favors; but when they increase, and compete with the laboring classes for a living, and especially when they begin to aspire to social equality, they cease to be 'interesting negroes,' and become 'niggers.'"

Toronto newspapers continued to report on American issues. In 1868, the *Globe* applauded when South Carolina's legislature became the first in the United States to have a black majority, with eighty-seven African American representatives to forty white ones. The editorial tone reflected a strong hope for Reconstruction, but the papers also recorded the actions of unrepentant Confederates who did everything possible to undermine gains made by the South's newly freed labor force. *The Irish Canadian* deplored President Andrew Johnson's pro-Southern sympathies, writing prophetically on October 4, 1865:

> The white population of the Slave States have been corrupted by vicious institutions, which have left them totally unfit to participate in the reconstruction of the Southern States on a basis of freedom and equality, and if the power of legislation is left to this class alone, . . . the colored people, who are the only truly loyal people of the South, will be deprived of the even nominal freedom which they now enjoy and remanded back into slavery.

Unlike white newspapers of an earlier day, the Toronto *World* regularly reported on events of interest that were happening in the black community, including concerts and lectures that were open to all. For all George Brown's partisan attitudes toward abolition, the *Globe* did not have the same interest in the quotidian life of the city's black community. The *World*, while hardly in the *Globe*'s league in terms of journalistic integrity or distribution, was far more in touch with the daily lives of the city's working people, including African Canadians. A certain degree of social responsibility is evident in its pages; the principal reporter on the police beat in those years was a young man named John Joseph Kelso, who founded the Toronto Humane Society and was the guiding light behind the development of the Children's Aid Society. Much of his concern came from his experiences among the impoverished folk of St. John's Ward.

The Blackburns' properties in St. John's Ward were to become a source of trouble to the elderly couple. In the 1880s, the district was losing the respectable character it once had, and would by the turn of the century deteriorate into a dilapidated slum known simply as the Ward. It was described in 1885 as "the notorious St. John's Ward, at once the negro quarter, the Five Points, and the St. Giles of Toronto. This description applies to its southerly half; its northern portion contains many elegant residences and handsome streets." York Street, outside the Ward to the south of Osgoode Hall, was one of the least savory quarters of the city. But the longest-standing residences and businesses of the old black families remained.

Undoubtedly there was criminality in St. John's Ward. The Toronto *World* was fond of describing police raids on houses of ill repute where "scantily clad damsels" were forced to parade through the streets to the station, and drinking and other forms of vice were common enough among the poor in this late-Victorian-era working class district. However, black people did seem to be singled out. A typical article published in the *World*, on September 7, 1885, described how "the police raided 16 Elizabeth Street late Saturday night and made a big catch of colored folks. Those arrested were John Tinsley, keeper." There is no mention of what the raid was for, but it is implied that John M. Tinsley's grandson and namesake might be operating a common bawdy house, although this may seem far-fetched since the house was right next door to the upright former Underground Railroad conductor, Thomas Smallwood, in Toronto a pillar of the Baptist

Church for fifty years. It was perhaps not coincidental that the police magistrate, George Taylor Denison, the same man who had entertained the Confederates at his Toronto home during the Civil War, also owned a number of rental properties in the Ward. Perhaps that had something to do with the severe sentences he imposed on blacks living in the district.

Even Thornton Blackburn managed to run afoul of the law in his later life. Apparently he was taken before Magistrate Denison in the police court on occasion for drunken behavior. His companions in the offenses were some of his neighbors from Corktown, all Irish. On the first occasion he was acquitted, and the second time he was forced to pay a small fine. However, his third charge seems to have been a matter of bad luck, or perhaps insufficient attention to the activities of his tenants. Apparently one of the houses he had owned for many years on Edward Street in St. John's Ward had been used for purposes of which the churchgoing Blackburns would not have approved. The newspaper report of March 14, 1882, says, "Thornton Blackburn was up on a charge of renting premises for the purpose of prostitution. As the occupants had vacated he was discharged." Court records make it clear that the Blackburns did not know that their rental property was serving as a brothel. Less than a year later, the same house, empty of tenants since the 1882 incident, burned to the ground, according to the *World* article of February 2, 1883.

In 1880, George Brown of the *Globe*, the old friend to black Canada, had passed away. He died a lingering death of a gunshot wound inflicted by a disgruntled former employee. Brown's funeral was the largest and most elaborate procession Toronto had ever seen. The city's African Canadian population turned out in force to honor the passage of the man who had been such a friend to the fugitive slaves in the province. His cortege wound its way down Winchester Street and turned in at the gate of the Toronto Necropolis. There, Brown is buried, mere steps from the Blackburn family grave site.

Perhaps one of Brown's greatest contributions after the founding of the Anti-Slavery Society of Canada and the role he played in Canadian Confederation was his championship of a man who rescued him from being plunged into the Don River when the horses pulling his carriage bolted. This was William Hubbard, a Toronto baker and son of a former slave. Hubbard's political acumen intrigued Brown, who took pains to foster the man's political ambitions. In 1894, Hubbard was elected to the city council and was Toronto's first African Canadian deputy mayor. So eloquent was he that his fellow politicians dubbed him "Old Cicero." He consistently fought for the little man, protecting the rights of Chinese laundry owners in the city and assisting Adam Beck, founder of Toronto Hydro, in ensuring that the power commission remain in public hands. Intermarried with the Toronto elite Abbott, Casey, and Lightfoot families, Hubbard would see his son become head of the Toronto Transportation Commission from 1930 to 1939. William Hubbard's portrait hangs in the Toronto City Hall, just as it did when it was first unveiled in 1913. He maintained he had never experienced racism in political office because he ran on his knowledge of real estate, rather than as a "Negro politician," and said, "I have always felt that I am a representative of a race hitherto despised, but if given a fair opportunity would be able to command esteem."

Before they died, Thornton and Lucie and their friends experienced the devastating disappointment of watching Reconstruction fail. The Civil Rights Act was passed, followed shortly by the Fourteenth Amendment to the U.S. Constitution, which guaranteed all men equal protection under the law; this was just eleven years after the Dred Scott decision had stated that blacks had no rights that "white men were bound to respect." The South was effectively subjected to Northern military rule, and Ulysses S. Grant became president in 1869. By 1876, the wonderful promise of Reconstruction had been destroyed as state after state had been "Redeemed," that is, returned to the white-controlled political and economic conditions that had prevailed before the Civil War. Blacks were progressively stripped of their recently won rights and protections. By 1883, the Civil Rights Act had been declared unconstitutional by the Supreme Court. It would be almost eight decades before black rights were formally reinstituted in the United States.

Many of the gains made in the first few years were lost in the resurgence of white supremacy and the rise of the New South. The old power base of wealth and privilege reasserted itself, and by 1880, a majority of former slaves were living under a new unwaged labor system, one, again, where whites held all the cards. It was called sharecropping. The progressive restrictions on black life undermined much of the advances made in social, educational, economic, and above all political development for African Americans. Convoluted laws that restricted political involvement effectively disenfranchised black voters. Toronto newspapers continued to trumpet black gains, such as when the *Evening Telegram* of June 2, 1885, reported that four African Americans were admitted to the South Carolina bar, but lynchings were becoming a regular feature of the news as well. Toronto newspapers also reported the ominous rise of the Ku Klux Klan.

Thousands of American black families were displaced when they moved en masse to the northern United States in search of employment. The great migration had begun, and the face of the industrialized north changed drastically. But here, too, blacks were disenfranchised in another way, for trade unions rejected their membership. Impoverished black laborers desperate for employment were brought in to work as scabs during strikes, further alienating European working-class immigrants. By 1890, segregation would be codified into the Jim Crow laws. The infection spilled over the Canadian border. Toronto blacks were soon to be found caricatured in art and advertising using names like Lemon John for a local ice cream vendor.

Nostalgic memorials such as *Our Mammy* painted an idealized picture of life in an Old South that existed only in the imagination, and advertising, comics, songs, and minstrel shows portraying black Americans as figures of ridicule became common in

Toronto, just as they were in the American South. The descendants of the old minstrel shows of the 1840s some fifty years later were still spreading their pernicious message of black inferiority and the "happy dancing slave" to audiences throughout North America. The Christy Minstrels, in blackface and using exaggerated Southern accents, played to sold-out houses at the Toronto Lyceum and Music Hall. The side of a building on Toronto's King Street in 1900 advertised Sunlight Soap with an immense image of a caricatured black baby, her face wreathed in the rays of a brilliant yellow sun. Hobberlin Bros. & Co. at 569 Queen Street West in Toronto advertised their new woolen pants "at half their worth" with a logo of a black child wearing diapers with the words "When I Grow Big I'll Wear Hobberlin's Pants." A few days later, the same company used the black child logo beside the words "In Black Goods We Show a Fine Line." A former slave named Nancy Green was hired by the predecessor to the Quaker Oats company in 1893 to serve as the quintessential "mammy" for their product, Aunt Jemima Pancake Mix. She and later actresses playing the same role visited the Canadian National Exhibition each year at Toronto to sell pancakes, a tradition that continued through the 1960s.

In Canada, black communities lost their cachet as havens for victims of American oppression and romantic fugitives on the Underground Railroad. Quasi-medical theories based on "scientific" evidence loosely derived from—or in direct contradiction to—Darwinian theories of human evolution purported that blacks were a separate, inferior race. Northern states and then Canada bought into the stereotypes that provided the ideological infrastructure for segregation and oppression based on skin color and ethnicity. Across the country, exclusionary policies based on custom, if never on law, meant that blacks were refused service in restaurants and hotels, excluded from membership in trade unions, turned down for housing and employment, harassed at the polls, and ill treated in public.

Mercifully, it was not until after their deaths that the Blackburns themselves were held up as objects of fun in Toronto. The Toronto Press Club in 1909 put on an immensely popular satire of an old play. Advertised in the Toronto *Globe* of June 14, 1909, the entertainment was mounted at Toronto's elegant Royal Alexandra Theatre and titled *Uncle Tom's Taxi-Cabin*. This was, of course, a thinly veiled spoof on the owners of Toronto's first taxi company. One of hundreds of blackface minstrel shows popular in the period, its libretto is, probably deservedly, lost to history.

When the Blackburns were very old, their comfortable home of so many years was threatened with demolition. The Palace Street School property a block to the south was too small to allow for expansion, for the Grand Trunk rail bed ran right past the building. The old Enoch Turner Schoolhouse beside Little Trinity Church was again pressed into service to deal with the overflow, but clearly a new school was needed. But every inch of Corktown was taken up with either industrial yards or the densely packed housing of the poor, the working class, and the aspiring shopkeepers who made up the district's population. The only large, relatively empty piece of land in the entire area was the corner of the street now called Eastern Avenue at Sackville Street. A double lot, it was occupied by only two elderly residents of a long, narrow old frame house, with peeling paint and a rickety barn, and a hayloft over one end, that used to house a taxi business more than twenty-five years earlier.

The records of the Toronto Board of Education indicate that the school board fully intended to expropriate the Blackburns' property in 1887. The same prominent Toronto architect who designed the central building of Osgoode Hall (1856–60) with its Palladian portico, W. G. Storm, was hired to design a utilitarian yellow brick building with a central porch and four rooms on each of two floors. With the building situated at the back of the large lot facing onto Eastern Avenue, there would be plenty of space for a playground in front. A shed would be built along the east side where the children could shelter from the weather. The basement was to be reserved as an apartment for the caretaker and his family. The Standing Committee of the school board decided on November 18, 1887, to expropriate "a lot north of Eastern Avenue . . . the frontage being of 110 feet on Sackville Street by 132 feet deep . . . owned by Mr. Thornton Blackburn . . . the cost was set at fifty dollars per foot being $5,500." Expenditures on the building itself were to be kept to a minimum. These were children of the poor Irish, after all, and most did not vote. The school board trustees intended to do their duty for the people of Corktown, but nothing above what was necessary. Only plank sidewalks were provided instead of the landscaping more common in well-to-do areas, and there were no trees or flowers planted to delight the eye of the little Irish children who would crowd the halls of Sackville Street School for generations.

The Blackburns must have been heartbroken when they received the news that the city was determined to force them to sell their property. They had lived in their little house for fifty-three years. Thornton was seventy-five years old and in ill health, and while his eighty-four-year-old wife was apparently well, the move was simply too much to contemplate. A careful reading of the school board's Properties Committee minutes makes it clear that some extreme pressure was brought to bear in the decisionmaking process. Perhaps the Blackburns appealed to their minister and the parishioners of the Anglican church they had supported since its founding. Little Trinity's pastor, the Reverend Alexander Sanson, was a longtime friend of the Blackburns, and the Reverend Sadler, an up-and-coming man in the missionary branch of the church, was Acting Curate. Also still part of the congregation was the powerful Gooderham family. William Gooderham was dead, but he had seven sons and six daughters and had also raised the five children of his dead partner and brother-in-law, James Worts. Together they represented a significant portion of the city's elite, and several members of the family served on the city school board.

Whatever influence Thornton and Lucie were able to attract, when it came time to build the Sackville Street School, only the rear halves of the two lots belonging to the Blackburns were purchased. The front strip along Eastern Avenue, 132 feet wide but only 80 feet deep, where the house, barn, and vegetable garden were located, was all that was left to the elderly couple. There is no explanation given in the minutes of the Properties Committee to account for the change in plans, although it was obvious that the school board was only biding its time.

The school building was constructed facing south, toward Eastern Avenue (the former South Park Street). As long as Thornton and Lucie occupied their home, the school's front door looked toward the back of their house. It was an odd arrangement, and one clearly intended to be temporary. The board paid the Blackburns $5,500 for this portion of their land, the same sum that had been proposed for the entire double lot, including the part they still occupied.

Perhaps Lucie and Thornton, having had no children of their own, found the children's shouts as they enjoyed their games of marbles, ball, hopscotch, and jump rope a pleasure rather than a nuisance. They certainly had visitors who were children in their later years, for archaeologists discovered broken bits of china dolls and chipped tea sets, as well as a quantity of alleys, or marbles, left behind or lost by those long-ago students of the Sackville Street School.

In 1888, the editor of the Toronto *Telegram*, John Ross Robertson, visited the Blackburns at their little house. A humanist and a philanthropist, he was charmed by the couple, who greeted him with great cordiality and talked of the old days when they operated the first taxi company in Toronto. It is curious that Robertson's article never mentioned that the Blackburns had been fugitive slaves, but focused instead on the success of their business venture. In an article titled "The First Cab in the City," Robertson described the Blackburn home and wrote that even in Thornton's old age, many people recognized him on the street:

> Mr. Blackburn, the first cab driver in the city, retired from the businesses with a competency a score of years ago, but he is not forgotten, for grey-haired men now (1888) fre-

quently greet him with the exclamation, "Ha! It is you who drove me to my wedding," or "You are the man who drove my eldest boy to his christening."

Thus, at the end of Thornton and Lucie's long lives, the city where they had made their home for more than a half-century acknowledged them, not for the refugee condition in which they'd arrived, but for the contributions their entrepreneurship had made.

EPILOGUE

Thornton Blackburn died on February 26, 1890. According to cemetery records, he was seventy-six, although Kentucky documents suggest he was at least two years older. According to Lucie's will, he was attended on his deathbed by the "Reverend Sadler, Acting Curate of Little Trinity Church." Thornton was buried two days later, on February 28, 1890. The funeral was led from the old house on Eastern Avenue that Thornton had shared with his wife since 1834 to the Toronto Necropolis. His obituary appeared in *The Evening Telegram*. It read simply, "BLACKBURN:—On Wednesday, 26th, at his residence, 70 Eastern ave., Thornton Blackburn, aged 76 years. Funeral Friday at 2 pm to Necropolis."

Beside the Blackburn plot is the gravestone of one of Canada's most important nineteenth-century figures: George Brown, Father of Confederation, publisher of the Toronto *Globe*, and the driving force behind the Anti-Slavery Society of Canada. Brown rests at the side of one of the fugitive slaves he so admired during his lifetime.

Lucie erected an imposing red granite obelisk to her beloved husband, close to the southern entrance to the Toronto Necropolis. It reads:

IN MEMORY OF THORNTON BLACKBURN,
DIED FEB. 26, 1890, AGED 76 YEARS.
A NATIVE OF MAYSVILLE, KENTUCKY, USA
BLESSED ARE THE DEAD WHICH DIE IN THE LORD.

Thornton's old taxi had been given during his lifetime to the historical society, the York Pioneers. It was used for many years as an outdoor exhibit in front of Scadding Cabin on the grounds of the Canadian National Exhibition. The old Blackburn cab, now devoid of its bright paint and itself "grey with wind and weather," remained with the society until about 1960, when it seems to have been discarded.

Thornton left behind a will signed simply with an "X." The document was witnessed by his physician and his attorney, William Henry Brouse, of Chadwick & Beatty, yet another one of the Gooderham clan. In one of those circular coincidences that seemed to follow the Blackburns throughout their lives, the man who registered the probate was James Lukin Robinson, son of the long-dead Chief Justice Robinson whose carefully worded legislation had allowed a pair of runaway slaves to go free fifty-seven years earlier.

Thornton left Lucie an estate totaling more than $18,000. This included the old house on Eastern Avenue, six rental properties scattered about the city, and $7,812 divided between accounts at the Merchants Bank of Canada and the Bank of Toronto. There was no old-age pension in the nineteenth century, and this remarkable old former slave and his wife had been living on their savings and investments for almost three decades. It had been a long way to come for a young slave boy owed $6 when his master, Dr. Gideon Brown of Hardinsburg, died in 1829.

Two years after her husband passed away, Mrs. Blackburn sold the remaining Eastern Avenue property to the school board, and the house where they had lived for more than half a century was demolished. The property was formally transferred to the Toronto Board of Education on June 1, 1892. The chimney was knocked down to fill in the root cellar and the ground leveled to add to the schoolyard. The remains of the Blackburn home and barn were buried under cinder and ash, then planking, and finally the asphalt of the Sackville Street School playground.

Lucie moved to a home a few blocks to the north, which she and her husband had purchased years before as an investment property. She shared her Bleecker Street home with two sisters, one a dressmaker and the other a "flower embalmer," the Misses Louisa and Minnie Berry. Their father, the elderly James Berry, a former carter, also lived at 73 Bleecker Street, occupying a "rear premises," perhaps a flat at the back of the house accessed through the yard or even a separate cottage along the laneway that ran across the back of the property. Across the street were the gardens of huge mansions, three of which belonged to Gooderham's, so the connections between that family and the Blackburns clearly continued into Lucie's later years.

When Lucie passed away in 1895, she left money and property worth $13,000, but she also owned six mortgages. They were let out at 6 and 7 percent interest, an extremely high rate of return. Lucie was about eighty-five when she began her career as a moneylender.

Lucie Blackburn was not, however, particularly generous to her friends in the end. Originally her will had provided substantial legacies to friends. Among the original beneficiaries were the acting curate of Little Trinity Church, "the clergyman who frequently attended [her] husband in his last illness," and the "widow of Robert Smith" and the couple's three children, Frank, Alfred, and Minnie. Their exact connections with the Blackburns are not known, although Robert Smith, a carpenter, from Louisiana was living with the Tinsley family on Agnes Street in 1861. Later a Robert Smith worked with Jim Jackson, one of Ann Maria's sons, at the Queen's Hotel in the 1860s. That his surname, Smith, was the same as that of Thornton and Alfred's first master may be entirely coincidental, but perhaps not.

Lucie's will was dated January 19, 1891. It was drawn up by the senior partner of Chadwick & Beatty, Edward Marion Chadwick. Like Thornton, Lucie signed her will and the attached codicils with an "X." On May 10 and 13 of the same year, she instructed her attorney to revoke the bequests, for, as she explained in the codicil, she did not feel the Smiths had treated her with "due consideration." In the minister's case, she said that she had been "mistaken" in him. Nothing was left in the will to either of the women with whom she shared her Bleecker Street home, but they did inherit the house.

Lucie died in early 1895, on one of the coldest days of the year. Her obituary in *The Evening Telegram* and the Toronto *World* read, "BLACKBURN—On Wednesday morning, February 6, 1895, Mrs. Lucy Blackburn, aged 90 years, widow of the late Thornton Blackburn. Funeral from her late residence, 73 Bleecker Street, to the Necropolis, on Thursday, the 7th inst, at 3 p.m. Friends and acquaintances are requested to accept this intimation." A day later the same newspaper announced that the opening of the new British Methodist Episcopal church on Chestnut Street was delayed owing to the profound cold and deep snow in the city. Mrs. Blackburn's body was not interred until April 9, no doubt because of the frozen ground. Interestingly, the physician listed on her death records was one of the most prominent of Toronto's medical men, Frederick Lemoine Grassett, who also attended the family of George Gooderham, William Gooderham's eldest son and principal heir.

The executor of her estate had also been a law student at Chadwick & Beatty. Walker Lewis Edward Marsh lived for a time on Bleecker Street a few doors from the Blackburn property and was the son of an attorney from London, Ontario. It was he who applied for probate. The real estate was valued at $2,500 and the inventory of property at $10,835.05. All but $35.55—the estimated value of Lucie's household effects—was lent out in mortgages. These were encumbrances on properties Lucie and Thornton had sold off in St. John's and St. Patrick's wards. When she sold the houses, Lucie had taken back the mortgages. The rest of the Blackburn estate was eventually divided among the administrators and the lawyer from Chadwick & Beatty who had drawn up the will.

Fourteen days after Lucie's funeral, Frederick Douglass died. The *Plessy v. Ferguson* ruling of the next year, stating that separate but equal facilities satisfied the requirements of the Fourteenth

Amendment to the U.S. Constitution, would usher in decades of segregation in schools, public facilities, and government services. It was the end of an era.

In Toronto, the Blackburns lay peacefully in their graves for almost a century. Their memory in Toronto slowly faded, until archaeologists unearthing their city's past brought it again to light. For a few short months over the summer in 1985, a downtown Toronto schoolyard was a hive of activity as schoolchildren, reporters, and tourists all flocked to see what the archaeologists were digging up at the Thornton and Lucie Blackburn Site. When the snow flew in the fall, the excavation was filled in, and the following spring a wildflower garden was planted there in Thornton and Lucie's memory.

The archaeologists at the Blackburn site made no shattering revelations, discovered no priceless treasure, and certainly unearthed no gold. Thornton and Lucie knew what it was like to be poor and, despite their prosperous business, remained frugal all their days. From the painstakingly collected findings of excavators and their young assistants, the tiny fragments of a preserving jar and the broken bone handles of inexpensive table spoons, crochet hooks, a loom weight, a needle, and a button still with a tiny bit of white thread attached, our imaginations paint the picture of Lucie Blackburn at her household tasks. How proud she must have felt to serve guests in her home with her new marble-ware tea set, purchased in about 1885, when the pattern was all the rage; how sad she would have been when a cup shattered, a saucer chipped, and then cracked, and was thrown out behind the house, into the old garbage dump. That house was hers. Never, from the time Lucie reached Toronto to the day she died, did she have to toil for any reason except that of the comfort of her husband and herself. On Canadian soil she was *Mrs.* Blackburn, a title she would never have been accorded in slavery. She had left Ruthie far behind.

Echoes of Thornton, too, were there, in the soil of his land, in the vegetable garden he worked and the stable he and Alfred built to house the cab that was both his pride and his livelihood. On the earthen floor of the stable was a burned and blackened patch of ground. When the archaeologists dug the site, they found the place where he used to shoe his horses, on an anvil whose placement was imprinted on the dirt. Bits of harness brass turned up under the trowel, and horseshoe nails. Part of a dog collar was found, too, evidence of a loved companion now gone to dust.

In the dirt were tiny bones, muskellunge, lake trout, salmon, remains of fish Thornton and Lucie brought back from their rambles through the rich marshlands at the mouth of the Don River. One of them, probably Thornton, liked to hunt, too. In the ashes of the hearth, cold now for more than a century, were bones of rabbits and ducks caught and brought home for their meals. Perhaps after they had their suppers at the end of a long working day, they had a pipe or two. The tobacco may have come from their farming friends at Buxton, in the old Elgin Association settlement where Thornton had helped to build the mill. Eventually, their white clay pipes broke and ended up in the root cellar underneath the house.

Temperance was throughout much of the nineteenth century an important pillar of the black leadership's crusade for "uplifting the race." The Blackburns, as they always did, had their own ideas. They served wine to their guests, for archaeologists recovered fragments of the glasses from under the floorboards of their home. When, as an elderly but still sociable and energetic man, Thornton had a drop too much with some of his Irish neighbors, perhaps his wife took the horsecar along the tracks of King Street to the police court to pay his fine.

So much can be learned about people from digging up places where they lived and worked in the past. Much is lost, though. All that Lucie and her husband of so many years felt, whom else they cared for, what they believed. The music, the loving, the anger, the laughter. These archaeologists cannot recover from the ground, for all their care.

Thornton and Lucie left neither papers nor children to carry on their legacy. Thornton was unable to write down his own feelings about freedom, but surely they must have matched those of another fugitive who made his home for a time in Toronto. His name was John Henry Hill, and he wrote a long series of letters to William Still of the Pennsylvania Anti-Slavery Society. In one, he expressed, perhaps best of all the runaways who came to Toronto in the years before the Civil War, what living as a free man, gaining an education, and having the chance to fight back against the American slave system meant to him:

> But . . . about your Republicanism. Our masters have told us that there was no living in Canada for a Negro but here we are able to earn our bread and money enough to make us comfortable. But I say give me freedom, and the United States may have all her money and Luxuries, yeas give me Liberty or Death. I'm in America, but not under Such a Government that I cannot express myself, speak, think or write. If I were able, and if my master had allowed me to have an education, I would make them American slave holders feel me, yeas I would make them tremble when I spoke, and when I took my Pen in hand their knees would smite together. My Dear Sir suppose I were an educated man. I could write to you something worth reading, but you know we poor fugitives whom have just come over from the South are not able to write much on any subject whatever. But I hope, by the aid of my God, I will try to use my midnight lamp, until I can have some influence upon the American slavery. If some one would say to me, that they would give my wife bread until I could be Educated I would stop my trade this day and take up my books . . . I want you to let the whole United States know we are satisfied here because I have seen more pleasure since I came here then I saw in the US the 24 years that I served my master.

Thornton Blackburn could not have known it, but in 1831, when he and Ruthie broke the chains of their own oppression, they changed the very world in which they lived. This modest couple rejected their own predetermined role in the system that, in so many ways, defined the southern United States. All alone, as a nineteen-year-old porter and a nursemaid, they had challenged the enormous power that at the time kept more than two million people in perpetual bondage. The Blackburns' path to liberty had been neither smooth nor straight. But every American slave who found refuge in Canada before the Civil War had reason to be thankful to Thornton and Lucie Blackburn. The decisions they made, and the adventures they shared on the difficult road north, helped make a safe home for runaway slaves at the end of the Underground Railroad.

Theirs is both an American and a Canadian story. What makes the Blackburns memorable—indeed, what makes the whole collective African American emigration called the Underground Railroad worthy of remembrance—is the implacable and unrelenting resistance of people of African heritage to slavery. The Blackburns were ordinary people who made choices that placed them, forever, among the extraordinary of history.

Surely Thornton and Lucie would have echoed his sentiments when John Henry Hill wrote: "Come Poor distressed men women and come to Canada where colored men are free. Oh how sweet the word do sound to me."

NOTES

INTRODUCTION

xiv   **"secreting themselves."** William Wells Brown, *National Antislavery Standard*, April 12, 1855; Jackson, *Her Parentage*, 6.

xv   **antebellum period.** Wayne, "Black Population of Canada West on the Eve of the American Civil War," 465–81, and Winks, *Blacks in Canada*, 484–93.

xv   **arm themselves.** The literature on slave resistance is vast: Aptheker, *American Negro Slave Revolts*, esp. ch. 3; Bauer and Bauer, "Day to Day Resistance to Slavery"; Blassingame, *Slave Community*; Finkelman, ed., *Rebellions, Resistance, and Runaways*; Genovese, *From Rebellion to Revolution* and also *Roll, Jordan, Roll*; Gutman, *Black Family in Slavery and Freedom*; Harding, *There Is a River*; Levine, *Black Culture and Black Consciousness*; Rawick, *From Sunup to Sundown*; Sobel, *The World They Made Together*; Stuckey, *Slave Culture*.

xv   **they ran away.** Berlin, *Many Thousands Gone*, 120–21; Franklin and Schweninger, *Runaway Slaves*, esp. chs. 8 and 9.

xv   **"happy in their chains."** The early proponent of this view was Thomas R. Dew, president of the College of William and Mary. Dew, *Review of the Debate in the Virginia Legislature of 1831 and 1832*; Stampp, "An Analysis of T. R. Dew's 'Review of the Debates in the Virginia Legislature,'" 380–87. For the connection between U.S. slavery and race, see Degler, "Slavery and the Genesis of Race Prejudice"; Fredrickson, *Black Image in the White Mind*; Jordan, *White over Black*.

xvi   **"body and mind."** Jefferson, *Notes on the State of Virginia*, 143.

xvi   **concept of race.** That slavery was a labor system justified rather than caused by racism was elucidated by Eric Williams in *Capitalism and Slavery*, while the anthropologist Eric Wolf in *Europe and the People Without History* demonstrated how colonial powers stripped those cultures they intended to exploit of heritage, pride, and self-identity. Barbara Jean Fields, who in 1990 wrote what many believe to be the definitive discussion of the subject, presents race as an ever-shifting ideological construct in "Slavery, Race, and Ideology in the United States of America." Race and what more recent historians call "the creation of whiteness" were used to place African Americans in a caste separate from even the poorest white. See Kolchin, "Whiteness Studies," and Roediger, *Wages of Whiteness.*

xvi   **"morally and intellectually."** John C. Calhoun, "Speech on the Reception of Abolition Petitions," U.S. Senate, Feb. 6, 1837, reprinted in McKitrick, ed., *Slavery Defended*, 12–16.

xvii   **those they loved.** Coleman, *Slavery Times in Kentucky*, 60. Drew, *Refugee*, contains numerous examples, as does Coffin, *Reminiscences*, 345–51. See also Franklin and Schweninger, *Runaway Slaves*, 50–55.

xvii   **sold far away.** For Kentucky, see Clark, "Slave Trade Between Kentucky and the Cotton Kingdom"; Coleman, "Lexington Slave Dealers"; and Lucas, *History of Blacks in Kentucky*, 84–100.

xviii   **enslaved African Americans.** Goodell, *Slavery and Anti-Slavery*, 382–99. The U.S. Census for 1830 gives the number of slaves as 2,009,043, as per Adams, *Neglected Period of Anti-Slavery in America*, 7.

xviii   **formed in 1833.** *Minutes and Proceedings of the First Annual Convention of the People of Color*, Philadelphia, 1831. See Davis, "Emergence of Immediatism in British and American Antislavery Thought"; and Quarles, *Black Abolitionists*, esp. ch. 1.

xix   **freedom road.** There has been much debate as to the character and even the existence of the systematized Underground Railroad, especially as presented in the works of Wilbur Siebert, its most thorough nineteenth-century chronicler (Siebert, *Underground Railroad*). Larry Gara in his landmark volume, *The Liberty Line*, wrote, "Although the underground railroad was a reality, much of the material relating to it belongs in the realm of folklore rather than history" (2).

xix   **recorded by abolitionists.** Starling in *Slave Narrative: Its Place in American History*, 337, estimated that 6,006 individuals are represented in all forms of American slave narrative. Also see Casmier-Paz, "Footprints of the Fugitive: Slave Narrative Discourse and the Trace of Autobiography." The reliability of slave narratives is argued in Blassingame, ed., *Slave Testimony*, xvii–lvi; Rawick, ed., *American Slave*, and *From Sundown to Sunup*, esp. intro.; and C. Vann Woodward, "History from Slave Sources," in Davis and Gates, Jr., eds., *Slave's Narrative*, 48–58. Also see Davis and Gates, eds., *Slave's Narrative*, 30 and 35–146.

xx   **"Suky, cook, 34."** "James Curry, a Fugitive Slave," *Liberator*, Jan. 10, 1840. Curry wrote of his mother, "It is not common for slaves to have more than one name, but my mother was a proud-spirited woman, and she gave her children two." For naming by owners, see Sobel, *World They Made Together*, 154–60.

xxi   **Smith and Brown.** Boles, *Black Southerners*, 43; Genovese, *Roll, Jordan, Roll*, 443ff.; Gutman, *Black Family in Slavery and Freedom*, 185–256. Singleton stated: "All the slaves on a plantation had the same name as their master . . . When a plantation changed owners the slaves changed their names," in *Recollections of My Slavery Days*, 3. In Detroit court records Thornton was called both "Thornton Smith" and "Thornton Brown," the names of his first and second owners.

KENTUCKY

1. WADE IN THE WATER, CHILDREN

3   **mistake her to be.** The suit launched by the Blackburns' owners
     against the captain and owners of the *Versailles* included sworn state-
     ments by just about everyone who encountered the runaways between
     July 3 and 4, 1831. The dispute was only settled by the federal court in
     Kentucky in 1846. The files, including countersuits, are in Jefferson
     County Chancery Court Records, Public Records Division, Kentucky
     Department for Libraries and Archives, Frankfort, and variously named:
     McKnight v. McFarland, McKnight v. Quarrier, and *McKnight v. the owners
     of the* Versailles, collectively listed as Case 2221; and *Oldham v. McFar-
     land, McKnight v. Quarrier,* and *McKnight v. the Owners of the* Versailles,
     Case 2222, in the same location. These are hereafter cited as Case 2221
     and Case 2222.

4   **current of the channel.** Not until the fall of 1831 did a steam ferry take
     over the Louisville-Jeffersonville run. See *W. T. Huff and the Heirs of
     William Oldham v. A. Wathen, Ephraim Gilman, James Thompson, Charles
     M. Strader, and the Heirs and Administrators of Charles Myers,* Jefferson
     County Chancery Court, Case 635. The diagonal path the ferry trav-
     eled to the Jeffersonville side is clearly marked on *A New Map of Ken-
     tucky, with Its Roads & Distances from Place to Place Along the Stage &
     Steam Boat Routes* (Philadelphia: H. S. Tanner, 1839).

5   **"servants" left behind.** For the use of brine and turpentine, see Drew,
     Refugee, 70 and 301, and Weld, *American Slavery as It Is,* 9, 62, and 69.

5   **so great a profit.** Bancroft, *Slave-Trading in the Old South,* esp. ch. 6;
     Berlin, *Generations of Captivity,* 61; Clark, "Slave Trade Between Ken-
     tucky and the Cotton Kingdom," 331–34; Coleman, *Slavery Times in
     Kentucky,* esp. ch. 5; Lucas, *History of Blacks in Kentucky,* esp. ch. 4.

7   **worked the river.** The abuse by slave traders of women under their
     control outraged slaves and free blacks as well as abolitionists. In *Soul by
     Soul,* Johnson cites disgusted commentary by several former African
     American slaves who wrote on the subject, including Solomon Northrup,
     William Wells Brown, and Lewis Clarke, 113–16 and 154–55.

7   **"for $300!"** The appraised value of Ruthie Blackburn is provided in the
     inventory of George Backus's estate, June 7, 1831, Jefferson County Es-
     tate Book 8, Jefferson County Courthouse, Louisville, Ky., 502–505; "1
     Negro Girl (Ruth), $300." The account of her sale and the price paid for
     her at auction are detailed in *Charles W. Backus v. George Backus' Admin-
     istrators,* Jefferson County Court, Case 2502.

7   **his and Ruthie's own names.** Jefferson County Judge John Pope Old-
     ham, whose sister-in-law Susan Brown was Thornton's legal owner,
     would later swear that "Thornton Blackburn, [did not have] in his pos-
     session, the record of any Court of the United States *properly* exempli-
     fied proving his right to freedom." Deposition of John Pope Oldham,
     March 5, 1841, *John P. Oldham, Exr. of Gideon Brown Dec'd v. Verdict of
     the Steam Boat* Versailles. The papers have never been found.

9 **visit to Indiana.** An 1823 Kentucky law required personal details and descriptions to be included on free papers. The purpose, of course, was to make it difficult for free papers to be lent for use in slave flight. See Hudson, "In Pursuit of Freedom," 292.

9 **for the same reasons.** See Deposition of Lloyd White, Oct. 18, 1837, Jefferson County Chancery Court, Case 635: "This happened more frequently on Sundays than on other days, because more were passing on Sundays than other days." Deposition of John Myers, Oct. 18, 1837, *W. T. Huff and the Heirs of William Oldham v. A. Wathen, Ephraim Gilman, James Thompson, Charles M. Strader, and the Heirs and Administrators of Charles Myers*, Jefferson County Chancery Court, Case 635; Catterall, *Judicial Cases Concerning American Slavery and the Negro*, 1:347.

9 **penitentiary at Frankfort.** An Act to Prevent the Masters of Vessels and Others from Employing or Removing Persons of Colour from This State, and An Act to Amend an Act Entitled "An Act to Prevent the Masters of Vessels and Others from Employing or Removing Persons of Colour from This State," Jan. 7, 1824, Feb. 12, 1828, in Morehead and Brown, *A Digest of the Statute Laws of Kentucky*, 1:259 and 260; also *Session Laws, 1823*, 178; *Session Laws, 1831–32*, 54–55, cited in McDougle, "The Legal Status of Slavery," 263. A stricter law governing ferries was passed in 1831 to deal with exactly the issues raised in the Blackburn escape; *Session Laws, 1831–32*, 54–55, cited in McDougle, *Slavery in Kentucky*, 53–54. The pertinence of these laws to the case against Captain Quarrier and the owners of the *Versailles* is outlined in the summary of the cases entitled *McKnight v. McFarland and Others*, Opinion and Order, and *Oldham v. McFarland and Others*, Jan. 5, 1841, Cases 2221 and 2222.

9 **Louisville jailer.** A similar case to the Blackburns' shows the penalties involved. See Chancery, Oct. 28, Fall Term, 1839, *Wathen and Others v. Oldham's Heirs*, Case 635, in Dana, *Reports of Select Cases*, 9:50–51.

10 **they were not.** "Persons of color are deemed to be slaves, prima facie from their color, and therefore require that they produce exemplifications of their freedom," *McKnight v. McFarland and Others*, Opinion and Order, and *Oldham v. McFarland and Others*, Jan. 5, 1841, Cases 2221 and 2222.

10 **Louisville berth.** Deposition of Monroe Quarrier, March 30, 1832, Case 2221. The boat was later impounded. *McKnight v. McFarland*, Nov. 3, 1831, Case 2221. For the Louisville firms dealing with the *Versailles*, see, for instance, *Louisville Public Advertiser*, Oct. 4 and 20, 1831.

11 **papers were genuine.** Deposition of Monroe Quarrier, March 30, 1832, Case 2221.

11 **"black silk goods."** Deposition of Thornton Bayless, clerk of the *Versailles*, May 24, 1832, Case 2221.

12 **slave South in 1831.** Deposition of Virgil McKnight, May 3, 1834, Case 2222. *McFarland v. McKnight*, June 1846, in Monroe, *Reports of Cases at Common Law and in Equity Decided in the Court of Appeals of Kentucky*, 6:500.

12 **"confined to its cabin."** Trollope, *Domestic Manners of the Americans*, 16.

13 **furnace above-decks.** Drago, *Steamboaters*, ch. 2, and Ford, "Life on the Ohio: A Captain's View," 19–26.

2. THERE IS A LAND BEYOND THE RIVER

15 **William Grimes.** *Life of William Grimes*, 9.

15 **"colored men are free."** Clift, *History of Maysville and Mason County*, 1:151–52; Collins, *Collins' Historical Sketches of Kentucky*, 27; Siebert, *Underground Railroad*, 27.

16 **"Underground Railroad."** There are several sources for this tale. In *Underground Railroad* (3–4), Mitchell wrote: "these damned abolitionists must have a railroad under the ground by which they can run off our negroes." Siebert, *Underground Railroad*, attributed the story to the Hon. Rush R. Solan of Sandusky, Ohio, "who was actively engaged in underground work," and who told the historian in the 1880s that the incident happened opposite Ripley, Ohio, in 1831.

17 **already moved west.** The exact date is known because Susan Smith Doniphan died in childbirth the day her family arrived at Maysville. See "Dr. Anderson Doniphan of Mason County, Ky., Family Bible Records," in the Doniphan File, Mason County Museum Center, Maysville, Ky.

17 **"whenever I think of Virginia."** Fedric, *Slave Life in Virginia and Kentucky*, 14.

18 **never own.** Coleman, "Old Lexington and Maysville Road Turnpike," 13–16; Friend, *Along the Maysville Road*, 2; Michaux, *Travels to the West of the Alleghany Mountains*, 3:237.

19 **America's first frontier.** Coleman, *Slavery Times in Kentucky*, chs. 1 and 2; Fischer and Kelly, *Away, I'm Bound Away*, 39–63 and 69–73; Lucas, *History of Blacks in Kentucky*, esp. prologue; Terry, "Sustaining the Bonds of Kinship," 61–64.

19 **Mount Vernon.** Ranke, *Blackburn Genealogy*, 21–31. Richard Blackburn acquired in 1741 a grant of 2,628 acres, formerly part of Lord Fairfax's enormous land holdings mainly in Loudoun County. Blackburn never lived there, but leased it on terms that ranged from a few years to the life of the tenants. Will of Richard Blackburn, *Tyler's Quarterly* 31, no. 1 (July 1949), 38–42. The farm on Bull Run was originally called Yorkshire Farm and willed to his son Thomas. On November 2, 1777, Colonel Thomas Blackburn of Prince William County sold off sixteen tracts of land, several of which were acquired by members of the Smith family. Thomas Smith and his son William purchased life leases on the land, which was not sold out of the family until the 1820s. Blackburn Papers, Virginia Historical Society, various. See also Black, "Rippon Lodge and the Blackburns," and Hogue, "History of the Blackburn Family," 1–8.

20 **named Sibby.** Hopkins, ed., *Index to the Tithables of Loudoun County, Virginia and to Slaveholders and Slaves, 1758–1786*, 137. There was only one female slave named Sibby who was both connected to the Blackburn family in Virginia and who bore a son named Thornton in Mason

County, Kentucky. Further corroboration comes from their mutual ownership by the Smith family of Washington, Kentucky; Thornton used the surname "Smith" as an alias in later years. Thomas Smith of Fairfax County on July 17, 1764, bequeathed to William, "Old Will, Sibby, Nell, Davy, Moses, Milley, and Little Will." This Sibby was clearly too old to be Thornton's mother. The lease to the lands located along the Bull Run and the Beaverdam Branch of Goose Creek were sold, complete with slaves, to a planter named David Evans, who died in 1783. The property, and Sibby now with a child, also named Sibby, reverted to William Smith, for the same slave names appear, as is demonstrated in the Will of William Smith, January 23, 1802, Mason County, Kentucky, Will Book B, 170–4; he owned slaves named Old Will, Young Will, Milley, as well as "Old Milley," Sibby and her child, John. Therefore records pertaining to the Smith family show at least two generations of female slaves named "Sibby." Clemens, *Virginia Wills Before 1779*, 32. See also Joyner, Jr., *First Settlers of Orange County, Virginia*, 97, 130–31, 194.

21 **of low water.** Harrison, "A Virginian Moves to Kentucky, 1793," 201–13; Terry, "Sustaining the Bonds of Kinship," 61–68.

21 **far from past.** Dorman, ed., *Genealogies of Virginia Families*, 4:716. Hamilton, *Ancestral Lines of the Doniphan, Frazee, and Hamilton Families*, 517.

22 **own destination.** Mason County Court Order Books, June Court 1802, 331; Dr. M. F. Adamson, "Reminiscences of Fifty Years Ago," *Maysville Republican*, September 20, 1879; Anderson Doniphan, 1764–1841, Day books, 1814–1844. BF/D683. 3 vols. Filson Historical Society, Louisville, Kentucky. See also Carson, "Transportation and Traffic on the Ohio," 26–38.

22 **west of the Alleghenies.** Collins, *Collins' Historical Sketches of Kentucky*, 428–29.

22 **family slaves.** Sibby Blackburn seems to have been a farm and field worker for the Smiths, for her name never appears with those of family's domestic servants in the account ledgers of Robert Tureman's store at Washington, where the Smith family did most of their shopping. Robert Tureman Ledger, Special Collections, Maysville Museum Center.

22 **"more slaves."** Fedric, *Slave Life in Virginia and Kentucky*, 17.

23 **slaves produce.** Inventory and Appraisement of the Estate of William Smith, Oct. 11, 1802, Mason Co. Will Book B, 194–95; Frazee, *Ancestral Lines*, 31–33; Mason Co. Deed Book P, Sept. 13, 1815, Anderson Doniphan and Samuel Owens.

24 **American economy.** Bancroft, *Slave-Trading in the Old South*, 9–10 and 340; Wright, *Political Economy of the Old South*, 13–14.

25 **Underground Railroad.** Winks, *Blacks in Canada*, 96–99.

25 **"with fathers."** Douglass, *My Bondage and My Freedom*, 51.

25 **"enjoyed considerable popularity."** Will of William Smith, Mason County Will Book B, Jan. 23, 1802, 170–74, proven Jan. 23, 1802; also Inventory and Appraisement of the Estate of William Smith, Court Orders, 1800–1803, November Court 1802, 121. There are twenty-six slaves listed in the inventory, of whom four were household servants. Hamilton, *Ancestral Lines*, 517–18.

26 **"never saw her more."** Fedric, *Slave Life in Virginia and Kentucky*, 42.

27 **their families.** Quarles, *Negro in the Making of America*, 80–82; Rose, ed., *Documentary History*, 107–36.

27 **land and workers.** Up to 1812, Robert Smith and his cousin Susan Hancock Smith, whom he had married in 1804, were still living in Washington, Mason County, and Sibby Blackburn and her son Alfred were with them, probably at the farm. The tax list for 1812 showed Robert as having four slaves above the age of sixteen and six slaves younger than sixteen. By 1813, official documents were calling Robert Smith the "late deputy sheriff" of Mason County, and he was steadily divesting himself of slaves.

28 **normally made.** Coleman, *Slavery*, 123–25; Eaton, "Slave Hiring in the Upper South," 672; Lucas, *History of Blacks in Kentucky*, 101–17; Wade, *Slavery in the Cities*, 48.

28 **Thornton Blackburn.** Slavery was hereditary: "The condition of the child follows the condition of the mother," or, in the Latin form, *partus sequitur ventrum*, a statute confirmed by the House of Burgesses of Virginia in 1662, Hening, *Statutes at Large*, 11:170.

28 **because of her pregnancy.** For example, see Roper, *Narrative*, 7.

29 **"drowned herself."** Brown, *Narrative*, 39–41.

29 **died in 1802.** John G. Hickman, "The Mortons," draft of speech delivered to the Mason County Historical and Scientific Society, Jan. 1876, Morton File, Mason County Museum Center, Maysville, Ky. Kinship may account for the fact that there survives no bill of sale for little Thornton Blackburn. See also Hamilton, *Ancestral Lines*, 33 and 45.

30 **"December 26, 1827)."** Mason County Deed Book O, June 17, 1815, 387; Hickman, "Mortons Genealogy, January 1876," MS, Morton File, Mason County Museum Center. Lucy Baylor Morton married the widowed William Murphy on June 20, 1815.

30 **"sho a scramble."** Work Projects Administration, the District of Columbia, *Kentucky Narratives*, vol. VII, typescript, Library of Congress, Washington, D.C., 1941. Interview with Mary Wright of Christian County, Ky.

31 **ten mechanics' shops.** Calvert and Klee, eds., *Mason County Fact and Folklore*, 66–67; Collins, *Collins' Historical Sketches of Kentucky*, 2: 56–57, and Lee, *Historical Sketch of Mason County, Kentucky*, 5–6.

31 **"lilies-of-the-valley."** Best, *Historic Past of Washington, Mason County, Kentucky*; Lee, *Historical Sketch of Mason County, Kentucky*, 10.

32 **"woman Esther."** Inventory and Appraisement of the Estate of William Murphy, Mason County Will Book G, July 6, 1829, 401–404. There were only three slaves left: Adam, a man worth $100, and two women, Kitt and Esther, valued at $150 and $100, respectively.

32 **eight children.** Young and Young, eds., *Mason County Deed Book Abstracts M–V*, book N, 2:112, Rudolph Black of Bracken County, Kentucky, and John Black of Mason County, Kentucky, sale of land. Joseph Doniphan passed away in early 1814. Included in the estate were slaves who had lived with Sibby when they all belonged to William Smith. Robert Smith, his wife, Susan Hancock, and his mother, Margaret Whitely Smith, moved to New Castle, Henry County.

32 **"handsomest towns on the river."** Edwin Adams Davis and John C. L. Andreassen, eds., "A Journey from Baltimore to Louisville in 1816: Diary of William Newton Mercer," *Ohio History* 45:4 (October 1936): 351–64.

32 **at their mothers' knees.** Blassingame, *Slave Community*, 72–73; Gaspar and Hine, *More Than Chattel*, 147–68, 154; Levine, *Black Culture and Black Consciousness*, 81–133; Stuckey, *Slave Culture*, 17–19.

33 **"she was gone."** Clarke, *Narrative*, 22; Douglass, *Narrative*, 3.

33 **"though I was but a boy."** Henson, *Autobiography*, 1881, 23.

33 **"teach them their duty."** Fedric, *Slave Life in Virginia and Kentucky*, 27.

33 **endure all their lives.** There were several slaves named Alfred listed in legal transactions in Washington, Kentucky, in this period; for example, see Will of Captain Thomas Marshall, Mason County Will Book D, March 4, 1817, 147–53. The Marshalls, Doniphans, Smiths, Mortons, and Murphys were interrelated as well as having business and land dealings both in Kentucky and in Virginia. Another Alfred is listed in the will of John Waugh, Will Book E, Jan. 1820, 77–79. Anderson and Joseph Doniphan's mother was a Waugh, as was George Morton's wife, so it is possible that Alfred, like Thornton, was passed between one or another family member without any bill of sale or hiring agreement being registered with the county clerk.

34 **black and white.** Francis Taylor in 1810 was the owner of eight slaves, of whom six were the Lightfoot brothers and their parents. 1810 U.S. Census, Mason County, Kentucky.

34 **slave one, Missouri.** Fogel, *Without Consent or Contract*, 290–93; Mc-Colley, *Slavery and Jeffersonian Virginia*, 174.

35 **"me to perform."** Clarke and Clarke, *Narrative of the Sufferings*, 16; Steward, *Twenty-Two Years a Slave*, 20.

35 **over the kitchen fire.** King, *Stolen Childhood*, 26–27; Schwartz, *Born in Bondage*, 118–20.

35 **"spoil the other slaves."** Fedric, *Slave Life in Virginia and Kentucky*, 10.

36 **"write at all."** Drew, *Refugee*, 152–53.

37 **"any feeling in me."** Campbell, *Bond and Free*, 2–3; *Life of William Grimes*, 9.

37 **"hot in our pockets."** Clarke, *Narrative*, 17; Henson, *Autobiography*, 1881, 49–50; Marrs, *Life and History*, 10.

38 **might bring.** Calvert and Klee, *Mason County Facts and Folklore*, 66; Clift, *History of Maysville and Mason County*, 145–46.

39 **prevent insurrection.** Coleman, *Slavery Times in Kentucky*, 76–77; Douglass, *Narrative*, 58–59; King, *Stolen Childhood*, 58–59.

40 **period of time.** Aptheker, *American Negro Slave Revolts*; Grable, "Racial Violence," 275–83; Kitson, "Towards Freedom," 175–87.

40 **"slave stealing."** Deed of emancipation for Anna, Eliza Jane, and Lucina Perkins, by Doctor Perkins, Sept. 13, 1824, Mason County Deed Book 29, 423; James M. Prichard, "Into the Fiery Furnace: Anti-Slavery Prisoners in the Kentucky State Penitentiary, 1844–1870," MS, 2001, Kentucky Department for Libraries and Archives, Frankfort, used with permission.

40 **Landing Place.** Jerry Gore, "Mason Is More than Gateway to the South; It Is the Gateway to Freedom," undated newspaper clipping, Slavery file, Mason County Museum Center.

40 **past seven years.** Martin, *Anti-Slavery Movement in Kentucky*, 89.

41 **"*in chains.*"** Stone was in business by about 1816, for he advertised: "EDWARD STONE, Living on the Limestone Road, 4 miles from Paris leading to Millersburg," *Western Citizen*, Lexington, July 24, 1816; Coleman, *Slavery Times in Kentucky*, 144ff; Rankin, *Letters on American Slavery*, 42.

41 **National Underground Railroad Freedom Center.** Shelly Whitehead, "Slave Jail Moving," *Cincinnati Post*, March 6, 2001; Patricia Leigh, "In a Barn, a Piece of Slavery's Hidden Past," *New York Times*, May 6, 2003.

42 **under the front porch.** Fedric, *Slave Life in Virginia and Kentucky*, 104–105; Lee, *Historical Sketch of Mason County, Kentucky*, 24; Jerry Gore, National Underground Railroad Museum, Maysville, Ky., personal communication, 2003.

42 **antebellum years.** Hagedorn, *Beyond the River*, 83–86; *Maysville Eagle*, March 28, 1827; "Slave Holders: We request to inform the slave-holders of Mason county, that a meeting of the description of persons will be held at the courthouse in Washington on SATURDAY, the 21st of July, inst., for the purpose of concerting measures for the better security of their property."

42 **"you were free."** Singleton, *Recollections of My Slavery Days*, 6.

43 **audiences cry.** "Interview of Professor W. H. Siebert with Captain R. C. Rankin, at Ripley, Ohio, Apr. 8, 1892," Wilbur H. Siebert Papers, Ohio Historical Society; Parker, *His Promised Land*, 12–13, and the notes on p. 162. For a modern rendering, see Hagedorn, *Beyond the River*, 136–39.

44 **as late as 1939.** "Slave Block Where Uncle Tom Was Believed Sold Is in Mason: Old Buildings Located There, First Postoffice in 'West' Is in Town," clipping marked "1939," unidentified newspaper, Washington File, Mason County Museum Center.

44 **nephews to freedom.** Henson, *Autobiography*, 1881, 107–20.

46 **"a new smith's shop."** Pennington, *Fugitive Blacksmith*, 4.

46 **Henry Clay.** Clift, *History of Maysville and Mason County*, 1:160–64. The letter from the Maysville town fathers to Henry Clay dated May 23, 1825, included William Murphy's signature.

3. ON JORDAN'S BANK

47 **"My Old Kentucky Home, Good Night."** The Kentucky state song was inspired by Stephen Foster's 1853 visit to Bardstown, Kentucky, where he observed slavery firsthand. The song is the lament of an elderly slave who has been sold away from Kentucky to the sugarcane plantations of Louisiana.

47 **from miles around.** For the weather conditions, see Jacob Rauschenberger, "Diary of Gnadenhutten, Beersheba, and Sharon, May 1816–Dec. 31, 1826," translated by Allen P. Zimmerman at Gnadenhutten, Ohio, 1955.

48 **forgot the sight.** Clark, "Slave Trade Between Kentucky and the Cotton Kingdom," 332; Weld, *American Slavery as It Is*, 92–93. For the

Stones' marketing practices, see Coleman, *Slavery Times in Kentucky*, 173–74.

48 **"in a jail of Breckinridge County."** Thompson, *History and Legend of Breckinridge County, Kentucky*, 72. They were indicted on October 17, 1826, and tried on the eighteenth, nineteenth, and twenty-first. Breckinridge County Circuit Court Book 7, 182, 183, 192, 194, 207, 208, 219, Breckinridge County Archives, County Courthouse, Hardinsburg, Ky.; *Paris (Ky.) Western Luminary*, Sept. 30, 1826.

49 **carted away for burial.** Gideon Brown was on several occasions appointed by the town to oversee conditions at the jail. See, for instance, Breckinridge County Court Minute Book 2, Feb. 1813–Aug. 1818, May 16, 1814, 59. On the next court day, ten of the Stone slaves were sold on the steps of the Hardinsburg courthouse. Administration of the Estate of Edward Stone, Bourbon County Order Book I, Oct. 2, 1826, 395, Kentucky Department of Libraries and Archives, Frankfort, Ky.

49 **Stone's widow.** Pen Bogert, librarian, Filson Historical Society, personal communication, 2000, for location of Edward Stone's grave; Bob Moorman, president, Breckinridge County Historical Society, personal communication, 2002, for Stephensport graves of the victims of the Stone massacre. See also A Deed of Manumission from the Heirs of Edward Stone to Lewis, Bourbon County Order Book I, Jan. 2, 1827, 429.

49 **remain to this day.** *Paris (Ky.) Western Luminary*, Oct. 11, 1826; Coleman, *Slavery Times in Kentucky*, 176.

50 **"fiddle almost continually."** Abraham Lincoln to Mary Speed, Sept. 27, 1841, in Basler, ed., *Collected Works of Abraham Lincoln*, 121.

51 **through the Maysville Landing.** Philip Lightfoot purchased "Samuel Stuckey's Tanyard," on March 15, 1827, Lot 36, one half acre "with the appurtenances" on the outskirts of Hardinsburg, adjacent to Gideon Brown's two-acre homestead property; Breckinridge County Deed Book H. The Lightfoots were a very old and prominent Virginia family, which had migrated from the Potomac to the district of Orange County that later became Culpeper, also the home of Dr. Gideon Brown's family. Slaughter and Green, comp., *Genealogical and Historical Notes on Culpeper County*, 69; Joyner, *First Settlers of Orange County, Virginia*, 194.

51 **protect their investments.** I arrived at this figure by examining a series of wills and estate appraisals in the Breckinridge County Archives for the appropriate period.

52 **them were slaves.** U.S. Census Bureau, 2000: Only 2.9 percent of the modern Breckinridge County population is black. By contrast, U.S. Census for Breckinridge County, 1830, listed white males 7,239; slaves, 1,691; free black 17. Most local residents came from Botetourt, Bedford, Fauquier, Loudoun, and Culpeper counties, the so-called back counties of Virginia. See Cook and Cook, *Breckinridge County, Kentucky: Records*, 1:1–2; Lucas, *History of Blacks in Kentucky*, xv–xix.

53 **"Linkhorn," or Lincoln.** "Lincoln and His Sister Were Fed by Slave When in Hardinsburg," undated newspaper clipping, vertical files, Breckinridge County Public Library, Hardinsburg. The story is repeated in *Kentucky: A Guide to the Bluegrass State*, 404.

53 **family home.** Tax rolls for Breckinridge County, 1813–1830, Breckinridge County Archives, Hardinsburg; U.S. Census, 1820 and 1830. U.S.
Census, Breckinridge County, 1820, shows Gideon Brown of Hardinsburg in possession of six slaves. No purchase agreements have been discovered, but a list of their names and values appears in the inventory for
Gideon Brown's estate. The land was bought in 1828; "Deed J. P. Oldham, executor of the estate of Dr. Gideon Brown, dec^d and Susan
Brown, widow of Dr. G. Brown, both of the City of Louisville, and
Charles Hambleton of the County of Breckinridge for $150 . . . June
20, 1832 . . . 2/3 of parcel in the Co. of Breckinridge on Hardin's Creek
near Hardinsburg . . . sold to Dr. Brown by Zachariah Mattingly by
deed May 24, 1828," Breckinridge County Archives.

54 **owners' stores.** Such pits have been found at Louisville's Oxmoor
Plantation, home to Kentucky's first Lieutenant Governor, Alexander
Scott Bullitt, and at former slave quarters in Virginia, including Thomas
Jefferson's Poplar Forest and Monticello. Heath, *Hidden Lives*, 37;
Kelso, "Archaeology of Slave Life at Thomas Jefferson's Monticello."

54 **"*without a shelter.*"** Green, *Narrative*, 5.

54 **Maryland farm.** Henson, *Autobiography*, 1881, 49.

54 **October 19, 1786.** See the Will of Thomas Brown, St. Mark's Parish,
Culpeper County, Va., Oct. 19, 1786, in Wulfeck, *Culpeper County, Virginia, Will Books B and C*, 64; James Brown, dec^d, Inventory of His Estate, 1815, Feb., Nelson Co. Archives, County Administrative Building,
Bardstown, Ky.

55 **that never healed.** Nelson County Deed Book 6, July 11, 1808, 769.

55 **rode into town.** Gideon Brown's name first appears in local records on
July 9, 1810, when he witnessed a military warrant. See Breckinridge
Commissioner's Deed Book 1, 43, Breckinridge Co. Archives.

55 **a comfortable home.** Brown bought the property, on which he had al-
ready built a house, for $25, Breckinridge County Deed Book C, Nov. 10,
1813, 272. Today, the site of the homestead lies on U.S. 60, west of
Hardinsburg, between Hardin's Creek and the subdivision known as
Gilbert Heights. Gideon Brown is cited in legal documents prepared for
Bill Hardin's signature, and also witnessed his will. Cook and Cook, *Breck-
inridge County, Kentucky: Records*, 4:35; for William Hardin, see Battle,
Perrin, Kniffin, *Kentucky: A History of the State* in Westerfield, ed., *Ken-
tucky Genealogy and Biography*, 1:108–11; Oldham Papers and Rogers C.
Ballard Thruston Papers, Filson Historical Society, Louisville, Ky.

56 **Breckinridge County.** John Pope Oldham's (1785–1858) name appears
repeatedly in the Breckinridge County Court Minute Books, vols. 2 and
3. He was trustee for the Town of Hardinsburg (Aug. 21, 1815, and May
20, 1816), a guarantor of various public officials (Jan. 15, 1816, and Jan.
19, 1818) and was appointed commonwealth attorney for the circuit
court (Nov. 18, 1817).

56 **Churchill Downs.** John Pope Oldham acquired his land by virtue of
the military exploits of his famous father, Colonel William Oldham,
who lost his life at St. Clair's Defeat in 1791, John Pope Oldham to Ly-
man Draper, Sept. 13, 1847, Draper Manuscript Collection, Wisconsin
Historical Society; Jennings, *Louisville's First Families*, 60–62.

56 **"Talbot's billiard table."** Murray, abst., *Logan County, Kentucky, Deed Abstracts, 1792–1813* (Dallas, privately published, 1993), 240.

56 **private academies.** Fletcher, *Genealogical Sketch*, 34–35.

57 **evident annoyance.** Susan Talbot was born at Russellville, Kentucky, in 1794 and died in Pewee Valley, Oldham County, Kentucky, in 1873, according to her burial records at Louisville's Cave Hill Cemetery.

57 **team in 1827.** Tax rolls for Hardinsburg, Breckinridge County, Ky., 1827, Breckinridge County Archives.

57 **"about the yard."** Watson, *Narrative*, 22.

57 **plants and herbs.** Murray to Brown's Heirs, Deed, June 9, 1829, Breckinridge County Deed Book 1, 16, Breckinridge County Archives; Fire Insurance Map for Hardinsburg, Breckinridge County, Kentucky (Pelham, N.Y.: Sanborn, 1916).

57 **four counties.** The size of the practice is inferred from the towns where patients who owed Dr. Brown money lived. See List of Debts Due, the Estate of Dr. G. Brown, Dec[d], June 21, 1830, Breckinridge County Estate Book 3, 39, Breckinridge County Archives.

58 **white patient again.** See, for instance, Green, *Narrative*, 12. For McDowell's involvement and discussion, see Goodson, "Enslaved Africans and Doctors in South Carolina," 225–33, and Savitt, "The Use of Blacks for Medical Experimentation and Demonstration in the Old South," 331–48.

59 **border state.** Jacobs, *Incidents in the Life of a Slave Girl*, 20. For Kentucky, see Coleman, *Slavery Times in Kentucky*, 61–62; *Louisville Daily Journal*, Oct. 17, 1839; and O'Brien, "Slavery in Louisville," 23–24.

59 **"Christmas week."** Brown, *Narrative*, 95–96; Coleman, *Slavery Times in Kentucky*, 68–76.

60 **"husked in one night."** Green, *Narrative*, 8.

61 **"allowance of whiskey."** Pennington, *Fugitive Blacksmith*, 65.

61 **physical punishment.** Rawick, *From Sundown to Sunup*, 61–65; Federal Workers of the Writers' Program of Virginia, comp., *Negro in Virginia*, 155–65.

61 **"fear of the consequences."** Green, *Narrative*, 23.

62 **"person receiving them."** Watson, *Narrative*, 12.

62 **"hurt or caught."** Robinson, *From Log Cabin to Pulpit; or, Fifteen Years in Slavery*, 78.

63 **his skill.** Rawick, *From Sundown to Sunup*, 71. For the archaeology, see Hamalainen, "Faunal Analysis," in Jamieson, ed., Smardz, Hamalainen, et al., "Thornton Blackburn House Site, AjGu-16," 92.

64 **"opposition to the other."** Faust, "Slavery in the American Experience," 15.

64 **usual duties.** Breeden, ed., *Advice Among Masters*, 122; Stampp, *Peculiar Institution*, esp. ch. 4.

65 **in this way.** "List of Debts Due the Estate of Dr. G. Brown, Dec[d], June 21, 1830," Breckinridge County Estate Book 3, 396, Breckinridge County Archives: "Black Man Thornton ac[coun]ts, $6.00." For resistance, see Bauer and Bauer, "Day to Day Resistance to Slavery"; Cheek, *Black Resistance*; Rawick, *From Sundown to Sunup*, 95–121.

65   **today's currency.** Samuel H. Williamson, "What Is the Relative Value?" *Economic History Services*, June 2006, eh.net/hmit/compare/ (accessed Aug. 10, 2006).

66   **"their own masters."** Douglass, *Narrative*, 5; George Fitzhugh, perhaps the best known of the proslavery apologists, in *Cannibals All! Or Slaves Without Masters* (Richmond, VA: A. Morris, 1857), unfavorably compared the lot of "wage slaves" in Britain to the happy, well-managed slave population in the American South.

66   **Civil War.** The literature on Jackson's presidency is vast. One of the most prolific authors is Robert Remini, who produced the useful *Andrew Jackson: A Bibliography* (Westport, Conn.: Meckler, 1991). Arthur Schlesinger, Jr., *The Age of Jackson* (Boston: Little, Brown, 1945), remains a classic work. The role of women in the South is the subject of Clinton's *Plantation Mistress: Woman's World in the Old South* and Fox-Genovese's *Within the Plantation Household: Black and White Women of the Old South.*

67   **complex land transfers.** See, for instance, "Indenture made this 25th day of October, 1825 between Charles H. Willman . . . and Dr. Gideon Brown," Breckinridge County Deed Book I, 317, Breckinridge County Archives; Cook and Cook, *Breckinridge County, Kentucky: Records*, 4:60.

67   **beside his house.** Brown's will stipulates that he is to be buried there with his children. Will of Gideon Brown, April 6, 1829, Breckinridge County Archives.

67   **"where he has gone to."** Drew, *Refugee*, 89.

68   **"the black man Thornton."** "List of Debts Due the Estate of Dr. G. Brown, Dec[d], June 21, 1830," Breckinridge County Estate Book 3, 396.

68   **went for $855.** Breckinridge County Deed, box 6, folder 7, June 29, 1832, Brown's executors, deed for two-thirds of fifty-nine acres to Charles Hambleton; "Inventory & Appraisement of Dr. G. Brown's Estate, made at his late residence, the 9th of June, 1829, filed 21st June, 1830," Breckinridge County Estate Book 3, Breckinridge County Archives.

69   **$2,160.39¾.** "Jno" is a nineteenth-century short form for the name John. "Sales Bill of the Personal Property of Gideon Brown, deceased, made 20th November, 1829, on 16 months credit," Breckinridge County Estate Book 3, Breckinridge County Archives.

69   **Serena $175.** "An Inventory & Appraisement of the estate of Dr. Gideon Brown dec'd made at his late residence this 9th of June 1829," Breckinridge County Estate Book 3, Breckinridge County Archives.

70   **taxable assets.** U.S. Census, Breckinridge County, Ky., 1830, 81–82. Rose was over forty-five according to the 1820 census, so she was at least fifty-five in 1830.

4. TROUBLING THE WATERS

71   **Frederick Douglass, 1849.** Holland, *Frederick Douglass*, 261.

72   **"salute the ear."** Atwater, *Remarks Made on a Tour to Prairie du Chien*, 11.

73   **Ohio River shipping.** Kreipke, "Falls of the Ohio and the Develop-
     ment of the Ohio River Trade." There are several good general histories
     of the city. See, for example, Casseday, *History of Louisville*; Johnston,
     ed., *Memorial History of Louisville*; Yater, *Two Hundred Years*.
73   **on the side streets.** Atwater, *Remarks Made on a Tour to Prairie du Chien*,
     11–12.
73   **"attachment to money."** Cited in Yater, *Two Hundred Years*, 36.
74   **"in every direction with plantations."** Postl, *Americans as They
     Are*, 45.
74   **population in 1832.** Dickens, *American Notes*, 356. For the prevalence
     of illness, see Stafford, "Slavery in a Border City: Louisville, 1790–1860,"
     46–48; Wade, *Urban Frontier*, 96–97; Yater, *Two Hundred Years*, 24.
74   **lumberyards.** Curry, *Free Blacks in Urban America*, tables A-1 and A-2,
     246–47.
75   **the upper floors.** No illustrations of this building survive, but it was
     undoubtedly similar to Federal-style terraced homes of the period that
     still stand on Fourth Street. The lot was twenty-three and a half feet
     wide but more than two hundred feet deep, according to the tax rolls for
     Louisville, Kentucky, in 1831. The property was initially rented. It and
     an adjacent lot were purchased on July 28, 1832. Jefferson County Deed
     Book EE, 105–106, Jefferson County Courthouse, Louisville, Ky.
75   **going to school.** U.S. Census, Louisville, Jefferson County, Ky., 1830;
     Fletcher, *Genealogical Sketch*, 36–39.
75   **or off the kitchen.** Jay Stottman, staff archaeologist, Kentucky Archae-
     ological Survey, "Consumer Market Access in Louisville's 19th-Century
     Commercial District," report, 2004; also Draft Report, "Excavations at
     the Commonwealth Convention Center Site, Louisville," 2004. Such
     slave quarters are clearly visible on the panoramic lithograph map of
     Louisville by J. T. Palmatary, 1855, reproduced in Yater, *Two Hundred
     Years*, 71–72; and the Sanborn Fire Insurance Maps (various), Louisville,
     Ky., 1892 and 1904, Special Collections, Margaret I. King Library, Uni-
     versity of Kentucky. For a detailed analysis, see O'Brien, "Slavery in
     Louisville," 18–24; Stafford, "Slavery in a Border City," 22–24; Wade,
     Slavery in the Cities, 55–79 and 111–13.
75   **to the rear.** The U.S. Census for Louisville, Jefferson County, 1830.
     There was, with the Oldham family, a total of seventeen people living at
     the post office property.
76   **born in the house.** U.S. Census, Louisville, Jefferson County, 1830.
     Fletcher, *Genealogical Sketch*, 36–38; Will of John P. Oldham, Jefferson
     County Will Book 2, Jefferson County Archives, 216–19.
76   **other employers.** Bancroft, *Slave-Trading in the Old South*, 145–64;
     Coleman, *Slavery Times in Kentucky*, 123–26; Eaton, "Slave Hiring,"
     663–78; Lucas, *History of Blacks in Kentucky*, ch. 5; Wade, *Slavery in the
     Cities*, 38–54, and *Urban Frontier*, 220–21.
76   **behind his own house.** A careful analysis of Louisville's annual tax rolls
     shows the Oldham household gaining a young man aged more than six-
     teen in 1829 and reduced by one person of the same description before
     the fall of 1831. For hired slaves living away from their owners, see
     O'Brien, "Slavery in Louisville," 23–24; Wade, *Slavery in the Cities*, 66.

77 **further passage.** Hudson, *Fugitive Slaves*, esp. ch. 6.

77 **"one hundred & ten dollars per year."** "John P. Oldham Exec. & Devisee of Gideon Brown, Bill, J. R. McFarland & Others," Jefferson County Chancery Court Files, box 3, Case 2222, Kentucky Department for Libraries and Archives, 1831.

78 **deal was struck.** Wallis and Tapp, eds. *Sesquicentennial History of Kentucky*, 512.

78 **Wurts & Reinhard's.** Yater, *Two Hundred Years*, 45.

79 **for white workers.** David R. Goldfield, "Black Life in Old South Cities," in Campbell, and Rice, eds. *Before Freedom Came*, 123–53; O'Brien, "Slavery in Louisville," 10–11, 29–32. Stafford, "Slavery in a Border City," 121–22.

80 **nurse for his children.** Otis, *Louisville Directory for the Year 1832*, and tax rolls, 1821–32, Jefferson County Archives, Louisville, Ky.

82 **"better off."** Douglass, *Narrative*, 34; Franklin and Schweninger, *Runaway Slaves*, 112; Wade, *Urban Frontier: Pioneer Life*, 124–26.

82 **"their legitimate results."** Hudson, "Crossing the 'Dark Line,'" 33–83.

83 **Judge Oldham's brother.** Coleman, *Slavery Times in Kentucky*, 104; Stafford, "Slavery in a Border City," 108; Johnston, ed., *Memorial History of Louisville*, 67.

83 **could be found.** Morehead and Brown, *Digest of the Statute Laws of Kentucky*, 1:610.

84 **in their own yards.** Coleman, *Slavery Times in Kentucky*, 120–21; McDougle, *Slavery in Kentucky*, 50–51; Stafford, "Slavery in a Border City," 153–56; Wade, *Slavery in the Cities*, 96–97.

84 **"devotion to their owners."** Forster, *Life of Charles Dickens*, bk. 3, *America*, www.lang.nagoya-u.ac.jp/~matsuoka/CD-Forster-3.html (accessed Aug. 12, 2005).

85 **"North was trying to do."** Singleton, *Recollections of My Slavery Days*, 6.

85 **"against our peace."** Cited in Wade, *Slavery in the Cities*, 87.

86 **antislavery movement.** "Constitution of the American Society of Free Persons of Color" (Philadelphia: J. W. Allen, 1831), in Carter, Ripley, et. al., eds., *Black Abolitionist Papers*, doc. 6714; "Minutes and Proceedings of the Second Annual Convention for the Improvement of the Free People of Color in These United States" (Philadelphia, 1832), in *Black Abolitionist Papers*, doc. 1977.

87 **in later years.** "J. C. Brown," in Drew, *Refugee*, 239–47. See also Adams, *Neglected Period of Anti-Slavery in America*, 24–28; Landon, "Diary of Benjamin Lundy" and "Wilberforce, an Experiment."

88 **begun much earlier.** Woodward, *Strange Career of Jim Crow*, esp. ch. 3; Yater, *Two Hundred Years*, 59 and illus. The song as first published is in the Lester S. Levy Collection of Sheet Music, Special Collections, Milton S. Eisenhower Library, Johns Hopkins University.

89 **never forget.** Lucas, *History of Blacks in Kentucky*, 107–17.

89 **severely restricted.** Berlin, *Slaves Without Masters*, esp. ch. 10.

89 **community organizers.** Butler, "Black Benevolent and Fraternal Societies"; Curry, *Free Black in Urban America*, 210–13.

90 **"claim her."** Swisshelm, *Half a Century*, 62–63.

90 **usually Cincinnati.** Hudson, *Fugitive Slaves*, 109–16; Lucas, *History of Blacks in Kentucky*, 68–69.

91 **it was done.** Lucas, *History of Blacks in Kentucky*, 109; "Our New Voters: Past History of the Colored People of Detroit," *Detroit Daily Post*, Feb. 7, 1870.

91 **in real estate.** Hudson, "African American Religion in Ante-bellum Louisville, Kentucky," 48; Lucas, *History of Blacks in Kentucky*, 112–13 and 128.

92 **"did this several times."** Interviews of Wilbur Siebert, typescript, 173, J. Winston Coleman Papers, Special Collections, Margaret I. King Library, University of Kentucky.

92 **more than twenty-five years.** Hicks, *History of Louisiana Baptists*, 21; Hudson, "African American Religion," 45; Lucas, *History of Blacks in Kentucky*, 123; Sobel, *Trabelin' On*, 196–97.

92 **fewer restrictions.** Hudson, "African American Religion in Antebellum Louisville, Kentucky," 45; Otis, *Louisville Directory for the Year 1832*, 48–49 and 112.

92 **moved to the city.** The Louisville directory for 1838 shows Susan Brown occupying a property owned by John Pope Oldham on the south side of Market Street, between Third and Fourth. She was consistently listed for taxation purposes as part of the Oldham household until the early 1840s, when she moved in with her daughter, Mary, who was the wife of prominent iron merchant James Alexander Miller. She lived with them until she died in 1870.

93 **yet another master.** The obituary for "Pretty Polly" Crewes Talbot was published in the *Huntsville (Ala.) Democrat*, April 16, 1830. Details of Clayton Talbot's movements come from Fletcher, *Genealogical Sketch*, 34–36.

93 **Northern states.** *John P. Oldham Exec. & Devisee of Gideon Brown, Bill, J. R. McFarland & Others*, Jefferson County Chancery Court Files, Case 2222; Deposition of Thomas J. Rogers, Jefferson County Chancery Court Files, Case 2222, June 5, 1833.

5. I'M BOUND TO GO

94 **Harriet Jacobs, 1861.** Jacobs, *Incidents in the Life of a Slave Girl*, 58.

94 **some years his senior.** There is great variation in the records, but the Census of Canada West, 1842 and 1861, and the Census of Canada, Ontario, City of Toronto, for 1871, 1881, 1891, indicate an age gap of nine years between Ruthie/Lucie Blackburn and her husband, with Mrs. Blackburn the elder of the two.

94 **George and Charlotte Backus.** George Backus (1799–1831) and Charlotte Backus (?–1831) were from Windham County, Connecticut. According to Backus, *Backus Families of Early New England*, 32–33, there were four children: George; Andrew; Mary Ann, who died in 1821; and Charles W. Backus.

95 **"West Indies."** "Trouble Among the Blacks," *Liberator*, July 13, 1833.

95 **Kentucky in 1829.** The voyage is described in *Charles W. Backus v.*

George Backus' Administrators, Dec. 8, 1831, Case 2505, 1833, Old Chancery Court, Jefferson County Courthouse, Louisville, Kentucky; hereafter cited as Case 2505. The year of their arrival is calculated based on the age of Henry Backus, their son, who was five when the family arrived from Connecticut. His sister was not yet born.

96 **United States in 1809 and 1810.** Berlin, "Creole to African," 251–88, and *Slaves Without Masters*, 63–65 and 81–85.

96 **expensive lawsuits.** Chancery Court File 19846, 1830, Jefferson County Courthouse. Tax rolls for Louisville, Jefferson County, 1829; *Louisville Public Advertiser*, March 2 and 19, 1830: "NOTICE: The copartnership before existing under the firm of Cozzens, Bell & Backus, was dissolved by the subscribers . . ." It was signed by Robert Bell and George Backus. See also "Cozzens, Brown," "Slave Era Insurance Registry: Names of Owners," California Department of Insurance, www.insurance.ca.gov/0100-consumers/0300-public-programs/0200-slavery-era-insur/slaveholder-names.cfm (accessed Oct. 14, 2006).

96 **that had employed Charles.** The information about Charles's character is from court documents filed after George Backus's death. Deposition of Anne Waldo, April 24, 1832, and Deposition of Robert Bell, May 20, 1836, *Backus v. Backus' Administrators*, Case 2505.

97 **elsewhere in Louisville.** Tax rolls for Louisville, Jefferson County, Ky., 1830.

97 **throughout the American West.** Backus, *Genealogical Memoir of the Backus Family*; Backus Family Papers, Virginia Historical Society; Woodbridge and Backus Papers, Baker Library, Harvard University.

97 **as well as the cooking.** Accounts of Frederick B. Ernest, Admr., Estate of George Backus, Aug. 1831, Jefferson County Courthouse, 228. Anacha was hired from July to July for each year, which suggests that the Backuses may have arrived in Louisville in the spring or summer of 1829, for they would have needed a house servant almost immediately.

98 **"the same as others."** Randolph, *Sketches of Slave Life*, 16. For a discussion, see Genovese, *Roll, Jordan, Roll*, 327–65; O'Brien, "Slavery in Louisville," 25–29; Wade, *Slavery in the Cities*, ch. 5.

99 **top floor of the house.** George Backus Inventory, June 7, 1831, Jefferson County Estate Inventory Book 8, Jefferson County Courthouse, 502–505. See also O'Brien, "Slavery in Louisville," 19–21.

99 **until that time.** Deposition of John Pope Oldham, June 5, 1833, "Thornton Blackburn, Fugitive Slave, 1833," Papers of the Secretary of State, RG 56–26, box 198, folder 9, Michigan Archives, Lansing, Michigan, hereafter cited as Blackburn File.

100 **"according to the gospel rule."** Bibb, *Narrative*, 38.

101 **"number of guests."** Keckley, *Behind the Scenes*, 49.

101 **black silk dress.** Personal interview with James V. Deane, ex-slave, Sept. 20, 1937, in *Slave Narratives: A Folk History of Slavery in the United States. From Interviews with Former Slaves: Maryland Narratives*, Works Progress Administration, e-book accessed July 2, 2006: "The bride's trousseau, she would wear the cast-off clothes of the mistress, or, at other times the clothes made by other slaves."

101 **"girl's master."** William R. Mays, Fourth District, Johnson County,

"Narrative of Henry Clay Moorman, Born in Slavery, Breckinridge-County, Kentucky," in *Slave Narratives: A Folk History of Slavery in the United States, from Interviews with Former Slaves: Indiana Narratives*, Work Progress Administration, e-book 13579 (accessed Oct. 2, 2004).

102 **"freedom and safety."** Douglass, *Life and Times*, 159.

102 **newcomers to Louisville.** "Mrs. Charlotte S. Backus, wife of George Backus of Louisville. Died in April, 1831," *Kentucky Register*, April 20, 1831. Also obituary of Charlotte Backus, "wife of George Bachus [*sic*] of the firm Bachus and Bell," *Louisville Daily Focus*, April 16, 1831.

102 **George Backus died.** Deposition of Anne Waldo, April 24, 1832, *Backus v. Backus' Administrators*, Case 2505.

102 **business correspondence.** Deposition of Robert Bell, May 20, 1836, *Backus v. Backus' Administrators*, Case 2505.

103 **was overextended.** Defendant Index, Chancery Court Records, Jefferson County Court, Books A–E, Jefferson County Courthouse, microfilm C987226.

104 **"making Cloathes [*sic*] for Henry," $2.75.** Accounts of Frederick B. Ernest, Admr., Estate of George Backus, Aug. 1831, Inventory Book 9, Jefferson County Courthouse, 228.

104 **New Orleans.** *George Backus v. His Creditors*, Louisville, First Judicial District Court (Orleans Parish), Suit Records, 1813–35, Cases 364 and 8804.

104 **August 23, 1831.** Deposition of Anne Waldo, April 24, 1832, *Backus v. Backus' Administrators*, Case 2505.

105 **relatives in Detroit.** *Detroit Daily Advertiser*, Sept. 16, 1857: "Henry Charles Backus, September 13, 1857, died 13th in his 34th year, at Louisville, Kentucky, a resident of Detroit in his early youth." Several relatives of the Backus family were living in Michigan, including the widow and children of Colonel Electus Backus, a first cousin of George Backus's father. He had been killed on June 13, 1813 while defending Sackets Harbor against British forces.

106 **"Methodist churches?"** Bibb, *Narrative*, 38.

106 **only be imagined.** Frederick B. Ernest's full accounting of Blair's escape and recapture is in *Robert Bell, Survivor of Bell & Backus, Accounts, v. Geo. Backus Adminr.*, Dec. 3, 1831, Chancery Court, Jefferson County, Case 20587.

106 **rest of the account.** Deposition of Larkin W. Wood, Davidson County Courthouse, Nashville, Oct. 3, 1832.

107 **start in Mississippi.** "Brief of Attorney James Guthrie, Administrator de *bonus non* of Charles W. Backus, deceased, n.d., filed at the December Court, 1836," Case 2505.

108 **Backus family's debts.** "Account of Sales of Household furniture &/c belonging to the Estate of George Backus," [signed] Frederick B. Ernest, June 1831, Inventory Book 9, Jefferson County, 228ff.; Deposition of Frederick B. Ernest, June 30, 1832, Case 2505.

109 **Ohio and Mississippi valleys.** Otis, *Louisville Directory for the Year 1832*, 133; Johnston, ed., *Memorial History of Louisville*, 1:413–15.

109 **Logan County is named.** Green, *Historic Families of Kentucky*, 161–67.

109 **"twinkled with fun."** Ibid., 166–67.

109 **reputation for integrity.** Casseday, *History of Louisville*, 195; Collins, *History of Kentucky*, 1:286; Johnson, *Memorial History of Louisville*, 1:413–14.

111 **"of his whereabouts."** Alexander, *Battles and Victories of Allen Allensworth, A.M., Ph.D., Lieutenant-Colonel, Retired*, 172–73.

113 **New Orleans market.** Bancroft, *Slave-Trading in the Old South*, 123–24; Johnson, *Soul by Soul*, 48–49.

114 **"living with Virgil McKnight."** Cook and Cook, *Jefferson County, Kentucky: Records*, 4:329.

114 **far-off land.** Indenture, John Murray of Meade County to Virgil McKnight and John Tevis, late merchants trading at Louisville, Nov. 3, 1833, Meade County Land Book B, Meade County Court House, Brandenburg, Ky.

115 **is graphic.** Baptist, " 'Cuffy,' 'Fancy Maids,' and 'One-Eyed Men.' "

115 **"housekeeper and mistress."** Clarke and Clarke, *Narratives of the Sufferings of Lewis and Milton Clarke*, 74–75.

116 **"so well off."** Pennington, *Fugitive Blacksmith*, vi.

6. NOW LET ME FLY

117 **Henry Bibb.** Bibb, *Narrative*, 30.

119 **"quarter of a mile."** Trollope, *Domestic Manners of the Americans*, 34.

119 **"intemperance and demoralization."** Sturge, *Visit to the United States in 1841*, 58.

119 **former did not.** Barnhart, "Southern Influence in the Formation of Ohio"; Litwack, *North of Slavery*, 69–75.

120 **their black competition.** Baily, "From Cincinnati, Ohio, to Wilberforce, Canada"; Wade, *Urban Frontier*, 40–42, 225–27; Woodson, "Negroes of Cincinnati Prior to the Civil War." On differential wage structures as the cause of racial tension, see Bonacich, "Advanced Capitalism and Black/White Race Relations," 34–51.

120 **"jails and penitentiaries."** John Malvin, quoted in Trotter, *River Jordan*, 27.

121 **Wilberforce settlement.** "J. C. Brown," in Drew, *Refugee*, 244. See also Curry, *Free Blacks in Urban America*, 104–105; Hepburn, "Following the North Star"; Landon, "Wilberforce, an Experiment"; Litwack, *North of Slavery*, 70–74; Wade, "Negro in Cincinnati."

122 **"about ten cents."** "Early Stagecoaches and Their Routes," Warren County, Ohio, GenWeb, www.rootsweb.com/~ohwarren/Bogan/bogan143.htm (accessed Sept. 12, 2005); "Summer Arrangement: Wheeling, Lake Erie & Cincinnati Lines of Post Coaches, Cincinnati 1829," *Cincinnati Directory for the Year 1831* (Cincinnati: Robinson & Fairbank, 1831), rear advertising section.

123 **"goes on wheels."** Dickens, *American Notes*, 378.

123 **for some time.** James Slaughter gave the date of the Blackburns' arrival at Detroit as July 18 or 19, Deposition of James Slaughter, June 15, 1833, before Judge Henry Chipman, doc. 3, Blackburn File.

124 **to the Blackburns.** Hudson, *Fugitive Slaves*, 110; Trotter, *River Jordan*, 42.

125 **"did not know her personally."** Deposition of William Oldham, Nov. 10, 1842, *Gideon Brown's Executors v. Steam Boat* Versailles *& Owners*, Case 2222, Jefferson County Circuit Court, hereafter cited as Case 2222.

126 **"Sandusky, Ohio."** Ibid.

126 **Thornton's escape.** "One who hires a slave agreeing to return him at a certain time is not liable where the slave runs away without negligence or fault of the hirer. *Singleton v. Carroll*, 28 Ky. 237; 6 J. J. Marsh, 527, 22 Am. Dec. 95," cited in *Kentucky Digest, 1785 to Date*, 17:8.

127 **"Thornton Blackburn did."** Deposition of Edward Wurts, May 3, 1834, *Brown's Admirs. v. McFarland et al.*, Jefferson County Circuit Court, Case 2221; hereafter cited as Case 2221.

127 **Jefferson County.** The vessel was jointly owned by John R. McFarland, William Christopher, Jacob Rinear, Jacob Darneal, and A. Kirkpatrick. *Virgil McKnight v. John McFarland &c.*, Nov. 3, 1831, Jefferson County Chancery Court, Case 2221. The owners put up a bond of $1,000 to have the ship released. *John P. Oldham v. McFarland &c.*, Nov. 3, 1831, Jefferson County Chancery Court, Case 2222.

127 **"probably in Canada."** Deposition of Virgil McKnight, May 3, 1834, Jefferson County Circuit Court, Case 2221.

128 **"all the time in Kentucky."** *Edwards v. Vail*, April 1830, 3:595, cited in Catterall, *Judicial Cases Concerning American Slavery*, 1:315. See also *Kentucky Digest, 1785 to Date*, 17:364. In *Oldham v. Wathen*, the operators of the steam ferry that started in 1833 between Jeffersonville, Indiana, and Louisville were prosecuted because a slave escaped by boarding the ferry.

128 **in the lawsuit.** Decision of Judge Henry Pirtle, Jefferson County Circuit Court, Nov. 3, 1831: "The Sheriff . . . shall take unto his care and custody the steam boat *Versailles* and her safe keep and have her forthcoming and subject to the decree of the court to be rendered in this cause."

128 **Sophia, now deceased.** Obituary for Sophia Bullock, *Louisville Public Advertiser*, May 6, 1829.

129 **being fugitive slaves.** Opinion and Order, *McKnight v. McFarland and Others*, and *Oldham v. McFarland and Others*, July 5, 1841, Cases 2221 and 2222.

129 **"the negro to go on."** Deposition of Monroe Quarrier, March 30, 1832, Jefferson County Circuit Court, Case 2221.

130 **in need of funds.** *Quarrier Answer Oldham*, March 30, 1832, Jefferson County Chancery Court, Case 2222.

130 **"as yet, unknown."** C. Elizabeth Bodley to William S. Bodley, June [?], 1836; Bodley-Clark Papers, Filson Historical Society, Louisville, Ky.

130 **Texas from Mexico.** T. C. Oldham and William Oldham, Audited Claims, Republic of Texas, #40004–40006 and 40007–40008, Texas State Library and Archives Commission.

131 **"on the river."** *McKnight & G. Brown's Executors v. Quarrier & S[team] B[oat]* Versailles, Dec. 7, 1843, Jefferson County Circuit Court, Case 2221.

132 **part of Virginia.** Response of Monroe Quarrier, Dec. 7, 1843, Jefferson

County Circuit Court, Case 2222. When lands north of the Ohio River were ceded to the Northwest Territory according to the 1787 ordinance, Virginia claimed the right of ownership over the Ohio River, as far as the shore of Illinois, Indiana, and Ohio. See Catterall, *Judicial Cases Concerning American Slavery and the Negro*, 1:273 and nn33 and 34.

132 **on the opposite shore.** *Handly's Lessee v. Anthony et al.*, 18 U.S. (5 Wheat.) 374, 379–80 (1820). See also Hubbard and Johnson, *Kentucky's Ohio River Boundary*, 15–18.

132 **"when they disembarked."** Act of Jan. 7, 1824, and Act of Feb. 12, 1828, in Morehead and Brown, *Digest of the Statute Laws of Kentucky*, 1:259 and 260, cited in Catterall, *Judicial Cases Concerning American Slavery and the Negro*, 1:273–74 and n35. The 1828 act amended this as follows:

> That the liabilities under said acts shall accrue whenever the person of color shall be taken on board any steam vessel from the shores of the Ohio river, opposite to this State, to the same extent as if they were taken on board from the shores or rivers within this State and the like liability shall occur for landing or suffering to go on the shore within, as without the State: Provided, Nothing in this act, or the act to which this is an amendment, shall be so construed, as to apply to any person of color who is not a slave.

133 **paid the fines.** *McFarland v. McKnight*, June 1846, in Monroe, *Reports of Cases at Common Law and in Equity Decided in the Court of Appeals of Kentucky*, 6:500, cited in Catterall, *Judicial Cases Concerning American Slavery and the Negro*, 1:375.

133 **survives today.** Monroe Quarrier's (1802–1856) urn is in the collection of the Avampato Discovery Museum, Charleston, West Virginia. See also Atkinson, *History of Kanawha County*, 282, and Craik, *Historical Sketches of Christ Church, Louisville*, 69–70.

134 **in this way.** Sarah Lubman, "State Releases Names of Slaves Who Were Insured," *Mercury News*, May 2, 2002; Dan Moran, "Slave Owners and Their Insurers Are Named," *Los Angeles Times*, May 2, 2002; California Bureau of Insurance, "Slave Era Insurance Registry Report to the California Legislature," May 2002, www.insurance.ca.gov/SEIR/main.htm (accessed Oct. 14, 2006).

134 **since at least 1837.** "Railroads, Rivers, and Bridges," SF2 D2, folder 30, "Recollections of Steamboats on the Tombigbee River" (Tombigbee Tennessee Waterway Association, 1949), Judd K. Arrington Coll., University of Western Alabama.

134 **Zack, $500.** Leslie E. Tick, senior staff legal council, California Department of Insurance, personal communication, 2004.

DETROIT

7. STEAL AWAY, STEAL AWAY, I AIN'T GOT LONG TO STAY HERE

139 **Harriet Tubman, 1856.** Drew, *Refugee*, 30.
139 **Detroit River.** MacCabe, *Directory of the City of Detroit*, hereafter cited as *Detroit Directory, 1837*, 18. See also Katzman, *Before the Ghetto*, 17–18.

Samuel Zug, "Detroit in 1815–16," *Report of the Pioneer Society of Michigan* 1 (1877):496–501.

140 **left every other day.** *Niles' Weekly Register*, n.d., cited in Parkins, *Historical Geography of Detroit*, 176–77; *Detroit Directory, 1837*, 36; Edward Channing and Marion Lansing, *The Story of the Great Lakes* (New York: Macmillan, 1909), www.usgennet.org/usa/ny/county/oswego/nyoswego/greatlakes.html (accessed Dec. 5, 2005).

141 **in Upper Canada.** Palmer, "Detroit in 1827 and Later On," 272–75. The description of Canadians at the Detroit market comes from Palmer's *Early Days in Detroit*, 1000.

141 **"taverns and gaming houses."** Jameson, *Winter Studies and Summer Rambles in Canada*, 307–308; Pierson, *Tocqueville in America*, 239.

141 **"fine-looking churches."** Neidhard, "Reise Nach Michigan," 36–43.

142 **technically enslaved.** Burton, Stocking, and Miller, eds., *City of Detroit*, 1:228; Katzman, *Before the Ghetto*, 5, and "Black Slavery in Michigan," 56–66; Douglas, *Uppermost Canada*, 16–17 and 212; McRae, "Early Blacks in Michigan," 159–75, and "Crossing the Detroit River," 35–39.

142 **by boat.** Weld, *Travels Through the States of North America*, 404.

143 **into the United States.** David M. Erskine to Sir Francis Gore, May 26, 1807, Executive Council Records, Upper Canada Sundries, RG1 E3, 6, National Archives of Canada; Riddell, "Notes on Slavery in Canada," 396–97.

143 **ruled to that effect.** William Hull to Augustus B. Woodward, Dec. 31, 1806, and Oct. 17, 1808, "Permission to form a military company with black commander Peter Denison," Woodward Papers, Burton Historical Collection, Detroit Public Library; see also Girardin, "Slavery in Detroit," 415–17; McRae, "Blacks in Detroit," 92 and 97–98.

144 **Northwest Ordinance.** Catlin, *Story of Detroit*, 294–97; Farmer, *History of Detroit and Wayne County and Early Michigan*, 3–4; Hemans, *Life and Times of Stevens Thomson Mason*, 59–60.

144 **in the 1830s.** Mary Mahan to Theodore Dwight Weld, Feb. 21, 1836, Barnes and Dumond, eds., *Letters of Theodore Dwight Weld*, 1:360–61; Katzman, *Before the Ghetto*, ch. 1; Kooker, "Anti-Slavery Movement in Michigan," 49–63. For Southern influence in the Old Northwest, see Cashin, "Black Families," 448–75; Meier and Rudwick, *From Plantation to Ghetto*, 91–92.

145 **lower-paying jobs.** Horton and Horton, *In Hope of Liberty*, 117–19.

145 **"condition of the place."** Hoffman, *Winter in the West*, 105–106.

146 **"a new existence."** Douglass, *Narrative*, 68.

146 **female population.** Cashin, "Black Families," 453; Jones, "My Mother Was Much of a Woman," 252–54.

147 **1 percent of the population.** Lumpkin, "'General Plan Was Freedom,'" 65; Kooker, "Anti-Slavery Movement in Michigan," 58–59.

147 **tends to be inaccurate.** Reid, "1870 United States Census and Black Underenumeration"; Russell, *Michigan Censuses*, 171–73.

147 **identified as slaves.** Woodson, *Free Negro Heads of Families in the United States in 1830*, 73.

147 **anti-importation bill.** An Act to Prevent the Further Introduction of

Slaves, and to Limit the Term of Contracts for Servitude Within This Province, 33 George III, c.7, July 9, 1793, in *Provincial Statutes of Upper-Canada*, 30–35.

147 **War of 1812.** Hesslink, *Black Neighbors*, 29–40; Siebert, "Light on the Underground Railroad," 455–63.

148 **Detroit in 1831.** "What Colonization Means," *Anti-Slavery Record*, July 1835; Frederick Douglass, "Colonization," *North Star*, Jan. 26, 1849; Quarles, *Black Abolitionists*, ch. 1.

149 **right to either.** Katzman, *Before the Ghetto*, ch. 1; Leach, *Second Baptist*, 21–23.

149 **time in Detroit.** *Detroit Directory, 1837*, 47; Friend Palmer's Scrapbook, 3:168, Burton Historical Collection, Detroit Public Library.

149 **great deal of real estate.** William Lambert Papers, Historical Records Survey, Papers of Blacks in Michigan: Collections in Private Hands, Burton Historical Collection, Detroit Public Library.

150 **Welch & Company.** Katzman, *Before the Ghetto*, 18.

150 **September 1831.** A Copy of Oral Testimony of Talbot Oldham, Benjamin G. Weir, and James Slaughter, Taken and Reduced to Writing by Henry Chipman, Esq., . . . June 14, 1833, doc. 3, Blackburn File.

151 **like the Blackburns.** Leach, *Second Baptist*, 14; Ripley et al., *Black Abolitionist Papers*, 3:397–400.

151 **"familiar with him."** Leach, *Second Baptist*, 14.

151 **way to Canada.** According to the official history of the church, Cooper, Brisol, and Bradby, comps., *History of Second Baptist Church Detroit*, 1, it was founded by "thirteen fugitive slaves." There is no evidence of either Lightfoot or French having been fugitives, else they would have been in as much danger as Thornton and Ruthie Blackburn were under the 1793 Fugitive Slave Law.

152 **Civil War.** W. P. Newman, "Second Baptist Church of Detroit, Eyewitness History," in Leach, *Second Baptist*, 7; McCrae, "Blacks in Detroit," 234; Shreve, *AfriCanadian Church*, 47, 51, and 54. See also "Madison J. Lightfoot," MS, frontispiece, Amherstburg Baptist Association Ledger #1, Baptist Church Archives, McMaster University Divinity School, Hamilton, Ontario.

152 **"social functions were given."** Palmer, "Detroit in 1827 and Later On," 280.

153 **black male suffrage.** "Second Baptist Church, Detroit, 150th Anniversary Historic Pictorial Record" (1986), in Second Baptist Church (Detroit) Records, Bentley Historical Library, University of Michigan; Formisano, "Edge of Caste," 25. French's inability to write is witnessed by his "mark," which he used to sign the articles forming Second Baptist Church, Leach, *Second Baptist Connection*, 5.

153 **"in my office."** His manumission was registered August 1, 1817. Emancipation papers for Willoughby, Pendleton County Deed Book C, Aug. 1, 1817, Pendleton County Courthouse, Falmouth, Ky., 169.

154 **homes in the city.** The Willoughbys lived at 269 Catherine Street. *Detroit Daily Post*, Feb. 7, 1870; Douglass, ed., *Colored People of Detroit*, Benjamin F. H. Witherell Papers, Burton Historical Collection, Detroit

Public Library. Benjamin Willoughby was dead by 1860, for his wife, aged eighty-five, was listed as living with William and Julia Lambert in the U.S. Census for 1860, Wayne County, Detroit.

154 **chapter in 1912.** William Lambert (ca. 1818–90) first visited Detroit in 1832 and moved there permanently in 1840. A good short biography of him is in Ripley et al., ed., *Black Abolitionist Papers*, 2:168–69n29. See also Lumpkin, "'General Plan Was Freedom'"; Harding, *There Is a River*, 208–209, and "Freedom's Railway," *Detroit Free Press*, Jan. 17, 1887.

155 **in good stead.** McRae, "Blacks in Detroit," 143n62; Landon, "Underground Railroad Along the Detroit River," 63–66.

155 **returned to work.** Ross and Catlin, *Landmarks of Detroit*, 380; "Winder's Memories: The Dreadful Cholera Visitations in '32 and '34, Detroit During the Plague," undated newspaper clipping, Burton Scrapbook, Burton Historical Collection, Detroit Public Library.

156 **to the claimant.** "An Act Respecting Fugitives from Justice, and Persons Escaping from the Service of Their Masters, approved February 12, 1793," and "A Bill to amend, and supplementary to, the act entitled 'An Act Respecting Fugitives from Justice . . .'" Brooks, *Compilation of the Laws of the United States and of States in Relation to Fugitives from Labor*, 3–9.

156 **"as aforesaid."** An Ordinance for the Government of the Territory of the United States Northwest of the River Ohio, 69th Cong., 1st sess., House doc. 398, in Carter, ed., *Territorial Papers of the United States*, 10:252–53 and 1123–1242; Hurt, *Ohio Frontier*, 386–87.

156 **"labor may be due."** An Act Respecting Fugitives from Justice, and Persons Escaping from the Service of Their Masters, *Annals of Congress*, 2nd Cong., 2nd sess., Nov. 5, 1792, to March 2, 1793. Michigan's first personal liberty laws were not instituted until after the much harsher Fugitive Slave Law of 1850 was passed. See Hayden, "History of the Negro in Michigan," MS, Historical Collections of Michigan, Bentley Historical Library, n.d., 26.

157 **free status.** Michigan, *Laws of the Territory of Michigan, Comprising the Acts, of a Public Nature*, 484–86; also *Laws of the Territory of Michigan*, 2:634; *Detroit Gazette*, April 10 and May 1, 1827. For the impact of the legislation, see Castellanos, "Black Slavery in Detroit," 51.

157 **to their owners.** Hayden, "History of the Negro in Michigan," 14.

158 **blacks for employment.** *Detroit Gazette*, Nov. 1, 1826, and May 1, 1827; also Michigan, *Laws of the Territory of Michigan*, 2:634–36.

158 **"satisfy myself."** Chardavoyne, "Michigan, and the Fugitive Slave Acts," 1–11; Deposition of Ezekiel Hudnell, Henderson County, Ky., Jan. 6, 1829, Clarke Historical Library, http://clarke.cmich.edu/detroit/hudnall1828.htm (accessed May 4, 2006).

159 **"deprived of their property."** Carter, ed., *Territorial Papers of the United States*, 12:30–31.

160 **Upper Canada.** Aptheker, *American Negro Slave Revolts*, 314–15; Dew, *Review of the Debate in the Virginia Legislature of 1831 and 1832*.

161 **"his wife in Detroit with him."** Depositions of John P. Oldham and Thomas J. Rogers, made before John C. Bucklin, Mayor of Louisville,

June 5, 1833, doc. 1, Blackburn File. Apart from the arrest warrants, the same documents are in Robert Simpson Jameson Papers, Executive Council Papers for Upper Canada, National Archives of Canada, RG1, 38, hereafter cited as Jameson Papers.

162 **act for him.** A Copy of the Oral Testimony of Talbot Oldham, Benjamin G. Weir, and James Slaughter, Taken and Reduced to Writing by Henry Chipman, Esq., . . . June 14, 1833, doc. 3, Blackburn File.

162 **Wayne County Circuit Court.** Farmer, *History of Detroit and Michigan*, 186. Henry Chipman's own files of the Blackburn trial do not survive.

8. TELL OLD PHARAOH TO LET MY PEOPLE GO!

163 **Henry Highland Garnet, radical abolitionist, 1843.** "An Address to the Slaves of the United States of America" (1843), in Birnbaum and Taylor, eds., *Civil Rights Since 1787*, 55–57.

163 **City Council.** Otis, *Louisville Directory for the Year 1832*, 130; and "Council Minutes for the City of Louisville, June 9, 1833," handwritten ledger, City of Louisville Archives. See also A Copy of the Oral Testimony of Benjamin G. Weir, Taken and Reduced to Writing by Henry Chipman, Esq., . . . June 14, 1833, doc. 3, Blackburn File. Weir also occasionally sold slaves. In the March 30, 1830, edition of the *Louisville Public Advertiser*, he and William A. Cocke advertised "A likely Negro Girl, 18 years old, acquainted with house work." This may have been an official duty, since Weir was on the city council and Cocke was marshall of Jefferson County at the time.

164 **"slaves for life."** *Detroit Courier*, June 19 and July 18, 1833, and Kooker, "Anti-Slavery Movement in Michigan," 64–65.

164 **Campus Martius.** Warrant issued by the said Henry Chipman, Esq., to the Sheriff of Wayne County for the arrest of Thornton Blackburn, June 14, 1833, doc. 4, Blackburn File. Farmer, *History of Detroit and Wayne County*, 215, states that the "old jail" was on the "site now occupied by the Public Library." This is not the present main branch on Woodward Avenue, but the Skillman Branch at 121 Gratiot Avenue.

164 **"Virgil McKnight."** A Copy of the Oral Testimony of Talbot Oldham, Benjamin G. Weir, and James Slaughter, Taken and Reduced to Writing by Henry Chipman, Esq., . . . June 14, 1833, doc. 3, Blackburn File.

164 **"George Backus, deceased."** Depositions of John Pope Oldham and Thomas J. Rogers, before John C. Bucklin, Mayor of Louisville, June 5, 1833, doc. 1, Blackburn File.

165 **"for the said Weir."** A Copy of Oral Testimony of Talbot Oldham, Benjamin G. Weir, and James Slaughter, June 14, 1833, doc. 3, Blackburn File.

165 **"of the Said Territory."** Warrant Issued by the said Henry Chipman, Esq., to the Sheriff of Wayne County for the arrest of Rutha Blackburn, dated June 15, 1833, doc. 5, Blackburn File.

166 **"this July coming."** Deposition of James Slaughter, before Judge Henry Chipman, June 15, 1833, doc. 3, Blackburn File.

167   **were set free.** *Detroit Journal and Advertiser*, July 19, 1833.

167   **governing slavery.** "The Memories of Winder: Henry Chipman, One
       of Michigan's Early Jurists," undated newspaper clipping ca. 1880 in
       Samuel Zug's Scrapbook, 3:np., Burton Historical Collection; Chip-
       man, *Chipman Family*, 105–106.

169   **"he or she fled."** An Ordinance for the Government of the Territory of
       the United States Northwest of the River Ohio, 69th Cong., 1st sess.
       House doc. 398, in Carter, ed., *Territorial Papers of the United States*,
       10:252–53 and 1123–1242.

169   **did not possess.** *Detroit Journal and Advertiser*, July 19, 1833. See
       Michigan, *Laws of the Territory of Michigan, Comprising the Acts, of a Pub-
       lic Nature*, 484–86; Michigan, *Journal of the Legislative Council*; Kooker,
       "Anti-Slavery Movement in Michigan," 56.

170   **journey back to Kentucky.** Deposition of John M. Wilson, sheriff of
       Wayne County, before Henry Chipman, Esq., Aug. 10, 1833, doc. 6,
       Blackburn File.

170   **June 17.** Kooker, "Anti-Slavery Movement in Michigan," 65; Samuel
       Zug's Scrapbook, 1:120; Stocking, "Slavery and the Underground Rail-
       road," 476.

172   **"at all hazards."** Deposition of Alexander McArthur, deputy sheriff of
       Wayne County, before Henry Chipman, Esq., Aug. 10, 1833, doc. 7,
       Blackburn File.

173   **"John Cook."** Larrie, *Makin' Free*, 19.

173   **abolitionist views.** Cleland occasionally borrowed money from
       Willoughby. In the William Lambert Papers, Burton Historical Collec-
       tion, Detroit Public Library, are two promissory notes dated May 23,
       1836, one for $120 and another for $60. Cleland also served as an agent
       to facilitate land purchases for Willoughby.

174   **into the evening.** "Our New Voters," *Detroit Daily Post*, Feb. 7, 1870.
       See also Woodson, "A Century with the Negroes," 33–39.

174   **in Ruthie Blackburn's place.** Hayden, "History of the Negro in
       Michigan," MS, Historical Collections of Michigan, Bentley Historical
       Libray, n.d., 15; Samuel Zug's Scrapbook, 1:120, Burton Historical Col-
       lection, Detroit Public Library.

175   **to die down.** Farmer, *History of Detroit and Wayne County and Early
       Michigan*, 480; Parker, *A Trip to the West and to Texas*, 5; Katzman, *Before
       the Ghetto*, 10n; Stocking, "Slavery and the Underground Railroad,"
       476.

175   **of his sentence.** McRae, "Blacks in Detroit," 134.

176   **"suburbs of the city."** McRae, "Crossing the Detroit River," 35–39.

176   **to the vessel.** *Democratic Free Press*, June 19, 1833; *Detroit Journal and
       Advertiser*, July 19 and 24, 1833; Palmer, *Early Days in Detroit*, 78.

176   **"of the civil authority."** See also Electus Backus to Judge B.F.H. With-
       erell, April 2, 1860, in Witherell, "Papers Relative to Insurrection of
       Negroes," 593. This part of the story may be apocryphal; contemporary
       reports do not mention the elderly lady leading the attack. However, the
       account does resemble the description of the riot in an 1887 letter from
       Electus Backus, who was present, to Judge Witherell, president of the

Historical Society of Michigan. Backus was responding to Witherell's request for his personal recollections. Benjamin F. H. Witherell Papers, Burton Historical Collection, Detroit Public Library, henceforth Witherell Papers. Hemans, *Life and Times of Stevens Thomson Mason*, 102, says that this procession led by an elderly woman was part of the protests against the imprisonment of the rioters on or about July 15, 1833. As for the riot, this second version also states that only a few blacks were present in the street in front of the jail beforehand, but that as soon as Thornton came to the door, those in hiding suddenly came forward and participated in the fray.

177 **"in the evening boat."** "Report of the Committee," *Detroit Journal and Advertiser*, July 19, 1833.

177 **at the sheriff himself.** Deposition of Talbot C. Oldham, Nov. 10, 1842, *Gideon Brown's Heirs v. McFarland et al.*, Jefferson County Chancery Court, Case 2222, Kentucky Department of Libraries and Archives, hereafter cited as Deposition of Talbot C. Oldham, Nov. 10, 1842, Case 2222; McRae, "Crossing the Detroit River," 38; Witherell, "Papers Relative to Insurrection of Negroes," 593.

178 **"could remove him."** McRae, "Crossing the Detroit River," 36.

178 **"back part of the head."** Deposition of Alexander McArthur, deputy sheriff of Wayne County, before Henry Chipman, Esq., Aug. 10, 1833, doc. 7, Jameson Papers.

178 **Blackburn incident.** See Hemans, *Life and Times of Stevens Thomson Mason*, 94–97. Stocking, "Slavery and the Underground Railroad," 1:475–76, says the sheriff sustained a fractured skull and had his teeth knocked out. An undated newspaper article in Samuel Zug's Scrapbook, 1:119–20, states that he died from his wounds "about a year later." However, Wilson was still alive in 1839 when the mantle of sheriff passed to Goodell.

178 **"remainder of the day."** Palmer, *Early Days in Detroit*, 708.

180 **"blacks and Mulattoes."** Deposition of Alexander McArthur, deputy sheriff of Wayne County, before Henry Chipman, Esq., Aug. 10, 1833, doc. 7, Blackburn File; also *Detroit Courier*, June 19, 1833; Palmer, *Early Days in Detroit*, 709.

180 **closer and closer.** Larrie, *Corners of Michigan Black History*, 57.

181 **Sandwich, Upper Canada.** Samuel Zug's Scrapbook, 1:119–20; Kooker, "Anti-Slavery Movement in Michigan," 69.

181 **"handkerchief from a canoe."** "Trouble Among the Blacks," *Detroit Courier*, June 17, 1833.

182 **about eight o'clock.** Deposition of Alexander McArthur, deputy sheriff of Wayne County, before Henry Chipman, Esq., Aug. 10, 1833, doc. 7, Blackburn File. See also Palmer, *Early Days in Detroit*, 708.

182 **were all black.** Burton, Stocking, and Miller, eds., *City of Detroit*, 2:1140.

182 **twenty and fifty-five days.** Alexander D. Frazier to Lieutenant Colonel Rowan (Secretary to Lieutenant Governor John Colborne), June 25, 1833, Jameson Papers, 77.

182 **incarcerated for weeks.** "The Blacks," *Detroit Courier*, June 26, 1833; Kooker, "Anti-Slavery Movement in Michigan," 71.

182 *"white men and negroes."* Deposition of Talbot C. Oldham, Nov. 10, 1842, Case 2222.

183 **"expected of him."** Palmer, *Early Days in Detroit*, 708.

183 **patrolled the streets.** Charles M. Bull to John Bull, Jr., July 23, 1833, Witherell Papers; Glazer, "In Old Detroit," 206–207; "Report of the Committee," *Detroit Journal and Advertiser*, July 19, 1833; *Detroit Courier*, July 24, 1833; Palmer, *Early Days in Detroit*, 708; Williams, "Sketch of the Life of General John R. Williams," 492–96.

183 **"for the last week."** Eliza B. Mason to Catherine Mason, June 22, 1833, in John Mason, Jr. Papers, Burton Historical Collection, Detroit Public Library.

184 **affair of 1833.** Catlin, *Story of Detroit*, 322.

184 **"open breach of laws."** *Detroit Courier*, June 19, 1833. It is indicative of Detroit's racialized atmosphere that even someone like Charles Cleland, with good friends in the black community, considered the violence that attended the Blackburn rescue as arising out of undue white influence over local African Americans, whom he regarded as essentially passive.

184 **as long as needed.** *Detroit Courier*, July 24, 1833; *Journal of the Proceedings of the Common Council of the City of Detroit, 1824–1843*, 243–47.

185 **returned to Detroit.** Leach, *Second Baptist*, 14–15. "Report of the Citizens' Committee," *Detroit Journal and Advertiser*, July 19, 1833.

186 **his clandestine trade.** "James Stewart," *Detroit Tribune*, June 28, 1896; also Farmer, *History of Detroit and Wayne County and Early Michigan*, 202. The watch cost the city $342.60.

186 **"public tranquillity."** Witherell, "Papers Relative to Insurrection of Negroes," 591.

187 **"mayor's court."** "Report of the Citizens' Committee," *Detroit Journal and Advertiser*, July 19, 1833.

187 **"for some time."** Eliza B. Mason to Catherine Mason, July 20, 1833, John Mason, Jr. Papers. See also McDavitt, "Beginnings of Theatrical Activities in Detroit," 44.

187 **"of the Indians."** Charles M. Bull to John Bull, Jr., July 20 and 23, 1833, Witherell Papers, Burton Historical Collection.

187 **to the ground.** Fuller and Catlin, eds., *Historic Michigan: Land of the Great Lakes*, 1:323–24; Larrie, *Corners of Michigan Black History*, 18.

188 **"[signed M. CHAPIN]."** Marshall Chapin to Lewis Cass, at Detroit, July 25, 1833, Witherell Papers, Burton Historical Collection.

188 **"an alarming extent."** Lewis Cass to Jefferson Scott, June 16, 1828, cited in Klunder, *Lewis Cass and the Politics of Moderation*, 47.

189 **all danger was past.** Lewis Cass to Brigadier General Hugh Brady, Offices at Fort Gratiot, July 26, 1833, and Lieutenant W. W. Morris to Marshall Chapin, July 30, 1833, Witherell Papers and Marshall Chapin Papers, Burton Historical Collection, Detroit Public Library.

189 **its black citizenry.** A special census of Michigan in 1834 showed only 136 "colored persons" in Detroit. See Fuller and Catlin, eds., *Historic Michigan: Land of the Great Lakes*, 1:323–24, and Hemans, *Life and Times of Stevens Thomson Mason*, 120.

189 **"fled to Canada."** Lieutenant W. W. Morris to Marshall Chapin, Aug. 7, 1833, Marshall Chapin Papers, Burton Historical Collection, Detroit Public Library; Witherell, "Papers Relative to Insurrection of Negroes," 591–92.

190 **"of the rioters?"** "Report of the Citizens' Committee," *Detroit Journal and Advertiser*, July 19, 1833; Detroit City Council, *Journal of the Proceedings*, 243–47.

CANADA

9. OH, FREEDOM!

193 **John Colborne, 1829.** Drew, *Refugee*, 244–45.

193 *Lucie* **Blackburn.** Many slaves changed their names when first freed. Frederick Douglass changed his name three times, while Sojourner Truth, the former Isabella Baumfree, said she would keep "nothing of Egypt on me . . . an' so I went to the Lord and asked him to give me a new name." See Stuckey, *Slave Culture*, 194–95.

194 **if he were mad.** Henson, *Autobiography*, 1881, 95.

194 **"next question."** Clarke and Clarke, *Narratives of the Sufferings of Lewis and Milton Clarke*, 39.

195 **Detroit jail.** George Cary to William Lloyd Garrison, May 15, 1834, in Carter, Ripley, et al., eds., *Black Abolitionist Papers*, microfilm doc. 312; Franklin and Schweninger, *Runaway Slaves*, 116–20; Landon, "Diary of Benjamin Lundy."

196 **and for all.** Similar judicial decisions terminated the practice in Nova Scotia and New Brunswick, and by the time of the War of 1812 nearly all of those still legally enslaved were working for wages. Winks, *Blacks in Canada*, 96–98.

196 **Servitude Within This Province.** An Act to Prevent the Further Introduction of Slaves, and to Limit the Term of Contracts for Servitude Within This Province, 33 George III, c.7, July 9, 1793, in *Provincial Statutes of Upper-Canada*. See Winks, *Blacks in Canada*, 96–98.

196 **"little argument."** Diary of John White, Baldwin Room, Toronto Public Library; Riddell, "Slave in Canada," 316–22.

196 **in search of liberty.** Green, "Upper Canada's Black Defenders"; Kelly, "Canada's Black Defenders"; Hill, *Freedom-Seekers*, 114–18.

197 **Niagara region.** Walker, *History of Blacks in Canada*, 51–52; Simpson, "Negroes in Ontario from Early Times to 1870," esp. 303–54; Thomas, *Niagara's Freedom Trail*; Winks, *Blacks in Canada*, 486.

197 **"that of Humanity."** Henry Goulbourn, Undersecretary of War for the Colonies, to Major George Hillier, Oct. 24, 1819, "private," Upper Canada Sundries, vol. 59, RG 1, National Archives of Canada. See also French, *Men of Colour*; Silverman, "Unwelcome Guests," 19; Hill, *Freedom-Seekers*, 117–18.

198 **from the United States.** Cooper, "Fluid Frontier: Blacks and the Detroit River Region"; Lajeunesse, *Windsor Border Region*, esp. intro.

198 **U.S.-Canadian border.** Landon, "Amherstburg," 165.

198 **criminals to justice.** "Our New Voters," *Detroit Daily Post*, Feb. 7, 1870; Palmer, *Early Days in Detroit*, 708; Neal, *Township of Sandwich*, 98.

198 **justices of the peace.** François Bâby (1768–1852) was a fur trader, merchant, and politician and held a number of civil service positions in the district of Sandwich. See John Clarke, "Baby, François," in *Dictionary of Canadian Biography*, 5:41–47.

199 **up to that time.** "Chief Justice Robinson's Report," Original Correspondence of the Secretary of State, Colonial Office Papers, series 42/439, 199–204, National Archives of Canada; also cited in its entirety in Leask, "Jesse Happy," 97–98. For an important discussion of the law, see David Murray, *Colonial Justice*, 181–82, and "Criminal Boundaries"; also Alexander Murray, "Extradition of Fugitive Slaves from Canada," and Zorn, "Criminal Extradition."

199 **seemed very near.** *Detroit Free Press*, reprinted in the *New York Standard* of June 29, 1833. See also Western District Court Records, Court of Quarter Sessions, Oct. 8, 1833, and Jan. 6, 1834, microfilm reel 12A, Windsor Museum.

200 **at Maysville.** The sketch is by William R. Rood, August 13, 1833, Macdonald Historical Collection, Windsor Community Museum, Windsor, Ontario; Neal, *Township of Sandwich*, 179–80.

200 **present stone structure.** Neal, *Township of Sandwich*, 37–39, 48, and 86–87.

201 **Western District authorities.** Deposition of Talbot C. Oldham, Nov. 10, 1842, *Gideon Brown's Executors v. Steam Boat Versailles & Owners*, Case 2222, Jefferson County Court, Kentucky Department for Libraries and Archives, Frankfort.

201 **in search of land.** Travelers in the very sparsely populated western fringes of Upper Canada as early as 1792 found that the largest proportion of local immigrants were from Massachusetts, New York, and Vermont. Isaac Weld, cited in Landon, "Our Joint Historical Heritage," 9.

202 **William Henry Harrison.** Klunder, *Lewis Cass and the Politics of Moderation*, 9–10.

202 **from their captors.** Lindsay, "Diplomatic Relations Between the United States and Great Britain," 417–19. William Bâby, "Upsetting the Hour Glass," *Amherstburg Echo*, Sept. 7, 1888.

202 **the Blackburns' behalf.** Deposition of Charles Cleland, presented to George Jacob, Esq., June 25, 1833; and Deposition of Alexander D. Frazier, presented to George Jacob, Esq., June 25, 1833, Jameson Papers, 78–79 and 82–84.

202 **public good.** Report of the Upper Canadian Attorney General, Robert Simpson Jameson, to the Executive Council at York, Sept. 12, 1833, 99, 137, Upper Canada Sundries, RG1, National Archives of Canada.

202 **prove invaluable.** Frazier came to be known as the father of the Michigan bar. He served as City Attorney from 1832 to 1833, city recorder in 1836 and 1839, and water commissioner from 1855 to 1871. See John Winder, "Alexander Frazier: Winder's Memories: The Bench and Bar in the '40s and '50s, Lawyers of Olden Times," unidentified Detroit

newspaper c. 1895, Friend Palmer's Scrapbook, 1:33ff., Burton Histori-
cal Collection, Detroit Public Library; also "Pictures Identified After
Many Years: Two Portraits Reproduced in News of Pioneer Lawyers,"
Detroit News, June 13, 1929.

203   **into publishing.** Cleland was an attorney originally from New England, but he was more fond of journalism than the law. He began his
career as publisher of the *Democratic Free Press* but resigned on May 9,
1831, after only a few months at the helm, to assume the editorship as
co-owner of the *Detroit Courier*, a weekly that had begun on December
23, 1830. The paper changed hands and partners several times, and on
January 5, 1832, Cleland wrote an editorial announcing himself editor
of the *Democratic Free Press and Michigan Intelligencer*. By May 10 of the
same year, however, the paper was defunct, and Cleland had hung out
his shingle as a counselor and attorney, with a new office over the Farmers and Mechanics' Bank. See Burton, "Detroit in the Year 1832," 167;
"Some Notes Respecting the Pioneer Newspapers of Michigan," 90–94.

203   **to no avail.** Winks, *Blacks in Canada*, 168; Hillier to Goulbourn, Sept.
24, 1819, cited in *Report on Canadian Archives, 1897* (Ottawa: National
Archives of Canada, 1898), 100.

203   **"in this Province."** John Beverley Robinson to Lieutenant Governor
Sir Peregrine Maitland, July 8, 1819, Upper Canada Sundries, RG 1,
cited in Riddell, "Notes on Slavery," 397–98.

204   **to be black.** Opinion of Chief Justice Robinson on the case of Jesse
Happy, a fugitive slave from the United States, Colonial Office Papers,
series 42/439, National Archives of Canada. For Robinson's rulings regarding slavery, see Riddell, "Notes on Slavery," 396–98.

205   **"Western Settlements."** John Quincy Adams to G. Crawford
Antrobus, June 11, 1819, Upper Canada Sundries, RG 5 A1, 40, National Archives of Canada.

205   **"becoming contagious."** For the diplomatic dispute, see Siebert, *Underground Railroad*, 299.

206   **"British ground."** Albert Gallatin to Clay, Sept. 25, 1827, *Niles' Weekly
Register*, Dec. 27, 1828.

206   **rebuffed in 1828.** Howe, *Refugees from Slavery in Canada West*, 13;
Siebert, *Underground Railroad*, 300.

206   **"proprietor of another."** Winks, *Blacks in Canada*, 168; Riddell, "Slave
in Upper Canada," 269.

208   **and 40,000 people.** Henry Bibb quoted in Landon, "Social Conditions
Among the Negroes in Upper Canada," 145; Drew, *Refugee*, esp. 17, 94,
118 and 147; Ward, *Autobiography*, 151 and 154. Even contemporary
abolitionists despaired of obtaining an accurate estimate owing to the
flawed state of Canadian census figures. In 1852, the Anti-Slavery Society of Canada's Annual Report placed the figure in Canada West alone at
30,000, but many impoverished, illiterate individuals were left out of the
official record. Wayne, "Black Population of Canada West on the Eve of
the American Civil War," 465–81; Winks, *Blacks in Canada*, 240–45.

208   **property by 1861.** Olmsted, *Cotton Kingdom*, app. B, 595; Rose, *Documentary History of Slavery in North America*, 141–50. The *New Orleans*

Commercial Bulletin on December 19, 1861, estimated the annual loss to the United States of fifteen hundred slaves over a fifty-year period at $40,000,000. Landon, "Canada's Part in Freeing the Slave," 78.

208 **high market value.** Gara, *Liberty Line*, 43–44; Conrad and Meyer, "Economics of Slavery," esp. the table beginning on p. 212, "Tabulation of Reported Slave Transactions and Valuations."

208 **from $1,350 to $1,400.** Johnson, *Soul by Soul*, illus. no. 4 following p. 116.

208 **to her owner.** For Virginia, see Hening, *Statutes at Large*, vol. 2, statute 170. Morris, *Southern Slavery and the Law*, 43–49. It was carried over to the other slave states as well. See, for instance, South Carolina's version of the same legal practice, *Huggins vs. Wright, November 1806*, in Wheeler, *Practical Treatise on the Law of Slavery*, 3.

209 **one generation to the next.** Shadd, "The Lord Seemed to Say 'Go,'" 40; King, "'Suffer with Them till Death,'" 146–68; Sutch, "Breeding of Slaves for Sale and the Westward Expansion of Slavery," in Engerman, Genovese, and Adamson, eds., *Race and Slavery in the Western Hemisphere*, 173–210.

209 **John Colborne.** Stevens T. Mason to Sir John Colborne, June 21, 1833, Jameson Papers, 31.

210 **out of danger.** Deposition of Alexander McArthur, deputy sheriff of Wayne County, before Henry Chipman, Esq., Aug. 10, 1833, doc. 7, Jameson Papers, 33. See also the *Detroit Journal and Advertiser*, July 19, 1833.

211 **slaves in 1833.** Sir John Colborne (1778–1863), 1st Baron Seaton, served until 1836. Alan Wilson, "Sir John Colborne," *Dictionary of Canadian Biography*, 8:137–44.

211 **teacher education.** Melville, *Rise and Progress of Trinity College, Toronto*, 26–38; John Strachan Papers, Archives of Ontario, F-982-1, 2, 3.

211 **fugitive slave extradition.** John D. Blackwell, "Robert Sympson Jameson," in "Robert Sympson Jameson," *Dictionary of Canadian Biography*, 8:426–28; Scadding, *Toronto of Old*, 34–35.

212 **"in its defense."** Charles Cleland to Alexander Chewett, June 23, 1833, Jameson Papers, 28. The comment about Thornton having been born in Africa is obviously an error.

212 **courtroom.** Alexander Chewett to George Jacob, June 23, 1833, Jameson Papers, 29.

213 **"sphere in life."** Deposition of Alexander D. Frazier, June 25, 1833, Jameson Papers, 77–81.

213 **"community of Detroit."** Deposition of Charles Cleland, presented to George Jacob, Esq., June 25, 1833, Jameson Papers, 78.

215 **next to his church.** The Reverend William Johnson was rector of St. John's between 1829 and 1840. *Sandwich District Advertiser*, May 2, 1835; Douglas, *Uppermost Canada*, 232.

215 **objectives very clear.** Petition of Thornton Blackburn on behalf of himself, and his wife, Ruth Blackburn, both people of colour, at present confined in the Gaol of Sandwich, Western District, June 22, 1833, Jameson Papers, 90–93.

217 **"Your Petitioner."** Thornton's possession of a letter stating that additional "respectable" witnesses were willing to come forward on his behalf matches the statement Cleland made in his presentation to Upper

Canadian officials on the same subject. It was likely Cleland, therefore, who visited the Sandwich jail and gave Thornton the letter. See Deposition of Charles Cleland, June 25, 1833, Jameson Papers, 82.

218 **John Gentle, Sr.** Amherstburg Bicentennial Committee, *Amherstburg, 1796–1996,* Book 1:205–10; Douglas, *Uppermost Canada,* 14, 91, 98, 107, 116–17, 135, 142, 172; Obituary of John Gentle, Jr., *Hamilton Evening Times,* March 30, 1892; *Western Herald,* Jan. 22, 1842, p. 3, col. 3.

220 **"no guarantee against slavery."** Petition from Madison Mason & others, people of Color, fugitives from The United States, confined in the Jail of the Western District, praying that they may not be surrendered to the authorities of that Country, Jameson Papers, 24–25.

10. ONE MORE RIVER TO CROSS

221 **S. J. Celestine Edwards, 1891.** *From Slavery to a Bishopric,* 122.

222 **"inexpedient" to do so.** An Act to Provide for the Apprehending of Fugitive Offenders from Foreign Countries, and Delivering Them up to Justice, passed Feb. 13, 1833, 11th Parliament, 3d Year William IV Cap. 7. A.D. 1833, Colborne, *Statutes of His Majesty's Province of Upper Canada,* 37–38.

223 **"persons demanded."** Attorney General's Opinion, to Colonel Rowan from Robert Simpson Jameson, July 19, 1833, Jameson Papers, 13–17.

224 **"against their being delivered up."** Robert Simpson Jameson to Lieutenant Colonel Rowan, July 16, 1833, Correspondence of the Civil Secretary, Upper Canada Sundries, July 1833, RG 5 A1, 130, National Archives of Canada.

226 **Underground Railroad to Canada.** Anderson Ruffin Abbott, untitled memoirs, 9:12, in Abbott Papers, Baldwin Room, Toronto Public Library; Landon, "Diary of Benjamin Lundy," 114; Troy, *Hair-Breadth Escapes,* 8–9.

227 **"It must be reciprocal."** George B. Porter to John Colborne, Aug. 12, 1833, Jameson Papers, 21.

228 **"the said prisoner Blackburn."** Deposition of Alexander McArthur, deputy sheriff of Wayne County, before Henry Chipman, Esq., Aug. 10, 1833, Jameson Papers, 50–53.

229 **"last session."** John Strachan, Minute in Council, Sept. 12, 1833, Jameson Papers, 99.

229 **"death alone excepted."** Robert Simpson Jameson to John Beikie, Esquire, Clerk, Executive Council, Sept. 14, 1833, Upper Canada Sundries, RG1, 99:148, National Archives of Canada.

229 **"Government of Michigan."** Executive Council at York, Sept. 17, 1833, Upper Canada Sundries, 64.

230 **for an opinion.** Jameson to Beikie, Sept. 14, 1833, Upper Canada Sundries, RG1, 99:148, National Archives of Canada. Strachan's note appears on the bottom of the page where Jameson's letter is recorded.

230 **own response.** Read, *Lives of the Judges,* 101–106 and 148–57; Hamilton, *Osgoode Hall,* 21.

230 **the first place.** Murray, "Criminal Boundaries," 347–50.

231 **"Slavery for life."** Judge's Report, Sept. 27, 1833, Upper Canada Sundries, RG1, 99:155–61.

232 **return to bondage.** Colborne to Porter, Sept. 28, 1833, Blackburn File.

234 **"main terminus of the Underground Railroad."** Amherstburg Bicentennial Book Committee, *Amherstburg, 1796–1996*, 1:64–65; Landon, "Amherstburg," 1.

234 **"can be seen."** Martineau, *Retrospect of Western Travel*, 1:251.

235 **"government of their choice."** Landon, "Diary of Benjamin Lundy," 112.

236 **public schools.** Silverman and Gillie, "'Pursuit of Knowledge Under Difficulties,'" 96ff; Winks, *Blacks in Canada*, 368–70.

236 **"steam vessel."** Josiah Henson to John Campbell, "Condition of the Blacks in Canada," *British Banner*, Aug. 25, 1852; Silverman, *Unwelcome Guests*, 36–38.

236 **it was so *polite*.** Samuel Ringgold Ward, "Canadian Negro Hate," *Voice of the Fugitive*, Oct. 21, 1852.

237 **was its president.** Katzman, *Before the Ghetto*, 32–33; Ripley et al., eds., *Black Abolitionist Papers*, 3:168n29.

237 **of the province.** The presence of the Blackburns in Brown's household is suggested by the town tax rolls, which show an increase in the size of his household by two adults for the period between 1833 and 1834. The number of adults is again reduced to its original two—Nelson Brown and his wife—in the records of 1835. This is the only Amherstburg household for which this is the case. See "Tax Rolls for Malden Township, 1847," Copyright © 2002, Joanne Noble, comp., OntarioGenWeb, welcome.to/ontariogenweb, NAC: H-1175. Brown and his wife were Baptists and had been in the country for nineteen years. For the Amherstburg True Band, see Ripley, et al., eds., *Black Abolitionist Papers*, 2:306–308; also *Provincial Freeman*, March 13, 1855.

238 **cause once more.** Stuart provided the link between British, American, and Canadian antislavery. Barker, *Captain Charles Stuart*; Landon, "Captain Charles Stuart."

238 **"during the summer."** Cited in Douglas, *Uppermost Canada*, 212.

238 **Great Lakes.** Amherstburg Bicentennial Book Committee, *Amherstburg, 1796–1996*, 1:73.

240 **Detroit riots.** The 1861 census for the town of Thorold shows that his wife's name was Lydia, a Wesleyan Methodist born in the United States. Both were listed as black rather than mulatto. There had also been a Peter Sands from the Niagara district convicted of a felony in 1838 and sentenced to one year in the penitentiary. Whether this was the same man is unknown. "Report on Provincial Penitentiary, 4th Sess., 13th Parl.," "Return of Convicts for 1838," in *Appendix to Journal of the House of Assembly of Upper Canada in the Second Year of the Reign of Queen Victoria*, 1829, vol. LL (Toronto: Robert Stanton, 1839).

11. WRESTLING JACOB

241 **Sir Francis Bond Head.** Glenelg to Sir George Arthur, enclosure, Fox Strangeways to the Undersecretary, Colonial Office, Feb. 28, 1838,

Colonial Office Papers, series 42/453, 84–87, National Archives of Canada.

242 **"very first opportunity."** Charles Elliot to Lieutenant Colonel Rowan, Aug. 25, 1834, Upper Canada Sundries, RG 1 E3, 49:40–41, National Archives of Canada.

243 **charge was horse theft.** Murray, *Colonial Justice*, 197–216; "Hands Across the Border," 187–209; Winks, *Blacks in Canada*, 170–71.

243 **few months earlier.** This was pointed out in petitions sent on Moseby's behalf to the Lieutenant Governor: "Petition of Gentlemen, freeholders, and other white inhabitants of the Province," 128 signatures, Executive Council Records, and "Petition of men of color to Sir Francis Bond Head," 168 signatures, Executive Council Records, Upper Canada Sundries, RG 1 E3, 35:215–16, National Archives of Canada.

243 **more than four years old.** Hagerman to the Executive Council, Sept. 9, 1837, Executive Council Records, Upper Canada Sundries, RG 1 E3, 35:213–14 and 228–31, National Archives of Canada; Murray, *Colonial Justice*, 197–216; Riddell, "Fugitive Slave," 344–45.

243 **Moseby's extradition.** Carnochan, "Slave Rescue in Niagara Sixty Years Ago," 8–17; Murray, *Colonial Justice*, 201–202.

243 **camped out around the prison.** Murray, *Colonial Justice*, 208–209.

244 **"jailhouse door."** Quoted in the *Colonial Advocate*, Oct. 4, 1837.

244 **"as to prevent misfiring."** Jameson, *Winter Studies and Summer Rambles*, 246–50, and *Sketches in Canada*, 55–58.

245 **recapture him.** Hill, *Freedom-Seekers*, 94; Power and Butler, *Slavery and Freedom*, 49–53; Riddell, "Fugitive Slave," 347–50.

245 **"shall be concluded."** Head to Lord Glenelg, Oct. 8, 1837, Colonial Office Papers, series 42/439, 170–73, National Archives of Canada; also included in Head, *Narrative*, 201–204.

245 **David Castleman.** Murray, *Colonial Justice*, 201–202 and 264n. See also Leask, "Jesse Happy," 95–96; Silverman, "Kentucky, Canada, and Extradition," 50–60.

245 **his property.** "Jesse Happy," Oct. 12, 1837, Executive Council Records, Upper Canada Sundries, RG 1 E1, 54:616–18, National Archives of Canada. The negotiations regarding the Happy case are in the Upper Canada State Papers, RG 1 E3, 35:207–37, National Archives of Canada.

246 **a U.S. courtroom.** W. Fox Strangeways to Sir Francis Bond Head, Feb. 28, 1838, Correspondence of the Civil Secretary, Executive Council Records, series 26C, 43:34, National Archives of Canada.

246 **been received.** Glenelg to Arthur, March 9, 1838, Head to Lord Glenelg, Oct. 8, 1837, Colonial Office Papers, series 42/455, 160, National Archives of Canada; Leask, "Jesse Happy," 97–98; Murray, "Extradition of Fugitive Slaves from Canada"; Riddell, "Fugitive Slave," 350–54. Alexander Murray attributes this precedent to the Nelson Hackett case of 1842, which again involved a fugitive incarcerated at the Sandwich jail. However, the Blackburn incident was nine years earlier, and it was actually Attorney General Jameson who initiated this line of reasoning. Zorn repeats the error in his "Criminal Extradition."

246 **been accused.** Lindsay, "Diplomatic Relations Between the United States and Great Britain," 391–419.

247 **at the slaveholder's request.** "No. 2—Petition of Nelson Hackett & Petition of Alfred Wallace, Sept. 21, 1841, transmitted by Robert Mercer, with depositions," *Journals of the Legislative Assembly*, 2 vols. (1842), vol. 2, app. S.

247 **too literally.** "Requisition of the Governor of Michigan for the Surrender of Nelson Hackett, with two depositions," *Journals of the Legislative Assembly*, 2 vols. (1842), vol. 2, app. S. "Nelson Hackett: His Escape, Capture, and Recapture," *Peoria Register*, reprinted in the *Anti-Slavery Reporter*, July 13, 1842; "Case of Nelson Hackett," *Anti-Slavery Reporter*, Sept. 1, 1842; Zorn, "Arkansas Fugitive Slave Incident and Its International Repercussions," and "Criminal Extradition"; Winks, *Blacks in Canada*, 172.

247 **welcomed into the province.** Bagot to Lord Stanley, Report No. 10, Jan. 20, 1842, Colonial Office Papers, ser. 42/488, 214–17, National Archives of Canada.

247 **governor of Arkansas.** William H. Draper, "Attorney General's Report," Sept. 29, 1841. Deposition of Nelson Hackett, Deposition of Alfred Wallace of the County of Washington, State of Arkansas, Merchant, and Deposition of George G. Grigg, Accompanying the last preceding Requisition, *Journals of the Legislative Assembly*, 2 vols. (1842), vol. 2, app. S. See also Winks, *Blacks in Canada*, 172.

248 **without due process.** "Annual Report of the Colored Vigilant Committee of Detroit," delivered at Detroit City Hall, Jan. 10, 1843, in Ripley et al., eds., *Black Abolitionist Papers*, 3:397–402.

248 **Detroit jail.** "Extraordinary Conduct of the Government of Canada," Detroit, Feb. 28, 1842, *Anti-Slavery Reporter*, June 15, 1842; Hiram Wilson, "The Case of Nelson Hackett," *Anti-Slavery Reporter*, Jan. 11, 1843; Douglas, *Uppermost Canada*, 181.

248 **"active in this matter."** Charles H. Stewart to Lewis Tappan, Aug. 9, 1842, *Anti-Slavery Standard*, Sept. 1, 1842. See also Joshua Leavitt to Joseph Sturge, Dec. 27, 1842, in Riddell, "Documents: Tappan Papers," 235–37.

248 **sold away to Texas.** Zorn, "Arkansas Fugitive Slave Incident and Its International Repercussions"; "Annual Report of the Colored Vigilant Committee of Detroit," in Ripley et al., eds., *Black Abolitionist Papers*, 3:397–402.

249 **in attendance.** Jones, *To the Webster-Ashburton Treaty*; Riddell, "Documents: Tappan Papers," 179–256; Zorn, "Criminal Extradition," 288.

250 **surrounding it.** *North Star*, Dec. 15, 1848. See Yzenbaard, "Crosswhite Case"; and Wilson, "Kentucky Kidnappers, Fugitives, and Abolitionists." See also "Death of George DeBaptiste," *Detroit Daily Post*, Feb. 23, 1875; "George DeBaptiste, His Death Yesterday," *Detroit Advertiser and Tribune*, Feb. 23, 1874; Katzman, *Before the Ghetto*, 14–15.

251 **out of office.** Peskin, ed., *North into Freedom*, 75–78; Ripley et al., eds., *Black Abolitionist Papers*, 2:384n2; Winks, *Blacks in Canada*, 174.

251 **of the writ.** Larry Gara; review of *The Odyssey of John Anderson*, by Patrick Brode, *Canadian Historical Review* 71, no. 4 (Dec. 1990), www.utpjournals.com/product/chr/714/odyssey10.html; Winks, *Blacks in Canada*, 174–77.

252 **"was imported."** J. Lindsey and Dan Fackart, quoted in Howe, *Refugees from Slavery in Canada West*, 11.

12. AT HOME IN THE PROMISED LAND

254 **October 30, 1853.** Still, *Underground Rail Road*, 194.
255 **"Law society."** Walton, comp., *York Commercial Directory*, iii.
256 **Upper Canada.** Forster, *Life of Charles Dickens*, bk. 3, *America*, www .lang.nagoya-u.ac.jp/~matsuoka/CD-Forster-3.html (accessed Aug. 12, 2005).
256 **horizon for miles.** For the growth of the city in these years, see *History of Toronto and County of York, Ontario*, 1:258; also West, *Toronto*, chs. 14 and 15. Further information on Toronto urban development is in Armstrong, *Toronto, the Place of Meeting*, and *A City in the Making*; Arthur, *Toronto, No Mean City*, 120ff.; Goheen, *Victorian Toronto*. For black Toronto, see Hill, *Freedom-Seekers* and "Negroes in Toronto: A Sociological Study of a Minority Group."
256 **name was Alfred.** There are no emancipation papers filed for a slave named Alfred of the appropriate age in the very complete Mason County, Kentucky, records for this period, or in those for any of the immediately adjacent counties, so I assume Alfred escaped rather than was set free. For the possible Ripley connection, see Hagedorn, *Beyond the River*, 41–42, and "Interview of Professor W. H. Siebert with Capt. R. C. Rankin, at Ripley, Ohio, Apr. 8, 1892," in Wilbur H. Siebert Papers, Ohio Historical Society. Richard Calvin Rankin was five years old in 1826.
257 **of his era.** Shreve, *Pathfinders*, 43–44. Washington Christian was a former Virginia slave ordained at New York's Abyssinian Baptist Church in 1822. He came to the Town of York in 1825 and died in Toronto in 1850. "Biographical sketch of Elder Washington Christian, Minutes of the Amherstburg Association, 1878–96," ledger 2, MS, before p. 1, Baptist Church Archives, McMaster University School of Divinity, Hamilton, Ont.
257 **modern Parliament Street.** Sutton, "Enoch Turner, the Benevolent Brewer," and tax rolls for St. Lawrence Ward, various years, Toronto Archives.
258 **"slave hunters are detested."** Sellar, *Scotsman in Upper Canada*, 117.
258 **fifty families.** Hill, "Blacks in Toronto," 77; Landon, "Social Conditions Among the Negroes in Upper Canada Before 1865," 146; Winks, *Blacks in Canada*, 251–52.
259 **land in Canada.** Hill, "Blacks in Toronto," 76–77, and "Negroes in Toronto, 1793–1856," 74–75; Walker, "African Canadians," 142–46, and *History of Blacks in Canada*, 28–34; Winks, *Blacks in Canada*, 32–33.
259 **"bagpipes to perfection."** Scadding, *Toronto of Old*, 117.
260 **black elite.** Armstrong, "Toronto Directories," 111–19.
260 **churches of other denominations.** Robertson, "The Baptist Body, Its History," in *Landmarks*, 5:422–30. The black Baptists in 1841 erected a permanent chapel at the corner of Victoria and Queen streets. See Guillet, *Toronto, from Trading Post to Great City*, 383; Hill, "Blacks in Toronto," 80–81, and *Freedom-Seekers*, 138–40.

260 **modest home.** Hill, "Blacks in Toronto," 75–105. Horton, in *Free People of Color*, 30–31, notes that fugitive slaves arriving in Boston sought out rooms in African American homes.

261 **"decorous and exemplary."** Birney to Lewis Tappan, Buffalo, July 14, 1837, in *Letters of James Gillespie Birney*, 395–96.

261 **their flocks.** All the city's clergymen were from the United States until the time of the Civil War. See Ripley et al., eds., *Black Abolitionist Papers*, 2:302n, 380n, 483n.

262 **"ebony-hearted slave-holders."** Mackenzie, *Sketches of Canada and the United States*, 190.

263 **"bottle of wine."** Riddell, "Legal Profession in Upper Canada," 70–72. See also Martyn, *View of Original Toronto*, 59; Rolph, *Brief Account*, 177.

263 **just over £2 per month.** Hamilton, *Osgoode Hall*, 70–72. According to the Osgoode Hall Archivist, personal communication, June 1998: in 1835, waiters received the equivalent of $1.50 per month, assistant waiters, $3 for three months.

263 **new building.** "Crown Patent issued to the Trustees of the York General Hospital, 1818," Index to Land Patents by District, 1793–1825, RG 53 2, MS 1, National Archives of Canada. The Park is shown on the 1813 George Williams map entitled "The Town of York," National Archives of Canada.

263 **for them.** "Report of the Provincial Hospital," *Journals of the House of Assembly of Upper Canada*, from the third day of December, 1839, to the tenth day of February, 1840, 311, National Archives of Canada; Robertson, "First Cab in the City," 2:677, and Instrument No. 30946, St. Lawrence Ward, City of Toronto Land Registry.

265 **any obstruction.** Phil DiBlasi, archaeologist, University of Louisville, personal communication, 1999; Vlach, "Sources of the Shotgun House"; "Shotgun House" and "Afro-Americans," in Dell Upton, ed., *America's Architectural Roots*, 43–47.

265 **set in a row.** Vlach, *By the Work of Their Hands*, 109–213. For the Archaeological findings, see Jamieson, ed., Smardz, Hamalainen, et al., "Thornton Blackburn House Site, AjGu-16," MS, Archaeology Branch, Ontario Ministry of Culture.

265 **sold away from them.** Heath, *Hidden Lives*, 36–38; Kelso, *Kingsmill Plantations*, 116–28, and "Archaeology of Slave Life at Thomas Jefferson's Monticello," 13–14; Singleton, "Archaeology of Slave Life," 150–51.

266 **builders' brick instead.** Jamieson, ed., Smardz, Hamalainen et al., "Thornton Blackburn House Site, AjGu-16," 301–302. "Report of Jas. Fitzgibbon, Toronto, 19th November, 1836," Upper Canada State Papers, 1836, RG 1 E3, 47–48, National Archives of Canada; Smardz and Schiavetto, "inSite: The Front Street Archaeological Project," 45. "Detailed Account of the Parliament Buildings," *Journals of the House of Assembly of Upper Canada*, 1832, 996–99, National Archives of Canada.

266 **kitchen hearth.** Richard Gerrard, "Stratigraphic and Feature Analysis," and Hamalainen, "Faunal Analysis: Hunting and Fishing," in Jamieson, ed., Smardz, Hamalainen, et al. "Thornton Blackburn House Site, AjGu-16," 11 and Fig. 3.5, 271–74.

266 **Sackville Street.** Tax assessment rolls for St. Lawrence Ward, various years beginning in 1841–1845, Toronto Archives.

267 **separate spheres.** James Oliver Horton found a similar phenomenon in Boston, *Free People of Color*, 25–40. For racism in Canada, see Josiah Henson to John Campbell, "Condition of the Blacks in Canada," *British Banner*, Aug. 25, 1852; Silverman, *Unwelcome Guests*, 36–38; Howe, *Refugees from Slavery in Canada West*, 24–40.

267 **streets of Montreal.** Georgano, *History of the London Taxicab*, 27.

268 **"first cab built in Upper Canada."** Robertson, "First Cab," *Landmarks*, 2:677–78.

268 **St. James's Cathedral.** *View of King Street, Toronto, 1846*, attributed to Thomas Young, Canadiana Collection, Royal Ontario Museum.

269 **"impertinent language."** "Cabs and Carters," in Lewis, *Toronto Directory and Street Guide for 1843–4*, 7–8; Guillet, *Toronto, from Trading Post to Great City*, 118.

269 **"houses in King Street."** "Report on the Toronto Negroes for Lord Sydenham, Toronto, the 5th April, 1841"; Strachan Papers, Letterbook, Letter to Rev. A. M. Campbell, Society for Promoting the Gospel in Foreign Parts, April 28, 1840, MS 35 R11, 13, Archives of Ontario.

270 **Underground Railroad.** "John M. Tinsley," *History of Toronto and County of York*, 2:162. John Henry Hill to William Still, Oct. 4, 1853, in Still, *Underground Rail Road*, 192–93. Hill, a runaway, wrote to his benefactor that he was going to work for "a man named Tinsley, who is a master workman in this city . . . Everybody advises me to work for Mr. Tinsley, as there is more steadiness to him." *Globe* (Toronto), "Almost as Old as the U.S.," Wed., July 30, 1890; "Impressions," Feb. 24, 1892; and "John M. Tinsley, Buried," Oct. 10, 1892.

271 **National Guard.** Davis, "Eastman Johnson's 'Negro Life at the South,'" 67–71; John Franzén and Ruth Ann Overbeck, "The Overbeck Tapes: An Oral History of Capitol Hill" (Sept. 28, 2001), 5:4; Morley, Jefferson, "Snow Riot," *Washington Post*, Feb. 6, 2005; Ripley et al., eds., *Black Abolitionist Papers*, 2:157.

272 **Civil War.** Hill, *Freedom-Seekers*, 205–206; Landon, "Social Conditions," 148–49; Winks, *Blacks in Canada*, 211–12, 255, 328–29.

272 **begun to be understood.** Cooper, "Doing Battle in Freedom's Cause," esp. ch. 4, and Stouffer, *Light of Nature and the Law of God*.

273 **British subjects.** 1st Session, 13th Parliament, 7th William IV. Feb. 27th, 1837, *Journals of the House of Assembly of Upper Canada*, from the eighth day of November 1836 to the fourth day of March 1837, 577–78.

273 **in 1834.** Most sources date the founding of the society to 1837. However, Anderson Ruffin Abbott, describing the annual Emancipation Day parade, wrote that there was a "blue silk banner on which was inscribed in gilt letters, 'The Abolition Society, Organized 1833.'" Typescript memoirs, vol. 9, Abbott Papers, n.d., Baldwin Room, Toronto Public Library.

274 **Upper Canada's history.** Landon, "Canadian Negroes and the Rebellion of 1837"; *Annual Report of the American Missionary Society* (Boston: *The Liberator*, 1837), 34–35.

274   **fifty volunteers.** Landon, "Canadian Negroes and the Rebellion of 1837";
      Hill, *Freedom-Seekers*, 118–23.

274   **Anderson Ruffin Abbott.** Hamilton, *Osgoode Hall*, 44; Fonds Level
      Description for Papers of Professor Gilbert Bagnani, Trent University
      Archives.

275   **served as well.** Hill, "Blacks in Toronto," 78, and *Freedom-Seekers*, 118,
      197, 206; "J. C. Brown," in Drew, *Refugee*, 247.

275   **"loyalty to the British Crown."** Ripley et al., eds., *Black Abolitionist Pa-
      pers*, 2:76–79.

276   **five years before.** There is a reference to Thornton Blackburn return-
      ing to Kentucky *ten years* after the riots in the *Detroit Daily Post* article
      from Feb. 7, 1870. The same article states that Thornton and his wife
      became "prominent and acquired considerable property," and that he
      went to Louisville in disguise. See also Stocking, "Slavery and the Un-
      derground Railroad," in Burton, Stocking, and Miller, eds., *City of De-
      troit*, 1:477. The main modern sources are Larrie, *Makin' Free*, and *Black
      Experiences in Michigan History*, 8.

276   **hope for escape.** Bibb, *Narrative*, 188–89; Hagedorn, *Beyond the River*,
      46; *Liberator*, May 9, 1859. Lewis Clarke also returned to get his three
      brothers from Kentucky, Clarke, *Narrative of the Sufferings of Lewis
      Clarke*, 58.

277   **age of twenty-one.** Henry R. Reeder, 20th day of January, 1837, Deed
      Book L, 76, Bracken County Court, Indenture, in Miller, ed., *African-
      American Records*, 1:20 and 234.

277   **left the district.** There was a connection between the Davis, Lightfoot,
      and Blackburn families; the 1850 U.S. Census for Maysville, Mason
      County, Kentucky, shows Lewis Lightfoot, aged seventy-five, as living
      with the household of Mary Davis, forty-five.

277   **"wonderful blessing."** Hughes, *Thirty Years a Slave*, 193–94.

278   **his elderly mother.** Peter Gallego, "Number of Coloured Persons
      Resident in the City of Toronto & Liberties," July 25, 1840, and "Re-
      port on the Toronto Negroes for Lord Sydenham," E. de St. Remy to
      Sydenham, April 5, 1841, Colonial Office Records series Q, pt. 3, 415,
      National Archives of Canada.

278   **in the community.** Tax assessment rolls for St. Lawrence Ward, 1842,
      Toronto Archives.

278   **shown as Sibby.** Census of the Canadas, Canada West, Toronto "Lib-
      erties," 1842. In 1851, her name is given as Mary, aged seventy, but it is
      a notoriously flawed census. Thornton's mother appears as Sibby in
      every other Toronto source, including her death records.

13. SOLDIERS IN THE ARMY OF THE LORD

280   **building in 1843.** See Hayes, *Holding Forth the Word*, 6–13. Lucie
      Blackburn was an annual donor to the church. See "Annual Subscrip-
      tion List," *Seventh Annual Report of the Church Society, Little Trinity
      Church, for the year ending March 31, 1849*, Toronto Diocese, Anglican
      Church of Canada Archives.

281 **"slavery for life."** Washington, *Frederick Douglass*, 168. For a full discussion of the law, see Foner, *History of Black Americans*, chs. 1–6; Ripley et al., eds., *Black Abolitionist Papers*, 2:116n3.

281 **as merchandise.** Landon, "Negro Migration to Canada After the Passing of the Fugitive," 22–36; Walker, *History of Blacks*, 55–56.

282 **set an example.** Collison, *Shadrach Minkins*; Gara, *Liberty Line*, 107–109 and 112; Ripley et al. eds., *Black Abolitionist Papers*, 2:180n and 341–42n.

282 **May 1851.** Gara, *Liberty Line*, 103; see also Landon, "Negro Migration to Canada," 26–27.

282 **after Appomattox.** *National Anti-Slavery Standard*, July 2, 1853, quoting *New-York Tribune*; Gara, *Liberty Line*, 131 and 132n42.

283 **Blackburn family.** Arthur, *Toronto, No Mean City*, 121; *Leader* (Toronto), Jan. 9, 1860, quoted in Masters, *Rise of Toronto*, 95; "Uncle Tom's Cabin, Royal Lyceum Theatre, Toronto, Feb. 6, 1857," playbill, Baldwin Room, Toronto Public Library; Landon, "Canada's Part in Freeing the Slaves," 74–75, and "When *Uncle Tom's Cabin* Came to Canada," 1–5.

284 **shortage of labor.** Martin, "British Officials and Their Attitudes Towards the Negro," 86.

284 **antislavery newspaper.** Cooper, "'Doing Battle in Freedom's Cause,'" esp. chs. 3 and 7; also "Fluid Frontier: Blacks and the Detroit River Region," and "Search for Mary Bibb"; Winks, *Blacks in Canada*, 395.

285 **for decades.** Careless, *Brown of the Globe: Voice of Upper Canada, 1818–1859*, 1:100–103; Stouffer, *Light of Nature and Law of God*, esp. chs. 2 and 3.

285 **"sign such a paper."** Hill, "Blacks in Toronto," 98.

285 **own burial.** Mount Pleasant Group of Cemeteries, Toronto Necropolis, Interment Cards for the Blackburns and George Brown.

286 **Mason-Dixon Line.** Pease and Pease. *Black Utopia*, 84–108; Bryan Prince, *I Came as a Stranger*, 119–20.

287 **Thomas Fowell Buxton.** *A Sketch of the Buxton Mission and Elgin Settlement, Raleigh, Canada West* (Birmingham: Printer and Law Stationer, ca. 1870); William King to Mr. Hamilton, Chatham Nov. 23rd, 1889; also "William King Diary," MS, MG 29 C 51, William King Papers, National Archives of Canada; see also his manuscript autobiography in the same repository. See also Landon, "Buxton Settlement in Canada," 360–67; Law, "'Self-Reliance Is the True Road to Independence': Ideology and the Ex-Slaves in Buxton and Chatham," 107–21; Robbins, *Legacy to Buxton*, esp. ch. 6.

287 **temperance principles.** "Autobiography of William King, Jan. 6, 1892," William King Papers, 274–75, National Archives of Canada.

287 **Buxton facility.** Howe, *Report to the Freedmen's Inquiry Commission*, 70–71 and 88ff; Rogers, *Slaves No More*; *Voice of the Fugitive*, March 12, 1851. See also James T. Rapier, Buxton, C. W., to John H. Rapier, St. Paul, Minn., Jan. 27, 1857, Rapier Papers, Moorland-Springharn Collection, Howard University, Washington, D.C.

288 **revised Fugitive Slave Law.** Anti-Slavery Society of Canada, "Annual Reports," beginning March 24, 1852, also "Constitution and By-Laws," Toronto, 1852, and later (partial set, Baldwin Room, Toronto Public Li-

brary); Landon, "Anti-Slavery Society of Canada"; *Globe*, Feb. 26, 1851, on subject of inaugural meeting of Toronto Anti-Slavery Society; also Stouffer, *Light of Nature and the Law of God*, 110–11; Winks, *Blacks in Canada*, 257ff. See also Ripley et al., eds., *Black Abolitionist Papers*, 1:338n9.

288   **a society secretary.** See Hill, *Freedom-Seekers*, 15–17; Landon, "Captain Charles Stuart," 205–10.

288   **deliberations of the society.** Drew, *Refugee*, 149–52; Ripley et al., eds., *Black Abolitionist Papers*, 2:20 and 2:303–304n3.

289   **antislavery movement.** Ruth Bogin and Jean Fagan Yellin, introduction to Yellin and Van Horne, eds., *Abolitionist Sisterhood*, 1–19; Tate, "Political Consciousness and Resistance Among Black Antebellum Women"; Winch, " 'You Have Talents, Only Cultivate Them,' " 101–18.

289   **male or female.** "Anti-Slavery Convention at Lockport," *North Star*, April 3, 1851.

289   **Society of Canada.** Rhodes, *Mary Ann Shadd Cary*; Ripley et al., eds., *Black Abolitionist Papers*, 2:276n6; Yee, "Gender Ideology and Black Women," 61. Coleman Freeman was on the executive board of the Provincial Union, a self-help organization founded by blacks in Canada West in the mid-1850s, and was also involved with the British-American Institute at Dawn. See also Bristow, " 'Whatever You Raise in the Ground You Can Sell It in Chatham,' " in Bristow, ed., *"We're Rooted Here and They Can't Pull Us Up,"* 69–142.

289   **every sphere of influence.** See "The Split in the Abolitionist Movement," in Aptheker, ed., *Documentary History of the Negro People in the United States*, 1:192–96; Cooper, "Doing Battle in Freedom's Cause," 184–86.

289   **reception and assistance.** *Globe* (Toronto), March 27, 1852. According to the ASC's annual reports, its meetings were well attended "by both sexes."

290   **"has been the consequence."** Michael Willis, Thomas Henning, Andrew Hamilton, Toronto, Canada West, July 15, 1852, "Statement in Regard to the Colored Population of Canada: For Circulation Abroad," letter to *Frederick Douglass' Paper*, Aug. 6, 1852.

291   **to Toronto.** Stouffer, *Light of Nature and the Law of God*, 113–17, and "Michael Willis and the British Roots of Canadian Antislavery."

291   **"bloodhounds" or not.** Stouffer, *Light of Nature and the Law of God*, 113–15 and 234n8.

292   **"it is now."** Reprinted in *Globe* (Toronto), Jan. 11, 1853.

292   **"shorthand writer."** John D. Tinsley was the son of John M. Tinsley. "Impressions," *Globe* (Toronto), Feb. 24, 1892.

292   **suffered persecution.** Cooper, "Doing Battle in Freedom's Cause," 169–87; Guillet, *Early Life in Upper Canada*, 64–68; "Proceedings of the North American Convention," *Voice of the Fugitive*, Sept. 24, 1851.

292   **white men presiding.** See Katzman, *Before the Ghetto*, 42; Silverman, "Unwelcome Guests," 27–28; Ripley et al., eds., *Black Abolitionist Papers*, 2:149–69 and 159n8.

293   **facilitate decision making.** Ripley et al., eds., Ibid., 2:100n, 141n5, and

175–76n; *St. Matthew's Episcopal Church, Detroit, Celebrates Its Centennial, 1846–1946: 100 Years of Service to God and His People* (Detroit, privately published 1946), 1–3, Bentley Historical Collection, University of Michigan.

293 **"as may be practicable."** Ripley et al., eds., *Black Abolitionist Papers*, 2:149–63.

294 **safe to congregate.** *Voice of the Fugitive,* July 20, Sept. 24, Oct. 8 and 22, 1851.

294 **black nationalism.** Ripley et al., eds., *Black Abolitionist Papers*, 2:397–98n12; Sterling, *Making of an Afro-American*, 160–63.

294 **American Colonization Society.** "The Pioneer National Convention, 1830," in Aptheker, ed., *Documentary History of the Negro People in the United States*, 1:98–107; Ripley et al., eds., *Black Abolitionist Papers*, 2:165n.

295 **in 1862.** Abraham Shadd (1801–1882), a shoe and boot maker in Delaware, had been active in the Underground Railroad since the 1820s. Hill, *Freedom-Seekers*, 202–205; Rhodes, *Mary Ann Shadd Cary*, esp. ch. 1; Ripley et al., eds., *Black Abolitionist Papers*, 2:165–66n26.

295 **to settle.** Mary Ann Shadd, the eldest of Abraham's thirteen children, was educated in Quaker schools in Delaware and taught school in New York state before moving to Canada. Bearden and Butler, *Shadd*; Cooper, "Doing Battle in Freedom's Cause," 322–25; Ripley et al., eds., *Black Abolitionist Papers*, 4:33n4; Walker, *History of Blacks in Canada*, 142–45.

295 *Voice of the Fugitive.* Cooper, "Doing Battle in Freedom's Cause," 232–34. This happened some time after a highly publicized break from the Bibbs, the reasons for which have never been entirely clear. See also Silverman, "'We Shall Be Heard,'" 54–69. For Shadd's paper, see Murray, "The *Provincial Freeman*," 25–31.

295 **Southern states.** Loguen, *Rev. J. W. Loguen*, esp. 344–45; Dorothy Porter, preface to Ward, *Autobiography*; Quarles, *Black Abolitionists*, 209–10; Ripley et al., eds., *Black Abolitionist Papers*, 2:198n13, 209–10; see also Jermain Wesley Loguen to Frederick Douglass, Aug. 11, 1851, *Frederick Douglass' Paper*, Aug. 21, 1851.

296 **"stop to it."** Anderson Ruffin Abbott Scrapbook, 2:299, Abbott Papers, Baldwin Room, Toronto Public Library.

296 **during Reconstruction.** Ripley et al., eds., *Black Abolitionist Papers*, 2:358–59n8; *Voice of the Fugitive*, April 22, 1852.

299 **"to sustain themselves."** Troy, *Hair-Breadth Escapes*, 108.

300 **"what was their color."** Silverman, "American Fugitive Slave in Canada: Myths and Realities," 220. George Brown's harsh rebuttal appeared in the *Globe* (Toronto), Sept. 25, 1851.

300 **"those who were able to labor."** Ure, *Handbook of Toronto*, 167.

300 *Underground Rail Road.* William Still's "Account Book of the Vigilant Committee of Philadelphia, 1854–1857"; Carter and Ripley, eds., *Black Abolitionist Papers*, doc. 15845, and "Treasurer's Account Book, Boston Vigilant Committee to Assist Fugitive Slaves," Oct. 21, 1850, to May 20, 1861, doc. 10946; Gara, "William Still and the Underground Railroad," 33–44; Still, *Underground Rail Road*, 475, 512–14.

302 **mail sorting.** "The Colored Postman," *World* (Toronto), May 30, 1882.

303   **store in the village.** Ripley et al., eds., *Black Abolitionist Papers*, 2:71–72n, 157n, 164n, 303–304n.

303   **by midsummer 1855.** *Annual Report of the Elgin Association* (Toronto, 1854), Baldwin Room, Toronto Public Library.

303   **put to work.** Rogers, "Slaves No More," 241–49.

304   **"on the Railroad."** Drew, *Refugee*, 296.

304   **mill machinery.** In his February 6, 1894, article in the *New York Age* on the Elgin settlement, Anderson Ruffin Abbott states that "in 1855, a good saw and grist mill was erected on a site granted by the late Wilson R. Abbott."

304   **seemed imminent.** Mount Pleasant Group of Cemeteries, Toronto Necropolis, Lot 100E, Oct. 27, 1855.

305   **"since the settlement commenced."** See also Drew, *Refugee*, 296–97.

305   **the association's purposes.** Ullman, *Look to the North Star*, 135; Ripley et al., eds., *Black Abolitionist Papers*, 2:164n; Anderson Ruffin Abbott Scrapbook, 2:298, Baldwin Room, Toronto Public Library.

306   **"same tyrannical principle."** Wilbur, *President Lincoln's Attitude*, 36.

307   **Brown's future plans.** *St. Matthews Episcopal Church Centennial Celebration*, 5–6. The meeting was held at 185 Congress Street, where Webb resided, and included George De Baptiste, Robert Banks, William Lambert, and others from the Detroit Vigilant Committee.

307   **took part.** Hamilton, "John Brown in Canada"; Hill, *Freedom-Seekers*, 20–23; Ullman, *Look to the North Star*, 189–98.

308   **impoverished widow.** Winks, *Blacks in Canada*, 269.

14. GIRD UP YOUR SWORD

310   **James T. Rapier, 1860.** Schweninger, "Fugitive Negro," 103.

311   **"He Canada would sever."** Winks, *Canada and the United States*, 50, 62–63.

312   **"normal condition."** Henry Cleveland. *Alexander H. Stephens in Public and Private: With Letters and Speeches, Before, During, and Since the War* (Philadelphia, 1886), 717–29, members.aol.com/jfepperson/corner.html (accessed Dec. 10, 2005).

313   **Union officer.** Collins, *History of Kentucky*, 557, 576, and 590; Hamilton, *Ancestral Lines*, 31–34, 49–54, 64–66, 520. See also Dr. Adamson, "Gentlemen of the Mason County Medical Association," *Weekly Maysville Eagle*, Jan. 5, 1875.

313   **had requested it.** Landon, "Our Joint Historical Heritage," 19; Walker, *History of Blacks in Canada*, 68.

314   **galvanized the war effort.** For black Canadian enlistment, the most reliable figures come from the Civil War historian Tom Brooks, "Black Canadians Who Fought in the Civil War."

314   **in the postwar years.** Lockett, "Lynching Massacre of Black and White Soldiers," 83–94.

315   **officer's uniform.** Hill, *Freedom-Seekers*; Slaney, *Family Secrets*, 52–58.

317   **heavy financial losses.** Winks, *Canada and the United States*, 308–10.

For Thornton's sentencing before the police court, see "Police News," *World* (Toronto), March 14, 1882; "Police Court Notes," *World* (Toronto), Feb. 2, 1993.

317 **"who were refugees."** Headley, *Confederate Operations in Canada and New York*; Hoy, *Canadians in the Civil War*, 231–34; Mayers, *Dixie and the Dominion*, 85–87.

319 **June 23, 1863.** Luke Pryor Blackburn to Major General Dabney H. Maury, June 23, 1863, Blackburn Papers, Filson Historical Society, Louisville, Ky.

319 **against the charges.** Stuart Robinson Papers, Filson Historical Society; Rescher, *Niagara-on-the-Lake as a Confederate Refuge*, 26.

320 **Upper Canada College.** Marion Spence, Upper Canada College Archives, personal communication, 2004; Howard, *Upper Canada College, 1829–1979*, 437–38.

320 **Emily Ann Churchill.** Emily Ann's sister, Julia, was the wife of Luke Pryor Blackburn, also living in Toronto in 1866.

321 **"never committed any crime."** "The German Peace Offer: An Address by Colonel George T. Denison Before the Empire Club of Canada, Toronto, December 28, 1916," in *The Empire Club of Canada Speeches, 1916–1917* (Toronto: Empire Club of Canada, 1917), 340–50.

322 **"chief cornerstone is slavery."** Ripley et al., eds., *Black Abolitionist Papers*, 2:513–14.

323 **"they are free men."** Howe, *Refugees from Slavery in Canada West*, 102. See also Stewart, *Holy Warriors*, 165, 172, 184, 195.

324 **"love of *home*."** Ibid.; Walker, *History of Blacks*, 102–103.

324 **Freedman's Bank, in 1876.** W.E.B. DuBois, "The Freedmen's Bureau," *Atlantic Monthly* 87 (1901): 354–65.

325 **to the United States.** Winks, *Canada and the United States*, 365–66.

15. OH, WASN'T THAT A WIDE RIVER?

327 **Benjamin Blackburn, 1855.** Drew, *Refugee*, 333.

328 **Howard University.** Hill, *Freedom-Seekers*, 203–205; Rhodes, *Mary Ann Shadd Cary*, 191; Ullman, *Look to the North Star*, 224–36.

328 **congressman in Alabama.** Taylor, "Negro Congressman: A Generation After," 134; Ripley et al., eds., *Black Abolitionist Papers*, 2:358–59n8.

328 **in Canada.** Ripley et al., eds., *Black Abolitionist Papers*, 2:369–70n1.

329 **Thornton and his wife.** Toronto Necropolis, Section E, Lot 100, June 10, 1863. Alfred is listed as fifty-five years old, but this conflicts with other sources, which suggest he was born in 1804. That would have made him a contemporary of Lucie Blackburn, who was about fifty-nine in 1863.

329 **farming town.** Ullman, *Look to the North Star*, 237–43.

330 **across the street.** C. E. Anderson and Company's *Toronto City Directory for 1868–9*, 104–105; Goad, *Goad's Atlas* (1883), plate 28.

330 **United States.** Goheen, *Victorian Toronto*, 91ff.

331 **"the Adonis he used to be."** "Our Colored Citizens/Pen Pictures of

Prominent Africans Resident in Toronto/Old Residents—Wealthy Citizens—White Sheep—Amazons," ca. 1885, *New York Age*, Abbott Papers, Baldwin Room, Toronto Public Library.

331 **Civil War.** According to the Census of Canada West, Toronto, Thornton no longer owned a horse after about 1868.

332 **Fasken Campbell Godfrey.** "Fasken Martineau: Toronto," www.fasken .com (accessed Jan. 16, 2006); Kyer, "Transformation of an Establishment Firm."

332 **home to Toronto.** "Deborah Brown," in Shadd, Cooper, and Frost, *Underground Railroad*, 5–9.

333 **"are the nestors."** "No Colour Line in Canada/The Refuge of Exiles from the Southern States," Toronto, March 5, 1905, *New York Age*, Abbott Papers, Baldwin Room, Toronto Public Library.

333 **to end slavery.** "Toronto Was Haven for Runaway Slaves." *Star* (Toronto), May 13, 1922.

334 **Toronto Necropolis.** Slaney, *Family Secrets*, 91.

334 **for thirty-three years.** Leach; *Second Baptist*, 11.

334 **age of thirty-eight.** "Death of 'Dick' Jackson," *World* (Toronto), June 3, 1885.

335 **half a mile to the east.** "City News Jottings," *Evening Telegram* (Toronto), June 4, 1885: "At their meeting last night, Peter Ogden Lodge, GVOOF, passed a resolution of condolence with the family of the late Richard Jackson."

336 **"and become 'niggers.'"** Howe, *Refugees from Slavery in Canada West*, 40.

337 **least savory quarters of the city.** *History of Toronto and County of York, Ontario*, 1:289.

339 **from 1930 to 1939.** Walker, *History of Blacks in Canada*, 121–22; Winks, *Blacks in Canada*, 332.

339 **"to command esteem."** Daniel G. Hill, "Toronto's Pioneer Black Politician All but Forgotten," *Globe & Mail* (Toronto), Feb. 14, 1976; "Oldest Former Controller Wm. P. Hubbard Is Dead," *Telegram* (Toronto), April 30, 1935; "City Renders Last Tribute W. Hubbard," *Telegram* (Toronto), May 3, 1935.

340 **ice cream vendor.** "Toronto Was Haven for Runaway Slaves: District Filled with Negroes Who Had Escaped by Underground Railway," *Star* (Toronto), May 13, 1922, describes "Lemon John" the ice cream vendor.

341 **the 1960s.** *Evening Telegram* (Toronto), Jan. 31 and Feb. 5, 1895; Goings, *Mammy and Uncle Mose*, 31ff.

341 **separate, inferior race.** Williamson, *A Rage for Order*, esp. ch. 3; Woodward, *Strange Career of Jim Crow*, esp. ch. 3.

341 **ill treated in public.** For Canada, see Walker, "African Canadians," 149–50, 154, and 160–65.

342 **lost to history.** Winks, *Blacks in Canada*, 294–95.

342 **twenty-five years earlier.** The possible expropriation of the Blackburn land was discussed by the Standing Committee on Sites and Buildings of the Board of Education in 1886, which recommended on April 7 that a new school site be explored for St. Lawrence Ward. "Minutes of Meet-

ing April 7, 1887, Toronto Board of Education, 1887," Archives and
Museum, Toronto District School Board.

343   **"per foot being $5,500."** Duncan Fraser, "Sackville Street Public
School, Toronto," typescript historical report for University of
Toronto, May 1980, and Standing Committee Minutes, July 26, 1887;
Nov. 18, 1887; March 22, 1890, Archives and Museum, Toronto Dis-
trict School Board.

343   **for generations.** Fraser, "Sackville Street Public School," 12; also see
"Sackville Street Public School," William George Storm, *Architectural
Drawings*, E. C. Horwood Collection, Archives of Ontario.

344   **still occupied.** "Sackville Street School," vertical file, Toronto District
School Board, Records and Archives Division; Instrument 2162, "Grant
10 November, 1887, from Thornton Blackburn of the first part and Lucie Blackburn of the second part to the Public School Board of the City
of Toronto of the 3rd part."

344   **Sackville Street School.** Jamieson, ed., Smardz, Hamalainen, et al.,
"Thornton Blackburn House Site, AjGu-16."

345   **"to his christening."** Robertson, "First Cab in the City," in *Landmarks*,
2:666–67.

347   **"wind and weather."** Robertson, "The First Cab in the City," *Landmarks of Toronto*, 2:677–78.

348   **moneylender.** Will of Thornton Blackburn, GS ONT 1-1017, York
Co. Will #7771, March 13, 1890, and Will of Lucie Blackburn, GS
ONT 101046, City of Toronto Will #10745, Jan. 19, 1895, Ontario
Archives.

348   **but perhaps not.** Census of Canada, Toronto West, Division 1, 1871;
tax assessment rolls for St. Thomas Ward, 1890; *Toronto City Directory*,
1893 and 1895.

351   **"uplifting the race."** Law, "'Self-Reliance Is the True Road to Independence,'" 115. For an extensive discussion, see Berlin, *Slaves Without
Masters*, 308–14.

352   **"my master."** Still, *Underground Rail Road*, 193–94. I have slightly
smoothed the spelling and grammar, for the eloquence of Hill's statement should be read without any interruption in its powerful flow.

BIBLIOGRAPHY

BIBLIOGRAPHICAL NOTE

Omitted from this bibliography are literally hundreds of land, court, marriage, birth, and death records that I consulted while piecing together the history of the Blackburns. Likewise, there are many maps, articles, genealogical compilations, local histories, architectural guides, historical newsletters, Web sites, archival guides, and other invaluable resources that are, unfortunately, not noted here. These all helped paint a picture of the world in which the Blackburns lived at each stage of their very eventful lives, but in the interests of keeping the references down to a (relatively!) reasonable number, this list is limited to primary and secondary sources cited in the text and a few major reference works.

Many of the slave narratives cited here are available on the Web site "Documenting the American South," of the University of North Carolina at Chapel Hill.

A Sketch of the Buxton Mission and Elgin Settlement, Raleigh, Canada West. Birmingham: Printer and Law Stationer, ca. 1870.

Abbott-Namphy, Elizabeth. "Nelson Hackett." *Dictionary of Canadian Biography, 1836–1850.* Toronto, Buffalo & London: University of Toronto Press, 1988, 7:363–65.

Adam, Graeme Mercer. *A History of Upper Canada College, 1829–1892.* Toronto: Rowsell & Hutchison, 1893.

Adams, Alice Dana. *The Neglected Period of Anti-Slavery in America, 1808–1831.* Williamstown, Mass.: Corner House, 1973.

Alexander, Charles. *Battles and Victories of Allen Allensworth, A.M., PhD., Lieutenant-Colonel, Retired.* Boston: Sherman, French & Company, 1914.

Amherstburg Bicentennial Book Committee. *Amherstburg, 1796–1996: The New Town on the Garrison Grounds.* 2 vols. Amherstburg, Ont.: Amherstburg Bicentennial Book Committee, 1996.

Angelo, Frank. *Yesterday's Detroit.* Miami, Fla.: E. A. Seemann, 1974.

Annual Report Presented to the Anti-Slavery Society of Canada by Its Executive Committee. Toronto: Brown's Printing Est., 1852.

Aptheker, Herbert. *American Negro Slave Revolts.* New York: International Publishers, 1943; repr., Millwood, N.Y.: Kraus Reprint Co., 1977.

———, ed. *Documentary History of the Negro People in the United States*. 2 vols. New York: Citadel Press, 1951.

———. *Nat Turner's Slave Rebellion*. New York: Grove Press, 1966.

Armstrong, Frederick H. *A City in the Making: Progress, Peoples and Perils in Victorian Toronto*. Toronto: Dundurn Press, 1988.

———. "The Toronto Directories and the Negro Community in the Late 1840's." *Ontario History* 61 (1969): 111–19.

———. *Toronto, the Place of Meeting*. Toronto: Ontario Historical Society and Windsor Publications, 1983.

Arthur, Eric Ross. *Toronto, No Mean City*. 2nd edition. Toronto: University of Toronto Press, 1974.

Atkinson, George W. *History of Kanawha County*. Charleston, W.Va.: West Virginia Journal Office, 1876.

Atwater, Caleb. *Remarks Made on a Tour to Prairie du Chien; Thence to Washington City, in 1829*. Columbus, Ohio: Jenkins & Glover for Isaac N. Whiting, 1831.

Bâby, William Lewis. *Souvenirs of the Past: with Illustrations*. Windsor, Ont., 1896.

Backus, Reno W. *The Backus Families of Early New England*. New England, 1966.

Backus, William W. *A Genealogical Memoir of the Backus Family: With the Private Journal of James Backus, Together with His Correspondence Bearing on the First Settlement of Ohio, at Marietta, in 1788*. Norwich, Conn.: Bulletin Co., 1889.

Baily, Marilyn. "From Cincinnati, Ohio, to Wilberforce, Canada: A Note on Antebellum Colonization." *Journal of Negro History* 58, no. 4 (1973): 427–40.

Bancroft, Frederic. *Slave-Trading in the Old South*. Baltimore: J. H. Furst Company, 1931.

Baptist, Edward E. "'Cuffy,' 'Fancy Maids,' and 'One-Eyed Men': Rape, Commodification, and the Domestic Slave Trade in the United States." *American Historical Review* (Dec. 2001), 1619–50. www.historycooperative.org/journals/ahr/106.5/ah0501001619.html (accessed Nov. 9, 2005).

Barker, Anthony J. *Captain Charles Stuart, Anglo-American Abolitionist*. Baton Rouge: Louisiana State University Press, 1986.

Barnes, Gilbert H., and Dwight L. Dumond, eds. *Letters of Theodore Dwight Weld, Angelina Grimké Weld, and Sarah Grimké, 1822–1844*. 2 vols. New York: D. Appleton-Century, 1934.

Barnhart, John D. "The Southern Influence in the Formation of Ohio." *Journal of Southern History* 3 (Feb.–Nov. 1937): 28–42.

Basler, Roy P. *Collected Worlds of Abraham Lincoln*, 9 vols., New Brunswick, N.J.: Rutgers University Press, 1953–55.

Basler, Roy P., ed. *Abraham Lincoln, His Speeches and His Writings*. Clevland, OH: World Publishing, 1946.

Battle, J. H., W. H. Perrin, G. C. Kniffin. *Kentucky, a History of the State*. 2nd ed. Easley, S.C.: Southern Historical Press, 1979.

Bauer, Raymond A., and Alice H. Bauer. "Day to Day Resistance to Slavery." *Journal of Negro History* 27 (1942): 388–419.

Bearden, Jim, and Linda Jean Butler. *Shadd: The Life and Times of Mary Shadd Cary*. Toronto: NC Press, 1977.

Berlin, Ira. "Creole to African: Atlantic Creoles and the Origins of African-American Society in Mainland North America." *William and Mary Quarterly*, 3rd Ser., 53, no. 2 (Apr. 1996): 251–88.

———. *Generations of Captivity: A History of African-American Slaves*. Cambridge, Mass.: Belknap Press of Harvard University Press, 2003.

———. *Many Thousands Gone: The First Two Centuries of Slavery in North America*. Cambridge, Mass.: Belknap Press of Harvard University Press, 1998.

———. *Slaves Without Masters: The Free Negro in the Antebellum South*. New York: Pantheon Books, 1975.

Best, Edna Hunter. *The Historic Past of Washington, Mason Country, Kentucky*. Cynthiana, Ky.: Hobson Book Press, 1944.

Bibb, Henry Walton. *Narrative of the Life and Adventures of Henry Bibb, An American Slave, Written by Himself*. New York: Author, 1849.

Birnbaum, Jonathan, and Clarence Taylor, eds. *Civil Rights Since 1787: A Reader on the Black Struggle*. New York: New York University Press, 2000.

Birney, James Gillespie. *Letters of James Gillespie Birney, 1831–1857*. Edited by Dwight L. Dumond. New York: Appleton-Century, 1938.

Black, Richard Blackburn. "Rippon Lodge and the Blackburns," typescript, Oct. 3, 1974, Prince William County Historical Society, Dumfries, Virginia.

Blassingame, John W. *The Slave Community: Plantation Life in the Antebellum South*. Rev. and enl. ed. New York: Oxford University Press, 1978.

———, ed. *Slave Testimony: Two Centuries of Letters, Speeches, Interviews, and Autobiographies*. Baton Rouge: Louisiana State University Press, 1977.

Blockson, Charles L. "Escape from Slavery: The Underground Railroad." *National Geographic* 166, no. 1 (July 1984): 3–39.

Boles, John B. *Black Southerners, 1619–1869*. Lexington, Ky.: University Press of Kentucky, 1983.

Bonacich, Edna. "Advanced Capitalism and Black/White Race Relations: A Split Labor Market Approach." *American Sociological Review* 41 (Feb. 1976): 34–51.

Breeden, James O., ed. *Advice Among Masters: The Ideal in Slave Management in the Old South*. Westport, Conn., & London, England: Greenwood Press, 1980.

Bristow, Peggy, "'Whatever You Raise In the Ground You Can Sell It in Chatham,' Black Women in Buxton and Chatham, 1850–1865." In Bristow, ed., *"We're Rooted Here and They Can't Pull Us Up,"* 69–142.

Brode, Patrick. *The Odyssey of John Anderson*. Toronto, Buffalo, and London: Osgoode Society, University of Toronto Press, 1989.

———. *Sir John Beverley Robinson, Bone and Sinew of the Compact*. Toronto: Osgoode Society, 1984.

Brooks, Jehiel. *A Compilation of the Laws of the United States and of States in Relation to Fugitives from Labor with the Clauses of the Constitution of the United States Involved in the Execution of the Same*. Washington: Taylor and Maury, 1860.

Brooks, Tom. "Black Canadians Who Fought in The Civil War." Paper presented at the First Annual African Canadian Historical and Geneva Conference, Durham, Ontario, May 4, 2002.

Brown, George. *The American Way and Slavery: Speech of the Hon. George Brown, at the Anniversary Meeting of the Anti-Slavery Society of Canada, held at Toronto, on Wednesday, Feb. 3, 1863.* Manchester, England: Union and Emancipation Society, 1863.

Brown, William Wells. *Narrative of William W. Brown, a Fugitive Slave, Written by Himself.* Boston: Antislavery Office, 1848.

Brown-Kubisch, Linda. *The Queen's Bush Settlement: Black Pioneers, 1839–1865.* Toronto: Natural Heritage Books, 2004.

Brown's Directory for the City of Toronto, 1846/7. Toronto: George Brown, 1847.

Brown's Toronto General Directory, 1856, Toronto: W. R. Brown, 1856.

Buchanan, Thomas C. *Black Life on the Mississippi: Slaves, Free Blacks, and the Western Steamboat World.* Chapel Hill, N.C.: University of North Carolina Press, 2004.

Burton, C. M. "Detroit in the Year 1832." *Michigan Pioneer and Historical Society* 28 (1900): 163–71.

Burton, Clarence Monroe, William Stocking, and Gordon K. Miller, eds. *The City of Detroit, Michigan, 1701–1922.* 5 vols. Detroit, Mich.: S. J. Clarke Publishing Company, 1922.

Butler, Anne S. "Black Benevolent and Fraternal Societies in Nineteenth Century America." In Tamara L. Brown, Gregory S. Parks, and Clarenda M. Phillips, eds., *African American Fraternities and Sororities: The Legacy and the Vision.* Lexington: University Press of Kentucky, 2005.

Calvert, Jean, and John Klee, eds. *Mason County Fact and Folklore.* Maysville, Ky.: Mason County Bicentennial Committee, 1992.

———. *Maysville, Kentucky: From Past to Present in Pictures.* Maysville: Mason County Museum, 1983.

Campbell, Edward D. C., Jr., and Kym S. Rice, eds. *Before Freedom Came: African-American Life in the Antebellum South.* University Press of Virginia, 1991.

Campbell, Israel. *Bond and Free or, Yearnings for Freedom from My Green Brier House: Being the Story of My Life in Bondage, and My Life in Freedom.* Philadelphia: the author, 1861.

Careless, J.M.S. *Brown of the Globe.* 2 vols. Toronto & Oxford: Dundurn Press, 1989.

Carnochan, Janet. "A Slave Rescue in Niagara Sixty Years Ago." *Publications, Niagara Historical Society* 2 (1897): 8–17.

Carson, Wallace. "Transportation and Traffic on the Ohio and the Mississippi River Before the Steamboat." *Mississippi Valley Historical Review* (1920), 26–38.

Carter, Clarence Edwin, ed. *Territorial Papers of the United States: The Territory of Michigan, 1805–1820.* 26 vols. Washington, D.C.: Government Printing Office, 1934.

Carter, George E., and C. Peter Ripley, et al., eds. *Black Abolitionist Papers, 1830–1865: A Guide to the Microfilm Edition.* Sanford, N.C.: Microfilming Corp. of America, 1981, and media (17 microfilm reels).

Cashin, Joan. "Black Families in the Old Northwest." *Journal of the Early Republic* 15, no. 3 (Fall 1995): 448–75.

Casmier-Paz, Lynn A. "Footprints of the Fugitive: Slave Narrative Discourse and the Trace of Autobiography." *Biography: An Interdisciplinary Journal* 24, no. 1 (Summer 2001): 215–25.

Cassaday, Ben. *The History of Louisville: From Its Earliest Settlement Till the Year 1852*. Louisville: Hull & Bros., 1852.

Castellanos, Jorge. "Black Slavery in Detroit." *Detroit in Perspective: A Journal of Regional History* 7, no. 2 (Fall 1983): 42–57.

Catlin, George B. *The Story of Detroit*. Detroit: Detroit News, 1923.

Catterall, Helen Honor Tunnicliff. *Judicial Cases Concerning American Slavery and the Negro*. 5 vols. Washington, D.C.: Carnegie Institution of Washington, 1926–37.

Chardavoyne, David G. "Michigan and the Fugitive Slave Acts," in *The Court Legacy, The Historical Society for the United States District Court for the Eastern District of Michigan* 12, no. 3 (Nov. 2004), 1–11.

Cheek, William F. *Black Resistance Before the Civil War.* Beverly Hills, Calif: Glencoe, 1970.

Chipman, Bert Lee. *Chipman Family: A Genealogy of the Chipmans in America, 1631–1920*. Winston-Salem, N.C.: Bert L. Chipman, ca. 1920.

Clark, Thomas D. "The Slave Trade Between Kentucky and the Cotton Kingdom," *Mississippi Valley Historical Review* 2, no. 3 (Dec. 1943): 331–42.

Clarke, Lewis. *Narrative of the Sufferings of Lewis Clarke During a Captivity of More Than Twenty-Five Years, Among the Algerines of Kentucky, One of the So-Called Christian States of North America. Dictated by Himself.* Boston: David H. Ela, Printer, 1845.

Clarke, Lewis, and Milton Clarke. *Narratives of the Sufferings of Lewis and Milton Clarke, Sons of a Soldier of the Revolution, During a Captivity of More than Twenty Years Among the Slaveholders of Kentucky*. Boston: Bela Marsh, 1846.

Clarke, Lewis Garrard. *Narrative of the Sufferings of Lewis Clarke, During a Captivity of More than Twenty-five Years, Among the Algerines of Kentucky, One of the So Called Christian States of North America*. Boston: David H. Ela, 1845.

Cleary, Francis. "Fort Malden or Amherstburg." *Ontario Historical Society Papers and Records* 9 (1919): 1–19.

Clemens, W. M. *Virginia Wills Before 1779*, 2nd ed. Baltimore: Southern Book Co., 1952.

Clift, G. Glenn. *A History of Maysville and Mason County*. Lexington: Transylvania Printing Company, 1936.

Clinton, Catherine. *The Plantation Mistress: Woman's World in the Old South*. New York: Pantheon Books. 1982.

Coffin, Levi. *Reminiscences of Levi Coffin, the Reputed President of the Underground Railroad*. Cincinnati: Robert Clarke, 1880.

Colborne, Sir John. *Statutes of His Majesty's Province of Upper Canada, Passed in the Third Session of the Eleventh Provincial Parliament of Upper Canada*. York, Ont.: Robert Stanton, Printer to the King's Most Excellent Majesty, 1833.

Coleman, J. Winston, Jr. "Lexington Slave Dealers and Their Southern Trade." *Filson Club History Quarterly* 12, no. 1 (Jan. 1938): 1–23.

———. "The Old Lexington and Maysville Road Turnpike." *The Kentucky Engineer* 4 (Dec. 1961): 13–16.

———. *Slavery Times in Kentucky*. Chapel Hill: University of North Carolina Press, 1940.

———. *Stagecoach Days in the Bluegrass*. Louisville, Ky.: Standard Press, 1935.

Collins, Lewis. *Collins' Historical Sketches of Kentucky.* Enlarged four-fold and brought down to the year 1874, by his son, Richard H. Collins. 1844. 2 vols. Repr., Frankfort: Kentucky Historical Society, 1966.

Collison, Gary. *Shadrach Minkins: From Fugitive Slave to Citizen.* Cambridge, Mass.: Harvard University Press, 1997.

Commemorative Biographical Record of the County of York, Ontario. Vol 1. Toronto: J. H. Beers and Co., 1899, 1907.

Conrad, Alfred H., and John R. Meyer. "The Economics of Slavery." In Genovese, ed., *The Slave Economies,* vol. 2, *Slavery in the International Economy,* 170–231.

Cook, Michael A., and Bettie Ann Cook. *Breckinridge County, Kentucky: Records,* vol. 4. Evansville, Ind.: Cook Publications, 1977.

Cook, Ramsay, and Réal Bélanger, eds. *Dictionary of Canadian Biography,* vols. 1–15. Toronto and Quebec: University of Toronto Press and Université Laval, 1959–present.

Cooper, Afua. "'Doing Battle in Freedom's Cause': Henry Bibb, Abolitionism, Race Uplift, and Black Manhood, 1842–1854." Ph.D. diss., University of Toronto, 2000.

———. "The Fluid Frontier: Blacks and the Detroit River Region: A Focus on Henry Bibb." *Canadian Review of American Studies* 30, no. 2 (2000): 129–49.

———. "The Search for Mary Bibb, Black Woman Teacher in Nineteenth-Century Canada West." *Ontario History* 83, no. 1 (March 1991): 39–54.

Cooper, J. Will, V. A. Brisol, and R. L. Bradby, comps. *History of Second Baptist Church.* Detroit: Bolar Printing and Publ. Co., 1936.

Craik, James. *Historical Sketches of Christ Church, Louisville, Diocese of Kentucky.* Louisville: John P. Morton, 1862.

Craven, Patricia. *From Out of the Dark Past Their Eyes Implore Us: The Black Roots of Nelson County, Kentucky.* Bardstown, Ky.: P. Craven, R. Pangburn, 1996.

Curry, Leonard P. *The Free Black in Urban America, 1800–1850: The Shadow of the Dream.* Chicago: University of Chicago Press, 1981.

Dana, James G. *Reports of Select Cases Decided in the Court of Appeals of Kentucky.* Louisville: Geo. G. Fetter, 1899.

Davis, Charles T., and Henry Louis Gates, Jr., eds. *The Slave's Narrative.* New York: Oxford University Press, 1985.

Davis, David Brion. "The Emergence of Immediatism in British and American Antislavery Thought." *Mississippi Valley Historical Review* 49 (Sept. 1962): 209–20.

Davis, Edwin Adams, and John C. L. Andreassen, eds. "A Journey from Baltimore to Louisville in 1816: Diary of William Newton Mercer." *Ohio History,* 45:4 (October 1936): 351–64.

Davis, J. C. *United States Reports: Cases Adjudged in the Supreme Court at Oct. Term, 1898.* New York: Banks Law Publishing Co., 1899.

Davis, John. "Eastman Johnson's 'Negro Life at the South' and Urban Slavery in Washington, D.C." *Art Bulletin* (March 1998): 57–92.

Dawson, Hilary. "The Life and Times of Alfred Lafferty: A Black Educator and Lawyer." *North Toronto Historical Society Newsletter* 29, no. 1 (April 2005): 4–5.

————. "Alfred M. Lafferty, 1829–1912: An Early Black Graduate of the University of Toronto." *Ontario History Black News* 20, no. 37 (Fall 1998): 5–6.

Degler, Carl N. "Slavery and the Genesis of American Race Prejudice." *Comparative Studies in Society and History* 2:1 (1959): 49–66.

Detroit City Council. *Journal of the Proceedings of the Common Council of the City of Detroit, 1824–1843.* Detroit: State of Michigan, 1844.

Dew, Thomas R. *Review of the Debate [on the Abolition of Slavery] in the Virginia Legislature of 1831 and 1832.* Richmond: T. W. White, 1832.

Deyle, Steven. *Carry Me Back: The Domestic Slave Trade in American Life.* New York: Oxford University Press, 2005.

"The Diary of John White, First Attorney General of Upper Canada (1791–1800)." *Ontario History* 47 (1955): 147–70.

Dickens, Charles. *American Notes and Pictures from Italy.* London: Chapman & Hall, 1880.

Dorman, John Frederick, ed. *Genealogies of Virginia Families.* 5 vols. Compiled from the *William and Mary Quarterly Historical Magazine,* 1982.

Douglas, R. Alan. *Uppermost Canada: The Western District and the Detroit Frontier, 1800–1850.* Great Lakes Books. Detroit: Wayne State University Press, 2001.

Douglass, Frederick. *My Bondage and My Freedom, Part 1: Life as a Slave* and *Part 12: Life as a Freeman.* New York: Miller, Orton & Mulligan, 1855.

————. *Narrative of the Life of Frederick Douglass, an American Slave.* Boston: Anti-Slavery Office, 1845.

————. *The Life and Times of Frederick Douglass.* 1881. Rev. ed., Boston: De Wolfe, Fiske, 1892.

Douglass, Rev. Wm., ed. *The Colored People of Detroit: Their Trials, Persecutions and Escapes.* Undated pamphlet. Repr. of "Our New Voters: Past History of the Colored People of Detroit with Exciting Scenes of the Riots in 1833, 1839, and 1850." *Detroit Daily Post,* Feb. 7, 1870.

Drago, Henry Sinclair. *The Steamboaters: From the Early Side-Wheelers to the Big Packets.* New York: Bramhall House, 1967.

Drew, Benjamin. *The Refugee; or, The Narratives of Fugitive Slaves in Canada. Related by Themselves, with an Account of the History and Condition of Colored Population of Upper Canada.* Boston & New York: J. P. Jewett & Co., 1856.

Eaton, Clement. "Slave Hiring in the Upper South." *Mississippi Valley Historical Review* 46 (March 1960): 663–78.

Edwards, S. J. Celestine. *From Slavery to a Bishopric; or The Life of Bishop Walter Hawkins of the British Methodist Church.* London: J. Kensit, 1891.

Ehrlich, Walter. *They Have No Rights: Dred Scott's Struggle for Freedom.* Westport, Conn.: Greenwood Press, 1979.

Elgin Association. *Annual Reports of the Directors of the Elgin Association.* Toronto, Ont.: The Association, 1851–1859. CIHCM/ICMH Microfiche series; no. 00255.

Eslinger, Ellen. "The Beginnings of Afro-American Christianity Among Kentucky Baptists." In Craig Thompson Friend, ed., "The Buzzle About Kentuck," *Settling the Promised Land,* 197–215.

————, ed. *Running Mad for Kentucky: Frontier Travel Accounts.* Lexington: University of Kentucky Press, 2004.

Farmer, Silas. *The History of Detroit and Michigan; or, The Metropolis Illustrated: A Chronological Cyclopaedia of the Past and Present, Including a Full Record of Territorial Days in Michigan, and the Annals of Wayne County.* Detroit: S. Farmer & Co., 1884.

———. *History of Detroit and Wayne County and Early Michigan (A Chronological Cyclopedia of the Past and Present).* Detroit: Silas Farmer and Co., 1890.

Farrell, John. "The History of the Negro Community in Chatham, Ontario, 1787–1865." Ph.D. diss., University of Ottawa, 1955.

———. "Schemes for the Transplanting of Refugee American Negroes from Upper Canada in the 1840s." *Ontario History* 52 (1960): 245–49.

Faust, Drew Gilpin. "Slavery in the American Experience." In Edward D. C. Campbell, Jr., and Kym S. Rice, eds., *African-American Life in the Antebellum South.* Richmond, Va.: Museum of the Confederacy, 1991.

Federal Workers of the Writers' Program of Virginia, comp. *The Negro in Virginia.* N1940. Repr., Winston-Salem, N.C.: John F. Blair, 1994.

Fedric, Francis. *Slave Life in Virginia and Kentucky; or, Fifty Years of Slavery in the Southern States of America.* London: Wertheim, Mackintosh and Hunt, 1863.

Fields, Barbara Jean. "Slavery, Race and Ideology in the United States of America." *New Left Review* 181 (May/June 1990): 95–118.

Finkelman, Paul, ed. *Fugitive Slaves.* Articles on American Slavery. Vol. 6. New York: Garland, 1989.

———. *Rebellions, Resistance and Runaways Within the Slave South.* New York: Garland, 1989.

———. "Slavery and the Northwest Ordinance: A Study in Ambiguity." *Journal of the Early Republic* 6 (Winter 1986): 343–70.

Firth, Edith G., ed. *The Town of York: A Collection of Documents of Early Toronto, 1815–1834.* 2 vols. Toronto: Champlain Society for the Govt. of Ontario, 1962.

Fischer, David Hackett, and James C. Kelly. *Away, I'm Bound Away: Virginia and the Westward Movement.* Richmond: Virginia Historical Society, 1993.

Fletcher, Robert Howe. *Genealogical Sketch of Certain of the American Descendants of Mathew Talbot, Gentleman.* Leesburg, Va.: privately published, 1956.

Fogel, Robert William. *Without Consent or Contract: The Rise and Fall of American Slavery.* New York: W. W. Norton, 1989.

Foner, Philip S. *History of Black Americans: From the Compromise of 1850 to the End of the Civil War.* Westport, Conn.: Greenwood Press, 1983.

Ford, Ashley L. "Life on the Ohio: A Captain's View." In *Queen City Heritage: Journal of the Cincinnati Historical Society* 57, no. 2/3 (Summer/Fall 1999): 19–26.

Formisano, Ronald P. "The Edge of Caste: Colored Suffrage in Michigan, 1827–1861." *Michigan History Magazine* 55, no. 1 (spring 1972): 19–43.

Forster, John. *Life of Charles Dickens.* http://www.lang.nagoya-u.ac.jp/~matsuoka/CD-Forster.html.

Fox-Genovese, Elizabeth. *Life in Black and White: Black and White Women of the Old South.* Chapel Hill, N.C.: University of North Carolina Press, 1988.

Franklin, John Hope, and Alfred A. Moss. *From Slavery to Freedom: A History of African Americans.* 7th ed. New York: McGraw-Hill, 1994.

Franklin, John Hope, and Loren Schweninger. *Runaway Slaves: Rebels on the Plantation.* New York: Oxford University Press, 1999.

Fredrickson, George M. *The Black Image in the White Mind: The Debate on Afro-American Character and Destiny, 1817–1914.* 1st ed. New York: Harper & Row, 1971.

French, Gary E. *Men of Colour: An Historical Account of the Black Settlement on Wilberforce Street and in Oro Township, Simcoe County, Ontario, 1819–1949.* Stroud, Ont.: Kaste Books, 1978.

Friend, Craig Thompson, ed. *The Buzzel About Kentuck: Settling the Promised Land.* Lexington: University of Kentucky Press, 1999.

———. *Along the Maysville Road: The Early American Republic in the Trans-appalachian West.* Knoxville: University of Tennessee Press, 2005.

Fuller, George N., and George B. Catlin, eds. *Historic Michigan: Land of the Great Lakes.* 2 vols. Lansing: Michigan Pioneer and Historical Society, 1924.

Gara, Larry. *The Liberty Line: The Legend of the Underground Railroad.* Lexington: University Press of Kentucky, 1996.

Gaspar, David Barry, and Darlene Clark Hine, eds. *More Than Chattel: Black Women and Slavery in the Americas, Blacks in the Diaspora.* Bloomington: Indiana University Press, 1996.

Genovese, Eugene D. *Roll, Jordan, Roll: The World the Slaves Made.* New York: Pantheon Books, 1974.

———. *From Rebellion to Revolution: Afro-American Slave Revolts in the Making of the Modern World.* Baton Rouge: Louisiana State University Press, 1979.

Georgano, G. M. *A History of the London Taxicab.* New York: Drake, 1973.

Gibb, Harley J. "Slaves in Old Detroit." *Michigan History* 18 (1934): 144–46.

Gilje, Paul A. *Rioting in America.* Bloomington: Indiana University Press, 1966.

Gill, Harold B., Jr., and George M. Curtis III, eds. "A Virginian's First Views of Kentucky: David Mead to Joseph Prentiss, August 14, 1796." *Register of the Kentucky Historical Society* 90 (Spring 1992): 117–39.

Girardin, J. A. "Slavery in Detroit." *Pioneer Collections: Report of the Pioneer Society of the State of Michigan* 1 (1900): 415–17.

Glazer, Sidney. "In Old Detroit (1831–1836)." *Michigan History Magazine* 16 (Spring 1942): 206–207.

Goad, Charles E. *Atlas of the city of Toronto and vicinity from special survey founded on registered plans and showing all buildings and lot numbers.* Toronto: Charles E. Goad, 1890.

Goheen, Peter G. *Victorian Toronto: Pattern and Process of Growth.* Chicago: University of Chicago, Dept. of Geography, 1970.

Goings, Kenneth W. *Mammy and Uncle Moses Black Collectables and American Stereotyping.* Bloomington: University of Indiana Press, 1994.

Goings, Kenneth W., and Raymond A. Mohl, eds. *The New African American Urban History.* Thousand Oaks, Calif.: Sage Publications, 1996.

Goodell, William. *Slavery and Anti-Slavery: A History of the Great Struggle in Both Hemispheres, with a View of the Slavery Question in the United States.* 1852. Repr., New York: Negro Universities Press, 1968.

Goodson, Martia Graham. "Enslaved Africans and Doctors in South Carolina." *Journal of the National Medical Association* 95, no. 3 (March 2003): 225–33.

Grable, Stephen W. "Racial Violence Within the Context of Community History." *Phylon* 42:3 (3rd Qtr., 1981): 275–83.

Green, Ernest. "Upper Canada's Black Defenders." *Ontario History* 37 (1931): 365–91.

Green, Jacob D. *Narrative of the Life of J. D. Green, a Runaway Slave, from Kentucky, Containing an Account of His Three Escapes, in 1839, 1846, and 1848.* Huddersfield, Eng.: Henry Fielding, Pack Horse Yard, 1864.

Green, Thomas Marshall. *Historic Families of Kentucky.* 1st ser. Cincinnati: Robert Clark & Co., 1889.

Grimes, William. *Life of William Grimes, the Runaway Slave, Written by Himself.* New York, 1825.

Guillet, Edwin C. *Early Life in Upper Canada.* Toronto: Ontario Publishing, 1939.

———. *Toronto, from Trading Post to Great City.* Toronto: Ontario Publishing, 1939.

Gutman, Herbert George. *The Black Family in Slavery and Freedom, 1750–1925.* New York: Vintage Books, 1977.

Hagedorn, Ann. *Beyond the River: The Untold Story of the Heroes of the Underground Railroad.* New York: Simon & Schuster, 2002.

Hallam, W. T., Mrs. [Lillian Gertrude Best]. "Slave Days in Canada." Toronto, Ont.: Canadian Churchman, 1919.

Hamilton, Frances Frazee. *Ancestral Lines of the Doniphan, Frazee, and Hamilton Families.* Greenfield, Ind.: Wm. Mitchell, 1928.

Hamilton, James Cleland. "John Brown in Canada." *Canadian Magazine* (Dec. 1894): 119–40.

———. *Osgoode Hall: Reminiscences of the Bench and Bar.* Toronto: Carswell, 1904.

Harding, Vincent. *There Is a River: The Black Struggle for Freedom in America.* New York: Vintage Books, 1983.

Harney, Robert F., ed. *Gathering Place: Peoples and Neighbourhoods of Toronto, 1834–1945.* Toronto: Multicultural History Society, 1985.

Harrison, Lowell H. *The Antislavery Movement in Kentucky.* Lexington: University Press of Kentucky, 1978.

———. "A Virginian Moves to Kentucky, 1793." *William and Mary Quarterly,* 3rd Ser., 15, no. 2 (April 1958): 201–13.

Harrison, Lowell H., and James C. Klotter. *A New History of Kentucky.* Lexington: University Press of Kentucky, 1997.

Hayden, Horace Edwin. *Virginia Genealogies: A Genealogy of the Glassell Family of Scotland and Virginia.* Wilkes-Barre, Pa.: E. B. Yordy, printer, 1891.

Hayden, Robert E. "History of the Negro in Michigan," MS, Historical Collections of Michigan, Bentley Historical Library, University of Michigan, n.d.

Hayes, Alan L. *Holding Forth the Word of Life: Little Trinity Church, 1842–1992.* Stratford, Ont.: Beacon Herald Fine Printing, 1992.

Head, Francis Bond. *A Narrative.* London: J. Murray, 1839.

Headley, John W. *Confederate Operations in Canada and New York.* New York: Neal Publishing Co., 1906.

Heath, Barbara J. *Hidden Lives: The Archaeology of Slave Life at Thomas Jefferson's Poplar Forest.* Charlottesville: University Press of Virginia, 1999.

Hemans, Lawton T. *Life and Times of Stevens Thomson Mason, the Boy Governor of Michigan.* 2nd ed. Lansing: Michigan Historical Commission, 1930.

Hening, William Walker. *The Statutes at Large: Being a Collection of All the Laws of Virginia, from the First Session of the Legislature in the Year 1619.* 13 vols. Richmond: W. Gray, 1819–23.

Henson, Josiah. *An Autobiography of the Rev. Josiah Henson (Mrs. Harriet Beecher Stowe's "Uncle Tom").* London, Ont.: Schuyler, Smith and Co., 1881.

Hepburn, Sharon A. Roger. "Following the North Star: Canada as a Haven for Nineteenth-Century American Blacks." *Michigan Historical Review* 25, no. 2 (Fall 1999): 91–126.

Hesslink, George K. *Black Neighbors: Negroes in a Northern Rural Community.* 2nd ed. Indianapolis: Bobbs-Merrill, 1974.

Hicks, W. M. *A History of Louisiana Negro Baptists, from 1804–1914.* Nashville, Tenn.: National Baptist Publishing Board, 1915.

Hill, Daniel G. "The Blacks in Toronto." In Robert F. Harney, ed., *Gathering Place: Peoples and Neighbourhoods of Toronto, 1834–1945, Studies in Ethnic and Immigration History.* Toronto: Multicultural History Society of Ontario, 1985, 75–105.

———. "Early Black Settlements in the Niagara Peninsula." In John Burtniak and Patricia G. Dirks, eds., *Immigration and Settlement in the Niagara Peninsula: Proceedings of the Third Annual Niagara Peninsula History Conference, Brock University, April 25–26, 1981.* Brock University, St. Catharines, Ont., 1981, 65–80.

———. *The Freedom-Seekers: Blacks in Early Canada.* Agincourt, Ont.: Book Society of Canada, 1981.

———. "Negroes in Toronto: A Sociological Study of a Minority Group." Ph.D. diss., University of Toronto, 1960.

———. "Negroes in Toronto, 1793–1856." *Ontario History* 55, no. 2 (1963): 73–91.

Hine, Darlene Clark, Wilma King, and Linda Reed. *"We Specialize in the Wholly Impossible": A Reader in Black Women's History.* Brooklyn, N.Y.: Carlson, 1995.

History of Toronto and County of York, Ontario. 2 vols. Toronto: C. Blackett Robinson, 1885.

Hite, Roger W. "Voice of a Fugitive: Henry Bibb and Ante-bellum Black Separatism." *Journal of Black Studies* 4, no. 3 (March 1974): 269–84.

Hoffman, Charles Fenno. *A Winter in the West, by a New Yorker,* 2 vols. New York: Harper & Brothers, 1835.

Hogue, Louisa D. F. "The History of the Blackburn Family." *Prince William Reliquary* 2, no. 1 (Jan. 2003): 1–8.

Holland, Frederick May. *Frederick Douglass, the Colored Orator,* rev. ed. New York: Funk & Wagnall's Co., 1895.

Hopkins, Margaret Lail, ed. *Index to the Tithables of Loudoun County, Virginia and to Slaveholders and Slaves, 1758–1786.* Baltimore: Genealogical Publishing Co., Inc., ca. 1991.

Horton, James Oliver. *Free People of Color: Inside the African American Community.* Washington, D.C.: Smithsonian Institution Press, 1993.

Horton, James Oliver, and Lois E. Horton. *Black Bostonians: Family Life and Community Struggle in the Antebellum North.* Rev. ed. New York: Holmes & Meier, 1999.

———. *In Hope of Liberty: Culture, Community, and Protest Among Northern Free Blacks, 1700–1860.* New York: Oxford University Press, 1997.

Howe, Samuel Gridley. *The Refugees from Slavery in Canada West: Report to the Freedmen's Inquiry Commission.* Boston: Wright & Potter, 1864.

Howard, Richard. *Upper Canada College, 1829–1979: Colborne's Legacy.* Toronto: Macmillan Co., 1979.

Hoy, Claire. *Canadians in the Civil War.* Toronto: McArthur & Co., 2004.

Hubbard, Stephen L. *Against All Odds: The Story of William Peyton Hubbard, Black Leader and Municipal Reformer.* Hamilton: Dundurn Press, 1987.

Hubbard, William O., and Joe Johnson. *Kentucky's Ohio River Boundary: From the Big Sandy to the Great Miami.* Informational Bulletin no. 81. Frankfort: Legislative Research Commission (Dec. 1969).

Hudson, J. Blaine. "African-American Religion in Antebellum Louisville, Kentucky." *The Griot: Journal of the Southern Conference on African American Studies* 17, no. 2 (1998): 43–54.

———. "Crossing the 'Dark Line': Fugitive Slaves and the Underground Railroad in Louisville and North-Central Kentucky." *Filson Club History Quarterly* 75, no. 1 (Winter 2001): 33–83.

———. *Fugitive Slaves and the Underground Railroad in the Kentucky Borderland.* Jefferson, N.C.: McFarland, 2002.

———. "In Pursuit of Freedom: Slave Law and Emancipation in Louisville and Jefferson County, Kentucky." *Filson History Quarterly* 76, no. 3 (Summer 2002): 287–325.

Hughes, Louis. *Thirty Years a Slave: From Bondage to Freedom. The Institution of Slavery as Seen on the Plantation and in the Home of the Planter.* Milwaukee: South Side Printing Company, 1897.

Hurt, R. Douglas. *The Ohio Frontier: Crucible of the Old Northwest, 1720–1830.* Bloomington: University of Indiana Press, 1996.

Hutchinson's Toronto Directory, 1862–63. Toronto: Lovel & Gibson, 1863.

Incorporating the City of Maysville and the Ordinances Now in Force. Maysville: L. Collins, 1833.

Jackson, Mattie J., dictated to Dr. L. S. Thompson. *Her Parentage—Experience of Eighteen Years in Slavery—Incidents During the War—Her Escape from Slavery: A True Story.* Lawrence: Sentinel Office, 1866.

Jacobs, Harriet. *Incidents in the Life of a Slave Girl, Written by Herself.* Boston: Published for the author, 1861.

Jameson, Anna Brownell. *Sketches in Canada, and Rambles Among the Red Men.* New ed. London: Longman, Brown, Green, and Longmans, 1852.

———. *Winter Studies and Summer Rambles in Canada.* London: Saunders and Otley, 1838, and New York: Wiley and Putnam, 1839.

Jamieson, Susan, ed., Karolyn E. Smardz, Peter Hamalainen, et al. "The Thornton Blackburn House Site, AjGu-16." Archaeological site report. Toronto: Archaeological Resource Centre, Toronto Board of Education, 1986. On file at the Ontario Ministry of Culture, Archaeology Branch.

Jefferson, Thomas. *Notes on the State of Virginia*. Edited by William Harwood Peden. London: Printed for J. Stockdale, 1787. Repr., Chapel Hill: Published for the Institute of Early American History and Culture, Williamsburg, Va., by the University of North Carolina Press, 1955.

Jennings, Kathleen. *Louisville's First Families*. Louisville: Standard Printing Company, 1920.

Jenson, Carole. "A History of the Negro Community in Essex County, Ontario, 1850–1860." Master's thesis, University of Windsor, 1966.

Johnson, Walter. *Soul by Soul: Life Inside the Antebellum Slave Market*. Cambridge, Mass.: Harvard University Press, 1999.

Johnston, J. Stoddard, ed. *Memorial History of Louisville from the First Settlement to the Year 1896*, 2 vols. Chicago: American Biographical Publishing Co., 1896.

Jones, Howard. *To the Webster-Ashburton Treaty: A Study in Anglo-American Relations, 1783–1843*. Chapel Hill: University of North Carolina Press, 1977.

Jones, Jacqueline. *Labor of Love, Labor of Sorrow: Black Women, Work, and the Family from Slavery to the Present*. New York: Basic Books, 1985.

———. "My Mother Was Much of a Woman: Black Women, Work, and the Family Under Slavery." *Feminist Studies* 8 (Summer 1982): 252–54.

Jones, Steven J. "The African-American Tradition in Vernacular Architecture." In Theresa A. Singleton, ed., *The Archaeology of Slavery and Plantation Life*. New York: Academic Press, 1985, 195–312.

Jordan, Winthrop D. *White over Black: American Attitudes Toward the Negro, 1550–1812*. New York: W. W. Norton, 1977.

Joyner, Ulysses P., Jr. *The First Settlers of Orange County, Virginia*. Baltimore: Gateway Press, 1987.

Katzman, David M. *Before the Ghetto: Black Detroit in the Nineteenth Century*. Urbana: University of Illinois Press, 1975.

———. "Black Slavery in Michigan." *Midcontinent American Studies Journal* (Fall 1970): 56–66.

Keckley, Elizabeth. *Behind the Scenes: or, Thirty Years a Slave and Four Years in the White House*. New York: G. W. Carleton, 1868.

Kelly, Wayne E. "Canada's Black Defenders: Former Slaves Answered the Call to Arms." *Beaver* 77 (April–May 1977): 31–34.

Kelso, William. "The Archaeology of Slave Life at Thomas Jefferson's Monticello: 'A Wolf by the Ears.'" *Journal of New World Archaeology* 6, no. 4 (1986): 5–21.

———. *Kingsmill Plantations, 1619–1800: Archaeology of Country Life in Colonial Virginia*. New York: Academic Press, 1984.

Kentucky Digest, 1785 to Date. Covering Cases from State and Federal Courts. St. Paul, Minn.: West Publishing Co., 1953.

King, Wilma. *Stolen Childhood: Slave Youth in Nineteenth-Century America*. Bloomington: Indiana University Press, 1998.

Kitson, D. "Towards Freedom: An Analysis of Negro Slave Revolts in the United States." *Phylon* 25 (Summer 1964), 175–87.

Kleber, John E., ed. *The Encyclopedia of Louisville*. Lexington: University Press of Kentucky, 2001.

Klunder, Willard Carl. *Lewis Cass and the Politics of Moderation*. Kent, OH: Kent State University Press, 1996.

Kolchin, Peter. "Whiteness Studies: The New History of Race in America."
    The Journal of American History 89, no. 1 (2002): 154–73.
Kooker, A. R. "The Anti-Slavery Movement in Michigan, 1798–1840: A Study
    in Humanitarianism on the American Frontier." Ph.D. diss., University
    of Michigan, 1941.
Kreipke, Martha. "The Falls of the Ohio and the Development of the Ohio
    River Trade, 1810–1860." *Filson Club Historical Quarterly* 54, no. 2 (1980):
    196–217.
Kulikoff, Allan. "The Colonial Chesapeake: Seedbed of Antebellum Southern
    Culture?" *Journal of Southern History* 65, no. 4 (Nov. 1979): 513–40.
Kyer, Ian C. "The Transformation of an Establishment Firm: From Beatty
    Blackstock to Faskens, 1902–1915." In Carol Wilton, ed., *Essays in the History of Canadian Law*, 9 vols. Toronto: Osgoode Society, 1996, 7:61–206.
Lajeunesse, Ernest J. *The Windsor Border Region: Canada's Southernmost Frontier.* Toronto: Champlain Society, 1960.
Landon, Fred: "Abolitionist Interest in Upper Canada." *Ontario History* 44, no.
    4 (1952): 165–72.
———. "Amherstburg, Terminus of the Underground Railway." *Journal of Negro History* 10 (Jan. 1925): 1–9.
———. "The Anti-Slavery Society of Canada." *Journal of Negro History* 4 (Jan.
    1919): 33–40.
———. "The Buxton Settlement in Canada." *Journal of Negro History* 3 (Oct.
    1918): 360–67.
———. "Canada's Part in Freeing the Slave." *Ontario Historical Society Papers
    and Records* 17 (1919): 74–84.
———. "Canadian Negroes and the Rebellion of 1837." *Journal of Negro History* 7, no. 4 (Oct. 1922): 377–79.
———. "Captain Charles Stuart: Abolitionist." In Edith Firth, ed., *Profiles of a
    Province: Studies in the History of Ontario, a Collection of Essays Commissioned by the Ontario Historical Society to Commemorate the Centennial of
    Ontario.* Toronto: Ontario Historical Society, 1967, 205–10.
———. "The Diary of Benjamin Lundy, Written During His Journey
    Through Upper Canada, January, 1832." *Ontario Historical Society Papers
    and Records* 19 (1922): 110–33.
———. "Documents Illustrating the Conditions of Refugees from Slavery in
    Upper Canada Before 1850." *Journal of Negro History* 1 (1916): 199–206.
———. "The Fugitive Slave Law and the Detroit River Frontier, 1850–61."
    Detroit Historical Society Bulletin 7, no. 2 (1950): 5–9.
———. "Henry Bibb: A Colonizer." *Journal of Negro History* 5 (Oct. 1920):
    437–47.
———. "The Negro Migration to Canada After the Passing of the Fugitive
    Slave Act." *Journal of Negro History* 5, no. 1 (Jan. 1920): 22–36.
———. "Our Joint Historical Heritage." *Michigan History* 33 (1940): 5–12.
———. "A Pioneer Abolitionist in Upper Canada." *Ontario History* 52, no. 2
    (1960): 77–83.
———. "Social Conditions Among the Negroes in Upper Canada Before
    1865." *Ontario Historical Society Papers and Records* 22 (1925): 144–61.
———. "The Underground Railroad Along the Detroit River." *Michigan History* 39 (March 1955): 63–68.

————. "When Uncle Tom's Cabin Came to Canada." *Ontario History* 44, no. 1 (1952): 1–5.

————. "Wilberforce, An Experiment in the Colonization of Freed Negroes in Upper Canada." *Transactions of the Royal Society of Canada*, sec. 2 (1937): 69–78.

Larrie, Reginald. *Black Experiences in Michigan History.* Lansing: Michigan History Division, 1975.

————. *Corners of Michigan Black History.* New York & Hollywood: Vantage Press, 1971.

————. *Makin' Free: African-Americans in the Northwest Territory.* Detroit: B. Ethridge Books, 1981.

Law, Howard. "'Self-Reliance Is the True Road to Independence': Ideology and the Ex-slaves in Buxton and Chatham." *Ontario History* 77, no. 2 (June 1985): 107–21.

Laws of the Territory of Michigan. 4 vols. Lansing, Mich.: S. George, 1871–84.

Leach, Nathaniel. *The Second Baptist Connection, Reaching Out to Freedom: History of Second Baptist Church of Detroit.* Rev. ed. Detroit: N. Leach, 1988.

Leask, J. Mackenzie. "Jesse Happy, a Fugitive Slave from Kentucky." *Ontario Historical Society Papers and Records* 54 (June 1962): 85–98.

Lee, Lucy C. *A Historical Sketch of Mason County, Kentucky.* Louisville: Mason Home Journal, 1928.

Levine, Lawrence W. *Black Culture and Black Consciousness: Afro-American Folk Thought from Slavery to Freedom.* New York: Oxford University Press, 1978.

Lewis, Francis. *Toronto Directory and Street Guide, 1843–1844.* Toronto: H. W. Rowsell, 1844.

Lewis, James K. "Religious Life of Fugitive Slaves and Rise of Coloured Baptist Churches, 1820–65." Ph.D. diss., McMaster University School of Divinity, 1965.

————. "Religious Nature of the Early Negro Migration to Canada and the Amherstburg Baptist Association." *Ontario History* 58, no. 2 (1966): 117–32.

Library of Congress, Manuscript Division. *The American Colonization Society: A Register of Its Records in the Library of Congress.* Washington, D.C.: Library, 1979.

Lindsay, Arnett G. "Diplomatic Relations Between the United States and Great Britain Bearing on the Return of Negro Slaves." *Journal of Negro History* 5 (October 1920): 391–419.

Littell, William, ed. *Principles of Law and Equity, Recognized and Established by the Court of Appeals of Kentucky, in the Various Cases Determined in That Court, Commencing with Its First Existence, and Concluding with the Close of the October Term, One Thousand Eight Hundred and Six (Except the Land Cases Published by James Hughes, Esq.), Digested and Arranged in Alphabetical Order.* Frankfort, Ky.: William Gerard, 1808.

————. *The State Law of Kentucky to 1816, Comprehending Also the Laws of Virginia and Acts of Parliament in Force in the Commonwealth.* 5 vols. Frankfort, Ky.: W. Hunter, 1809–19.

Litwack, Leon F. *North of Slavery: The Negro in the Free States, 1790–1860.* Chicago: University of Chicago Press, 1961.

Lockett, James D. "The Lynching Massacre of Black and White Soldiers at Fort Pillow, Tennessee, April 12, 1864." *Western Journal of Black Studies* 22, no. 2 (1998): 84–93.

Loguen, Jermain Wesley. *The Rev. J. W. Loguen, as a Slave and as a Freeman: A Narrative of Real Life.* New York: Negro Universities Press, 1968.

Lucas, Marion P. *A History of Blacks in Kentucky,* vol. 1. *From Slavery to Segregation, 1760–1891.* Lexington: Kentucky Historical Society, 1992.

Lumpkin, Katherine DuPre. "'The General Plan Was Freedom': A Negro Secret Order on the Underground Railroad." *Phylon* 28 (Spring 1967): 63–77.

Lundell, Liz. *The Estates of Old Toronto.* Erin, Ont.: Boston Mills Press, 1997.

MacCabe, Julius Bolivar. *Directory of the City of Detroit.* Detroit: William Harsha, 1837.

Mackenzie, Alexander. *The Life and Speeches of Hon. George Brown.* Toronto: Globe Printing, 1882.

Mackenzie, William Lyon. *Sketches of Canada and the United States.* London: E. Wilson, 1833.

Manning, William R., ed. *Diplomatic Correspondence of the United States, Canadian Relations. 1784–1860.* Vol. 2, 1821–1835. Washington, D.C.: Carnegie Endowment for International Peace, 1942.

Mansfield, J. B., ed. *The History of the Great Lakes.* 2 vols. Chicago: J. H. Beers, 1899.

Marrs, Elijah P. *Life and History of the Rev. Elijah P. Marrs, First Pastor of Beaugrass Baptist Church.* Louisville, Ky.: Bradley & Gilbert Co., 1885.

Martin, Asa Earl. *The Anti-Slavery Movement in Kentucky Prior to 1850.* Louisville, Ky.: Standard Printing Company, 1918.

Martin, Ged. "British Officials and Their Attitudes Towards the Negro." *Ontario History* 66, no. 1 (March 1974): 79–88.

Martineau, Harriet. *Retrospect of Western Travel.* 2 vols. London: Saunders and Otley, 1838.

———. *Society in America.* 3 vols. London: Saunders and Otley, 1837.

Martyn, Lucy Booth. *The Face of Early Toronto: An Archival Record, 1797–1936.* Sutton West, Ont.: Paget Press, 1982.

———. *A View of Original Toronto: The Fabric of York/Toronto Circa 1834.* Sutton West, Ont.: Paget Press, 1983.

Masters, D. C. *The Rise of Toronto, 1850–1890.* Toronto: University of Toronto Press, 1947.

May, Trevor. *Gondolas and Growlers: The History of the London Horse Cab.* London: Alan Sutton, 1995.

Mayers, Adam. *Dixie and the Dominion: Canada, the Confederacy and the War for the Union.* Toronto: Dundurn Press, 2003.

Maysville City Council. *Incorporating the City of Maysville and the Ordinances of Same City Adopted by the Board of Councilmen, and Now in Force.* Maysville: L. Collins, City Printer, 1833.

McColley, Robert. *Slavery and Jeffersonian Virginia.* Champaign: University of Illinois Press, 1964.

McDavitt, Elaine Elizabeth. "The Beginnings of Theatrical Activities in Detroit," *Michigan History* 31, no. 1 (March 1947): 35–47.

McDougle, Ivan E. "The Development of Slavery," *Journal of Negro History* 3, no. 3 (July 1918): 214–39.

————. "The Legal Status of Slavery," *Journal of Negro History* 3, no. 3 (July 1918): 240–80.

————. *Slavery in Kentucky, 1792–1865.* Westport, Conn.: Negro Universities Press, 1970.

McEvoy, Henry C., comp. *C. E. Anderson & Co.'s Toronto City Directory for 1868–9.* Toronto: C. E. Anderson & Co., 1869.

McKitrick, Eric L., ed. *Slavery Defended: The Views of the Old South.* Englewood Cliffs, N.J.: Prentice-Hall, 1963.

McRae, Norman R. "Blacks in Detroit, 1736–1833: The Search for Freedom and Community and Its Implications for Educators." Ph.D. diss., University of Michigan, 1982.

————. "Crossing the Detroit River to Find Freedom." *Michigan History* 67, no. 2 (March/April 1983): 35–39.

————. "Early Blacks in Michigan, 1743–1800." *Detroit in Perspective: A Journal of Regional History* 2, no. 3 (Spring 1976): 159–75.

Meier, August, and Elliott M. Rudwick. *From Plantation to Ghetto.* 3rd ed. New York: Hill and Wang, 1998.

Melville, Henry. *The Rise and Progress of Trinity College, Toronto: With a Sketch of the Life of the Lord Bishop of Toronto, as Connected with Church Education in Canada.* Toronto: Henry Rowsell, 1852.

Michaux, François André. *Travels to the West of the Alleghany Mountains.* Repr. in 1904 in Reuben Gold Thwaites, ed., *Early Western Travels, 1748–1846.* Cleveland: Arthur H. Clark, 1904.

Michigan. *Journal of the Legislative Council.* 1st Council, 1st session (January 28, 1824), 6th Council, special session (August 20, 1835). Detroit: Sheldon & Reed, 1824.

Michigan. *Laws of the Territory of Michigan.* 4 vols. Lansing: W. S. George & Co., Printers to the State, 1871.

Michigan. *Laws of the Territory of Michigan, Comprising the Acts, of a Public Nature.* Detroit: Sheldon & Wells, 1827.

Middleton, Jesse Edgar. *The Municipality of Metropolitan Toronto: A History.* 3 vols. Toronto: Dominion Publishing, 1923.

Miller, Caroline, ed. *African-American Records, Bracken County, Kentucky, 1797–1999.* Vol. 1. Brooksville, Ky.: Bracken County Historical Society, 2000.

————. *Slavery in Mason County, Kentucky: A Century of Records, 1788–1888.* Vol. 1. Maysville, Ky.: National Underground Railroad Museum, 2001.

————. *Slavery in Newsprint: Central Ohio River Borderlands.* Vol. 1, 1797–1839, Ohio and Kentucky. Augusta, Ky.: Caroline R. Miller, 2003.

Minutes and Proceedings of the First Annual Convention of the People of Color, Held by Adjournments in the City of Philadelphia, from the Sixth to the Eleventh of June, Inclusive, 1831. Philadelphia: Published by Order of the Committee of Arrangements, 1831.

Mitchell, Reverend William M. *The Underground Railroad.* 2nd ed., 1860. Repr. Westport, Conn.: Negro Universities Press, 1970.

Monroe, Benjamin. *Reports of Cases at Common Law and in Equity Decided in the Court of Appeals of Kentucky.* Vols. 1 and 6, 2nd ed. Cincinnati: Robert Clarke, 1846.

Monroe, Benjamin, and James Harlan. *Digest of Cases at Common Law and in Equity, Decided by the Court of Appeals of Kentucky, from Its Organization in*

1792 to the Close of the Winter Term of 1852–53. Frankfort, Ky.: A. G. Hodges, 1853.

Morehead, C. S., and Mason Brown. *A Digest of the Statute Laws of Kentucky, of a Public and Permanent Nature.* Frankfort, Ky.: A. G. Hodges, 1834.

Morely, Jefferson. "The 'Snow Riot.'" *Washington Post.* Feb. 6, 2005.

Morris, Thomas D. *Southern Slavery and the Law, 1619–1860.* Chapel Hill, N.C.: University of North Carolina, 1996.

Morrison, Neil. *Garden Gateway to Canada: One Hundred Years of Windsor and Essex County, 1854–1954.* Toronto: Ryerson Press, 1954.

Murray, Alexander L. "The Extradition of Fugitive Slaves from Canada: A Re-evaluation." *Canadian Historical Review* 43, no. 4 (1962): 298–313.

———. "The *Provincial Freeman:* A New Source for the History of the Negro in the United States and Canada." *Journal of Negro History* 60 (April 1959): 123–35.

Murray, David. *Colonial Justice: Justice, Morality, and Crime in the Niagara District, 1791–1849.* Osgoode Society for Canadian Legal History. Toronto: University of Toronto Press, 2002.

———. "Criminal Boundaries: The Frontier and the Contours of Upper Canadian Justice, 1792–1840." *Canadian Review of American Studies/American Review of Canadian Studies* 26, no. 3 (Autumn 1996): 341–66.

———. "Hands Across the Border: The Abortive Extradition of Solomon Moseby." *Canadian Review of American Studies* 30, no. 2 (2000): 187–209.

Murray, Joyce Martin, abst. *Logan County Kentucky Deed Abstacts, 1792–1813.* Dallas, Texas: Privately published, 1993.

Neal, Frederick. *The Township of Sandwich (Past and Present) Illustrated.* Windsor, Ont.: Record Printing Co. Limited, 1909.

Neidhard, Karl. "Reise Nach Michigan." Translated by Frank X. Braun. Edited with an intro. by Robert Benaway Brown. *Michigan History* 25 (1951): 36–43.

Newby, Dalyce. *Anderson Ruffin Abbott: First Afro-Canadian Doctor.* Canadian Medical Lives. Markham, Ont.: Associated Medical Services and Fitzhenry & Whiteside, 1998.

O'Brien, Mary Lawrence. "Slavery in Louisville During the Antebellum Period, 1820–1860: A Study of the Effects of Urbanization on the Institution of Slavery as It Existed in Louisville, Kentucky." Ph.D. diss., University of Louisville, 1979.

Olmsted, Frederick Law. *The Cotton Kingdom: A Traveller's Observations on Cotton and Slavery in the American Slave States, 1853–1861.* Edited by Arthur M. Schlesinger. New York: Da Capo Press, 1996.

Otis, Richard W. *The Louisville Directory for the Year 1832.* Louisville, Ky.: James Virden, Printer, 1832.

Palmer, Friend. "Detroit in 1827 and Later On." *Michigan Pioneer and Historical Collections* 35 (1907): 272–83.

———. *Early Days in Detroit: Papers Written by General Friend Palmer of Detroit: Being His Personal Reminiscences of Important Events and Descriptions of the City for Over Eighty Years.* Detroit: Hunt & June, 1906.

Parker, Amos Andrew. *A Trip to the West and to Texas, Comprising a Journey of Eight Thousand Miles, Through New York, Michigan, Illinois, Missouri,*

Louisiana and Texas, in the Autumn and Winter of 1834–5; Interspersed with Anecdotes, Incidents and Observations. Concord, N.H.: White & Fisher, 1835.

Parker, John. *His Promised Land: The Autobiography of John P. Parker, Former Slave and Conductor on the Underground Railroad.* Edited by Stuart Seely Sprague. New York: Norton, 1996.

Parkins, Almon Ernest. *The Historical Geography of Detroit.* Lansing: Michigan Historical Commission, 1918.

Pease, Jane H., and William H. Pease. *Black Utopia: Negro Communal Experiments in America.* Madison: State Historical Society of Wisconsin, 1963.

——. "Opposition to the Founding of the Elgin Settlement." *Canadian Historical Review* 38 (1957): 202–18.

——. *They Who Would Be Free: Blacks' Search for Freedom, 1830–1861.* Urbana: University of Illinois Press, 1974. Repr. 1990.

Pemberton, Ian. "The Anti-Slavery Society of Canada." Ph.D. diss., University of Toronto, 1967.

Pennington, James W. C. *The Fugitive Blacksmith; or, Events in the History of James W. C. Pennington, Pastor of the Presbyterian Church, New York, Formerly a Slave in the State of Maryland, United States.* London: Charles Gilpin, 1849.

Peskin, Allan, ed. *North into Freedom: The Autobiography of John Malvin, Free Negro, 1795–1880.* (1879). Repr., Cleveland: Press of Western Reserve University, 1966.

"Petition for the Establishment of a Settlement in Canada, 1828: Test," *Journal of Negro History* 15 (Jan. 1930): 115–16.

Phillips, John T. *Historian's Guide to Loudoun County, Virginia: Colonial Laws of Virginia and County Court Orders, 1757–1766.* Vol. 1. Leesburg, Va.: Goose Creek Productions, 1996.

Phillips, Ulrich Bonnell. *Life and Labor in the Old South.* Boston: Little Brown, 1929.

Pierson, George Wilson. *Tocqueville in America.* Baltimore: Johns Hopkins University Press, 1996.

Postl, Karl [Charles Sealsfield]. *Americans as They Are: Described in a Tour Through the Valley of the Mississippi.* London: Hurst Chance, 1828.

Poulton, Ron. *The Paper Tyrant: John Ross Robertson of the Toronto Telegram.* Toronto: Clarke, Irwin, 1971.

Power, Michael, and Nancy Butler. *Slavery and Freedom in Niagara.* Niagara-on-the-Lake, Ont.: Niagara Historical Society, 1993.

Price, Lucy Montgomery Smith. *The Sydney-Smith and Clagett-Price Genealogy.* Strasburg, Va.: Shenandoah Publishing, 1927.

Prince, Bryan. *I Came as a Stranger: The Underground Railroad.* Plattsburg, N.Y.: Tundra Books of Northern New York, 2004.

The Provincial Statutes of Upper-Canada, Revised, Corrected, and Republished by Authority. York, Ont.: R. C. Horne, 1816.

Quaife, Milo. "When Detroit Invaded Kentucky." *Filson Club History Quarterly* (Jan. 1927): 53–57.

Quarles, Benjamin. *Black Abolitionists.* 1969. Repr., New York: Da Capo Press, 1991.

————. *The Negro in the Making of America.* 3rd ed. New York: Simon & Schuster, 1996.

Rael, Patrick. *Black Identity and Black Protest in the Antebellum North.* Chapel Hill: University of North Carolina Press, 2002.

Randolph, Peter. *Sketches of Slave Life, or, Illustrations of the "Peculiar Institution."* Boston: Published for the author, 1855.

Ranke, Vinetta Wells, comp. *The Blackburn Genealogy,* with notes on the Washington Family through intermarriage. Washington, D.C.: 1939.

Rankin, Reverend John. *Letters on American Slavery, Addressed to Mr. Thomas Rankin.* 5th ed. Boston: Isaac Knapp, 1838.

Rawick, George P., ed. *The American Slave: A Composite Autobiography.* Westport, Conn.: Greenwood, 1977.

————. *From Sundown to Sunup: The Making of the Black Community.* Westport, Conn.: Greenwood, 1972.

Read, David B. *The Lives of the Judges of Upper Canada and Ontario from 1791 to the Present Time.* Toronto: Rowsell & Hutchison, 1888.

Reid, Richard. "The 1870 United States Census and Black Underenumeration: A Test Case from North Carolina." *Social History* 20, no. 56 (Nov. 1995): 487–99.

Reinders, Robert. "The John Anderson Case, 1860–1: A Study in Anglo-Canadian Imperial Relations." *Canadian Historical Review* 56 (1975): 393–415.

"Report on the Buxton Mission." *Ecclesiastical and Missionary Record for the Presbyterian Church of Canada* 9 (July 1853): 132.

"Report on the Buxton Mission." *Ecclesiastical and Missionary Record for the Presbyterian Church of Canada* 10 (Aug. 1854): 146.

Rescher, Nicolas. *Niagara-on-the-Lake as a Confederate Refuge.* Niagara-on-the-Lake, Ont.: Niagara Historical Society, 2003.

Rhodes, Jane. *Mary Ann Shadd Cary: The Black Press and Protest in the Nineteenth Century.* Bloomington: Indiana University Press, 1998.

Riddell, William Renwick. "Additional Notes on Slavery, Reciprocity of Slaves Between Michigan and Upper Canada." *Journal of Negro History* 7 (Jan. 1932): 368–77.

————. "Documents: Records Illustrating the Condition of Refugees from Slavery in Upper Canada Before 1860." *Journal of Negro History* 15 (Jan. 1930): 199–206.

————. "Documents: The Tappan Papers." *Journal of Negro History* 12 (April 1927): 389–554.

————. "The Fugitive Slave in Canada," *Journal of Negro History,* 5 (1920): 340–58.

————. "Interesting Notes on Great Britain and Canada with Respect to the Negro." *Journal of Negro History* 13 (April 1938): 185–207.

————. *The Legal Profession in Upper Canada in Its Early Periods.* Toronto: Law Society of Upper Canada, 1916, 70–72.

————. "Notes on Slavery in Canada." *Journal of Negro History* 4 (Jan. 1919): 396–408.

————. "The Slave in Canada." *Journal of Negro History* 5 (1920): 261–375.

————. "The Slave in Upper Canada." *Journal of Negro History* 4 (Oct. 1919): 372–95.

Ripley, C. Peter, et al., eds. *The Black Abolitionist Papers.* 5 vols. Chapel Hill: University of North Carolina Press, 1985–92.

Robbins, Arlie C. *Legacy to Buxton.* Chatham, Ont.: Ideal Printing, 1983.

Robertson, John Ross. *Landmarks of Toronto.* 6 vols. Toronto: J. R. Robertson, 1894–1898.

Robinson, C. Blackett, ed. *History of Toronto and County of York, Ontario.* 2 vols. Toronto: C. Blackett Robinson, 1885.

Robinson, Gwendolyn, and John W. Robinson. *Seek the Truth: The Story of Chatham's Black Community.* Chatham, Ont., 1989.

Robinson, William H. *From Log Cabin to the Pulpit; or, Fifteen Years in Slavery.* Eau Clair, Wis.: James H. Tifft, 1913.

Roediger, David R. *The Wages of Whiteness: Race and the Making of the American Working Class.* The Haymarket Series in North American Politics and Culture. New York: Verso, 1991.

Rogers, Sharon A. "Slaves No More: A Study of the Buxton Settlement, Upper Canada, 1849–1861." Ph.D. diss., SUNY at Buffalo, 1995.

Rolph, Thomas. *A Brief Account, Together with Observations, Made During a Visit in the West Indies, and a Tour Through the United States of America, in Parts of the Years 1832–3; Together with a Statistical Account of Upper Canada.* Dundas, U.C.: G. H. Hackstaff Printer, 1836.

Roper, Moses. *Narrative of the Adventures and Escape of Moses Roper, from American Slavery.* Berwick-Upon-Tweed: Warder's Office, 1848.

Rose, Willie Lee, ed. *A Documentary History of Slavery in North America.* Athens: University of Georgia Press, 1999.

Ross, Robert B., and George B. Catlin. *Landmarks of Detroit: A History of the City.* Detroit: Evening News Association, 1898.

Russell, Donna Valley. *Michigan Censuses, 1710–1830, Under the French, British, and Americans.* Detroit: Detroit Society for Genealogical Research Inc., 1982.

Savitt, T. L. "The Use of Blacks for Medical Experimentation and Demonstration in the Old South." *Journal of Southern History* 48, no. 3 (Aug. 1982): 331–48.

Scadding, Henry. *Toronto of Old.* Edited by Frederick H. Armstrong. Toronto: Dundurn Press, 1987.

Schwartz, Marie Jenkins. *Born in Bondage: Growing Up Enslaved in the Antebellum South.* Cambridge: Harvard University Press, 2000.

Schweninger, Loren. "A Fugitive Negro in the Promised Land: James Rapier in Canada, 1856–1865." *Ontario History* 67 (June 1975): 91–104.

Sellar, Robert. *A Scotsman in Upper Canada: The Narrative of Gordon Sellar.* Toronto: Clarke, Irwin, 1969.

Shadd, Adrienne. "The Lord Seemed to Say 'Go': Women in the Underground Railroad Movement." In Bristow, *"We're Rooted Here and They Can't Pull Us Up,"* 41–68.

Shadd, Adrienne, Afua Cooper, and Karolyn Smardz Frost. *The Underground Railroad: Next Stop, Toronto!* Toronto: Natural Heritage Books, 2002.

Shadd, Mary Ann. *A Plea for Emigration; or, Notes of Canada West.* Edited by Richard Almonte. 1852. Repr., Toronto: Mercury Press, 1998.

Shirreff, Patrick. *A Tour Through North America.* Edinburgh: Oliver and Boyde, 1835.

Shreve, Dorothy Shadd. *The AfriCanadian Church: A Stabilizer.* Jordan Station, Ont.: Paideia Press, 1983.

————. *Pathfinders of Liberty and Truth: A Century with the Amherstburg Regular Missionary Baptist Association.* Privately published, 1940.

Siebert, Wilbur Henry. *The Underground Railroad from Slavery to Freedom.* With an intro. by Albert Bushnell Hart. New York: Macmillan, 1898.

————. "Light on the Underground Railroad," *American Historical Review* 1, no. 3 (April 1896): 445–63.

Silverman, Jason H. "Kentucky, Canada and Extradition: The Jesse Happy Case." *Filson History Club Quarterly* 54 (1980): 50–60.

————. *Unwelcome Guests: Canada West's Response to American Fugitive Slaves, 1800–1865.* Millwood, N.Y.: Associated Faculty Press, 1985.

Silverman, Jason H., and Donna J. Gillie. "'The Pursuit of Knowledge Under Difficulties': Education and the Fugitive Slave in Canada." *Ontario History* 74 (June 1982): 95–112.

Simpson, Donald George. "Negroes in Ontario from Early Times to 1870." Ph.D. diss., University of Western Ontario, 1971.

Singleton, Theresa A., ed. *"I Too, Am American": Archaeological Studies of African-American Life.* Charlottesville: University Press of Virginia, 1999.

Singleton, Theresa A. "The Archaeology of Slave Life." In Charles E. Orser, Jr., ed., *Images of the Recent Past: Readings in Historical Archaeology.* Walnut Creek, Calif.: AltaMira Press, 1996, 141–65.

Singleton, William Henry. *Recollections of My Slavery Days.* Pamphlet. Peter-skill, N.Y., 1922. Reprinted with intro. by Katherine Mellen Charron and David S. Cecelski. Raleigh, N.C.: Department of Cultural Resources, 1999.

Slaney, Catherine. *Family Secrets: Crossing the Colour Line.* Toronto: Natural Heritage Books, 2003.

Slaughter, Rev. Philip, and Raleigh Travers Greeen, comp. *Genealogical and Historical Notes on Culpeper County.* Baltimore: Southern Book Company, 1958.

Smardz, Karolyn, and Carole Schiavetto. "inSite: The Front Street Archaeological Project, Historical Report on the Parliament Buildings of Upper Canada: Part 1, the Construction." MS, Ontario Ministry of Culture, Tourism, and Recreation, Culture Branch, 1987.

Smardz Frost, Karolyn. "Let Your Motto Be Resistance! Fugitive Slaves Thornton and Lucie Blackburn, 1833–1855." Ph.D. diss., University of Waterloo, 2003.

Sobel, Mechal. *Trabelin' On: The Slave Journey to an Afro-Baptist Faith.* Westport, Conn.: Greenwood Press, 1979.

————. *The World They Made Together: Black and White Values in Eighteenth-Century Virginia.* Princeton, N.J.: Princeton University Press, 1987.

"Some Notes Respecting the Pioneer Newspapers of Michigan." *Michigan Pioneer Collections* 1 (1873): 385–95.

Stafford, Hanford D. "Slavery in a Border City: Louisville, 1790–1860." Ph.D. diss., University of Kentucky, 1987.

Stampp, Kenneth. "An Analysis of T. R. Dew's *Review of the Debates in the Virginia Legislature.*" *Journal of Negro History* 27 (1942): 380–87.

————. *The Peculiar Institution: Slavery in the Ante-bellum South.* New York: Knopf, 1956.

Starling, Marion Wilson. *The Slave Narrative: Its Place in American History.* Washington, D.C.: Howard University Press, 1988.

Sterling, Dorothy. *The Making of an Afro-American: Martin Robison Delany, 1812–1885.* Garden City, N.Y.: Doubleday, 1971.

Stevenson, Brenda E. *Life in Black and White: Family and Community in the Slave South.* New York: Oxford University Press, 1996.

Steward, Austin. *Twenty-Two Years a Slave, and Forty Years a Freeman: Embracing a Correspondence of Several Years While President of Wilberforce Colony, London, Canada West,* 1856. Repr., New York: Negro Universities Press, 1983.

Stewart, James Brewer. *Holy Warriors: The Abolitionists and American Slavery.* Rev. ed. New York: Hill and Wang, 1996.

Still, William. *The Underground Rail Road: A Record of Facts, Authentic Narratives, Letters, &C., Narrating the Hardships, Hair-Breadth Escapes and Death Struggles of the Slaves in Their Efforts for Freedom, as Related by Themselves and Others, or Witnessed by the Author; Together with Sketches of Some of the Largest Stockholders and Most Liberal Aiders and Advisers of the Road.* Philadelphia: Porter & Coates, 1872. Repr. Chicago: Johnson, 1970.

Stocking, William. "Slavery and the Underground Railroad." In Burton, Stocking, and Miller, eds., *The City of Detroit, Michigan,* 475–84.

Stouffer, Allen P. *The Light of Nature and the Law of God: Antislavery in Ontario, 1833–1877.* Montreal: McGill-Queen's University Press, 1992.

———. "Michael Willis and the British Roots of Canadian Antislavery." *Slavery and Abolition* (Great Britain) 8 (1987): 294–312.

Stowe, Harriet Beecher. *A Key to Uncle Tom's Cabin: Presenting the Original Facts Upon Which the Story Is Founded, Together with Corroborative Statements Verifying the Truth of the Work.* Boston: J. P. Jewett, 1853.

Stuckey, Sterling. *Slave Culture: Nationalist Theory and the Foundations of Black America.* New York: Oxford University Press, 1987.

Sturge, Joseph. *A Visit to the United States in 1841.* Boston: Dexter S. King, 1842.

Sutton, Jane Macaulay. "Enoch Turner, the Benevolent Brewer." *York Pioneer* 88 (1993): 3–15.

Swisshelm, Jane Grey Cannon. *Half a Century.* Chicago: J. G. Swisshelm, 1880.

Tate, Gayle T. "Free Black Resistance in the Antebellum Era, 1830–1860." *Journal of Black Studies* 28, no. 6 (July 1998): 764–82.

———. "Political Consciousness and Resistance Among Black Antebellum Women." *Women and Politics* 13, no. 1 (1993): 67–89.

Taylor, Alrutheus A. "Negro Congressmen a Generation After." *Journal of Negro History* 7, no. 2 (April 1922): 127–71.

Terry, Gail S. "The Breckinridge Slaves Move West to Kentucky: Family, Community and a Trans-Appalachian Migration, 1790–1815." Seminar paper.

———. "Sustaining the Bonds of Kinship in Trans-Appalachian Migration: 1790–1811." In John Saillant, ed., *Afro-Virginian History and Culture.* New York: Garland Publishing Inc., 1999, 61–84.

Thomas, Owen A. *Niagara's Freedom Trail: A Guide to African-Canadian History on the Niagara Peninsula.* 2nd rev. ed. Thorold, Ont.: The Corporation, 1996.

Thompson, Colin. *Blacks in Deep Snow: Black Pioneers in Canada.* Don Mills, Ont.: J. M. Dent, 1979.

Thompson, William. *History and Legend of Breckinridge County, Kentucky*. Utica, N.Y.: McDowell Publications, 1976.

Trollope, Frances M. *Domestic Manners of the Americans*. New York: Knopf, 1904.

Trotter, Joe W., Jr. *River Jordan: African American Urban Life in the Ohio Valley*. Lexington: University Press of Kentucky, 1998.

Troy, William. *Hair-Breadth Escapes from Slavery to Freedom*. Manchester: W. Bremner, 1861.

Turner, Frederick Jackson. *The Significance of the Frontier in American History, Proceedings of the State Historical Society of Wisconsin*. (Dec. 14, 1893.)

Twain, Mark. *Life on the Mississippi*. New York: HarperCollins, 1950.

Tyler-McGraw, Marie. *At the Falls: Richmond, Virginia, and Its People*. Chapel Hill: University of North Carolina Press, 1994.

Ullman, Victor. *Look to the North Star: A Life of William King*. Boston: Beacon Press, 1969.

Upper Canada. *The Statutes of Upper Canada, to the Time of the Union*. Toronto: R. Stanton Queen's Printer, 1843.

Ure, George P. *Handbook of Toronto*. Toronto: Lovell and Gibson, 1858.

Vlach, John Michael. *Back of the Big House: The Architecture of Plantation Slavery*. Chapel Hill: University of North Carolina Press, 1993.

———. *By the Work of Their Hands: Studies in Afro-American Folklife*. Charlottesville: University Press of Virginia, 1991.

———. "The Shotgun House: An African-American Architectural Legacy." In Dell Upton and John Michael Vlach, eds., *Common Places: Readings in American Vernacular Architecture*. Athens: University of Georgia Press, 1986, 58–78.

———. "Sources of the Shotgun House: African and Caribbean Antecedents for Afro-American Architecture." Ph.D. diss., Indiana University, 1975.

Wade, Richard C. "The Negro in Cincinnati, 1800–1830." *Journal of Negro History* 39, no. 1 (Jan. 1954): 43–57.

———. *Slavery in the Cities: The South, 1820–1860*. New York: Oxford University Press, 1967.

———. *The Urban Frontier: The Rise of Western Cities, 1790–1830*. Harvard Historical Monographs 41. Cambridge, Mass.: Harvard University Press, 1959.

Walker, James W. St. G. "African Canadians." In Paul R. Magocsi, ed., *Encyclopedia of Canada's Peoples*. Toronto: Published for the Multicultural History Society of Ontario by the University of Toronto Press, 1999, 139–76.

———. *A History of Blacks in Canada: A Study Guide for Teachers and Students*. Ottawa: Minister of State Multiculturalism, 1980.

———. *On the Other Side of Jordan*. Ottawa: Canadian Historical Association, 1978.

Walker, Juliet E. K. "The Legal Status of Free Blacks in Early Kentucky, 1792–1825." *Filson Club History Quarterly* 57, no. 4 (1983): 382–95.

Wallis, Frederick A., and Hambleon Tapp. *A Sesquincentennial History of Kentucky*. Hopkinsville, Ky.: The Historical Record Association, 1945.

Walton, George, comp. *York Commercial Directory, Street Guide and Register, 1833–4, with Almanack and Calendar for 1834*. York, U.C.: Printed by Thomas Dalton, 1834.

Walton, Jonathan William. "Blacks in Buxton and Chatham, Ontario, 1830–1890: Did the 49th Parallel Make a Difference?" Ph.D. diss., Princeton University, 1979.

Ward, Samuel Ringgold. *Autobiography of a Fugitive Negro.* 1855. Repr., New York: Arno Press, 1968.

Ward, William S. *A Sesqui-Centennial History of Kentucky.* 4 vols. Hopkinsville, Ky.: Historical Record Association, 1945.

Washington, Booker T. *Frederick Douglass.* London: Hodder and Stoughton, 1906.

Watson, Henry. *The Narrative of Henry Watson, a Fugitive Slave, Written by Himself.* Boston: Bela Marsh, 1848.

Wayne, Michael. "The Black Population of Canada West on the Eve of the American Civil War: A Reassessment Based on the Manuscript Census of 1861." *Histoire Sociale/Social History* 28, no. 56 (Nov. 1995): 465–81.

Weld, Isaac. *Travels Through the States of North America, and the Provinces of Upper and Lower Canada, During the Years 1795, 1796, and 1797.* 2nd ed. London: John Stockdale, 1799.

Weld, Theodore Dwight. *American Slavery as It Is: Testimony of a Thousand Witnesses.* New York: Anti-Slavery Society, 1839.

West, Bruce. *Toronto.* Toronto: Doubleday Canada, 1967.

Westerfield, Thomas W., ed. *Kentucky Genealogy and Biography.* Vol. 1. Owensboro, Ky.: Genealogical Reference, 1970.

Wheeler, Jacob D. *A Practical Treatise on the Law of Slavery, Being a Compilation of All the Decisions Made on That Subject in the Several Courts of the United States and State Courts, with Copious Notes and References to the Statutes and Other Authorities.* New York: A. Pollock, 1837.

Wilbur, Henry Watson. *President Lincoln's Attitude Towards Slavery and Emancipation; with a Review of Events Before and Since the Civil War.* New York: Biblo and Tannen, 1970.

Wilentz, Sean, ed. *David Walker's Appeal in Four Articles.* New York: Hill and Wang, 1968.

Williams, Eric. *Capitalism and Slavery.* 2nd ed. Chapel Hill: University of North Carolina Press, 1994.

Williams, John R. "Sketch of the Life of General John R. Williams." *Collections and Researches Made by the Michigan Pioneer and Historical Society* 29 (1901): 492–96.

Winch, Julie. "Philadelphia and the Other Underground Railroad." *Pennsylvania Magazine of History and Biography* 3, no. 1 (Jan. 1987): 3–25.

Winks, Robin W. *The Blacks in Canada: A History.* Montreal: McGill-Queen's University Press, 1971.

———. *The Canadian Negro: A Historical Assessment: The Problem of Identity: Part II. Journal of Negro History* 54, no. 1 (Jan. 1969): 1–18.

———. *Canada and the United States: The Civil War Years.* 4th ed. Montreal: McGill-Queen's University Press, 1998.

———. "'A Sacred Animosity:' Abolitionism in Canada." In Martin Duberman, ed., *The Antislavery Vanguard: New Essays on the Abolitionists.* Princeton, N.J.: Princeton University Press, 1965, 301–42.

Winks, Robin W., Josiah Henson, William Wells Brown, Austin Steward, and Benjamin Drew. *Four Fugitive Slave Narratives.* Reading, Mass: Addison-Wesley, 1969.

Witherell, Judge B.F.H. "Papers Relative to Insurrection of Negroes." *Michigan Pioneer and Historical Collections* 12 (1887): 591–93.

Wolf, Eric. *Europe and the People Without History.* Berkeley: University of California Press, 1987.

Woodson, Carter G. *A Century of Negro Migration.* Washington, D.C.: The Association for the Study of Negro Life and History, 1918.

———. *Free Negro Heads of Families in the United States in 1830.* Washington, D.C.: Association for the Study of Negro Life and History, 1925.

———. "The Negroes of Cincinnati Prior to the Civil War." *Journal of Negro History* 1 (1916): 1–22.

Woodson, June Barber. "A Century with the Negroes of Detroit, 1830–1930." *A.M.E. Church Review* 68 (1953): 38–49.

Woodward, C. Vann. *The Strange Career of Jim Crow.* 3rd rev. ed. New York: Oxford University Press, 1974.

———, ed. *Mary Chesnut's Civil War.* New Haven, Conn.: Yale University Press, 1981, 29.

Woodward, Judge. "Letter from Judge Woodward, Relative to the Subject of Slavery." *Michigan Pioneer and Historical Collections* 12 (1888): 511–22.

Work Projects Administration. Vol. 7 of *Kentucky Narratives. Slave Narratives: A Folk History of Slavery in the United States from Interviews with Former Slaves.* Washington, D.C., 1941.

Wright, Gavin. *The Political Economy of the Old South: Households, Markets, and Wealth in the Nineteenth Century.* New York: Norton, 1978.

Wulfeck, Dorothy Ford. *Culpeper County, Virginia, Will Books B and C, Court Suits, Loose Papers, Instructions.* Privately printed, 1965.

Yater, George H. *Two Hundred Years at the Falls of the Ohio: A History of Louisville and Jefferson County.* Louisville, Ky.: Filson Club and Liberty National Bank, 1987.

Yee, Shirley J. "Gender Ideology and Black Women as Community-Builders in Ontario, 1850–70." *Canadian Historical Review* 75 (1994): 53–73.

Yellin, Jean Fagan, and John C. Van Horne, eds. *The Abolitionist Sisterhood: Women's Political Culture in Antebellum America.* Ithaca, N.Y.: Cornell University Press, 1994.

Young, Florence Nelson, and Virgil D. Young, eds. *Mason County Deed Book Abstracts.* Denver: Western Heraldry Organization, 1973.

Yzenbaard, John H. "The Crosswhite Case." *Michigan History* 53 (Summer 1969): 131–43.

Zorn, Roman J. "An Arkansas Fugitive Slave Incident and Its International Repercussions." *Arkansas Historical Quarterly* 16 (Summer 1957): 139–49.

———. "Criminal Extradition Menaces the Canadian Haven for Fugitive Slaves, 1841–1861." *Canadian Historical Review* 38 (1957): 284–94.

PRIMARY SOURCES

REPOSITORIES IN CANADA

Library and Archives of Canada

Acts of the Parliament of Upper Canada
Askin Family Papers
George Brown Papers
Mary Anne Shadd Cary Papers
Census Return for Upper Canada, Canada West and Canada, 1842–1891
Colonial Office Papers
Sir John Colborne Papers
Colonial Office Papers
Executive Council of Upper Canada Records and Upper Canada State Papers:

> Correspondence of the Civil Secretary
> Lieutenant Governor's Correspondence
> Minutes of the Executive Council
> Papers of the Attorney General
> State Submissions to the Executive Council
> Upper Canada Sundries

Daniel G. Hill Papers
Journals of the Legislative Council of Upper Canada
Journals of the House of Assembly of Upper Canada
Journals of the Legislative Assembly of Upper Canada, State Book J
William King Collection
George Williams Map of Toronto, 1813

Archives of Ontario

Benchbooks of Justice Sir John Beverley Robinson
Death Registers, Ontario. General Index Books, A–Z, 1890, 1895
George Taylor Denison Fonds

J. Eaton Company Fonds
William Hands Papers
Daniel G. Hill Papers
Mackenzie-Lindsey Papers
Alvin McCurdy Papers
John Beverley Robinson Family Papers
Simcoe Family Fonds
John Strachan Papers
Hiram Walker Collection
Western District Court Judgment Rolls and Filings
Western District Court Minute Books
Wills of Thornton and Lucie Blackburn

Baldwin Room, Toronto Public Library

Anderson Ruffin Abbott Papers
Annual Report Presented to the Anti-Slavery Society of Canada by Its Executive Committee. Toronto: Brown & Co., 1851.
Constitution and By-laws of the Anti-Slavery Society of Canada. Toronto: George, 1852.
George Taylor Denison Papers
Elgin Association Annual Reports, 1852–55
Map, Photograph, and Art Collection (esp. John Ross Robertson Collection)
Elizabeth Russell Diary
Larratt William Smith Diary

City of Toronto Archives

Fire Insurance Maps and Historic Map Collection
Minutes of Toronto City Council
Petition from Toronto blacks for ban on minstrel shows, 1842
Photograph Collections:

   Department of Public Works, Ser. 372
   City Engineer's Department Photographs, Ser. 376
   James Sammon Collection, Fonds 1231

Toronto business and street directories, various years
Toronto Tax Assessment Rolls
Toronto Police Court Records

Toronto District School Board Archives

Duncan Fraser, "Sackville Street Public School, Toronto," typescript historical report for University of Toronto, May 1980
Minutes of the Board of Trustees, 1887–95
Minutes of the Properties Committee, 1887–95
Minutes of the Sites and Buildings Committee, 1887–95
Vertical files: Enoch Turner Schoolhouse, Palace Street School, Sackville Street School

Buxton National Historic Site and Museum

William King Daybook
Map and Photograph Collection
Mary Jane Robinson Correspondence, 1854
Abraham Doras Shadd Account books
Garrison Shadd Store ledger
A Sketch of the Buxton Mission and Elgin Settlement, Raleigh, Canada West. Birmingham: Printer and Law Stationer, ca. 1870
Tax Assessment Rolls for Kent County
Henry K. Thomas and James Rapier Family files

Chatham-Kent Black History Society, W.I.S.H. Centre

John Brown Convention papers and records
Martin R. Delany files
Map and Photograph Collection
Vertical files: Blackburn, Jackson, Smith families

Marsh Collection Society (Essex County History)

William R. Woods. Sketch of Sandwich, from Springwells, Michigan, August 13, 1833

Mount Pleasant Group of Cemeteries

Toronto Necropolis: Interment Cards for the Blackburns and George Brown

McMaster University, School of Divinity, Hamilton, Ontario

Amherstburg Baptist Association Minute books
Sandwich Baptist Church Minute book

North American Black Historical Museum, Amherstburg

Maps and Photograph Collections
Vertical files: Blackburn, Jackson, Nelson, Smith families

D. W. Weldon Library Special Collections, University of Western Ontario

Black Canadian Research Project Papers, 1972–76
Fred Landon Collection
William McClure Diary
Alexander Lovell Murray Papers
"Papers and Letters of Annie Straith Jamieson, Author, Concerning Reverend William King of the Elgin Settlement, Raleigh Township, 1859, 1870, 1895–1941, 1859."

Windsor Community Museum and Archives

Fort Malden "Black History" File
Hiram Walker Collection

REPOSITORIES IN THE UNITED STATES

District of Columbia

National Archives, Washington, D.C.

An Ordinance for the Government of the Territory of the United States
    North-West of the River Ohio, passed July 13, 1787
United States Census, various years

*Howard University, Moorland-Spingarn Research Center,
Washington, D.C.*

Mary Anne Shadd Cary Papers
James T. Rapier Papers

Michigan

Bentley Historical Collection, University of Michigan

Robert E. Hayden, "History of the Negro in Michigan," MS, Historical Col-
    lections of Michigan
William Lambert Papers, Historical Records Survey, Michigan, Papers of
    Blacks in Michigan: Collections in Private Hands
Michigan Supreme Court Records
Nathan Macy Thomas Papers, 1818–89
Stevens Thomson Mason Papers, 1812–43. File No. 23. "Addresses and Mes-
    sages, 1834–1840, undated."
"Works Progress Administration," Michigan, Papers and Records

Burton Historical Collection, Detroit Public Library

Census of Detroit, Fifth Census of the United States, 1830
Charles Askin Papers, 1801–36
John Askin Papers, 1704–1891
Marshall Chapin Papers and correspondence, 1828–40
George Catlin Papers
Clarence M. Burton Scrapbooks
Detroit city and business directories, various years
Detroit City Council Minutes, 1833
William Douglass. "The Colored People of Detroit: Their Trials, Persecu-
    tions and Escapes, Containing Sketches of the Riots of 1833, 1839, 1850,
    and 1863 . . ." Pamphlet. Repr. of articles from the *Detroit Daily Post*, Jan.
    and Feb. 1870
Friend Palmer's Scrapbook

Historical Newspaper Collection
Historical Map and Image Collection
Journal of the Common Council for the City of Detroit, 1824–43, 243–47
William Lambert Papers: "Negro" File, Historical Records of Michigan,
    Michigan Historical Collections
John Mason, Jr., Papers, 1818–1910
Stevens Thomson Mason Correspondence, 1831–42
Benjamin F. H. Witherell Papers
William Woodbridge Papers Burton Historical Collection, Detroit Public
    Library
Augustus Brevoort Woodward Papers and Correspondence
Samuel Zug's Scrapbook

W. L. Clements Library, University of Michigan, Ann Arbor

Theodore Dwight Weld Papers

Michigan State Archives, Lansing, Michigan

"Thornton Blackburn, Fugitive Slave, 1833." Papers of the Secretary of State,
    RG 56–26, box 198, folder 9
Journal of the Legislative Council of the Territory of Michigan. Monroe, Mich.,
    1827.
Laws of the Territory of Michigan. 4 vols. Detroit, 1827

Kentucky

Bracken County Courthouse

Deeds and Land registry abstracts
Indenture for apprenticeship of Franky Davis

Breckinridge County Archives

Deeds for Alexander, Brown, Hardin, and Oldham properties
Guardian bonds
Land registry abstract books
Order books
Plat map of Hardinsburg
Tax assessment rolls
Will and probate records, Gideon Brown

City of Louisville Archives

Louisville City Council Minutes, 1833

Cave Hill Cemetery, Louisville

Burial records of Brown, Bullock, Churchill, Oldham, and Talbot families

Filson Historical Society

Blackburn Family Papers
Bodley-Clark Papers
John Cabell Breckinridge Papers and Photographs
Churchill Family Papers
Anderson Doniphan Daybooks
Genealogical Collections. Families: Ballard, Brown, Churchill, McKnight, Oldham, Rogers, Weir
Map, Photograph, and Art Collections
Records of St. Paul's Episcopal Church, Louisville, Ky.
Stuart Robinson Papers
Rogers Clark Ballard Thruston Papers

Jefferson County Department for Historic Preservation and Archives

Commissioners' deed books and index
Death registers
Louisville city and business directories
Map and photograph collection
Marriage bonds and registers
Probate records, wills of George Backus, Virgil McKnight, John Pope Oldham, Malinda Oldham
Tax assessment rolls

Kentucky Department for Libraries and Archives

Kentucky Vital Statistics, 1852–59
Files of Jefferson County Courts

Kentucky Historical Society

H. S. Tanner. *A New Map of Kentucky, with Its Roads & Distances from Place to Place Along the Stage & Steam Boat Routes.* Philadelphia: H. S. Tanner, 1839.
Vertical files: Blackburn, Brown, McKnight, Rogers, Smith, Morton, Murphy, Oldham, Talbot, Weir. Also counties, including Bracken, Breckinridge, Hardin, Jefferson, Mason, Meade, Nelson, and Oldham

Mason County Museum Center

Deeds, Wills, Orders, Marriages for Mason County
Cemetery records
Slave sales, deeds, and emancipation records
Maysville directories, various
Tax assessment rolls
Vertical Files: Blackburn, Brown, Doniphan, Duke, Lashbrooke, Marshall, Morton, Murphy, Smith, Taylor

Meade County Courthouse

Deeds: Alexander, Brown, Oldham, and Washington families
Guardian bonds
Land registry abstract books
Slave importation declarations
Slave sales, deeds, and emancipation records

University of Kentucky, Margaret I. King Library, Special Collections

Breckinridge Family Papers
J. Winston Coleman Papers
Thomas Henry Hines Papers
Photograph, Map, and Art Collections
Washington, Kentucky, Trustees' Minutes

Virginia

Thomas Balch Library, Leesburg, Va.

Land registry abstracts
Vertical files: Davis, Blackburn, and Smith families

Virginia Historical Society

Backus Family Papers
Brown Family Papers
Mason Family Papers
Vertical Files: Blackburns, Rippon Lodge, Prince William County, Virginia

Miscellaneous Repositories

California Department of Insurance

Records of companies that insured the lives of slaves

Houghton Library, Harvard University, Cambridge, Mass.

Samuel Gridley Howe Papers
"Statement of Property Owned by Coloured Persons in the Ward of St. John
Together with the Assessed Value and the Amount of Taxes Paid for
1862," in American Freedmen's Commission Records.

New Jersey Historical Society

Benjamin Drew Letters

Ohio Historical Society

Wilbur H. Siebert Papers, Ohio Historical Society

Pennsylvania Historical Society

Pennsylvania Anti-Slavery Society Collection
William Still Papers

Schomberg Collection, New York Public Library

Robin W. Winks Papers

Texas State Archives and Libraries Commission

Republic of Texas Claims

Wisconsin Historical Society

Draper Manuscripts

ACKNOWLEDGMENTS

Fugitive slave history is a complex and time-consuming field of research. Still more so is reconstructing the personal lives of individuals who, like the Blackburns, experienced lifelong illiteracy. Photographs of neither Thornton and Lucie nor of the African Americans and African Canadians who helped them in their quest for liberty have surfaced. I hope the people who worked so hard to help me find images over the years know how much I appreciate their efforts.

The idea of writing about the Blackburns came about during the archaeological excavations at their home in 1985. Noted scholars of African America Drs. James Oliver Horton and Lois E. Horton flew to Toronto after hearing about the dig on a Washington, D.C., radio program. This volume was their idea, and I thank them from the bottom of my heart.

The Ontario Ministry of Culture provided substantial early funding, as did the Toronto Board of Education, Multiculturalism Canada, and the Ontario Heritage Foundation. Nola Crewe, Ron Halford, Edward McKeown, Audrey Howard, Rob Mewhinney, and later on Ron Kendall of the Toronto Board of Education made possible Canada's first Underground Railroad dig and the educational programs that developed out of it. Board Archivist Donald Nethery and his partner, Gary Moriarity, were there for me from the beginning, and it is a great sorrow that Donald never lived to see the final results.

Special thanks are due to Peter Hamalainen, my archaeology and education partner for more than a decade, material culturalist Ellen Blaubergs, the late Rod Crocker, and all the staff and students of Toronto's much-lamented Archaeological Resource Centre. We all miss Duncan Scherberger, whose public relations talents made Thornton and Lucie come alive for so many people in the summer of 1985. Christopher Koch was site photographer, and I am honored by his friendship to this day. In addition to the hardworking Ministry of Culture archaeologists, especially Roberta O'Brien, who discovered the site with me, I have always been very grateful for the support of the Ontario Black Historical Society. President Emeritus Dr. Daniel Hill, President Paul Anderson, and executive directors Lorraine Hubbard and Glace Lawrence contributed materially to the success of the project, and particularly to ensuring its high public profile. Many years later, Rosemary Sadlier of the OBHS petitioned to have the Blackburns designated Persons of National Historic Significance. In Kentucky, Celeste Lanier and Diane Wells were responsible for the Blackburn plaque erected in Louisville in April 2002.

Dr. Anne Butler of Kentucky State University hosted me for literally months at her home, arranged the Blackburn celebrations in Louisville, and shared both her own research and her dedication to truth in history with me. The Kentucky African-American Heritage Commission, chaired by Dr. Blaine Hudson of the University of Louisville and directed by Nicole Harris, funded my study of the Blackburns' lives in slavery. Don Ball, formerly of the U.S. Army Corps of Engineers, befriended me, put me up, and "did history" with me whenever I was in Louisville. Kentucky archaeologists Anne Bader, Nancy O'Malley, and Phil DiBlasi provided assistance at important points in the process.

The staffs of Louisville Filson Historical Society (thanks, Jim Holmberg, Pen Bogert, and Becky Rice!), the Kentucky State Archives (Jim Pritchard, I appreciate everything you do for me), the Kentucky Historical Society, the Breckinridge County Archives (Karen Schafer and Sylvia Hinton, you have been so helpful), and Maysville's Kentucky Gateway Museum Center deserve endless thanks. Alicestyne Turley-Adams and Dr. Lindsey Apple of Georgetown College in Kentucky, as well as Jerry Gore of Maysville's National Underground Railroad Museum, have given crucial assistance. My "genealogy buddies," some known only over the Internet, are legion, but I will mention here Anne Huntsman, Jim Hancock, Mary Ann Dickerson Shoemaker, Patricia Duncan, and especially Farris Womack, who manages the Talbot family Web site and helped me locate descendants of the slaveholders involved in the Blackburn story. As for the Chovil family and Susan Curran White, her brother, and her sister, I can't thank them enough for sharing the Brown and Oldham portraits with the world.

Further afield, a Mellon Fellowship from the Virginia Historical Society made research in Richmond possible, where the VHS Director for Library Services, Frances Pollard, deserves special mention, as does my dear friend and perennial Virginia hostess, Martha Williams. The late John Hemphill and his wife, Dr. Gail Terry, were extremely helpful. I must thank the excellent people at the National Archives and Library of Congress in Washington, D.C. Peter Hanes of the U.S. Parks Service has been both enthusiastic and caring, while independent historian Charles Brewer has shared his prodigious knowledge and his time. I also received a fellowship from the Anderson Centre at Red Wing, Minnesota, and while at the Institute for Minnesota Archaeology I spent hours ruminating over my research with Dr. Clark Dobbs and Rhoda Gilman. Ellen Eslinger, thanks for sharing your unpublished research with me.

My appreciation and admiration go to Michigan historian Dr. Norman McRae, who has been so generous with his own superbly researched Blackburn data. The staffs of the Burton Historical Collection at the Detroit Public Library, the Michigan State Archives at Lansing, and the Clement Library and the Bentley Historical Collection at the University of Michigan have been very helpful, and the Bentley also provided research funding. I hope Dr. David Katzman will accept my thanks for his critical review of the relevant chapters. To the late Norman Leach and to Bobbie Fowlkes-Davis of Detroit's Second Baptist Church, I offer both thanks and praise for your lifelong dedication to preserving so valuable and unique a heritage.

In Toronto, the people at the Baldwin Room (especially Christine Mossop and Alan Walker) and the City of Toronto Archives (thanks, Karen Teeple, John Huxil, Steve MacKinnon, and Glenda Williams) have gone above and beyond the call of duty to assist in this research. I miss Leon Warmski at the Archives of Ontario, who passed on many tidbits of history. My friends and coauthors on other projects, Dr. Afua Cooper and Adrienne Shadd, have argued at length the finer points of black history research with me, for which I am ever grateful. I also learned much from Shannon Ricketts, Derek Cook, and Owen Thomas at Parks Canada. I would be remiss not to mention my friend Judith McErvel, who has shared both her archival expertise and many wide-ranging conversations about history with me. Tom Brooks, I truly appreciate your depth of knowledge about Canadians in the U.S. Colored Troops.

I am particularly indebted to the enormous depth and breadth of knowledge of Canada's preeminent historian of race, Dr. James W. St. G. Walker, which informs this work throughout. His assistance to the research began well before I first became his doctoral student at the University of Waterloo in 1997. My costudent and dear friend Stephanie Bangarth has always been there to listen, critique, and argue, something I greatly value. Thanks also to secretaries Irene Majer and Nancy Birss at the History Department, for absolutely everything. The Social Sciences and Humanities Research Council of Canada funded my doctoral and postdoctoral work on the Underground Railroad, and University of Waterloo Alumni Fund bursaries always arrived just in the nick of time. I would like to thank Dr. Leslie

Sanders at York University's Atkinson College for her friendship and unfailing support.

The former fugitive slave communities of Southwestern Ontario remain today lasting memorials to the courage, ingenuity, and dedication to the freedom of their ancestors. While studying the Blackburns, I have traveled tens of thousands of miles but in no place have I received a warmer welcome than among my North Buxton family. My deepest love to Alice Newby, Blair and Quinn, and to Duane Newby, whom we lost far too soon. The Dudleys, Princes, Middletons, and all my other friends there know they hold my heart, always. I will never forget the help I have received from Bryan Prince, who for almost fifteen years has freely given his prodigious knowledge of Ontario's African Canadian heritage to help make this book a reality. This volume is also presented in loving memory of Margot Freeman. To Gwen and John Robinson in Chatham, Elise Harding-Davis in Amherstburg, Barbara Carter and Steven Cook at Uncle Tom's Cabin in Dresden, and Wilma Morrison at Niagara Falls, thank you so much for welcoming me, and for not allowing even the smallest detail of this proud history to be forgotten.

To my agent, Denise Bukowski, and to my editors at FSG, John Glusman, and his assistants Aodaoin O'Floinn and Corinna Barsan, and, most recently and wonderfully, Courtney Hodell and her assistant, Zachary Woolfe, I cannot express how grateful I am for the years of hard work that helped bring this project to fruition. Sarah Russo and Kathy Daneman, bless you for your talent and enthusiasm as publicists. Patrick Crean, publisher at Thomas Allen Books in Toronto, has become a close friend, and I do appreciate Janice Zawerbny's and Liza Zaritzky's efforts on my behalf. My employers at the Ontario Historical Society have been generous both with their support and in making time available to me, and I am grateful.

On a personal note, I want to thank my oldest friends Peggy Tuitt, Anita Zijdemans, and my godbabies. I wish that my incredibly supportive mother, Laura Smardz, who taught the most challenged of Toronto's children for almost thirty years, my father, Stanley Smardz, a concentration camp survivor and hero of the French Resistance, and my first husband, Bruce Heyding, who always believed, were all alive today to see that "Karolyn's book" is finally finished.

Above all, I must thank my perfect husband, Norm Frost. He is an awesome researcher in his own right, has pored over every word I have written, and loves me no matter what. Norm, you enrich my life every day and I could not have done this without you. My beautiful stepchildren, Jamie, Sara, Graham, and Jason, are enormously proud of me, and are really, really glad that *I've Got a Home in Glory Land* is finally done.

INDEX

Abbott, Anderson Ruffin, 272–74, 287, 288, 296, 315, 328, 330–31, 333, 393*n*, 398*n*

Abbott, Ellen Toyer, 271, 287, 315

Abbott, Wilson Ruffin, 271, 275, 287, 288, 296, 297, 303, 315, 334

Abbott family, 332, 339

abolitionist movement, xii, xviii, xxiv, 42–43, 85–87, 97, 123, 163, 238, 271, 310, 313; in Britain, 209, 249–50; in Canada, 194–97, 211, 219, 238, 260, 261, 272, 273, 281, 284–86, 288–94,312; Fugitive Slave Law and, 281, 282; fund raising in, 297; in New England, 156; Quakers in, 35, 97, 235, 248; Southern diatribe against, 151; support for John Brown in, 307; women in, 65, 90, 289–90

Act to Prevent the Further Introduction of Slaves, and to Limit the Term of Contracts for Servitude Within This Province (Canada, 1793), 24, 196

Act to Regulate Blacks and Mulattoes, and to Punish the Kidnapping of Such Persons (Michigan Territory, 1827), 157, 163, 169

Act of Union (Canada, 1841), 246

Adams, Henry, 92, 101, 260

Adams, John Quincy, 205

Aetna Insurance Company, 134

Allen, Robert, 149

Allensworth, Colonel Allen, 110

American Anti-Slavery Society, xviii, 248, 294

American Colonization Society, 65, 86, 148, 238, 294

American Revolution, xiii, xvi, xxviii, xx, xxiv, 19–20, 153, 208, 310; Canada during, 140, 195, 207, 259

American Society of Free Persons of Color, 294

Amherstburg Baptist Association, 155, 236, 334

Anderson, John, 251

Anderson, John W., 41

Anderson, Osborne, 308, 313

Anderson, Robert, 309

Anglicans, 211, 215, 217, 230, 260–61, 280, 291, 331–32, 343

antislavery movement, *see* abolitionist movement

Anti-Slavery Society of Canada (ASC), 288–91, 295, 339, 346, 385*n*

Ashburton, Lord, 249

Askin, Charles, 218

Askin, John, 218

Atwater, Caleb, 72, 73

Augusta, Alexander T., 315

Austin, Lewis, 177, 179, 180, 193, 201, 219, 225, 228, 229, 239

Bâby, François, 198, 202, 214, 217, 219, 224, 248, 384*n*

Bâby, Jacques, 200

Backus, Charles W., 96–97, 102, 104–107

Backus, Charlotte, 94, 95, 97–102, 104, 106, 107, 146, 166

Backus, Colonel Electus, 146, 189, 372*n*, 380*n*

Backus, George, 94–104, 106, 107, 127, 146, 164, 166, 371*n*

Backus, Henry, 95, 102–106, 128, 146

Bacon's Rebellion, 20

Bagot, Charles, 247, 248

Bancroft, Frederic, 114

Bank of Kentucky, 109–11, 131

Bank of the United States, 109

Banks, Robert, 149, 292
Baptists (black), 33, 106, 155, 213, 334,
   388*n*, 391*n*; in Detroit, 141, 150–52, 173,
   236, 239; in Louisville, 92, 94, 101, 124;
   in Toronto, 257, 259, 261, 270, 278, 280,
   311, 337–38
Barber, Charles, 328–29
Barry, James, 348
Barry, Louisa, 348
Barry, Minnie, 348
Bayless, Thornton, 11, 127
Beatty (fugitive slave), 180, 193, 219, 225,
   229, 239
Beatty, Charlotte Louisa, 332
Beatty, William Henry, 332
Bell, Robert, 94, 96, 102, 103, 105, 134–35
Bell & Backus, 94–98, 102–106, 134
Ben (fugitive slave), 158
Berlin, Ira, 148
Bibb, Henry, 105–106, 117, 172, 250, 284,
   288, 291, 293, 295–97
Bibb, Mary, 284, 295, 409*n*
Birney, James G., 260
Bishop, Paul, 268
Blackburn, Alfred (Thornton's brother), 40,
   42, 45, 66, 114, 160, 261, 263, 276, 283,
   311, 312, 330, 348, 350, 361*n*, 362*n*; birth
   of, 25–26; childhood of, 27, 32, 33; death
   of, 329, 399*n*; employment in Toronto of,
   257, 275, 280; escape of, 14, 256; health
   problems of, 304; reunion of Sibby and,
   277–78; reunion of Thornton and,
   256–58; during Upper Canadian Rebellion, 274, 275
Blackburn, Benjamin, 327
Blackburn, John (Thornton's brother), 25
Blackburn, Julia Churchill, 318–20, 399*n*
Blackburn, Lucie (Ruthie), xi–xiii, xxi,
   250–52, 327, 328, 339, 350–53; in
   Amherstburg, 195, 226, 234–37, 258; in
   antislavery movement of, 283, 286, 289,
   290, 294, 297, 305; arrest and trial in
   Michigan of, 162–70; arrival in Canada
   of, 193–94, 196; cab company of xi–xii,
   268–69, 341; during Civil War, 311, 314;
   death of, 341–42, 348–49; in Detroit,
   139–51, 154–55, 152, 160–61, 255; escape
   from slavery of, xiv, xvii–xviii, xxii–xxv,
   3–4, 6–14, 117–29, 131–35, 159, 309,
   352–53; extradition case against,
   198–204, 210–33, 240, 252–53; financial
   success of, 269–71, 276, 286, 331, 332,
   337, 347; Jackson family and, 300, 301,
   334; in Louisville, 94–100, 102–105, 146,
   255; marriage of Thornton and, 99–102;

monetary value placed on, 6, 7, 108, 208;
   name change of, 194; old age of, 342–45,
   346–48; origins of, 95; religious affiliation
   of, 150, 152, 213, 261, 280, 331–32, 343;
   rescue of, xii, xxiv, 172–75, 180–90, 198,
   225, 228, 243, 249, 307; sale of, 6–7, 103,
   106–109, 111–16; Sibby and, 277–78,
   304; in Toronto black community, 269,
   271, 281, 332, 335; Toronto home of,
   xxiv, 263–67, 278, 287, 329–31, 342–44;
   white connections of, 279–80, 285, 331,
   332
Blackburn, Luke Pryor, 317–20, 399*n*
Blackburn, Richard, 359*n*
Blackburn, Sibby (Thornton's mother), xxi,
   21–23, 44, 66, 114, 160, 257, 311–13,
   318, 360*n*, 361*n*; birth of, xviii, 19; birth
   of sons of, 25–26, 28, 147, 359*n*; childhood separation of sons from, 27, 31–33,
   51; death of, 304, 329, 334; hiring out of,
   27–29, 32; in migration from Virginia to
   Kentucky, 17, 20; rescue of, 14, 275–78
Blackburn, Colonel Thomas, 19, 318, 359*n*
Blackburn, Thornton, xi–xiii, xvi, xxi, 252,
   327, 328, 339, 350–53; adolescence of,
   36, 45–55, 57, 59–69; Alfred reunited
   with, 256–58; in Amherstburg, 226,
   234–37, 239, 258; in antislavery and self-
   help movement, 283, 285–86, 290, 292,
   294–98, 302–305, 328; arrest and trial in
   Michigan of, 162–70; arrival in Canada
   of, 193–97; birth of, 15, 28, 153; cab
   company of xi–xii, 268–69, 318–20, 331,
   332, 341, 350; childhood of, 5, 29–40, 43;
   during Civil War, 311, 312, 314, 317,
   319, 320; death of, 341–42, 346–47; in
   Detroit, 139–52, 154–55, 158, 160–61,
   255; employment at Osgoode Hall of,
   262–63, 267; escape of, xiv, xvii–xviii,
   xxii–xxv, 3–4, 6–14, 117–29, 131–35, 159,
   309, 352–53; extradition case against,
   198–204, 210–33, 240, 252–53; financial
   success of, xi–xii, 269–71, 276, 286, 331,
   332, 337, 347; hiring out of, 76–77;
   Jackson family and, 300, 301, 334; Lightfoot family and, 34, 44, 151–52, 334; in
   Louisville of, 69–89, 91–96, 255, 318;
   marriage of Ruthie and, 99–102; monetary value placed on, 51, 69, 208; naturalization of, 272; old age of, 316, 330,
   337–38, 342–45, 351; petition of, 215–18;
   religious affiliation of, 33, 92, 150, 151,
   213, 261, 280, 331–32, 343; rescue of, xii,
   xxiv, 170–90, 195, 198, 209, 225, 227–28,
   239, 243, 249, 307; and sale of Ruthie,

103, 111–12, 114, 116; Sibby rescued by, 274–78; in Toronto black community, 269, 271–73, 281, 332, 335; Toronto home of, xxiv, 263–66, 277–78, 287, 329–31, 342–44, 250; white connections of, 279–80, 285, 331, 332

Blackburn Riots (Detroit, 1833), xii, xxiv, 176–90, 225, 239, 240, 244, 249, 257, 276; demands for return of participants in, 222, 229; evidence on, in extradition case, 210, 213, 217, 219, 223, 227–28, 232

Black Code (Code Noir), 120–21, 156–58

Black Hawk War, 143–44, 155

Black Loyalists, 207, 259

Black Nationalism, 315

Black Refugees, 207

Blair (slave), 99, 106

Bleeding Kansas, 305–306

Bodley, William S., 130

Bond Head, Francis, 241, 243, 245, 246

Boone, Daniel, 16, 20, 52

Boone, Jacob, 16

Boone, Rebecca, 20

Booth, John Wilkes, 320

Brady, General Hugh, 146, 189

Breckinridge, Issa Desha, 317–18

Breckinridge, John Cabell, 243, 318, 362n

British-American Anti-Slavery Society, 272, 289

British American Institute, 283, 286, 303

British antislavery movement, 65, 209, 211, 267

British law, freedoms guaranteed by, 203–207

Brooks, John W., 292

Brouse, Henry, 347

Brown, Ellen, 237

Brown, George, 285, 287–88, 296, 308, 311, 314, 325, 336, 338, 346

Brown, Gideon, 51, 53–55, 58–59, 63–64, 125, 162, 364n, 365n, 377n; death of, 67, 165, 216, 347; estate of, 63, 64, 67–69, 77, 78, 93, 128, 129, 368n; marriage of, 56–57; medical practice of, 49, 54–55, 57, 368n

Brown, James, 54–55

Brown, James Charles, 86–87, 121, 260, 275, 292

Brown, John, 154, 306–308, 313, 322, 328

Brown, Joseph, 302

Brown, Nelson, 237, 388n

Brown, Susan Talbot, 53, 59, 92–93, 125, 131, 168, 219, 357n, 370n, 387n; and

Blackburns' marriage, 99; household slaves and, 58, 63–64; marriage of, 56–57; Thornton hired out by, 10, 76, 78; Weir as agent for, 162–63; widowhood of, 68–70, 165

Brown, William Wells, xiv, 29, 59

Brown family, 285

Buchanan, James, 243, 318

Bucklin, John C., 163–64

Bull, Charles M., 187

Bullock, Sophia Oldham, 75, 128, 130

Bullock, William Fontaine, 75, 128, 130

Bull Run, Battle of, 311

Burnett, M., 149

Burns, Anthony, 282

Burwell family, 100–101

Bush, William, 149

Butler, Alexander, 180, 193, 219, 225, 229, 239

Butler, Ann, 149

Butler, William, 149, 150, 239

Buxton, Thomas Fowell, 287

Caldwell & Ernest, 104

Calhoun, John C., xvi, 66, 270

Campbell, Israel, 36

Canada, Confederation of, 325–26

Canadian Mill and Mercantile Association, 296, 298, 302–305, 328

Canadian National Exhibition, 341, 347

Cary, Mary Ann Shadd, 289, 295, 297, 307, 313, 315, 328, 397n

Cary, Newton, 273

Cary, Thomas, 313

Casey family, 339

Cass, Lewis, 141, 188–89, 201–202

Castleman, David, 242–43, 245

Catholics, 51, 141, 260

Chadwick, Edward Marion, 348

Chadwick & Beatty, 331, 332, 347–49

Chapin, Marshall, 163, 182, 183, 186, 188, 190, 198

Charles, John, 274

Chesnut, James, 28

Chesnut, Mary Boykin, 28

Chewett, Alexander, 212

Children's Aid Society, 336

Chinese immigrants, 339

Chipman, Henry, 162, 167, 171, 174, 216, 227; arrest and return of Blackburns ordered by, 164, 165, 169; Frazier's case against, 202, 213; riots as response to decision of, 189, 190, 222

Christian, Washington, 257, 259–61, 272, 273, 278, 391n

Christianity, 33, 160; *see also specific denominations*
Christy Minstrels, 341
Churchill, Abigail Oldham, 318, 320
Churchill, Emily Ann, 320, 399*n*
Churchill, Samuel, 320
Churchill family, 56, 80, 128
Church of England, *see* Anglicans
Civil Rights Act (U.S., 1866), 339
Civil War, xviii, 49, 52, 66, 207, 251, 310–22, 329, 338; black soldiers in, 110–11, 272, 313–15; events leading to, 305–309; outbreak of, 204, 309, 310; Union victory in, 325
Clark, Ephraim, 149
Clark, General George Rogers, 78
Clark, William, 78
Clarke, Lewis, 32, 37, 194
Clarke brothers, 115
Clarkson, Thomas, 65
Clay, Henry, xvi, 34, 46, 65, 201, 205, 280
Cleland, Charles, 169, 173, 174, 179, 184, 202–203, 380*n*, 382*n*, 385*n*; extradition of fugitive slaves fought by, 202, 212–13, 219, 223, 233–34, 242, 248, 386*n*
Cockburn, George R. R., 320, 321
Cockburn, Mary Eliza Zane, 320
Cocke, William A., 379*n*
Code Noir, *see* Black Code
Colborne, John, 209, 211–12, 214–15, 227–29, 239, 243; African Americans welcomed to Upper Canada by, 121, 193, 211; extradition of Blackburns denied by, 223–25, 231, 232, 240; return of fugitive slaves opposed by, 211, 222, 252–53; Thornton's petition to, 215–19
colonization, xviii, 65
Congress, U.S., 34, 155, 204, 270, 280, 288, 305, 313, 327
Constitution, U.S., 163; Thirteenth amendment, 327; Fourteenth amendment, 327, 339, 350; Fifteenth amendment, 327
Constitutional Act (1791), 24
Convention of Colored Freemen (North American Convention), 291–94
Cook, John, 173, 185
Cooley, Chloe, 195–96
Cooper, Afua, 155
Copper, Peter, 149
Coquillard, Thomas, 144, 239
Cornish, Samuel E., 206
cotton agriculture, xvii, 24; British textile industry and, 310; expansion of, 86, 208
cotton gin, xvii, 24
Creoles, 95
Creole affair, 249, 400*n*

Crosswhite, Adam, 250
Curry, James, 36, 356*n*
Custaloe, Reuben, 334
Custaloe, William, 270

David (fugitive slave), 158
Davis, Franky, 277
Davis, Jefferson, 100, 308, 315, 321, 325
Davis, Sibby, 277
Davis, Varina, 100
Dearborn, General Henry, 223
De Baptiste, George, 250, 284, 297
Delany, Martin R., 294, 307, 315, 335
Denison, George Taylor, 316–17, 321, 325, 338
Derrick, Alfred, 292
Desha, Joseph, 317
Detroit Anti-Slavery Society, 183
Detroit Vigilant Committee, 151–53, 237, 247, 249, 250
Dew, Thomas R., 160
Dewson, George Oscar, 316
Dickens, Charles, 74, 84, 122–23, 256
Doniphan, Alexander W., 312–13
Doniphan, Anderson, 20–23, 27, 41, 200, 362*n*
Doniphan, Anne Fowke Smith, 20, 32, 312–13
Doniphan, Joseph, 20–23, 32, 312, 361*n*, 362*n*
Doniphan, Susan Smith, 20, 21, 359*n*
Douglass, Frederick, 25, 39, 71, 102, 145, 250, 292, 294, 383*n*; in Canada, 291; childhood of, 32–33; on city versus plantation slaves, 82; death of, 349; on Fugitive Slave Law, 281; Lambert and, 154, 307; parents of, 25, 66
Draper, William H., 247
Dred Scott decision (1857), 306, 339
Drew, Benjamin, 35–36, 67
DuBois, W.E.B., 324
Duke, Basil W., 312

education: in Canada, 323, 328, 330; during Reconstruction, 327–28
Edwards, S. J. Celestine, 221
Edwards v. Vail (1830), 128
Edwoods, William Henderson, 273
Elgin, Lord, 283–84, 287
Elgin Association, 279, 287, 295, 298, 303, 329, 351; *Annual Reports* of, 303, 305
Eliza (fugitive slave), 43
Elliot, Charles, 241–42
emancipation: gradual, xviii, 86, 196, 258–59; immediate, *see* abolitionist movement

Emancipation Day (British, West Indian), 273, 297
Emancipation Proclamation, 208, 313–14
Empire Club (Toronto), 321
epidemics, 319; in Detroit, 155; in Louisville, 74
Episcopalians, 141; *see also* Methodist Episcopal church
Ernest, Frederick B., 103–108
Erskine, David M., 142
Evans, John, 91–92
extradition protocols, Canadian: *see* Fugitive Offenders Act; Webster-Ashburton Treaty

Fairfax, Lord, 359*n*
Family Compact, 211, 274, 334
fancy girls, trade in, 6, 111
Fedric, Francis, 17, 26, 35, 42
Fields, Barbara Jean, 355*n*
Fillmore, Millard, 281–82
Filson Historical Society, 320–21
First Nations, *see* Native peoples
Fisher, John T., 271, 293, 296
Fisk University, 327
Foreign Enlistment Act (British), 313
Forrest, Nathan Bedford, 314
Foster, Stephen Collins, 47, 363*n*
Founding Fathers, 23
Frazier, Alexander D., 165, 166, 169, 171, 173–75, 233–34; extradition of Blackburns fought by, 202, 212–14, 219, 223, 384*n*; prosecution of rioters by, 182, 202, 225
free blacks, 40, 81–83, 88–90, 147, 152, 259, 269, 271; abolitionist, xviii, 85; documents of, *see* Manumission papers; enslaved under Fugitive Slave Law, 282; exodus of, after Nat Turner rebellion, 226, 260; fugitives slaves aided by, xiv, 42, 90–92, 124, 154; kidnapped and sold into slavery, 159, 202; laws limiting, 160; urban culture of, 148–49; white animosity toward, 120, 121
Freedman's Bank, 324
Freedmen's Bureau, 324, 327–28
Freedmen's Inquiry Commission, 91, 322–24, 332
Freedom's Journal, 86
Freeman, Barbara, 289
Freeman, Coleman, 289, 396*n*
Freeman, Thomas, 292
Frémont, John C., 312
French, Caroline, 150, 173–75, 185, 194, 225
French, George W., 150–52, 173–75, 180, 185, 225, 276, 377*n*

French family, 149, 151, 234, 236, 237, 250, 284
Fugitive Offenders Act (Canada, 1833), 199, 204, 210, 221–22, 229–33, 242, 246, 251, 280
Fugitive Slave Law (U.S., 1793), xix, 126, 155, 161–62, 193, 214, 276, 377*n*; local and state ordinances supporting, 121, 156, 163; northern evasion of, 202; passage of, 23–24; penalties under, 224; requirements of, 165
Fugitive Slave Law (U.S., 1850), xix, 280–84, 288, 290, 292, 295, 333, 378*n*

Gallego, Peter, 277
Gara, Larry, 356*n*
Garnet, Henry Highland, 163
Garrison, William Lloyd, xviii, 42, 43, 87, 183, 289
Genius of Universal Emancipation, 86
Gentle, John, Sr., 218–19
Georgian Affair, 316–17
German immigrants, 80, 119, 141
Germantown (Kentucky), 22, 41
Glenelg, Lord, 245, 246
Goodell, Lemuel, 170, 174, 177, 181, 227
Gooderham, George, 349
Gooderham, William, 258, 343, 349
Gooderham family, 257–58, 280, 330, 332, 343, 347, 348
Gooderham & Worts, 257–58, 265, 329, 330
Goodlett, John, 54
Gordon, James Wright, 247
Gore, Francis, 142
Grace, Daddy, 178–80, 182
Grant, Ulysses S., 312, 339
Grassett, Frederick Lemoine, 349
Gray, John T., 74
Great Exhibition (London), 303
Great Western Railway, 298
Greeley, Horace, 282
Green, Nancy, 341
Grey, Lord, 284
Grimes, William, 15, 37
Guthrie, James, 106, 128

Hackett, Nelson, 246–49, 389*n*
Hagerman, Christopher Alexander, 243
Haitian Revolution, 95, 264
Hampton University, 327
Handly's Lessee v. Anthony et al. (1820), 132
Hands, William, 198, 219, 225
Happy, Jesse, 245–46, 285*n*
Hardin, Big Bill, 55

Harpers Ferry, John Brown's raid on, 154, 307–308, 313, 322; planned in Canada West, 307
Harris, Eliza, 43
Harrison, William Henry, 175, 200, 202, 250
Hasbrook, Abram, 114
Headley, John W., 317
Henning, Thomas, 288
Henson, Josiah, 33, 37–38, 44, 45, 54, 193–94, 236, 275, 283, 286, 292, 303, 313
Hill, Horace Buckner, 131
Hill, John Henry, 254, 352, 353, 393n
Hill, Susan Oldham, 75, 131
hiring out of slaves, 76, 79, 83
Hoffman, Charles Fenno, 145
Holly, James Theodore, 293
household slaves, conditions of, 34–37, 97
House of Representatives, U.S., 34, 66, 206
Howard University, 327, 328
Howe, Julia Ward, 322
Howe, Samuel Gridley, 322–24, 332, 336
Hubbard, William, 339
Hudnell, Ezekiel K., 158–59
Hughes, Louis, 277

immigrants: Chinese, 339; European, 80, 119, 120, 141, 158, 245, 285, 329, 330, 338, 343, 351; Irish, 245, 280, 329, 330, 338, 343, 351
Indians, see Native peoples; specific tribes
Indian War (1676), 20

Jackson, Albert, 302
Jackson, Andrew, 30, 56, 65, 66, 86, 109, 141, 143
Jackson, Ann Maria, 300–302, 334, 335, 348
Jackson, James Henry, 302, 348
Jackson, John, 302
Jackson, John Andrew, 36
Jackson, Mattie J., xiv
Jackson, Richard M., 302, 334–35
Jacob, George, 199, 202, 212–14, 217, 218
Jacobs, Harriet, 94, 100
Jameson, Anna Brownell, 244
Jameson, Robert Simpson, 211–12, 217, 219, 223–25, 228–29, 244, 253, 262, 389n
Jamestown colony, xiv
Jay's Treaty, 140, 219
Jefferson, Thomas, xv–xvi, 24, 34, 78, 188, 270, 308
Jerry (fugitive slave), 282, 295
"Jim Crow," coinage of term, 87–88
Jim Crow segregation, xiii, 88, 321, 340
Johnson, Abraham, 241

Johnson, Andrew, 336
Johnson, William, 215, 217
Johnston, Albert Sidney, 312
Jones, A. Beckford, 288
Jones, Jehu, 275

Kansas-Nebraska Act (1854), 305–306
Keckley, Elizabeth, 101
Kelso, John Joseph, 337
Kemp, James, 206
Kenton, Simon, 16
Kentucky Colonization Society, 40, 80
Kentucky Derby, 56
Kentucky slave code, 1798, 27
King, William, 279, 286–87, 296, 297, 303, 307
King's College Medical School, 272, 328
Kirkpatrick, Andrew, 128
Knox College, 287, 288, 328
Ku Klux Klan, 314, 340

Lafayette, George Washington, 46
Lafayette, Marquis de, 46
Lambert, Benjamin Willoughby, 154
Lambert, Julia Willoughby, 150, 154
Lambert, William, 154, 237, 250, 284, 292, 297, 307
Lanton, Archie, 250
Larned, Charles, 175
Larrie, Reginald, 173
Lee, Robert E., 316, 320
Lewis, Meriwether, 78
Lewis, Phillip, 149
Liberator, The, xviii, 183, 282
Lightfoot, James, 44
Lightfoot, Madison J., 150–53, 173–75, 177, 180, 185, 249, 276, 334, 377n
Lightfoot, Philip, 51, 152, 364n, 364n
Lightfoot, Tabitha, 150, 173–74, 185
Lightfoot family, 34, 149, 152, 250, 332, 339, 362n; in Baptist church, 236, 237; escape from slavery of, xiii, 44–45, 283; and Thornton Blackburn, xxiii; Underground Railroad activities of, 234, 284
Lincoln, Abraham, 50, 243, 306, 310–13, 319, 321–22; assassination of, 325; and black soldiers, 315; childhood of, 53; elected president, 308; Emancipation Proclamation of, 208, 313–14; Stowe and, 43
Lincoln, Mary Todd, 101
Lloyd, John, 180, 193, 201, 219, 225, 229, 239
Logan, Ben, 109
Loguen, Jermain Wesley, 295

London Anti-Slavery Society, 288
Louisiana Purchase, 24, 78
Loyalists, *see* Black Loyalists; United Empire Loyalists
Lucifer, Nero, 149
Lundy, Benjamin, 86, 87, 235, 260

Macaulay, James Buchanan, 230–32, 242, 260, 262
Macaulay Town, 230, 260, 263, 269
Macdonald, John A., 313
Mackenzie, William Lyon, 262, 274, 275
Mackenzie Rebellion, *see* Upper Canada Rebellion
Maitland, Peregrine, 197, 205
Manifest Destiny, 311
Manumission papers, 11, 83, 153, 216
Marsh, Walker Lewis Edward, 349
Marshall, John, 132
Martineau, Harriet, 234
Mason, Eliza, 183, 187
Mason, George, 143
Mason, John Thomson, 143, 159
Mason, Madison J., 180, 193, 219, 225, 229, 239
Mason, Stevens Thomson, 143, 175, 209–10, 226, 241
Maury, General Dabney H., 319
May, Samuel J., 291
McArthur, Alexander, 171–73, 177, 178, 180, 181, 209–10, 227–29
McDowell, Ephraim, 58
McFarland, John R., 128
McFarland v. McKnight (1846), 132
McHenry, William "Jerry," rescue of, 282, 295
McKnight, Anne Logan, 109, 110, 114
McKnight, Sheldon, 184
McKnight, Virgil, 7, 108–14, 124–32, 135, 161–66, 168, 171, 201, 210, 214, 240
McMullins, P., 201, 218, 219
McMurtrie, Henry, 73
McRae, Norman, 177–78
Methodist Episcopal church, 260, 311
Methodists, 92, 106, 141, 292, 322, 334–35, 349
Middle Passage, 18, 264
Miller, James Alexander, 370*n*
Miller, Mary Brown, 370*n*
Minkins, Shadrach, 281–82
minstrel shows, blackface, 87–88, 340–42
Missouri Compromise, 66, 306
Mitchell, William M., 359*n*
Mohawk Indians, 255

Monroe, William C., 151, 307
Monroe Doctrine, 201
Morris, Lieutenant W. W., 188, 189
Morton, George, 25, 29–30, 153, 362*n*
Moseby, Solomon, 242–45
Mott, Lucretia, 97
Mountjoy, Captain Thomas, 153
Murphy, George Morton, 29–31, 35, 45
Murphy, William, 30, 31, 33–36, 38, 45, 46, 57, 97, 153, 312
Murray, Alexander, 389*n*

National Association for the Advancement of Colored People (NAACP), 154
National Guard, U.S., 271
National Underground Railroad Freedom Center (Cincinnati), xxi, 42
Native peoples, 16, 18, 20, 21, 55, 66, 78, 141, 198, 200; removal of, 86, 143–44; enslavement of, 142, 195
Nautilus Insurance Company, 134
Neidhard, Karl, 141
Nelson, Mrs. Harry, 334
Nelson, Thomas, 25
New England Anti-Slavery Society, xviii
New York Life Insurance Company, 134
Niger Expedition, 315
North American League, 293
Northrup, Solomon, 358*n*
North Star, The, 290, 291, 294
Northwest Ordinance (1787), 142, 144, 156, 167
nullification crisis, 66

Ohio (steamboat), 141, 170, 171, 175, 176, 183
Oldham, John Pope, 7, 55, 75–76, 81–83, 85, 107, 240, 318, 320, 357*n*, 370; appointed postmaster of Louisville, 74–75; and Blackburns' marriage, 99, 101; country estate of, 92; as executor of Brown's estate, 67–69, 93, 77, 129, 365*n*; and leasing of Thornton to Wurts & Reinhard's, 77–78; pursuit of Blackburns initiated by, 124–25; return of Blackburns sought by, 161–65, 168, 201, 210, 214; Thornton brought to Louisville by, 70, 71; *Versailles* owners sued by, 126–32; wealth and connections of, 56
Oldham, Malinda Talbot, 55, 56, 81, 92, 93, 130, 131, 318, 320
Oldham, Richard, 83, 84
Oldham, Talbot Clayton, 63, 75, 76, 81, 92–93, 131, 162; in Canada to secure extradition of Blackburns, 201, 212, 213;

Oldham, Talbot Clayton (*cont.*)
in Detroit to recover Blackburns, 162,
164–66, 168, 169, 171, 174–77, 181–82,
227
Oldham, William (John Pope Oldham's
son), 63, 75, 76, 81, 92–93, 125–26
Oneida Institute, 238
Osgood, William, 196

Palace Street School (Toronto), 330, 342
Palmer, Friend, 178, 183
Panic of 1837, 109
Parliament, British, 209, 211
"paterollers," 27
Patriot War, *see* Upper Canadian Rebellion
Penn, Shadrach, 82
Pennington, James W. C., 45–46, 115–16
Pennsylvania Anti-Slavery Society, 270, 352
Perkins, "Doctor," 40
Philadelphia Vigilance Committee, 300
Phillips, Robert, 322
Phillips, Wendell, 42
Pickering, Joseph, 238
plantations, xvi, xvii, 18–19, 23, 82; inade-
quate food on, 37; in Kentucky, 80, 81;
slave houses on, 265; Stowe's portrayal
of, 283
Plessy v. Ferguson (1896), 349–50
Pope family, 56, 80
Porter, George B., 144, 226–29, 231, 232
Presbyterians, 83, 125, 141, 206, 286, 288,
317
Prince, Colonel John, 250–51
Prosser, Gabriel, 26, 160
Protestants, 280; *see also specific denominations*
Provincial Freeman, 295, 297–98, 300, 307
Provincial Union, 396*n*

Quakers, xxiv, 35, 67, 86, 97, 147, 235, 248
Quarrier, Monroe, 10–12, 117, 119,
125–35, 167, 216, 309
Queen's Light Infantry, 274

Rankin, John, 42–43, 27, 256
Rapier, James T., 296, 310, 328
Reconstruction, 296, 321, 327–28, 336, 339
Reeder, Henry R., 276
Reinhard, John, 77–78, 80, 126, 130
Reinhard, Paul, 77–78
Reinhard family, 318
Republican party, 243
Revolutionary War, *see* American
Revolution
Rice, Thomas D., 87–88
riots, racial, 120, 121, 159, 271; in Canada,
243–44; *see also* Blackburn Riots of 1833

Robertson, John Ross, xii, 263, 268, 275, 335,
344
Robinson, James Lukin, 347
Robinson, John Beverley, 199, 203–204,
222, 230–32, 247, 262, 274, 334, 347
Robinson, John Beverley, Jr., 274
Robinson, Stuart, 317–19
Rogers, Thomas, 78, 79, 93, 160–61, 164,
171, 227
Russwurm, John B., 206

Sackville Street School, 343–44, 347
Sadler, Reverend, 343, 346, 348–49
Sands, Lydia, 388*n*
Sands, Peter, 180, 193, 199, 219, 225, 229,
239–40, 388*n*
Sandusky, Ohio, 119, 121, 123, 126, 140,
166
Sandwich jail, 199–201, 225, 254
Sandwich Mission, 286
Sanson, Alexander, 343
Scadding, Henry, 259
Scott, Dred, 306
Scott, William, 151
Scottish immigrants, 285
Second Baptist Church, 151–52, 235, 236,
384*n*
Second Great Awakening, 33
"Secret Six," 307, 322
segregation, xiii, 88, 321, 340, 349–50
self-help activities, African Canadian, 237,
273, 281, 283, 286, 291–92, 295–98, 300,
302–305, 328, 396*n*; True Band, 237,
398*n*
Senate, U.S., xvi
separate but equal, doctrine of, 349–50
Seward, William, 311
Shadd, Abraham Doras, 294–95, 315, 328
Shadd, Emaline, 328
Shadd, Isaac, 307, 328
Shadd, Mary Ann, *see* Cary, Mary Ann
Shadd
sharecropping, 340
Shawnees, 200
Sheldon, Thomas, 158
Sherwood, Levius Peters, 230–32, 262
shotgun houses, 264–66
Siebert, Wilbur Henry, 91, 356*n*, 359*n*
Simcoe, John Graves, 24, 147, 195–96, 210,
230, 255, 256, 258, 263
Singleton, William Henry, 42, 85, 356*n*
Slaughter, James, 123, 139, 150, 165–66,
227, 379*n*, 383*n*, 387*n*
slave jail, Germantown, Ky., 41
slave trade, 29, 40–41, 43, 46, 50, 113–16,
267; Atlantic, 18, 24, 195, 264; auctions,

5–7, 43–44, 81, 108, 208–209; monetary value of, 208; during Revolutionary War, 142

Sloan, John, 238–39

Smallwood, Thomas, 337

Smith, Margaret Whitely, 17, 22, 27, 361*n*

Smith, Robert (fugitive slave), 270, 348

Smith, Robert (slave owner), 22, 25–29, 32, 143, 147, 200, 361*n*

Smith, Susan Hancock, 28, 361*n*

Smith, Thomas, 359*n*, 360*n*

Smith, William, 17, 20–22, 25, 312–13

Smith family, 348

Snow, R. Beverly, 271, 292

Solan, Rush R., 359*n*

Somerset, James, 203

Spradling, Washington, 91, 124

Starling, Marion Wilson, 356*n*

Stephens, Alexander, 312

Sterne, Charles, 153

Steward, William and Susannah, 239–40

Stewart, Charles H., 248–50

Still, William, 254, 270, 300–302, 322, 352

Stone, Edward, 40, 41, 48, 49

Stone massacre, 48–49

Storm, W. G., 342

Stowe, Harriet Beecher, 43–45, 283

Strachan, John, 211, 223, 225, 228–30, 253, 263

Stuart, Captain Charles, 237–38, 250, 288

Sturge, Joseph, 119

Sumter, Fort, 309

Supreme Court, U.S., 132, 306, 340

Surratt, John, 320

Swisshelm, Jane, 90

Talbot, Clayton Merriwether, 56, 65, 67, 93

Talbot, Polly Crewes, 56, 93

Talbot, Sophia, 93

Talbot, Thomas, 56

Taney, Roger, 306

Tappan, Lewis, 248

Taylor, Francis, 33–34, 45, 362*n*

Tecumseh, Chief, 200

Thames, Battle of the, 200

Thomas, Henry K., 296, 328

Thompson, George, 291

Thompson, Jacob, 317

Thornton, Anna, 271

Tilly (fugitive slave), 258

Tinsley, John D., 270, 292

Tinsley, John M., 270, 292, 296, 297, 303, 334, 337, 393*n*

Tinsley family, 332, 348

Tocqueville, Alexis de, 140–41

Toronto, University of, 287

Toronto Board of Education, 342–44, 347, 400*n*

Toronto General Hospital, 333

Toronto Humane Society, 337

Toronto Ladies Association for the Relief of Destitute Colored Refugees, 289–90

Toronto Liberating Society, 283

Toronto Necropolis Cemetery, xii, 304, 329, 346, 349

Toronto Normal School, 287, 296, 328

Toronto Press Club, 342

Toronto Rolling Mills, 330

Toronto Transit Commission, 268, 339

Toussaint-Louverture, 264

Transylvania University, 143

Trent Affair, 311

Trollope, Frances, 12, 118

Troy, William, 299

Truth, Sojourner, 289, 383*n*

Tubman, Harriet, 139, 290, 295, 307, 314–15

Tucker, G. W., 149

Tureman, Robert, 356*n*

Turner, Enoch, 257, 280

Turner, Nat, 159, 226, 260, 333

Tyler, John, 249

Uncle Tom's Cabin (Stowe), 43–44, 282–83

Underground Railroad, xiv, xix, xxiv–xxv, 135, 281, 292, 293, 298–300, 314, 341, 356*n*; in Canada, xi, xii, 25, 196, 207, 226, 234, 269, 270, 294, 316; cost to South of, 207–209; in Detroit, 124, 144, 226, 234, 237, 250; in Indiana, 76–77; in Kentucky, 42–44, 63–64, 90, 91, 122; in Ohio, 97, 119, 256; peak traffic on, 284; Quakers and, xxiv, 147; secret code of, 16

United Empire Loyalists, 195, 198, 201, 204, 218, 230, 274, 318

Unsworth, Abraham, 200–201, 218

Upper Canada College, 320

Upper Canadian Rebellion, 245, 275

Ure, George P., 300

U.S. Colored Troops, 49, 314, 315

Van Buren, Martin, 159

Versailles (steamboat), 4, 8, 10–13, 111, 117–19, 125–33, 167, 216, 309, 357*n*, 374*n*

Vesey, Denmark, 39

Victoria, Queen, 274

Voice of the Fugitive, 236, 284, 292, 293, 295–97, 408*n*

Wade, Jerry, 90
Walker, David, 85, 313
Walker, James St. George, 313
Wallace, Alfred, 247
Ward, Samuel Ringgold, 236, 295
War of 1812, 143, 147, 175, 183, 204, 219, 237, 317, 391*n*; black Canadian troops in, 196, 197, 207, 230, 259; invasion of Upper Canada in, 200–202, 223; outbreak of, 27
Washington, Charles A., 334
Washington, George, 19, 221
Washington, D.C., riots, 271, 292
Watson, Henry, 57
Watson, John Gowie, 218
Webb, William, 307
Webster, Daniel, xvi, 249
Webster-Ashburton Treaty, 249–51
weddings, slave, 100–101
Weir, Benjamin G., 162–66, 168–70, 174–76, 182–83, 212, 213, 227, 379*n*
Welch, Elizabeth, 150
Weld, Isaac, 142
Weld, Theodore Dwight, 238
Wellington, Arthur Wellesley, Duke of, 211
Wells, Frank, 25
Westward Movement, xx, 17–20, 50–52, 140
White, John, 196
white supremacy, ideology of, 148, 340
Whitney, Eli, xvi, 24
Wickliffe, Robert, 40–41
Wilberforce, William, 65, 86, 195
Wilberforce settlement, 86–87, 121, 197, 211, 260
Wilkinson, John Alexander, 218–19
William and Mary University, 160
Williams, Eric, 355*n*
Williams, General John R., 183
Williams, Prince, 180, 193, 199, 219, 225, 229, 239

Willis, Michael, 288, 290
Willoughby, Benjamin, 149–54, 237, 250, 276, 380*n*; Cleland and, 203, 388*n*; in Kentucky, 152, 153; rescue of Blackburns orchestrated by, 172–73, 180, 185, 307
Willoughby, Deborah (Devon), 151, 154, 307
Willoughby, Frances, 151, 154
Willoughby family, 234
Wilson, Hiram, 286, 292, 301
Wilson, John M., 167, 169–70, 172, 173, 175, 183, 198, 210, 223, 227–29; Blackburns arrested by, 162, 164, 165; Frazier's case against, 202, 213–14, 224; injuries sustained by, 178, 179, 181, 231–32; during riot, 176–78
Wingfield, Rowland, 239
Witherell, Benjamin F. H., 159, 380*n*
Wolf, Eric, 355*n*
women: in abolitionist movement, 65, 90, 289–90; in Civil War, 314–15; employment of, 146, 262; in protest against extradition, 244
Wood & Crutcher, 106
Woodward, Augustus, 143
World Anti-Slavery Convention, 249
World War I, 321
Worts, James Gooderham, 332, 343
Worts family, 257, 280, 332
Wurts, Charles, 77–78, 80, 126, 130
Wurts, Daniel, Sr., 77–78, 80
Wurts, Edward, 126
Wurts family, 318
Wurts & Reinhard's, 3, 10, 77–80, 91, 93, 95, 108, 109, 126, 160, 161, 171

Yellow Fever Plot, 319
York Pioneers, 347

Zug, Samuel, 381*n*